Partners-in-Crisis:
The Untold Story of
Pat and Richard Nixon

To Cathy Thompson

Best wishes,

Helin M. Montgomery

January 23, 2004

Partners-in-Crisis: The Untold Story of Pat and Richard Nixon

People of Courage

Helen M. Montgomery

To order additional copies of this book, contact:
Xlibris Corporation
1-888-795-4274
www.Xlibris.com
Orders@Xlibris.com
18649

Contents

Dedicated to the Memory
of
James Darrell Montgomery

To Julie and Tricia
and to Pat and Richard's grandchildren Jennie,
Alex, and Melanie Eisenhower and Christopher Cox.

Chapter 1

REMEMBERING
A SPECIAL TIME

In the late 1950's, I had just arrived in Chicago from the hill country of Appalachian Mountains of Kentucky. At that time I didn't realize that my change of scenery and vocation to the State of Illinois would soon alter the direction of my life. This change of direction really began when I met Pat and Richard Nixon.

I was working in Chicago when Pat and Richard Nixon made a visit to Wheaton-College in a nearby suburb. One friend, a co-worker, Ruth said," Helen, why don't we take time off from work and visit the Vice-President. He's coming to speak to the students at the college and to anyone else who cares to listen to his talk."

"Well", I said, "which one?" My mind was on other things and far away.

My friend replied, "Which one! Silly. It is the Vice-President Richard Nixon. The Second Lady, Pat Nixon, will be with him. This is a rare occasion because the children will be with them. Coming?"

Then, I really perked up at the mention of their names. I told my friend, "Ruth, you mean Richard Nixon—the man who helped expose Alger Hiss as a spy. Why didn't you say so in the first place?" So my friend dragged me over there. At first glance, Richard Nixon did not remind me of a glamorous movie star but of a small town young man, quiet and reserved. The thick eyebrows, projected jaw and the up-swept nose were characteristic of his mother's side of the family. When Nixon rose to address the audience, all of us soon forgot his unglamorous appearance and became enthralled with what he had to say. I wasn't disappointed.

Nixon's voice was resonant and strong. There was something spellbinding about what he said. He spoke to the heart, and it inspired me as well as others to be a better citizen. As I listened enchanted, I knew Nixon was a man of destiny, especially talented for a very important task in history.

Then, I was amazed. Nixon did not use any notes at all to refer to when he was speaking. None of the college professors I knew could do that.

Afterwards, my friend steered both of us through the crowds to shake hands and to talk with them. We were standing at the end of a long line, wondering and hoping, if we would be fortunate to meet them. I thought the crowds would never get smaller. Eventually, our turn finally arrived.

Richard Nixon was outgoing, friendly and attractive. One of the things I liked about Nixon was that he didn't talk about himself or his accomplishments. Somehow this man was different from others, he told me why it was important for persons to get involved in working for the good of the country. Then, he mentioned his mother, Hannah, Pat, his wife, and Julie and Tricia, his two daughters, and what they meant to him.

Pat Nixon, the Second Lady, showed personal warmth and charm. She became interested in what we had to say. Her two children were an example of which we all could be very proud.

As memories took me back to that distant time, I remembered the past again-especially of two people, Pat and Richard Nixon, who made a difference in my life. Some of those memories would be pleasant—some fraught with suffering or distress of body or mind.

That day as we shook hands and talked—in that magic moment—a special friendship began. It started with Pat and I corresponding with each other and to become pen pals. This was the beginning of a special time of memories in my life. At that moment I never realized where my journey would eventually take me, or how these two partners would survive in crisis one after another.

Chapter 2

PEOPLE OF COURAGE

In 1958, the recession was still across the land. Many persons were scurrying around here and there looking for a job. It was difficult in finding one. The economy was on everyone's mind.

President Dwight Eisenhower had received word that the Communists in South America were planning demonstrations and protests against United States policies. He was pressuring Richard Nixon and Pat to go to South America on another goodwill trip. After a recent tour of nineteen other countries, Pat and Richard Nixon did not want to go on another trip. They wanted a little peace and quiet and to enjoy their children at home. Many official functions kept them away from Julie And Tricia more than they liked. Pat longed to spend more time with the girls and help them on their homework from school.

Richard" Dick" Nixon had become the most active of all Vice-Presidents and added the art and practice of conducting negotiations between nations to his many other tasks. Because of President Eisenhower's health problems, Dick and Pat had to step in and take over many responsibilities, which were delegated, to Ike and Mamie, as President and First Lady.

More and more they were in view of everyone across the land.

But, April 1958 came around too quickly. Pat and Dick had to leave on their South American goodwill trip. It was a trip, they didn't desire to take, but duty for country prevailed. Once again, Julie and Tricia said farewell to their mother and daddy.

Pat and Dick made stops in Uruguay, Argentina, Paraguay, and Bolivia without encountering any hostility. However, in Lima, Peru, two thousand Communist demonstrators blocked the entrance to San Marcos University where Nixon as Vice-President was suppose to visit. Somehow Dick sensed that there was danger in the air, he persuaded Pat to continue to stay at Grand Hotel Bolivar. The mobs were still shouting, "Death to Nixon" and throwing rocks and fruit.

At lunchtime, I remembered watching news on television with one of my coworkers. Halfway through my lunch of soup and sandwich, a special news bulletin flashed on the television that Vice-President Richard Nixon and Pat Nixon, Second Lady, had been assaulted by an unruly crowd in Lima, Peru. I had a difficult time in finishing my lunch. Felt sick inside. My heart was heavy with fear.

Then, I learnt that the Nixons would continue their trip to Caracas, Venezuela by May. There were rumors around the country of the plot to kill the Nixons in Venezuela. All I could do was to pray. "God please protect Pat and Dick Nixon from all harm."

In Caracas, Venezuela, Pat's courage and compassion were never more apparent than in the thick of heavy concentration of rocks and vociferated abusive words. She walked up to a barrier, which held a horde of angry, violent, spitting people and extended her hand and gently clasped the hand of a girl who was one of the more fervent of the haters. Tears suddenly rose up in the girl's eyes and she turned away shamefaced.

There, in Caracas, the fanatical, screaming crowd

surrounded Richard Nixon's vehicle, rocked it and smashed the car windows. Rocks, garbage and spit were showered on them. Pat was in the second car behind Dick's car. The unruly crowd cursed and ejected spit. The saliva covered their clothing and windshields. Dick decided abruptly to cancel the rest of the Venezuelan trip and headed for a safe haven at the Embassy residence. That judgment rescued Pat and Dick from danger.

Many bombs were found placed near the wreath-laying ceremony. The moment that Pat and Dick arrived there, they would have been killed along with others in the retinue. I was glad that God answered my constant prayer for their protection and saved them from the Communist murder plot.

In this time of crisis, Pat and Richard Nixon showed courage and calmness under fire. However, at the White House, President Eisenhower was frustrated and in a state of uncertainty. He could not reach Nixon by telephone or the radio. Even cabled messages could not get through. To wait might be dangerous for Vice-President Nixon and Pat, the Second Lady. So, as a safety measure, President Eisenhower rushed marines and paratroopers to Puerto Rican and Cuban bases, in case the Venezuelan government requested assistance from the violent mobs there.

Nixon accepted the apology of the Venezuelan government for the incident. He had turned his other cheek and in public showed his self-control. Nixon saw first hand the violence, which was sowed by a Communist who held an important position in the Venezuelan government. He repeated his respect and friendship for the people of Venezuela. After all this ordeal and frustration, Dick finally let his inner anger boil to the top. He then felt better knowing it would be his last night in Venezuela, and he would be going home soon.

I was really proud of Pat and Richard Nixon. The rest of the country echoed my sentiments about the Nixons. More and more my admiration for them had grown. Their courage in very troublesome incidents, calmness in a crisis, and the strength of mind, which enabled them to meet danger in Venezuela, won the hearts of the American people.

May 15,1958, Pat and Richard Nixon came home. The reception at the airport was one of the largest ever recorded for a Vice-President. Julie and Tricia were there to greet their mother and father, as well as President Eisenhower and Senator Lyndon Johnson. In my heart, I knew this couple would be making more history in the near future.

By November, Republicans were defeated in Congressional races, and the Democrats controlled the government for ten years. It was demoralizing. By spring, 1959, the economy turned up.

However, on July 23,1959, the newspaper headlines burst forth that Vice President Richard Nixon and his wife, Pat, would be going to Moscow in the Soviet Union to meet with Nikita Khrushchev. Officially, they were there to open the American Exhibition at Sokolniki Park. It was another goodwill trip tour of Russia and Siberia. President Eisenhower had confidence that Nixon would do a good job of defending United States policies there. Also, Nixon was counted on to break the chilling relations between the two countries and to emphasize that Americans only wanted peace.

In Moscow, no crowds met them at the airport. Bands or Russian national were absent. The streets were empty as they were driven to meet Khrushchev. No people or cars were there.

At first, Khrushchev was friendly and pleasant. Nixon knew he could not change any U.S. policy under any circumstance, but he defended our country's policies. So Nixon determined to listen more instead of talking a lot. Quickly, he learned early that Khrushchev was a foxy person and didn't play by fair rules.

But then, Khrushchev suddenly accused United States of

dangerous agitation by enacting the Captive Nations Resolution. This was the Captive Nations Week Resolution, which the U.S. Congress passed before the Nixons departed for the Moscow trip. It only asked President Eisenhower to pray for enslaved people under Communist rule and make known our support for them.

Vice President Nixon reminded Khrushchev that our country was composed of people who came from all of Europe, and that these same people make their views known to Congress. This resolution was not hatched up on the spur of the moment by Congress, but they were only acting on the public opinion views of the people in our country. Khrushchev was angry and still could not understand why Congress acted as it did. Finally, when Nixon calmed Khrushchev down, their conversation became more amicable.

When the Nixons and Khrushchev were progressing around the exhibitions, they finally reached the model American home exhibit with all of its laborsaving appliances, which the average American family could own. Khrushchev didn't think much of the washing machines there. He thought the money should be spent on State rockets.

Then Khrushchev noticed the television cameras. He immediately took advantage of the moment to encounter Nixon in a verbal attack again on the captive Nations Resolution. Khrushchev was rude and insulting, but Nixon stood his ground and kept his temper in control.

When I heard Nixon's "Kitchen Debate" with Khrushchev about that his grandchildren would someday live in freedom, it made me feel proud to be an American. The story was in all the newspapers and on the radio. It was the talk of the land. He sure shook up the Russians, but Dick made a diplomatic triumph for the United States.

While there in Moscow, Pat visited a market, a school, and a hospital. At the hospital she visited with the children there, because she knew how children loved someone to visit them when they are ill. She was so down-to-earth and so genuine, even the Russian women and children knew they met a real lady of grace, tact, and diplomacy.

It was time to leave Moscow, and they returned enroute to the United States via Poland. Since no one had told the Polish people that the Nixons would be in Warsaw, Radio Free Europe beamed the direction of the Nixon route from the airport. As the motorcade progressed, Millions of Poles cheered the Nixons and threw bouquets of flowers. Many wept. This time it was different! Flowers not rocks. Pat and Richard Nixon represented freedom and America. My American patriotism overwhelmed me and I cried too.

But, as Nixon returned to the States, he was convinced that negotiation with the Soviet Union could only succeed for peace if we first established a position of strength. His popularity soared and surged ahead. Many people thought Richard Nixon should run for President, and so did I.

Therefore, I sent him a note that he should make a run for the presidency. I realized that the odds against any Republican winning in 1960 were about five to one. To win, we would have to get practically all the Republican voters, five million Democrat votes, and more than half of the independent votes. I thought Richard Nixon would have the best chance of winning the presidency.

At that time, Len Hall, chairman of the Republican National Committee, recognized that Richard Nixon was presidential timber, too. The March, 1958 Gallup Poll had published that Republicans nationwide favored Richard Nixon for President. I was happy that others felt as I did.

Chapter 3

1960-CLOSES RACE
IN HISTORY

Of all Richard Nixon's campaigns for public office, the one I remember most vividly was his 1960 presidential race for the White House, which ended in defeat—not victory. It was the longest and most strenuous. The economy had turned up in the spring of 1959, but the odds of any Republican elected were five to one. However, Nixon was a favorite of sixty-four per cent of Republicans nationwide according to the Gallup poll. This happened two years before the Republican and Democrat conventions and no other candidate of either party had that distinction.o

Nixon thought if an effective campaign was wagered before the election things could change. A presidential campaign requires planning years ahead and to organize many workers. He knew that to win in 1960 for President, he would have to win thirty per cent of all the Republican voters, forty-seven per cent of the Democrats and garner twenty-three per cent of the independent voters over to his side.

The campaign would take much money and organization, so Leonard Hall, Chairman of the Republican National

Committee, stepped in and began organizing early on Nixon's 1960 campaign bid for the residential nomination at that time, J. Clifford Folger, who was the ambassador to Belgium and an investment banker, became the finance committee chairman for the Nixon campaign. Nixon's choice for campaign director was Robert H. Finch. Finch was a lawyer and had been the Los Angeles Republican Area Chairman.

Bob Finch had considerable political experience. He was a mature, trustworthy, thirty-five year old individual, with sound judgment and had the full confidence of Nixon. In turn, he was completely loyal to Nixon as a candidate. Bob was objective and had the ability to remain calm under great pressure, and in addition, to control the campaign and yet keep it on the move at all times. Finch realized that Nixon made his own decisions how to run the campaign and was his own severest critic.

Pat and Richard Nixon were a team. The people across the land admired them both for their stamina and courage. Pat was a remarkable Second Lady. But the press followed her around everywhere trying to get a story about her. Then, Pat realized that she was now a public figure and privacy was limited. Also, she had to be careful what she did or what she said. The media would write about her clothing and what she would wear the next day. When they found out she pressed Dick's trousers, the newspapers let everyone know about it. I thought that was silly! She was one of us and was only doing what was natural for the women to do then. My mother and grandmother always did that for their husbands. I continued the practice when I got married. Perhaps, they thought Second Ladies shouldn't do that.

However, there was a growing movement nationwide to make Pat Nixon First Lady. People loved her. Pat was not aware of the Republican National Committee's women division activities to start a separate campaign built around her. I was one of the members of the National Federation of

Republican Women, and I was swept up in the excitement about doing this. Pat said we are electing Dick as President—not me as First Lady. I knew Pat was uncomfortable about this. It really was embarrassing for her. She wanted the spotlight to be on her husband—not her.

The wheels of the Pat Week were already in motion by October third. Pat would attend coffees and teas and small precinct meetings. Pat for First Lady buttons were manufactured. Everywhere I went people were wearing those buttons.

Then, I realized for the first time, perhaps Pat would be the first woman in American history to change the direction of a presidential election. After all, Pat was an experienced team worker, and she represented America wherever she went. I thought after all these years as an exceptional Second Lady; she would be qualified unlike any other First Lady. Everyone wanted to meet her. They loved her as I did. So the campaign was going on the road.

Nixon wanted all his personal friends to have a part in his campaign bid for the White House. Thus, I received word from Pat and Dick that they wanted me to be part of the campaign. They knew I would be a loyal worker and do more than was required for Nixon to win. The task, which lay ahead as an assistant Volunteer Coordinator, appeared at first an awesome assignment for me. But, as an enthusiastic person I knew I had to inspire others to action and motivate them to come back, time and time again to tackle the burgeoning jobs as the campaign moved and progressed ahead.

Most persons do not realize how many daily tasks there are to be performed in a campaign—research, publicity, door-to-door canvassing, telephone canvassing, mailing cards and letters, recruiting other volunteer members, coffee hours, and speaking engagements—just to name a few. It is WORK! Perhaps, that is why some do not like that four-letter word—Work. It involves, a lot.

In spite of all the things we had to think about during the campaign, Nixon saw Nelson Rockefeller, Governor of New York, as an obstructionist to his ambition to be president. It really worried him. Rockefeller wanted to be President, too, and he didn't think Nixon was the one for the office of president. However, Rockefeller backed off when he discovered Nixon had the delegates and practically had the nomination sewed up. He issued a withdrawal statement that he would not be a candidate for the nomination for the presidency. That was final, Rockefeller said.

But, in Mid-May, Rockefeller said he would accept if he were drafted for President. Nixon did not believe what he said. By June 1960, Rockefeller blasted Nixon and all in the Republican Party who held Nixon's views. Even, President Eisenhower urged Rockefeller to support whoever was nominated at the Republican Convention. Rockefeller couldn't take that advice. He continued to solicit delegates even if it became a fruitless campaign. So Rockefeller resumed his activities against the Nixon wing of the Republican Party to help weaken Nixon's chances for the presidency.

While Nixon kept his eye on Rockefeller's movements, he centered his attention on the Democrats. If John F. Kennedy was to be his opponent, Nixon feared Kennedy's ruthlessness as an adversary. He remembered what Kennedy did in the Wisconsin Democrat primaries against Senator Hubert Humphrey. One of Kennedy's staff flooded malicious anti-Catholic leaflets postmarked in Minnesota. Everyone thought Humphrey had done it, and this caused a strong adverse reaction. Humphrey lost. Then, it leaked out what the Kennedy aide had done, but John F. Kennedy did not reprimand the aide for this vicious course of action.

On July 6, John F. Kennedy was the choice of the Democrat Party. After all the stories I heard about the Kennedy's, I was more determined to work more arduous for

Richard Nixon. I was wondering what dirty tricks the Kennedy's would be up to in the campaign. I kept my eyes and ears open for any leaks or gossip in the rumor mill. Did not want to discount anything. Kennedy had personal wealth and unlimited money for organizing a successful campaign. His liabilities were inexperience, wealth, his youth and religion. But, as true in politics today, no one can beat anybody with a nobody.

Then, to my amazement, on July 22, Friday Nixon flew to New York to meet with Rockefeller at his apartment on Fifth Avenue. I was wondering what was going on. Meanwhile, at the Chicago Sheraton-Blackstone Hotel, Charles Percy, Chairman of the Republican Platform Committee was waiting there for the rest of the committee's reports. By late evening, Chuck Percy received a call from Nixon and Rockefeller-much to his surprise.

"The Compact of Fifth Avenue" was the outcome of the Nixon-Rockefeller meeting. Nixon and Rockefeller publicly agreed on the wording of some of fourteen points, which actually came from the draft of the Platform Committee. On the national defense plank, the compact only added sixty-two more words to the original draft of five hundred forty words.

In reading over the "Compact" at that time, I couldn't see what the fuss was all about. Barry Goldwater, a conservative with libertarian views, labeled the Nixon-Rockefeller pact "a surrender." I asked myself, who surrendered what? As far as I could tell Rockefeller and Nixon agreed on all points.

Outside the Republican Convention, Dorothy Kennedy, a friend of mine stood outside the door to catch a glimpse of Nixon. She had been waiting so long; her feet became very sore and tired. The Chicago papers shot a picture of her standing in her bare feet and holding her shoes. It read: "Nixon will have this Kennedy's vote."

However, inside the convention the most intense platform committee fight in Republican history started. It really surprised Nixon with all this fuss. The 1960 Republican Platform Committee did not know that they were to only approve the platforms—not to make them. The committee thought that Rockefeller and Nixon were trying to tell them what to do, and they didn't like that.

It was disgusting to hear all the squabbling about this and that. There I found out some Republicans, who disagree with other Republicans, have an extreme urge to destroy them. Their methods put a bitter taste in my mouth, and I don't like that side of politics today. An army shouldn't attack its own troops. It should level its firearms at the enemy—the other side. Stick with the issues and not deal in regard to personalities.

July 25, 1960, Nixon found twenty six hundred delegates and alternates enraged and defiant in Chicago. Protests were heard when Barry Goldwater urged the delegates to go out and support Nixon. He did not permit the Goldwater name to be voted on as a candidate. Barry admonished them by saying, "Let's grow up conservatives. If we want to take this party back—and I think we can someday—lets go to work." So Nixon met with all the delegates and set the account straight after he answered each charge, he won them over and they agreed to make Nixon their nominee for president. Two days later the platform was approved and Nixon became officially the Republican Party president nominee. When I heard the announcement that became the happiest days of my life!

Several names were on Nixon's Vice President's list— Walter Judd, Thruston Morton, Gerald Ford, Jim Mitchell, Fred Seaton, and Henry Cabot Lodge. Walter Judd was my choice. He was the son of medical missionaries overseas. When I ever heard him talk I recognized a real leader. However Judd thought would be would better help to Nixon as a Congressman.

Thruston Morton also held the same views as Nixon. They had become close friends in Congress since 1947. Morton told Nixon that Lodge would be the better choice because he was from the East and we needed Eastern support. Also President Eisenhower thought Lodge would be the man to select. There it became the Nixon/Lodge ticket.

The three days in Chicago was exhausting for Nixon and all of us who worked for him. There were platform committee meetings, posing for photos for delegates and candidates, and more delegation meetings.

At the convention Nixon had to make a speech to unite all the Republican voters also to capture the Democrat voters as well, to defend President Eisenhower's record. He took the time to think over what he had to say.

When the convention convened, Rockefeller introduced Richard Nixon as a man of vision, judgment, and courage. Then Dick came to the podium and gave his acceptance speech. The last portion of the speech inspired and held us spellbound: "One hundred years ago in this very city Abraham Lincoln was nominated for President . . . The question then was freedom for the states and survival of the nation. The question then was freedom for the slaves and survival of the nation. The question now is freedom for all mankind and the survival of civilization.

We shall build a better America . . . in which we shall see the realization of the dreams of millions of people not only in America but throughout the world-for a fuller, freer, richer life than men have ever known in the history of mankind.

What we must do is to wage the battles for peace and freedom with the same dedication with which we wage battles in war. The only answer to a strategy of victory for the communist world is a strategy of victory for the free world. Let the victory we seek be the victory of freedom over tyranny of plenty over hunger, of health over disease, in every country of the world.

"When Mr. Khrushchev says our grandchildren will live under communism, let us say his grandchildren will live in freedom.

Our answer to the threat of Communist revolution is renewed devotion to the great ideals of the American Revolution that still live in the minds and hearts of people everywhere.

I believe in the American dream, because I have seen it come true in my own life.

Abraham Lincoln was asked during the dark days of the tragic war between the States whether he thought God was on his side, His answer was "My concern is not whether God is on our side, but whether we are on God's side," may that ever be our prayer for our country. And in that spirit-with faith in America, with faith in her ideals and in her people, I accept your nomination for President of the United States."

This speech Nixon gave at the Republican Convention was one of the best speeches I ever heard him make. Nixon critics thought it was remarkable. At that time Goldwater changed his mind, which he rarely did. It also made an impact on the country. After the Republican Convention the Gallup Poll showed Nixon/Lodge ticket had pulled ahead 53% to Kennedy/LBJ, 47%. All that TV exposure and the newspapers paid off, but the real work was just ahead. It would be an intense campaign and the election would be very close. Many Democrats called in to let us know they were supporting the Nixon/Lodge ticket after hearing Dick speak. I guess we will never know who is listening to television and radio.

Nixon promised at the convention that he would carry his campaign in all 50 states. Many of us on the staff disagreed with Nixon's about this decision. We thought he should concentrate on the states with the highest electoral votes to be assured of victory.

Also many Republican officials were disturbed by Nixon's idea to set up Nixon/Lodge volunteer clubs for Democrats and independents to help in the campaign. He knew most of them wouldn't be comfortable in coming into a Republican headquarters to work for him. Dick assimilated all the others into his campaign because he knew there were only 33 million Republicans to 50 million Democrats in the country. Each vote does count whoever it is!

Richard Nixon was tied down in Washington after the Republican Convention. Lyndon B. Johnson had adjourned the Congress before the Democrats Convention, and then commenced it again after the Republicans had theirs. This delayed Nixon's campaign.

Kennedy and Lyndon B. Johnson arranged a "live pair" to protect their position in the Senate. Their vote would be recorded anyway while they were both out campaigning during the week. That way they knew Nixon couldn't leave—except on the weekends-to campaign. That was not fair but what could one expect of those two men. All this conniving by the Kennedy's made me more determine to work and labor diligently for Nixon to win.

Dick Nixon was defending the Eisenhower administration record, but Kennedy kept hammering away at it. Then the Kennedy crowd wanted Nixon to debate him. Kennedy had already accepted NBC offer to debate Nixon. Then the rest of the networks offered free time only to Kennedy and Nixon. All other candidates from other small political parties could not have a part in it. Therefore Nixon consented to debate Kennedy.

Wherever Pat and Richard Nixon went the crowds were enormous. Pat was the drawing card! She loved to meet people and every stranger became a friend. Pat did not show signs of weariness—unlike Dick during the campaigns. The visited Nevada, California, Hawaii, Washington and Maine. However Nixon's plan to go to Alaska or visit Mississippi and Louisiana, and the rest of the remaining states was briefly changed when an unfortunate accident happened.

It happened in Greensboro, North Carolina, August 17, a very large crowd wanted to see Nixon. They shoved and pushed to meet him. Dick accidentally slammed his knee on a car door. The injured knee became so painful he decided to call the physician, Dr. Walter Tkach at the White House. At the Walter Reed hospital they discovered that a hemolytic staphylococcus infection had occurred in the banged knee. It meant that Nixon would have to spend two weeks in the hospital and no campaigning. No one could imagine the frustrated and the intense pain Dick was going through.

Pat, Julie and Tricia visited him every evening and tried to update on certain events, which were going around the country. The press had put a picture of Nixon in the newspaper and the magazines depicting him in very loud pajamas. "People were surprised that their Vice-President had that kind of taste in clothes.Some laughed at the picture. Others said Nixon was one like them. And so he was.

We urged people to send in cards and letters to him. And they did. Thousands of get-well cards and letters flowed into the hospital, as well as the Vice-President's office. Many school children sent in their thoughts of encouragement. I remember the one letter from a twelve-year-old Maryland girl which encouraged and cheered up Nixon. It was the best one of all the letters, which poured in.

It read, "God sometimes makes us to lie down so that we can look up to him more." This really was a lesson we all could learn. Now, Nixon understood that it was better that his illness happened at this time instead of another time closer to the election in November.

But, another political bombshell developed which Nixon had no control over. One morning in the hospital Nixon was reading the newspaper and discovered that a personal friend of the family, Dr. Norman Vincent Peale, had signed a statement listed there in the paper which communicated uneasiness over whether a Catholic President could detach himself from the power of the Pope. People urged Nixon to denounce Peale.

He found out that Peale did not personally form the statement, but only signed it as a group member sharing the same general opinions of that day. Many Protestant ministers and others did not want any party or anyone connected with the Roman papal power. They did not want anyone church to tell them what to do or to influence their thinking.

Around Chicago many churches and schools held prayer meetings regarding the presidential election, and the movement spread around the country. After all I couldn't discuss the topic of religion, but Dick didn't say a word to us about telling others to pray about it. Therefore, I told inquirers to go back to their churches and synagogues and pray who was the better man for the country. This was an explosive issue at that time.

Bob Finch gave us a memo from Nixon laying down instructions regarding the religious issue: "Anyone or any group will not be a part of the Nixon campaign who supports solely on religious reasons."

I had to tell my volunteers that no literature on the issue of religion from any source—even if it came from any local Republican organization would not be distributed at any campaign headquarters. Bob reminded us that all of us—staff and volunteers—were not to discuss it anywhere or anytime because the Kennedy's might interpret this as a contemplated campaign.

Kennedy had made a speech at Houston, Texas to the ministerial association there that he believed in the absolute separation of Church and State. But, I was skeptical of what Kennedy said. He was a ruthless adversary, and in the past he used any method to further his cause. Nixon was trying to be honest and fair and to stick to the issues, which affected the country.

But, across the country, the Democrats were concentrating

on the Catholic vote in key electoral states and major cities. They knew that many Democrat Catholics voted for Eisenhower, and so Kennedy focused his attention on all Catholic voters—Democrat and Republican alike. As Nixon found out later, Kennedy was using the religious issue in reverse. He determined he would be silent about this issue and not stoop to the level, which Kennedy was doing—even it cost him the election.

All of us pleaded with Dick to cancel his fifty state pledges because of his stay in the hospital. We thought we would have Pat Nixon on our side, but we didn't. Pat believed when a person makes a promise, one should keep his pledge. She was torn on exactly what to do. But, she agreed that the rest of the campaign would be exhausting for them, as well as the other campaign workers. After talking it over with each other, Pat urged Dick to keep his pledge. I was astonished, but I questioned the wisdom of that decision.

The hospital stay had left Nixon weaker than he realized. When Pat and Dick left the hospital, they covered fourteen states in the most intense campaign at anytime. The heavy schedule cut into Nixon's sleep—was fatigued—became bone tired. It made it difficult for him to get up in the morning for those early scheduled appointments.

But, on the campaign trail, Dick started shaking like a leaf in a windstorm. He developed a raging fever of 103. His doctor gave him some antibiotics and aspirins. The fever finally broke. But Dick was very weak again. We became so worried about him.

But, Nixon insisted that he should go the next morning to the International Association of Machinists national convention and deliver his speech for the first time before a labor union. He told the labor union he would be President of all the people and would not set groups against each other. What was important for both of their goals was to be what was good for all America. In spite of his weaken condition, the press, who was following him everywhere in his campaign, thought Nixon had expressed himself very well. According to them, they thought it was the best speech they had heard during the whole campaign.

At that time, there were more Democrats registered than Republicans—three to two. The Democrats had thirty-four governors in power. In both houses of Congress, the Democrats had the majorities. In twenty-nine states, the legislatures were predominately Democrats. Even the Democrats controlled one hundred twenty eight of the cities mayors, and one of those cities was Chicago. After looking at these statistics, I understood the odds Nixon was up against in his battle for the presidency race, and why he had to fashion a strategy to win.

In the farm belt in the Mid-West, things were more encouraging for Nixon. The Nixon farm plan was favored by the farmers. They liked that part of his farm program, which would give more control to the farmers instead of the bureaucrats in Washington. They didn't like the Kennedy plan, which provided the increase of controls by the government over every farmer in the country. Finally, the farm vote was shifting to Nixon away from Kennedy.

Kennedy offered a federal government program for every problem with increased controls. It would cost the taxpayers, but he forgot to tell them about that. Nixon thought the role of government should be limited and to support and activate the private sector. Individuals should have free choice and equal opportunity for all.

September 26, Monday, Nixon was to debate Kennedy on all the TV networks from Chicago. Pat decided to go to Washington to watch the debates with Julie and Tricia there. She had been absent from them almost two weeks. Dick thought he would be able to go to sleep before the debates. But Dick's plans did not work out, as he wanted. Five thousand people met Nixon at the Chicago airport at 10:30 a.m.

Republican officials planned five-ward street rallies enroute from the airport to Hotel Pick-Congress. Dick would stop only fifteen minutes in each ward. I remembered those large crowds, and how Nixon was so very tired. I wondered how long he would be able to stand up with this hectic campaigning. He finally tumbled into bed by one o'clock Monday morning.

The Carpenter's Union, a labor organization, had invited him to come to speak there at 11:00 a.m. Dick thought it was important to accept the union's invitation. There were many who reflected the Republican view in the union. Nixon asked them to look to the man, what he stands for, and will the man of your choice for president provide the leadership, which our country needs. But Dick Nixon discovered a hostile audience there, and it became very rough.

That afternoon Dick studied material on all the issues his staff had prepared for him. This cramming made him more completely ready than anytime in his political career. When other men had to have notes when speaking, Nixon did not. This man had an amazing mind, which caused him to photograph facts, figures, and other material. I really stood in awe of Dick's ability to say the right things without having notes in front of him.

However, Nixon was not aware of Kennedy's dirty tricks. Through the grapevine we learned that they had bugged Dick's hotel room, and also hired someone to pass out anti-Catholic and anti-Negro literature in certain neighborhoods. According to the Kennedy's, it was all right for them to do these ruthless things, but everyone else would be guilty if they did like wise.

At the TV studio, Nixon was on the set where the technicians were checking out the lighting and sound for him. Then a few minutes later, Kennedy walked in. My mouth dropped open. I couldn't believe my eyes! This was the first time I had seen him in person—up close. He was so becoming. Looked a picture of health with his beautiful suntan. Although

Kennedy was a very charming man, his eyes showed me a dark side, which the public was not aware of at that time. This troubled me.

Then I looked at Nixon. He looked so tired, pallid and weak. Unfortunately, he cracked his knee once again when coming into the TV studio. That infection took its toll. I wished he hadn't decided to debate Kennedy. Someone recommended that Dick should wear makeup. But, he rejected that idea. He only asked for some stick powder to conceal his" five-o'clock-shadow". Often, Dick had to shave two or three times a day, and a few minutes after he shaved it still looked obvious. The television cameras would be sure to pick it up. And it did. The weak knee and the studio's warm temperature were getting to Nixon. Dick Nixon tended to perspire more than most people. To stand on that weaken leg was excruciating! It took real courage for Nixon to go through the first debate with Kennedy.

Kennedy started off in the first debate. He attacked the Eisenhower administration on the elderly who could not afford medical care, discrimination against the minorities, the unemployed—all were their responsibility. Kennedy tried to convince the public Nixon did not care about these problems. He said it was time to get moving again. As I listened, I was wondering how Kennedy would do all these things. How much would it cost us as taxpayers? Would he keep all what he promised? I figured he wasn't going to spend his money, but mine, and the rest of the people's money.

I was glad Nixon took Kennedy on point by point. He pointed out that Kennedy proposed big federal government programs, and it would be paid right out of the taxpayer's pocket, as well as the people who needed help. Also, there should be limited government action and encourage private enterprise to solve the problems. Dick suggested what do we want—a free society or one, which is run by bureaucrats?

When I arrived back home, my friends called and asked if

Nixon was sick. They said he looked white and exhausted on TV—what was wrong? Even Nixon's mother called the office and inquired if Richard was sick. This made Nixon question others about it, too. The press wasn't sure who really won the debate. They were relying on what substance the candidates said. On the radio Nixon's message came across loud and clear and definitely won over the listeners. They thought Nixon was the better of the two. Dick realized that appearance was important as the message, and he strived to do something about it in the remaining three debates with Kennedy. In the fourth debate Nixon raised foreign policies differences between Kennedy and himself. Kennedy thought the Quemoy and Matsu Islands near China were not worth defending. Nixon said these two islands stood for freedom. We should not force our Chinese Nationalist allies off and let the Communists take over. Then, Kennedy made a campaign issue of Cuba and Castro. It involved the Cuban exiles and the CIA who wanted to overthrow Castro. The press applauded Nixon's decision to call the Kennedy plan irresponsible and to endanger the lives of Cuban exiles.

On the campaign trail crisscrossing the country, large enthusiastic crowds were evident wherever Pat and Richard Nixon went. Everyone loved Pat. She was an asset as usual to Dick's campaign. It was important that they would see as many people as they could.

It was an exhausting campaign—little food and sleep. All who were connected with the campaign felt pressed, shoved, and wore out. We all wondered if we could take more week. Pat was concerned about each one involved in the horrendous schedule. However I was worried about her. She was exhausted as the rest of us who worked. Pat was the one who encouraged us and inspired the rest of us to hang in there.

Ever since the Alger Hiss days, Richard Nixon had been attacked and maligned in the eastern press unfairly. It was difficult for me to listen to the lies and distortions. But I read everything and filed it under the name who wrote it. Pat was deeply hurt by it. How she lived with it, I'll never know. I knew she was alarmed by the Kennedy's mercilessness determination to win by any plan they could fashion.

One reason Nixon did not put women in top campaign offices very often, because he thought they couldn't stand the onslaught and cruelty of political life. However, I developed a thick skin and learned to dish it back with truth and facts. Pat wasn't that enthused about politics, but she was the best campaigner and always for her husband. She would give advice and criticism. Pat may have been a perfectionist, but anyone, who looked back on her life, would come to the conclusion she was one of us, who came up the hard way, too. Her stamina and courage was an inspiration to us all.

Just shortly before the November election, Martin Luther King, Jr. the black Negro, Baptist preacher, had a sit-in demonstration at an Atlanta, Georgia restaurant and was arrested. The judge had sentenced him to four months in jail because he had violated his parole some weeks before driving without a legal license. That really made a stir in the black Negro community.

But John F. Kennedy wanted the black Negro vote. So he seized the opportunity immediately and called Coretta King to pledge he would help get her husband out of jail. Then, Bobby Kennedy, John's brother, called the judge and urged him to release Martin Luther King, Jr., because he could be lynched there in jail.

Since Nixon was a lawyer, he thought it was an improper act to contact the judge in Atlanta. It would oppose the rules of professional conduct set by the American Bar Association.

Therefore, Nixon privately contacted the Justice Department to probe the situation to see if King's constitutional rights were violated. This did not get any publicity because the media did not have any information about it. The Attorney General asked President Eisenhower for approval, but he didn't get it. Because of Nixon's so-called silence, the King family condemned him and switched their votes. They urged all of the Negroes to vote for Kennedy instead of Nixon.

The Kings forgot Nixon's record on civil rights and the 1957 Civil Rights Act, which Nixon helped, get through in Congress for them. As the Israelites lost their memory of what God did for them to get out of Egypt, the black leaders neglected to remember who was their savior of the past. Kennedy fueled the incident by his money and shifty tactics.

Every time Nixon tried to do the right and proper thing, it was turned against him. He learned that the Democrats would play both sides of any issue as well as the race issue. I was in favor of exposing some of their shady maneuvers and schemes. Pat was disturbed by the methods, which Kennedy was using, and she was wondering how they could let the American people know the truth.

Just before the 1960 election, there was another economic slump. President Eisenhower was concerned about the country's unemployment. He asked Republican leaders to come to a White House luncheon for their suggestions on how to turn around the unemployment, and also how to promote the Nixon campaign. The campaign polls showed Kennedy and Nixon running neck-to-neck. Eisenhower did not want John F. Kennedy in the White House and desired to get out on the campaign hustling himself.

However, "Ike" was not aware of the telephone call which Mamie, his wife, had made to Pat Nixon the night before. She urged Pat to tell Dick to not let "Ike" to take on any extra campaign appearances because of his frail health. Mamie did not want her husband to know she had made the call to the Nixons.

Then, Howard M. Snyder, Eisenhower's doctor, called Nixon and asked if he could talk to him before the luncheon at the White House. Nixon found out the President was not well, and any additional campaign appearances would be disastrous on Eisenhower's health and maybe his life. After pondering on these two revelations, Nixon was wondering how he could handle this situation and persuade Eisenhower not to do any more campaigning.

Of course, this was the best-kept secret. Even Len Hall the Republican National Chairman, did not know have one inkling about it. Hall was angered at Nixon for this odd presentation. Eisenhower wanted to take on another assignment for his country. So he was quite disturbed and disappointed when Nixon would not let him add on any more states to his campaign schedule. It was an abrupt stunning announcement.

President Eisenhower wondered did Richard Nixon really want to be President? Was he throwing it all away? "Ike" was perplexed about it all. Those of us, who knew about the secret revelations given to the Nixons, were convinced that Nixon would rather lose the election than have President Eisenhower sacrifice his life. Again, Nixon put his country first instead of his ambitious plan. This was a courageous thing he had done. How many other people would have done it differently?

Eisenhower was disappointed and confused by not having more assignments. Therefore, he concentrated on the campaign appearances he was supposed to make. Eisenhower became fired up and attacked Kennedy's political views. The crowd loved it! Kennedy was no match for Eisenhower's scorn. Ike turned everything around what Kennedy said and hammered it home. The last person he wanted to see in the White House was John Kennedy! I wondered would the campaign be this close or way ahead, if Eisenhower had been allowed to go the extra miles to travel from place to place?

On the pinnacle of adversities, the economy began to slide, and higher interest rates developed just before the election. Pocket-book issues do have an effect on voters. However, this election was running neck-to-neck. It was too close to call. Who would really win?

In the last few days of his campaign, Nixon was pondering over and over in his mind concerning the issue of Kennedy's religion. Should he discuss the religious subject he had forbidden any campaign worker to exploit? All of us on the staff were pressuring him to take some action regarding what the leaders in Kennedy's campaign were saying and doing on the religious issue. The Catholics on Nixon's staff were most shocked about what the other side was doing against their boss. They said the Kennedy's staff was using reverse bias against Nixon, and they didn't like the tactics used. Their insistence to do something about it really touched Nixon.

Nixon did not believe that the Catholic religion was a valid important issue on Kennedy's qualifications for the presidency. He had vetoed a proposed endorsement by Billy Graham, the evangelist. His endorsement was based on Nixon's experience in foreign policy and not necessarily on a religious issue. Everyone knew that Richard Nixon often participated in Billy Graham's Crusades around the country, and he gave his personal religious testimony of what God meant to him.

Since Billy Graham and Richard Nixon were friends along time and had a close relationship, Nixon's staff thought Billy Graham's statement would be very helpful. Here again, Nixon would not use Billy Graham's support and vetoed the idea to inject it in the last days of the campaign.

However, it did not prevent the Democrats from using it against Nixon. The news media made the most of it and kept the issue alive on the front page. Nixon, once again, was trying to be fair about the whole thing. I never knew him to overstep the limits of fair play. He never defamed or persecuted others.

Nixon fulfilled his pledge to visit all fifty states in his

campaign. Two days before the election he flew to Alaska. No one thought Alaska would go for Nixon. When it was all over, Alaska had pulled over in the Nixon column. From Alaska, Pat and Dick left for Madison, Wisconsin enroute to Detroit, Michigan. Wisconsin, which was another close narrow margin state. Even though, the temperature was five degrees above zero, an enthusiastic crowd was jam-packed in an airline hangar there. Then Pat and Dick flew to Detroit.

I really don't know how Pat kept up with the hectic pace. All of us were exhausted, and so I knew she had to be, too. Also, Nixon was tired physically, but he was mentally alert for the nation-wide telethon at WXYZ-TV. Detroit, Michigan. For this telethon, he took questions for four hours from all over the country. As everyone analyzed the telethon results, they gave Nixon the edge in this election out-come. The last two weeks of this grueling race would make a difference they thought.

Nixon was known for his thoughtfulness. He took time from his busy campaign schedule to thank all the women who had manned the phone banks for the telethon. Nixon always realized that he could not do everything alone. He was grateful for everyone—great or small—who had a part in his campaign. Through the years, he developed friendships with those in low and high places. They never forgot Dick Nixon and the small kindness he bestowed on them.

At last, their Chicago telecast would be the end of an exciting campaign for Pat and Dick. Outside the Chicago studio five thousand enthusiastic volunteers rallied support for the Nixon team. To everyone's surprise, most of the crowd were college and university young people. It really warmed their hearts to feel the love, support, and loyalty of the crowd.

Inside the television studio, Nixon urged everyone to put America first, regardless of Party. He emphasized to vote for the man, who will support the needs of the American people, what is best for America and the world.

Finally, Pat and Richard Nixon said goodbye to everyone in Chicago at the airport. Enroute to Los Angeles, Pat and the children, Julie and Tricia, fell asleep on the airplane. Pat's physical and moral endurance had been greater than Dick's. I never had seen any other candidate's wives who could outdo Pat as a most gracious lady and an enthusiastic campaigner. For Nixon he inspired all of us never to give up in spite of adversity.

Instead of landing at the Los Angeles International airport, it was planned that the plane would come down at the Ontario airport. Fifteen thousand cheering people welcomed Pat and Dick back home to California. It was cold at two a.m., but the excited crowd warmed their hearts. They were glad to be home, and best of all to be able to go to bed.

However, for them sleep time was short. They had to rise early to go to Whittier to vote, and also pose for photographs at the precinct voting booths. Pat decided to go back to the Ambassador Hotel to rest and catch up on some mail she had been unable to answer. Pat always thought that her husband would win this election. She never considered the American people would ever decide to vote for a man like Kennedy.

Even Nikita Khrushchev of theSoviet Union got in his two cents worth of thoughts before the election. He rejected both Kennedy and Nixon, as a "pair of boots—which is better, the right boot or the left boot?

The early returns first came in from New Hampshire and Connecticut showing Kennedy was taking an early lead. At the Chicago campaign headquarters, I told some of the workers not to worry. The first returns didn't mean a thing— just to wait until more results would come in from the Midwest, California, Arizona, Utah, Ohio, Texas, and New

York. Time will tell-this will be a horse race—won by a nose—too close to call.

NBC and CBS were broadcasting confidently that it would be a Kennedy victory. I was ready to junk all those newsmen into the Potomac—always guessing and predicting. By seven, I hollered—Oklahoma, Vermont, and Kentucky moved into the Nixon column along with Indiana (Nixon's mother home state.) Some of the large states, which had more electoral votes, were starting to come in. I was watching the board for New York, Ohio, Texas, Pennsylvania, Michigan, California, and Illinois returns. The excitement was getting too much!

In the Midwest states, Nixon had moved into the lead, but in Illinois it was neck-to-neck. Kennedy was ahead for a while and then Nixon was in the lead. It seesawed back and forth all night. The suspense was killing me! We all had worked so hard until we were to the point of exhaustion. Now Florida, Tennessee, and Arizona had propelled over into the Nixon column. By 8:30 a.m. NBC was predicting that there would be a Kennedy electoral landslide. But I was praying for something different.

Then Ohio slid over into the Nixon column. It was discouraging to see the state of Texas in the Kennedy column. There would be still many states votes to be recorded. It didn't look good at this point, but I refused to let Kennedy have a victory at this time.

When CBS said Kennedy would take California, I noticed the tally board showed only eight per cent of the vote was in. Not yet said I! By 9:45 p.m., Nebraska, Iowa, North and South Dakota joined the other states in the Nixon column. I cheered when Kansas, my home birthplace, pulled over for Nixon.

The news media, Democrats, and some Republicans wanted to declare Nixon the loser and Kennedy the winner. By 10:30 p.m. it wasn't over yet. The states of Colorado, Wyoming, and Washington finally were added for Nixon. When I heard Nixon wanted to make a statement of some kind, I told him, "Don't make a concession statement. Not all Illinois votes are in—wait please." Even Senator Everett Dirksen of Illinois called Dick that the downstate Illinois votes were not in yet. Many wired and called Nixon not to concede until every last vote was counted.

The media was calling Nixon a poor loser because he didn't have the courage to say he lost. That really made me angry! It wasn't over until that one last vote was in! I didn't mind telling them so.

Pat didn't want her husband to make any kind of statement until all the results were in. She was not ready to give up the election victory to Kennedy. Pat was determined her husband would be victorious.

Then Bob Finch brought in a report that the popular vote had narrowed to a thin trickle. He opposed Nixon making any kind of concession announcement. This time Pat was on our side. She opposed Dick making a statement. Texas and Illinois were having problems with their ballot boxes and voting machines. Pat wanted to win. She was confident, if Illinois and Texas would clear up their voting irregularities, Dick Nixon would be the winner. But this was not to be!

The clock chimed the midnight hour. The waiting was terrible. The minutes were creeping slowly by. Richard Nixon was weighing in his mind what to do next. Should he make a statement? When he discussed it again with Pat, she still opposed the idea. What would he tell all those faithful workers and friends? She did not want Dick to declare Kennedy the victor. She was torn emotionally and refused at first to go with her husband. However, something inside her said she should be with him. Wasn't Dick hurting, too? Therefore, Pat gathered herself together and retained her composure.

As Pat and Dick walked onto the Ambassador Hotel platform, the crowd shouted words of encouragement and was applauding a long time. It was an enthusiastic crowd of friends, workers, and supporters.

As the people became quiet, Nixon began slowly to speak. It was difficult for him to say anything. He told them if the current trend continues, Senator Kennedy would be the next President of the United States. Tears were in Pat's eyes and she tried to control it desperately. Even Bob Finch cried, too, as well as many did in the crowd. All didn't want Nixon to give up the fight. Tears flowed down my cheeks. That night there were so many hugs and greetings with one another. It would be a night to remember.

Pat was badly hurt by the results of the 1960 presidential campaign. She thought Dick should challenge the results because of the Illinois and Texas vote frauds. Senator Everett Dirksen and President Eisenhower thought Nixon shouldn't have made a statement until all the votes were in, and now they wanted a recount. Without the Illinois and Texas electoral votes, Kennedy would not have been the winner.

The TV and radio broadcasters were changing their tune who was actually the winner. Now they were saying Kennedy was ahead or it looked like he had won. What a switch! Weren't they part of the problem by their actions? If California and Illinois were to move over in the Nixon column, the outcome would be different.

I knew what the Democrats in Cook County were doing in Illinois. Their game was to hold back certain precincts and waiting to see how the people down state would be voting. The popular vote continued to narrow. The unofficial election returns in Illinois listed Kennedy down to eight thousand votes. The absentee ballots were counted in California and Nixon won his home state vote. After losing the state of Minnesota votes, Nixon sent a formal concession telegram to Kennedy.

Days after the election, thousands of letters and telegrams poured in for them. Pat and Dick appearance on television engendered an enthusiastic response all through the country. Even in their defeat, the people showered them with their love and respect. They wanted them not to be discouraged but to continue the fight.

There was massive vote fraud in Illinois and Texas. Because he loved his country more, Nixon did not throw the case into court. The law would have allowed the case trial to run for a year or more in the courts, and the United States would have been without a President for that length of time. Richard Nixon set a proper example of conduct even in defeat. He knew that defeat was a greater test of his character than if he had won. His serenity in time of disappointment and defeat stemmed from his religious and moral training.

But God had other plans. Sometimes He lays people aside, so they can look up to Him for dependence, guidance, and help. Surely, Nixon had done a lot of soul-searching and was assured that his cause was right. When at the right time— God's time—he would be permitted to run for the presidency again.

Even though, Nixon thought no one could steal the election, I was determined to show the country it really did happen and set out to prove it.

Chapter 4

VOTE FRAUD;
A CONSTITUTIONAL CRISIS

As a woman I found it very difficult to accept this defeat, especially when I knew the election had been stolen. I had committed myself to the Nixon battle with all my heart and being. I knew Nixon had won. So did Pat, Julie and Tricia think as I did and could not reconcile themselves that their father and husband had lost. Julie insisted that we should have a recount in Chicago. I supported that statement.

Even, Hannah, Richard Nixon's mother, and his secretaries didn't want him to give up the fight. Tricia and Julie scolded their father harshly. Dick found out that women were more loyal and committed than men. In his defeat, it was the women who did not forsake him in his battle for the presidency.

Although, Nixon once said no one can steal an election. This time I disagreed with him. Since I lived in Chicago I knew this city's politics much better than those who lived outside the state of Illinois. Election fraud is a way of life here. Every person is guaranteed the right to vote, but where is the guarantee that his vote would be counted?

Despite the secret ballot and the voting machine, vote

stealing was an old and dishonorable trade. Nixon was deprived of the Presidency by widespread vote frauds in key states such as Illinois and Texas. Also, Benjamin Adamowski who ran for Illinois State's attorney and lost in a very close race, asked for recount. But, as his re-count probe progressed, it became obvious that the perplexing laws and methods and shortage of time in which to reverse an apparent fraud, not to refer to the gigantic cost involved, all were consolidating to have effect against this ratification of injustice.

It would be difficult to slash through the statutory muddle and to win control over the action of a forceful political machine. I realized that it would not be simple—even with all the evidence supplied—to nullify the outcome of the vote declared officially by the controlled Democrat county election machine.

The painful procedure to obtain that end had begun with the termination of the recount expose. The Democrats on the Chicago canvassing board had walked out on the petition that they make right the vote in agreement with the recount. A writ was issued in the Circuit Court against the Chicago and Cook County canvassing boards to compel them to act upon it. The members of the boards were commanded to attend court under penalty for failure to do so. Then, the Illinois state electoral board was asked not to verify Kennedy as the winner of the electoral votes in Illinois.

Was the vote stolen from Richard Nixon? Yes, it was. What we discovered was nothing like the Florida punch card voting debacle for the Gore/Bush 2000 Presidential race. Apparently, in Florida certain persons could not read or to follow instructions. In Illinois in 1960, the case was quite different. What did we find? Nixon was deprived of an honest vote count by the actions of others. This is what we found:

Certain names were pulled from precinct binders, so they would be deprived of their right to vote. The voting machines, which registered the tallies automatically, were deliberately counted incorrectly. Marked ballots were deposited. Paper ballots tallies were missing and falsified in certain precincts. In certain parts of Chicago, paper ballots were used. Some voters sold their vote before hand. Before going into the polling place, a marked ballot was given to them. Inside the voting booth the marked ballot was cast. The clean ballot, which they received inside the polling place, was given to the men outside who gave them the marked ballot originally. This is what we called chain balloting.

Then, we found out that persons were hired as Republican judges in name only in precincts and were secretly in pay of the Democrats. All the votes were recorded for the Democrats with no regard how the persons voted.

Before the polls opened in the morning, the voting machines tallies were run up before any voters had registered their vote. I discovered several machines had 1000 votes registered before hand. Also voting machines were jammed. The fewer machines operating, it was better for the corrupt Democrat machine to continue their operations, If a voter of not of their persuasion who was waiting in a long line, they hoped they would give up and go home without voting for Nixon.

Did you ever hear of ghost voting? You ask what is that? If a person who is listed at a certain address to vote, and then they either die or move away, without having his name removed from the poll list. This way anyone could visit several polling places and vote for dead persons or someone who has moved out of state.

When ballot boxes were found empty, we wondered where the missing ballots were. The ballots would eventually show up somewhere after the corrupt people had a chance to tamper with the ballot boxes. The precincts charged with vote fraud, their ballots mysteriously disappeared from the election commissioner's safe.

Another thing we discovered the election judges told the

voters how to vote when they were assisting voters. Crooked information was given. You see Chicago was divided into ethnic-foreign groups, such as German, Spanish, Polish, Swedish, Italian, etc. Interpreters were provided at the polling places to tell each voter in their own language how to vote the straight Democrat ticket. Since the ethnic voter did not have the special ability in understanding of the English language, he bought the word of the election worker who had given him voter information. Later, the voter found he was deceived and cheated out of his vote.

Poll watchers were prohibited the right to examine and count the unused ballots in the precincts. After the election many believed that ballots were marked and used to replace others. No wonder the official tally was not correct. Ballot boxes were discovered with their seals broken and some seals did not have the judge's signatures written on it. That would make anyone wonder if the contents were tampered with there in.

They could not challenge or throw out spoiled ballots or ballots which did not have the judge's initials or misplaced somewhere in a different area. In the original precinct count, Republican ballots were thrown out or spoiled and not tallied in the re-count. Evidence showed they were deliberately spoiled. How were we to take account of those who voted several times and paid voting, and those who used false names, or of improper removal of registered voters from voting registration lists?

Eight University of Chicago students were disillusioned and very angry. They witnessed vote fraud on a large scale and were powerless to do much about it. What they saw was more disgraceful than they had ever imagined. This group of students set out to question this trickery and to be vigilant as watchers at the polls. They thought this sort of thing wasn't supposed to happen. All the books they had read didn't tell them about this kind of chicanery.

The fourth ward was controlled by the Democrat machine,

as well as part of the south side bloc of wards by the Democratic leader Dawson. These students found eight persons with the same last names; even some had the same first names. And behold, these persons were listed as living in the same one block. Six were listed at the same address. However, these students could find only two persons with that name in the block.

Then, they discovered voters whose names were listed on the election commission books as nonqualified voters. To their amazement, the election judges failed to compare the voter's signatures on the ballot applications with the polling place binder's signatures. When the judges were questioned about this, they claimed to know everyone in the precinct. Therefore, they didn't have to check this out, the judges said. These volunteer poll watchers were told to mind their own business. Because the Democrat precinct captains were running the election, they knew exactly what they were doing. Also, some of the student watchers with proper credentials were ordered out of certain precincts. These university students learned a lot, and said they would be back for the next election to save more votes from theft.

Yet, the Democrat canvassing board chaired by Sidney Holzman admitted irregularities were due to human error. But, I wondered why he decided to announce he was summoning the election judges for questioning, if it was due just to human error. Republicans demanded that four hundred sixty election judges appear before the canvassing board of Chicago to answer questions and verify if the tallies were correct. When Holzman invited the judges into a little room, it became a most disorganized, unruly crowd. After displaying the tallies for each precinct to be verified by the judges, he finally dismissed them after nonsensical questioning about it.

It was decided that only the five member canvassing board would be responsible for re-counting each precinct. This was the strategy to slow the task to a crawl. However, the new

Democratic county judge ordered twenty-five tally clerk teams to accelerate the job.

The best that was possible was to confirm the totals in counting all ballots the precinct election judges had determined to be authentic whether or not the ballots were false, defective or invalid. No ballot was nullified in the precinct, even if it had been marked deliberately, was permitted in the recount. The canvassing board refused the revision of the voting totals—showing admitted errors.

Now, we had established sufficient evidence for bring a court suit for an official recount because of voter fraud. We would have to rely on a Republican volunteer committee to watch and be on the constant alert. If the recount were carried out, all candidates who protested the outcome of the election would have to bear the cost of hundreds of thousand dollars. We were advised by our lawyers that the recount would take a year and a half to be completed and the country would be in limbo without a President.

We knew we didn't have much time. December 19th was the deadline for certification of Illinois twenty-seven electoral votes for John F. Kennedy or Richard Nixon? What were we to do? We knew what we had discovered. However, this was a constitutional crisis.

Mayor Richard Daley, Sr. and the Cook County Clerk were the two Democrats on the three member county canvassing board. Much earlier they had already signed the declaration that Cook County went for Kennedy and other Democrat candidates who were also in this controversy. Our difficulty was getting an honest voting report of the results to the Springfield state board. I was wondering if those men had a conscience. What would induce them to recall the former declaration and replace it with the correct list? I was hoping the courts would force them to do so.

The existing Illinois election procedure was insufficient to procure an honest vote count or protect the ballot's integrity. The election law offered almost no recourse to any candidate who lost by default in an election. Every registered person has the right to vote and have that vote to be counted honestly. I was determined to have the election law system revamped in Illinois, which I considered corrupt.

Julie and Tricia were convinced that their father had won the election in Illinois. They decided to send all their Christmas money gifts to us for the recount.

In Texas the immense vote was manipulated for the Kennedy/Johnson ticket, too. In the election machinery there were Democrats who dictated every function from the state board of canvassers to the tally clerks in the precincts. The state board was made up of three Democrats. Two of them were directors of the Kennedy campaign in Texas. Because of their underhanded tricks and questionable conduct, ballot-box stuffing existed and jammed voting machines misread votes for Republicans, and the Democrats had their votes counted double.

For example, in Angelina County, Texas eighty-six persons cast their ballots. However, the official showed twenty-four votes for the Nixon/Lodge ticket and one hundred forty eight for the Kennedy/Johnson ticket. There were many thousand precincts in Texas like the Angelina County, which were approved without question by the Texas Election Board of Canvassers. Where was the media in Illinois and Texas? Were they involved and only looked the other way when something was happening? At that time Texas was one of the states, which had a poll tax. Before every election voters had to re-register. To determine who could vote, all one had to do was to check the poll tax list and count names.

Of course, Texas has to do something unusual. Under their Texas election law a voter could delete the candidates he didn't want—just the opposite of what we usually do in other states. If a voter failed to cancel out any other minority party candidates, the Nixon ballot was thrown out. The votes tallied for Kennedy did not take place. With all the evidence before Nixon and more flooding in his office, we assumed Nixon would take legal action. But he did not. Nixon was not going to take the country down the road of a constitutional crisis because of this election result. Again he put the country first instead of self. This was a different case then the 2000 Gore and Bush presidential race. Who was most courageous—Gore or Nixon?

To many there will be a memory of a decisive Kennedy victory in 1960. As things turned out it was really two occurrences, which denied the presidency to Richard Nixon and gave it to John F. Kennedy. The state of Illinois was one occurrence and the 1960 census was the other.

In Illinois Nixon carried ninety-three of the one hundred counties. Only the downstate counties of Alexander, Gallatin, Clinton, St. Clair, Madison, Macoupin, Christian and the counties of Rock Island and Cook County upstate were carried by Kennedy. The downstate counties gave Kennedy 999,503 votes. Nixon won over Kennedy in those counties with 1,309,381 total votes. Cook County delivered 1,376,343 votes for Kennedy, but Nixon received only 1,059,607 votes. When the total was completed for Illinois Kennedy received 2,377,846 votes and Nixon 2,368,988.

The popular vote nationwide was Kennedy 34,227,096 49.7 %) and Nixon was 34,108,546 (49.5 %) Kennedy had 23 states-303 electoral votes and Nixon had 26 states—219 electoral votes. This made a difference of 118,550 votes nationwide. It was a squeaker election. If Illinois had gone victorious for Nixon I was wondering whether this would have been sufficient to swing the election to Nixon. As memories faded regarding the 1960 election, mine did not.

The number of Congressmen determines the Electoral College membership. A census is taken every ten years by the federal government for each state's entitlement to certain number of congressmen, as well as other concerns. The 1960

Nixon/Kennedy election was held on the premise of the Electoral College with the 1950 census calculations. The census figures were not finished until after the election in November. If the 1960 census figures had been used, the election between Nixon and Kennedy would have been even closer than anyone thought. The States, which cast electoral votes for Kennedy, would have lost ten electoral votes. Those States carried by Nixon would have gained nine more. Therefore, Kennedy would have received only 293 electoral votes instead of the 303 he was supposed to have. Had the 1960 census been used, the loss of Illinois would have made a huge difference.

If Nixon had the state of Illinois in his vote column, Kennedy would have one electoral vote short of the majority needed. Then the election would have gone to the House of Representatives to decide the outcome. If Senator Harry F. Byrd received fifteen electoral votes, this would have prevented Nixon from getting the necessary majority.

Either way my dream of victory for Nixon was shattered completely. Should I accept the verdict when I knew first hand what really happened? For now, I had to do it.

Nixon was a statesman—fought clearly and fairly—and put decency before politics. On January 6, 1961, Dick's last official responsibility as Vice-President of the United States was to oversee the joint congressional meeting and to declare the Electoral College votes for President. As the votes were tallied, Nixon reminded us to support those who win and accept the outcome. Then, he announced that John F. Kennedy was the official elected President of the United States.

Richard Nixon realized that soon he would be a private citizen. He would have no job or pension. All he had was a used Oldsmobile car and several thousands in savings. How would he earn a living? Tricia and Julie would be going to college soon. That was something else for him to think about.

There were telephone calls and letters urging him to be a baseball commissioner, a commentator on television, a college president or an influential lobbyist in Washington. Should he stay in Washington or go to California? As he pondered all these things, Nixon knew either one of these job offers would pay well and provide a satisfactory livelihood for his family. However, he still wanted to be a part of the Republican Party and give his expertise in public affairs.

The closing down of his Vice-President's office was an arduous job. Staff personnel were dwindling and so it became more strenuous. Tons of mails, telegrams, and telephone calls enlarged and flooded in every week after the election. No one could keep up with the mail. It just kept coming in from people all over the country, as well as statesmen from other parts of the world.

After examining carefully all the job opportunities, Nixon decided to accept the offer of a Los Angeles law firm of Adams, Duque, and Hazeltine as a lawyer. His earnings were to be established on professional service charges from persons who engaged Nixon personally. This way Richard Nixon could choose which clients he wanted to work with and to distribute his time proportionately.

The day before the inauguration of John F. Kennedy, the remaining staff members were still trying to sort and pack thousands of letters and files. They were hoping to be completely packed because January 20,1961 date would be there tomorrow to vacate Nixon's office. Before leaving Washington Nixon set up a special postal box—P.O. Box 6539 in Los Angeles 55, California, to receive mail. It was never ending. Pat and Dick tried to catch upon their mail. It was an immense task, and it would take months and months to answer it all.

That night Pat and Dick said goodbye to all of their staff at a farewell party at the Capitol. The unexpected, heavy snow blizzard complicated travel. A thirty-minute trip became a three-hour journey. When everyone arrived, each one looked out at the pretty view of the Lincoln Memorial and other sights in Washington. At night Washington, D.C. is a beautiful vision to behold. It brought back pangs of sadness, in spite of the marvelous time together. For some it would be the last time to see each other and to look at the beautiful view of Washington. It was difficult.

All of the staff was devoted to the Nixons. As Pat and Dick left the Capitol, the workers who took care of the building came out to say goodbye. Some had a sad look and others had tears in their eyes. Their kindness really touched Pat and Dick. It was something they would never forget.

After the Kennedy inauguration ceremony and luncheon, Pat and Dick and a few friends flew to the Bahamas for a much needed vacation. Then, I took off to Arizona for a two-week vacation of relaxing and meditating in the Valley of the Sun. When I arrived back to Chicago, I decided to consult with other Republicans in Illinois and map out plans for vote reform and to eliminate vote fraud in Chicago or where ever else it might happen. Down deep down in my heart, I knew Richard Nixon would run again for the presidency. Next time I was determined he would not be denied victory again.

Chapter 5

TIME OF REBUILDING

The Nixons planned a lazy vacation in the Bahamas for a month. However, the slow quiet life of the islands was too lethargic for Dick. He was not use to being that inactive. So Pat and Dick concluded that they should go back to their mortgaged Washington home. Visitors came to their home. There was a constant parade of people, as well as many telephone calls and mountains of mail.

The private life for Nixon began when he departed for Los Angeles to begin working with the law firm of Adams, Duque, and Hazeltine. Pat went along to look for a new house. She found out it wasn't easy as she thought to find in one week the house of their dreams. Dick was expected to travel a lot, so a place near an airport or one with a view of the ocean would be fine. They discovered those kind of houses eluded them. Therefore, Pat and Dick determined to build a house like they wanted it.

Pat had decided that Julie and Tricia should stay in school in Washington until the end of the school term. Dick went to Los Angeles and Pat stayed behind in Washington with the girls. What a way to start a new life! Personally, I thought Pat, in reviewing the past events, considered she had made a wrong decision this time. Pat and Dick missed each other. Dick was unhappy and lonely, and he could not concentrate. The children wanted to be with their daddy, and Dick wanted to be with Pat and the girls.

Pat enjoyed being Second Lady, but not the political aspects connected with it. The 1960 presidential campaign outcome totally shattered her. She kept the pain inside and never wanted to discuss it with anyone again. All she wanted was to be a good mother to Julie and Tricia and a wonderful wife to her husband. She firmly believed that back home in California they could spend more time together as a family.

For now, Julie and Tricia were still enrolled at Sidwell Friends, a private Quaker school, in Washington. I remembered how Julie and Tricia were so broken up by their father's defeat. They loved their father and wondered why everyone else didn't. Julie and Tricia were appalled by a few of their classmates who went out of their way to make political attacks on their father. It really hurt. Then, they discovered that those students were connected with the Kennedy administration.

Tricia was more restrained. She just kept everything inside and didn't always show her emotion. But, Julie was different. She was like a little "tiger-in-a-tank." Never would give up on anything. She believed that her father won the election. Julie wanted a recount. At school she would put up with classmates taunts regarding her dear father, but at home she would let it all out and weep. Julie and I both thought the same way about the stolen election, and so we ended up in the same "club" determined to do something about it.

Meanwhile, Nixon had rented another set of offices two blocks from his law office to take care of the huge amount of mail inundating his post office box 6539 and the research for other writings he was making. Rosemary Woods had already come to the California law offices as his personal secretary. Loie Gaunt would be in charge of the second office place.

Pat sent an Easter card to me with the latest news. She always remembered me on Easter and Christmas. She was always a thoughtful person remembering others. On Easter vacation from school, Julie and Tricia came out with their mother to California. They had a good time on the beach at San Monica and loved the warm weather there.

Dick often commuted between Los Angeles and Washington. Since he would make speeches regarding foreign policies, Nixon always wanted to be up-to-date on any information about foreign affairs. He was disturbed about President Kennedy's foreign policy actions connected with the Communist attacks in Laos. It was time for Dick to speak out. Just before he left for Washington one day in April, the newspapers exploded with the news about the invasion of Cuba by anti-Castro insurgent forces.

Then, after I read about the disastrous Bay of Pigs landing in the "Chicago Tribune," I remembered what Kennedy said in October of the 1960 campaign, "We must attempt to strengthen the non-Batista democratic anti-Castro forces in exile, and in Cuba itself . . . thus for these fighters for freedom have had virtually no support from our government."

However, when Kennedy became President, he waffled on the Cuban issue. The Cuban expatriates were authorized an invasion undertaking without air protection aid from the United States. Kennedy revoked this part of the invasion plot, without informing the anti-Castro aggressors. As the invasion started, President Kennedy proclaimed to the whole world that our Armed Forces would not invade under any circumstance, thereby preventing any revolt in Cuba.

What did this do to United States prestige abroad? Again I remembered what Kennedy said during the 1960 campaign-"Rebuilding our prestige must be the primary concern of our next President." Now, the American prestige endured smashing damage to our allies support because of Kennedy's actions in Laos and Cuban disaster. Foreign leaders were questioning Kennedy's leadership.

President Kennedy knew he was in deep trouble. The Castro bombers had annihilated the landing forces. How could he face the survivors? The relatives were very angry. It would be difficult.

Then, Kennedy called Nixon's home in Washington and wanted Dick to come to the White House. Nixon had not arrived yet, so Tricia took the message for her father. She knew Kennedy must be in real trouble for him to call her father for help. Tricia didn't mind saying so.

Kennedy thought he obtained bad advice from some of the men he trusted. But, I was wondering if Dick were President would Kennedy go out of his way to support him and not use it in a partisan way? I think not. However, Dick gave him some advice what he would do in Laos and Cuba. At all times, if we make a commitment we must back it up with United States forces. It should be in our national interest—not based on public opinion. They departed amicable.

In May of 1961, Nixon began a speaking tour from California to certain states throughout the country. We convinced him to make his first stop in Chicago at the Executive Club luncheon and in the evening at our Republican Citizens League of Illinois. Also, he had decided to write ten articles for the Times Mirror Syndicate. It was carried in one hundred forty five newspapers. One was in the "Chicago Sun Times." It was real informative, and I saved each one, which was published. I was really proud. Dick was telling it like it should be.

May 5, 1961 in Chicago, Dick was attending the Executive Club luncheon. Charles Carpentier, our Illinois Secretary of State, was sitting next to him. They had some fun toasting each other in tomato juice.

I remembered Dick stressing in his speech that we should

be constructive in our criticism attacks on the Kennedy administration—just stay on issues and not on personalities. Dick Nixon was really perturbed about the way Kennedy handled the Cuban invasion Bay of Pigs. He said we should not start something anywhere in the world, unless we provide the necessary power to finish it. Also, he was concerned that Kennedy should have the backbone to stand up against the Communists in Laos, Vietnam or the Far East, or anywhere else for that matter.

After the 1960 election many people were aroused around the country, especially Cook County, Illinois. James Worthy, who used to be in the Eisenhower administration, as well as one of the directors of the United Republican Fund of Illinois, was deeply concerned about the vote fraud in Illinois. He wanted to organize concerned citizens. I volunteered my time to help in anyway to get this grassroots movement, the Republican Citizens League, on the road.

The turn out that night at McCormick Place even amazed me. There was a new spirit abroad in our state and country and within the Republican Party. I would not have predicted a few months ago that a meeting such as this could be held in a non-election year, especially by the Republicans recently defeated at the polls. I never would have guessed there would be such a spontaneous enthusiasm for everyone there who resolved what happened November 8,1960 would not occur again. It was a tribute to Richard Nixon.

When Dick approached the podium, the crowd went wild and applauded him along time. Of course, that made me happy. It was a time of rebuilding.

Dick bluntly criticized Democrat programs and lashed out at Kennedy's actions regarding Laos and Cuba. Then he reminded us that if he had an organization parallel to that of the Democrats in all big cities and in key electoral states in 1960 we would have been assured of victory. But we did not.

He told us that the responsibilities of citizenship go

beyond merely going to the polls to cast a vote. Asked us to be concerned with the courthouse race as we are with the presidential election contest, with the aldermanic race, or with the United States Senator's office. Work not for personal reward but from a sense of personal service. That we must be a "Gideon's Army" concerned for good government and forward the principles for which the Republican Party stands. In conclusion, Dick said that the Republican Party had a historic mission to perform. Principles are important and so are candidates. But neither can prevail unless we have a powerful organization support. As citizens we could provide manpower and womanpower to give victory to our candidates and meaning to our principles.

Dick asked us to go to work and so we did. Thousands of people who heretofore had taken little personal part in politics, never held an office, or official party position became a part of the Republican Citizens League—a working group for the Republican Party. There were young people, vigorous and dedicated, and women deeply concerned with what was happening around them and wanted to do something about it. The retired blue-collar and the white-collar workers became the most effective enthusiastic volunteers to restore the Republican Party strength in Illinois. Wherever Dick spoke he inspired us to work for a cause, party unity and morale.

I remembered what President John Kennedy said the week before at McCormick Place to Mayor Richard Daley, Sr. and the Democrat Party in Illinois. Here Kennedy admitted in his own words whom to thank for that achievement. The news media chose not to connect Kennedy with the election skullduggery.

After Nixon's speaking engagements, he returned to California. He realized he was now backing in the center of public attention. Dick only wanted to spend more time with Pat and the girls, but the obligations of his law work, writing articles for the newspapers, and the inevitable political

Partners-in-Crisis: The Untold Story of Pat and Richard Nixon

journeys around the country caused him to spend little time with Pat, Julie and Tricia. Then, to all of this, Dick added the responsibility of writing a book "Six Crises" We all wondered how he would be able to do it.

Walter Lang, director of FOX studios, had solved Pat and Dick's problem where to live, until their house at 410 Martin Lane, in Trousdale Estates was ready to occupy in Beverly Hills. The Langs were pleased to rent to the Nixons a furnished, vacated English Tudor house on North Bundy Drive in Brentwood, just for the upkeep cost. Of course, Pat and Dick were delighted with the offer and accepted Lang's proposal at once. Since they would not be overlooking the ocean, the Lang property had a large swimming pool, which would be a good substitute.

Julie and Tricia's school ended in the middle of June. They realized that they would be leaving their friends there. It would be difficult. Although, the girls had been to California often, their home had always been in Washington, D.C. Moving away and not seeing their friends was something else. Julie was affected especially by the soon departure.

Dick returned to Washington in June to complete the real estate escrow papers for the sale of their Washington home. He helped Pat with the packing for their move to California. Checkers, the famous black and white, cocker spaniel dog and the two cats, Puff and Nicki, were to be transported in a special portable kennel cabs via the airline cargo system to California. Finally, Pat and Dick with the girls were once again one family.

63

Chapter 6

CRISIS OF 1962
GOVERNOR'S RACE

After dwelling a few months in their rental home in Brentwood, the Nixon's moved into their new home at 410 Martin Lane. Tricia and Julie's youthful friends from Washington came as guests. Pat thought there were a lot of young people coming and going. In the new Nixon home the atmosphere resembled a miniature hotel. There were swimming pool contests, lots of chatter, and plentiful food and snacks.

Dick usually worked twelve hours or more at the office, but sometimes he did some of his work at home. One time he was at home, Dick noticed that Tricia was becoming interested in boys, and the boys were attracted to Tricia. That really got his attention. For the first time he realized Tricia was growing up and not a little girl anymore.

He had seen the girls less in that year in California than all the time he was in Washington. With his busy schedule, when would he have more time to spend with the children? Dick had an active life. Sometimes he felt like a juggler in a circus. The pressures and responsibilities he faced were almost overwhelming, yet some people wanted him to still keep taking on more and more. It was his hope to spend more time with his daughters, Tricia and Julie. He made every effort to do so. However, it wouldn't be easy.

Throughout the summer time and the fall Nixon dedicated himself to finish his book "Six Crises." Often he would seclude himself and be absorbed in writing, oblivious of anyone or everything around him. The book was taking longer than the scheduled plan. The deadline, which the publisher set, was coming closer and closer. His scribbled notes were dictated into his tape machine and then transcribed by one of his secretaries. The strain and fatigue of writing the book, as well as his other duties, took its toll on Nixon. He lost weight and became short-tempered at the office and home, and just rundown generally. All these extra activities drained all the creativity, productivity, and energy from his very being.

Dick was so tired that he was unable to make the proper decision regarding the pressures from some Republican friends wanting him to run for the office of Governor. California politics was trying to interrupt his private life. The pressure continued. He had no intention to run as a candidate for Governor of California. Repeatedly, Dick told everyone, who approached him about it, that he was not interested in the job.

I remembered even President Eisenhower told him it was his obligation to run. If the state were taken over by the Democrats, Dick would be blamed because he did not run or do anything to stop what was going on. Even, Barry Goldwater got into the act, too, and he told Dick his influence in the Republican Party would fade if he didn't hold a public office. Len Hall told him the same thing. He even received advice from ex-President Herbert Hoover and General Douglas MacArthur that he should run for Congress instead. Therefore, Dick was between a rock and a hard place on what to do.

However, some of us did not believe this was the time and place for him to run for the governor's office, and we told him so. Also, Pat was not in favor of Dick running for any office now. She wanted him to spend more time with Julie and Tricia during their teenage years. So Dick kept mulling over everyone's opinions and advice. How would he approach Pat?

Pat was happy to be out of politics. She enjoyed gardening and the California sunshine, and to spend more time with her family. Julie and Tricia were attending a private Marlborough School for girls in Los Angeles. Pat reviewed their homework with them each evening. She helped them with their studies when necessary. They were not permitted to watch TV on school nights. With school assignments and book reports from a required list, Julie and Tricia did not have the pleasure of reading other stories until vacation periods. After they finished their homework on the weekends, they were allowed to watch television.

Pat wanted her two girls to grow up gracious and feminine. If anyone expected them to be pampered, they discovered that they were not. Julie and Tricia were regular teenagers. They would swim and sometimes eat more than they should. However, they enjoyed skits and like to act in plays. Julie was the inquisitive one. She asked questions about everything. Both of the girls were up on the latest current events, and they were doing things, which other teens their age were doing. Pat was a remarkable fine mother and Julie and Tricia were her two good examples. Dick and Pat gave both of the girls love and security in their home. In turn, Julie and Tricia developed the same feeling for their parents and wanted them to be proud of what ever they did or said. They were considerate and thoughtful of Pat and Dick, as well of others around them.

Wherever Pat and Dick went, people would tell them how nice and friendly and warm their daughters were. That made them very proud.

Dick went to father-daughter events and tried to make up for anytime he was separated from the girls. His daughters and his wife were all important to him. Pat said Dick never said a harsh word to the girls. She was the one who was the disciplinarian.

She participated in a car pool with other parents driving to school with their girls. Pat attended Parent-Teacher Association (PTA) meetings and went to all school fairs and bazaars, as well as the Girl Scout meetings. Both of them were concerned about their children and showed by example they cared.

The girls loved baseball games. They would sit in on baseball games and cheer themselves sick. One time at school Julie was hit on the head with a bat during a girls' softball game. She was sitting on a bench watching the ball game. The girl at bat swung wildly at the pitched ball and struck Julie on the left side of the head. Pat took her to the doctor. The doctor said Julie endured a broken blood vessel and a lump on the left side of her head, and that she should go home to rest. From then on, Julie didn't stay too close to the batter box.

Dick was not an impulsive thinker and doer. He would take everyone's advice, and then ponder over it before acting on it. That summer the pressure to run for the Governor's race tripled. He thought over about the political powers that would oppose him if he should decide to run.

Southern California was regarded as Republican territory, but the northern half of California usually voted Democratic. The Democrats surpassed the Republicans by more than a million registered voters. However, the voters in California were not reliable and were unstable.

Then, Dick realized that the Kennedy administration would oppose him and would do anything to stop him if should make a decision to run for the office of Governor. Also, he could not count on California ultra-conservative Republicans to help him out or give money to his campaign. They called him a "loser." There were two factions—Goldwater and Rockefeller—very divisive and divided and fighting one another.

Dick hated to bring the subject up with Pat and the girls. Therefore, he decided to call a family meeting after dinner. He summarized the pros and cons of the advice he had been given. Dick said he wanted to know what they thought about him running for Governor before he finally made up his mind.

Pat did not want to give up her private life. She wanted to enjoy life as she saw it. To her—she wanted to only walk down a street without being recognized, to cook and clean a house without servants, and not be disturbed many times a day.

All three voted down Dick's decision to run for Governor. Dejected, he went to his room to write out a press release that he would not be a candidate. Tricia saw how her father's face looked, so she mentioned to her mother maybe we should change our votes.

Pat thought about it for a while. She was convinced it would be a big mistake for Dick to run. Disappointed, she told her husband that she would be by his side campaigning as she had in the past—if that was what he really wanted to do. Julie and Tricia said they would approve whatever their father decided to do. In talking with Pat, I agreed with her that Dick's decision would be a mistake, but I would support him anyway.

On September 27,1961 at the Statler Hilton Hotel in Los Angeles, Nixon announced at a press meeting he would be a candidate for Governor of California in 1962,and also he would not be a candidate for President of the United States in 1964. After hearing Nixon's announcement, Pat Brown, the Democrat Governor of California, accused Richard Nixon of using the governor's office as only a stepping-stone to further his future plans to become President someday.

Dick had only three more months to complete his book, "Six Crises." Now he had a deadline from the publisher regarding it. He was wondering how he could devise tactics and plan his campaign for Governor and finish his book, too. However, he managed to complete it. The book was a masterpiece.

The Republican primary election was to be held June 5, 1962. Nixon's opponent was Joseph C. Shell, the California Assembly Minority Leader. He was an attractive man who wasn't short of money either.

Dick always had a rule—never attack another Republican. Aim your ammunition at the person you have to defeat in the general election in November. Therefore, he concentrated on Governor Brown instead of Shell.

Pat predicted that the primary campaign would be hateful and ruthless. And so it was. Dick was use to the far left badgering him wherever he went, but this would be the first time he would get this kind of treatment from the far right. Several Republican groups had been infiltrated by the John Birch Society members. Robert Welch, the founder of the group, had accused President Eisenhower and John Foster Dulles as agents of the Communist conspiracy, and that Nixon was soft on Communism.

When I heard that I couldn't believe my ears! What were they up to by saying those things? Wherever Dick was campaigning they showed up asking complicated questions. They only helped the Democrat cause. So he took a stand and publicly disowned the John Birch Society's statements. Even though it would cost him the election, he obeyed the only choice of his conscience regarding Welch's accusations.

I realized that some were so concerned in voting against Nixon—one of their own number—who they thought was straying from the fold—that they worked to keep the ultra liberal in power whom they asserted to fear above all else. They decided to punish Dick by staying away from the polls or by voting against him without thinking of what the re-election of Governor Brown may convey on the principles they avow to hold dear.

When they have been successful, those groups only elect a Democrat farther to the left then the defeated man. Then, this man will never vote as they might want, but the defeated man would consider their views and act on them. Everyone has the right to gripe and to vote for the man of their choice, but they must consider this point—will I be double crossing myself?

Pat knew if she was to be at her husband's side on the campaign trail, she would have to hire some servants to take care of the household. A Cuban couple, Manolo and Fina Sanchez came for the job interview and was hired. They were very helpful and dependable. When Pat and Dick were gone, the Sanchezs watched over Julie and Tricia.

In the June primary Shell lost by 37 per cent to Nixon's 63 per cent. Dick was the winner of the primary election. However, this would be disastrous for him. As a candidate for governor, he would have to get 90 per cent of the Republican vote. If the voters for Shell defected, Dick would be in deep trouble for the general election. Some Republican headquarters refused to have Richard Nixon's picture posted there. Apparently, they wanted to re-elect Governor Brown. I don't think they knew what they were doing. Since Dick had a problem with the defection of Shell voters, he found out raising money for his campaign was also evaporating. Therefore, he had to operate on a shoestring limited budget.

On July 1,1962, Richard Nixon accompanied by Pat flew into Copenhagen, Denmark. By invitation he was to make a Fourth of July speech at Rebild National Park in Northern Jutland. U.S. Ambassador William McCormick Blair, Jr. welcomed them on their arrival at the Kastrup airport.

Dick came as a private citizen. He felt that when Americans go abroad. They go as Americans—not as

Democrats, Independents, or Republicans. Nixon kept emphasizing to reporters there that this visit was a private one—not a political one in anyway.

Some Danish newspapers attacked the choice of Nixon to speak at the Rebild festival—Denmark's observance of United States—Danish of American Independence Day held once a year. They debated that Nixon, as an adversary of the administration of President John F. Kennedy, should not have been requested to participate In the Rebild festival or share a platform with King Frederik IX and other prominent Danish politicians. Dick was not embarrassed by all the controversy the newspapers raised. It would take an unpleasant result to mortify him.

Pat and Dick were honored to be there for this historic occasion. The festival was the concept of Danish Americans who paid for the land and gave it to Denmark some fifty years before. A well-known American was always invited to speak at the festival. Richard Nixon was the first Vice-President requested to address there at Rebild. Now the invitation was repeated. Nixon had not asked to come there again. Tom Knudsen, a member of the Rebild committee, was a Los Angeles businessman who had issued the invitation for this private organization. What really marred the Danish fete of the fifty-anniversary observance of America's Fourth of July was that the son of the founder of the celebration, Henry Henius, fell unconscious and died on the speaker's platform.

While Nixon was there at the festival, Pat wanted to go sightseeing on Sunday. There would not be any time left for taking a Sunday nap. On July 4, Pat and Dick flew back to the United States to be with Julie and Tricia, and to continue the campaign for the governor's office.

Nixon usually liked to participate in important, stimulating thought-provoking conversation. He didn't relish trifling, unimportant talk. This was a concern for all of us because we knew that in a state campaign there would be many trivial discussions regarding schools, highways, taxes, and much more. Also, if he should win, a Democrat legislature would be attacking him on every point of issue.

Then, Nixon and his campaign staff neglected to file his primary campaign personal expense account by the July deadline time at the Secretary of State's office in Sacramento. They had to petition the Superior Court for an extension of time to file the account. Shell's campaign expenses totaled $457,617, of which $800.000 was his own money; Gov. Edmund G. Brown spent $500,000 for the campaign, while Nixon campaign filed expenditures of $453,000 on his behalf in the campaign. If Nixon hadn't filed for an extension of time, he could have been disqualified from the race for governor.

Dick was alarmed about the growth of crime in California. The state of California was number one in states for crimes committed—more than several states combined. He would attempt to make serious reforms about crime and taxes. He thought the people of California had the most heaviest tax load in the country. It concerned him that California businesses were failing and so many were bankrupt. He urged retired persons to volunteer their time and expertise to train young people who dropped out of high school.

In a California radio broadcast Nixon blasted Governor Brown for disregarding Communist efforts to infiltrate the state of California. The liberal press accused Nixon of dredging up an old red herring. However, many Washington investigators were aware of the rising Communist activities up and down the West Coast. Then, the Democrats admitted that about thirty-five Communists could have infiltrated their local Democrat Party groups.

Reactions among the voters were mounting. Nixon recommended that the Fifth Amendment witnesses should be prohibited to talk in schools supported by taxpayers. Brown denied that no subversives had turned upon any campus as long as he had been Governor. Then, Nixon disclosed an itemized list of persons who had been speaking in the California state schools and hid behind the Fifth Amendment.

One of the persons listed was Clinton E. Jencks, a teaching assistant, at University of California Dept. of Economics. In 1959 Mr. Jencks had appeared at the House Un-American Activities Committee, and he was one who invoked the Fifth Amendment.

Harry Bridges' International Longshoremen's and Warehousemen's Union had been kicked out of CIO for sympathizing with the Communists. He showed up in Brown's list of endorsements.

Nixon, in 1951, had helped write in Congress the Subversive Activities Control Act. He did not believe in giving the Communists a forum to those who pledged to destroy our constitutional government by any means.

But, Pat was busy out on the campaign trail, too. Whenever she would appear, the crowds would come. Everyone wanted to meet her and shake hands. Pat was an asset to Dick's campaign for Governor. Brunches, teas, and coffee receptions were held. This was a popular way of entertaining by many political groups. The young and the old, Republicans, Democrats, and Independent women came.

However, the first week of October Pat slipped on the floor of a bathroom in a San Fransico hotel. She cracked three ribs. A doctor was called in and taped her injured ribs, and she continued campaigning despite the pain. Pat had intense pain for a few days. It was painful for her to shake hands and be on her feet for hours. There would be many thousand women waiting in line. She did it because she didn't want to disappoint any of the women who came out to see her. Pat was a gracious, courageous lady and the people loved her wherever she went.

But, Pat was disturbed by the persistent criticism of Dick's honesty, and how many questions were brought up which didn't relate to him. The liberal press kept re-hashing the Hughes Tool Company loan to Nixon's brother, Donald. Somehow in their little minds, reporters thought Dick had gotten some money out of the deal. It involved his brother borrowing $205,000 from that company because of his financial hardship. Don did not consult or ask Dick about it. It was Hannah, their mother, who put up the store and service station as collateral. Even when the press and the Democrats knew the facts, they continued their badgering.

When I first heard about it, I told my only brother never to borrow any money. For if I ran for any office, someone would dig up something about you and then apply it to me. That would be guilt by association.

The press and the Democrats kept attacking and needling Dick about everything in the world. Where did he get money for his Martin Lane house? Are you getting a divorce from Pat Nixon? Why aren't you sending your daughters to public school? Do you know why your tax returns are being examined by the IRS? Why have you opposed equal rights for minorities? Didn't you sign a limited compact on your Washington home? It went on and on. Personally, I don't know how they both stood it all.

Some newspaper reporters realized they could make Richard Nixon touchy and perturbed if they mentioned anything involving his family. Therefore, they kept it up.

Then, on October 22, President John Kennedy told us on the television news that the Soviet Union had moved nuclear missiles ninety miles offshore into Cuba. He asked the Soviets to remove the missiles immediately and ordered a naval blockade of Cuba. Dick supported Kennedy's actions regarding Cuba, but he knew that the timing of the Cuban missile crisis made him lose the election. The voters had their attention distracted from California's state issues to the strained international crisis. Pat and Dick were both aware of the problem in Cuba. The Senate had been discussing it for weeks prior to President Kennedy's announcement. Therefore, we all were astonished why President Kennedy deliberately waited until now to make his announcement. Dick's narrow lead over Brown was vanishing.

By the next morning, Brown was confirmed the winner. Dick lost by 297,000 votes out of 6 million votes cast at the polls. Two defeats in a row were heart wrenching. It was the second saddest day for all of us.

Dick Nixon sent Herb Klein down to read his concession statement. The reporters demanded Nixon to appear. They were down right insulting. It was a highly charged emotional scene. The press was still arrogant and shouting, "Where's Nixon?" "Is he afraid to come down here?" When Dick saw that scene on his own television, the exasperation and disappointment boiled up inside. He said to himself, I'll go down and talk to them, and so he did. I noticed once again that Dick had not shaved. It showed the five o'clock shadow, and the fatigue made him look worse than ever.

I remember that telecast like it was yesterday. I kept a copy of Nixon's speech that day. I felt like he did, and Pat echoed the same feeling about the news media's bias reporting. Nixon believed reporters should write the facts fairly and objectively, and not take it out of context.

Nixon battled for the things he believed in. In his speech, he said, "I did not win. It is the people's choice. They have chosen Mr. Brown. They have chosen his leadership, and I can only hope that leadership will now become more decisive, that it will move California ahead, and so that America can move ahead economically, morally, and spiritually—so that we can have character and self reliance in this country. This is what we need. This what we need to move forward."

Nixon continued, "I think that it's time that our great newspapers have at least the same objectivity, the same fullness of coverage, that television has. And I can only say thank God for television and radio for keeping the newspapers a little more honest."

The press did not forget Nixon's speech, nor did I. However, from then, the press would only remember the part of his speech, which Richard Nixon said toward the last, and they recorded it over and over.—"I want you to know, just think how much you are going to be missing, you won't have Nixon to kick around anymore, because, gentlemen, this is my last press conference."

Pat and the rest of us applauded Dick's response. He did what we wanted to do all along. From then on, the press realized Dick would not take it anymore and would fight back. This election outcome was heart breaking. We all shed tears, but we knew life goes on in spite of obstacles and defeat.

Chapter 7

THE POLITICAL
OBITUARY OF
RICHARD NIXON

When Nixon made the statement: "Thank God for radio and television. They will make newspapers more honest." he under estimated the television media of the American Broadcasting Corporation (ABC) wanting to out-do the newspapers in California.

On Sunday, after the election on November 11, Veteran's Day, ABC quickly manufactured a put-together program called "The Political Obituary of Richard Nixon." This show was a replacement for a previously planned Veterans Day program. The initial program was dedicated to the memory of those who battled and died in war so that our constitutional republic would continue. The ABC network considered the Nixon story the most important political account in 1962. Therefore, they decided this was the time to change programs.

However, ABC did not count on the uproar and protests, which started before the show aired, and what happened afterwards. When word got around about the program switch, avalanche of protests and disapproval poured in against ABC broadcasting company. Switchboards of ABC offices all over the country lit up with thousands of telephone calls. Hundreds of telegrams were received. Many ABC television stations had their phone lines swamped and others had theirs tied up for two hours before the airing of the show.

Seventy ABC stations were scheduled to carry the new program about Nixon. Four stations in Philadelphia, Pennsylvania, New Haven, Connecticut, and the stations in Cincinnati and Columbus, Ohio cancelled the program.

Howard K. Smith, an ultra liberal news commentator on ABC, had invited Alger Hiss, a convicted traitor to appear on the television program and letting him denounce Richard Nixon. James Hagerty, Vice President of ABC News had put his stamp of approval on the show. The irony of that decision, Hagerty use to be President Eisenhower's press secretary.

In 1948 Nixon was a member of the House committee on Un-American Activities. He helped to expose Alger Hiss, an official In the U.S. State Department. Hiss was convicted of perjury involving the practice of spying for the Soviet Union and served a period of time in prison at Lewisburg, Pennsylvania.

Hiss, on the program, expressed that Nixon was motivated by ambition, personal self-serving, and was carried along politically. He thought he was a victim of Nixon's ambition. Hiss did not have any personal affection for Nixon.

However, in looking back at the record, it showed Richard Nixon braved political disaster, rather than promoting his political career in pressing forward in his investigation of Alger Hiss. As time went by, memories fade through the years. Some may wish to forget the facts of the Alger Hiss case, but I did not. It was like it had happened yesterday—so vivid.

The biggest mistake Alger Hiss made was when he hastily brought legal action against Whittaker Chambers, another confirmed spy for the Soviet Union for slander and vilification. His goading compelled Chambers to bring forward factual evidence to corroborate Hiss was really a spy for the Soviets, too. The House Committee on Un-American Activities called Chambers to appear before them about Communist activities in our government. No one on the committee, including Nixon, was not informed that Chambers would name Hiss as a Communist. It was a bombshell! Certain members of the Un-American committee, after hearing Hiss's constant denial of the charges, were persuaded to apologize to Hiss and dismiss the case. But, Richard Nixon and Karl Mundt were two Congressmen on the committee who did not believe Hiss was telling the truth. Both were aware if their continued investigation was proven wrong, they would be dead politically.

After the Alger Hiss conviction, Nixon went on to the U.S. Senate, and then on to the Vice-Presidency. Because of this case, Dick Nixon acquired a multitude of enemies who never forgave him for his part in this famous Hiss case.

Across the country, newspaper editors took only an offhand concern for the Hiss case. They were not alarmed much less shocked. The only paper to defend Alger Hiss was "The Washington Post," and they continued their harangue against Nixon wherever he went.

At that time, "The Chicago Tribune" had a more comprehensive account of what happened than any other newspaper. It led the press in honest and courageous reporting. They thought it was their duty to investigate the circumstances, which made ABC network to consider Hiss as a suitable person to be on the program.

Richard Nixon alerted his family and friends not to watch the TV program. But, we did watch for thirty minutes. It was painful and disturbing. We were shocked at the inaccuracies and the bias, which marked the program.

A few hours before the airing of the show, President Eisenhower had called on the telephone to James Hagerty, the news chief for the ABC network. He was totally amazed to the nature of the program which Hagerty had allowed Hiss to assail Nixon. Television stations in California and Missouri, which carried the show, received threats to bomb and burn the stations.

The Veterans of Foreign Wars and American Legion commanders published protests against the ABC network for allowing Alger Hiss, a traitor, to be on the program. They demanded the network to apologize to all veterans for their disservice.

Some companies tried to cancel their contracts with ABC because of the poor taste and judgment in having Alger Hiss on the program. Other companies refused to sponsor news programs because of the Hiss incident. Others decide to cancel their plans to advertise on ABC. The appearance of Hiss attacking Nixon was the epitome of vilification to these companies for their withdrawal of economic plans.

I was flabbergasted, too, as well as the rest of the country, at ABC, which permitted Alger Hiss a market place to attack the character of Richard Nixon. As far as I was concerned ABC's action was an insult to all of us who loved this country, as well as the lack of good taste and fairness. Overshadowed by the Hiss appearance was Congressman Jerry Ford and Murray Chotiner, two longtime Nixon friends, who were also were part of the four-guest panel. ABC even had Jerry Voorhis, a former California Democrat Representative, who once was defeated in 1946 by Nixon for Congress, to appear on the telecast and viciously condemn Nixon. Voorhees was displeased when learned that Hiss was to be on the same program, and he objected to ABC.

What caused considerable public outrage was the fact that Alger Hiss, a remorseless fabricator, was asked to express his feelings about Nixon's personal character. But, what was more startling how close Hiss and Howard K. Smith were in concord on Nixon's character. Smith accused Nixon of discrediting his political adversaries reputation with innuendos and calling certain Democrats "traitors". Nor did Smith allow any rebuttal to his own charges by those he interviewed on the program or by anyone who called into protest.

I was curious about ABC Vice-President James C. Hagerty's role in this whole affair. Eighty thousand protests had come into the ABC network. As he went on the air the next Sunday evening, he tried to calm the tempest of criticism directed toward him and the ABC network. However, what he had to say didn't make much sense. What perturbed me when Hagerty said all of us who protested the show did not believe in the freedom of speech and the press. That his company had the right to express free speech. As far as I was concerned Hagerty and Smith were guilty of abusing that freedom. In the letter I wrote him I told him he should have a greater sensibility of responsibility on his part of broadcasting.

All the people who sent in protests were deeply offended by Alger Hiss, a convicted liar and spy to attest to the motives of Nixon who was responsible for showing what Hiss really was. As far as I was concerned the standard of what they did was not socially acceptable in conduct and speech. All of us questioned what Hagerty said. In fact he didn't offer an adequate answer on the air or in the answer I received from him in the mail. No good reason was given. It was my suspicion to what the real purpose was to kick Dick Nixon when he was down at his lowest ebb and to stomp on his political grave.

(Hagerty letter in the Montgomery collection at the Nixon Library file.)

Richard Nixon sent a telegram to the "Chicago Tribune" thanking them for their objective news coverage and recent editorials on his sixteen years in public life. Mr. W. D. Maxwell, the Editor, had it printed on the front page of the newspaper, November 16, 1962, for everyone to see and read.

"As I begin a long delayed vacation I want to thank you

for your recent editorials and the objective news coverage of my activities during the sixteen years. I have been in public life.

'As I finish my last campaign for public office, I shall always be grateful for the opportunity that has been accorded of serving as a Congressman, as a Senator and as Vice President of the United States for eight years."

At that time, Nixon thought this would be his last campaign, but he was grateful for the opportunity to serve the people all those years.

In the future, he only hoped he could voice his ideas and opinions to preserve the freedoms and opportunities for all Americans.

Nixon was encouraged by the letters and telegrams, which flooded in for him from patriotic Americans. It meant more to him than the Hiss attack.

I remember what Richard Nixon said afterwards," It is not whether we win or lose that counts but whether we fight to the best of our abilities for the cause in which we believe."

On the same day, "Time" magazine put it this way: "Barring a miracle Richard Nixon can never hope to be elected to any political office again." In response to their article, I wrote a letter to the editor of "Time" magazine. They did not publish my letter. However, much to my surprise I received a letter from the top editor of "Time" magazine regarding what I said. Dick had said he never had complained to any newspaper or news magazine, but he never said I couldn't or anyone else could not. To this very day, I became an avid letter writer to newspaper editors for Richard Nixon.

With Dick's experience, knowledge and integrity, I knew someday he would be back. We, who were his friends, had not given up. "The Political Obituary" television program had brought him back from the bottom of the political pit, and he would arise again to the top. God sometimes leads us through the wilderness that we might learn from our mistakes and look up to Him for renewed strength and faith.

("Time" editor letter in Montgomery collection at the Nixon Library.)

Chapter 8

A NEW BEGINNING

As far as Pat was concerned, the 1960 and the 1962 campaign defeats were best forgotten. She did not want to discuss it ever. Julie and Tricia did not want to go back to school. They dreaded to meet their classmates. Pat was ready to go anywhere except stay in California. After talking it over with Pat, Julie, Tricia, and friends about what to do, Dick decided they should move to New York City. He knew that opportunities for a lawyer would be better there than any other place in the United States. Pat and the girls were excited about the move to New York.

In the spring of 1963 Pat and Dick flew to New York City to look for a house. Wherever they searched no house appealed to them. Houses in the suburbs would involve commuting to the city. Neither one wanted that chore. Then, they decided to look at some apartments.

When discouragement almost managed to get the best of them, the last place on their list—the Fifth Avenue Co-op Building, a ten room cooperative at the corner of 62nd. Street and Fifth Avenue was the size they wanted. It needed a little painting. Pat was good at decorating and she would make all things she touched amazingly beautiful. Both were elated that they found a place they would enjoy. The apartment had a view of Central Park. The park would be ideal for Dick to walk "Checkers", his dog, and also read the morning paper there.

On May 2,1963, Dick announced he would join the Manhattan law firm—Mudge, Stern, Baldwin and Todd. Even, this printed statement was given to the press as well as friends at the Waldorf-Astoria hotel in New York.

My copy read:

"On June 1, 1963, I shall move my residence to New York City and shall become counsel to the firm of Mudge, Stern, Baldwin, and Todd. After I have met the six-month residence requirement of the New York law I shall apply for admission to the New York bar. When admitted to the bar, I shall become a general partner in the firm. Pending my admission to the New York bar, I shall engage principally in matters relating to the Washington and Paris offices of the firm."

Many were questioning Dick's motives to move from California to New York City. At that time Dick felt he had no chance to win for any office in the political field. Some of his so-called friends thought he was a two-time loser, but I did not. I did not share their view. Abraham Lincoln lost many political offices but went on to win the presidency. I knew that someday Richard Nixon at the right time would become an international leader. Those of us, who believed that, were working in the political underground across the country toward that end.

On June 7, many thousands of business and civic leaders, Democrats and Republicans crowded the Biltmore Hotel bowl in Los Angeles to bid farewell to Pat and Richard Nixon and the children. This happened several hours before President Kennedy's arrival on a political stint there.

Mayor Samuel Yorty of Los Angeles, an independent Democrat who supported Nixon in his 1960 bid for the White

House, presented the Nixon with a color television as a farewell gift from his friends in California. Therefore, the Democrat California state committee treated Yorty with contempt and refused to invite him to greet President Kennedy or even to attend the dinner for him at the Beverly Hilton Hotel the same night.

Art Linkletter, a TV entertainer, was the master of ceremonies for the special event. He made us laugh when he said, "Dick and Pat got their California exit visa just in time. They are racing a deadline, trying to get out of California before Governor Brown gives it away."

When Democrat Governor Pat Brown heard that Nixon was moving to New York, he repeated what he said during the campaign for governor. This confirmed his view that Dick was using California as a stepping-stone, which would lead to the presidency back East.

Pat and Dick said goodbye to California and headed for New York City for a new beginning. Julie and Tricia were looking forward to the trip. Checkers, their black and white cocker spaniel dog, was to make the journey on the airline, too. That dog had lived in so many places. In doggy years, Checkers was in his eighties, and was regarded as a senior famous dog. Manolo and Fina, their Cuban refugee servants, came along to New York to continue to work in the Nixon's new home.

Dick decided not to own a car in New York. He leased a LeBaron Imperial car and would be chauffeured wherever he wanted to go.

Before settling down into his new law practice, Dick had promised Pat and the girls he would take them on a trip through Europe and the Middle East. Prior to their departure to New York, Dick had gone to Washington to get a state department briefing on countries they planned to visit in Europe. The press found out he was in town and followed him everywhere for an interview. Dick informed them he was just "a leader of opinion." in the Republican Party and the country. He had no plans to run for President and would not dictate who would be the best candidates for national or state offices.

Finally, on June 12th, the Nixons departed on their summer vacation touring Europe. Every time I picked up a newspaper, there was a picture of Pat and Dick. Everyone in Europe thought he was still Vice President and treated him as such. They didn't think he was a loser. Neither did I.

Pat and Dick's sightseeing tour with Tricia and Julie was full and rigorous. Along the way Dick had meetings and talks with foreign leaders as well. Generalissmo Fransisco Franco invited them to his Barcelona, Spain dwelling. In Paris, Pat and Dick had lunch with President de Gaulle and visited the Eiffel Tower. As they stood on a platform in West Berlin, Germany, and looked over the barbed wire barrier into East Berlin at Potsdammer Platz, Dick deplored division of Germany and urged freedom for the entire universe. When they entered East Berlin at Checkpoint Charlie, the Communists attempted to harass him, and to engage Dick in heated wrangling.

The Nixons saw the Aswan high dam in Cairo, Egypt as a guest of President Gamal Abdel Nasser of the United Arab Republic. The dam was being built to control the intense power of the Nile River.

As Pat and Dick toured a market in Budapest, Hungary, they were crowded by hundreds of Hungarians presenting them with fruit and bouquets of flowers. They were touched by the demonstration of friendship by the Hungarian people.

They had an audience with the Pope in Rome, and they rode in gondolas in Venice; and they visited the Parthenon ruins in Athens, Greece. Pat and Dick made news on their vacation trip, but it was time for Dick to go home to New York to be a Wall Street lawyer.

Pat enjoyed being able to walk and shop without being recognized. Occasionally, some would gawk and go out of their way to take a second look. Others would guess, "Is that Pat Nixon? Are you sure? It can't be—must be someone who resembles her." Then someone would ask her, "Are you Pat Nixon, the Vice-President's wife?" Pat was happy with her private life and just to be out of politics. Anyone around her was cautioned not to bring up the subject of politics. And so I never did in letters, or in person.

As a practicing lawyer in California, Dick did not have to take an examination as an admission to the New York bar. However, he was required to write a 500-word essay on the question: "What do you believe the principles underlying the form of government of the United States to be?" Usually, these admission papers are sealed by the court. Since Dick Nixon wrote the best essay of admission to the New York bar in twenty-eight years, the chairman of the state appellate division's committee on character and fitness decided to make it public. The actual wording off Dick's essay was the following:

"The principles underlying the government of the United States are decentralization of power, separation of power, and maintaining a balance between freedom and order.

'Above all else, the framers of the Constitution were fearful of the concentration of power in either individuals or government. The genius of their solution in this respect is that they were able to maintain a very definite but delicate balance between the federal government and the state government, on the one hand, and between the executive, legislative, and judicial branches of the federal government, on the other hand.

'By contrast, in the British system, the Parliament is supreme. In this present French system the primary power resides in the executive, and some older civilizations the judges were predominant. Through out American history there have been times when one or the other branches of government would seem to have gained a dominant position, but the pendulum has always swung back and the balance over the long haul maintained.

'The concept of decentralization of power is maintained by what we call the federal system. But the principle is much broader in practice. Putting it most simply, the American ideal is that private or individual enterprise should be allowed and encouraged to undertake all functions, which it is capable to perform. Only when private enterprise cannot or will not do what needs to be done should government step in. When government action is required, it should be undertaken if possible by that unit of government closest to the people. For example, the progression should be from local, to state, to federal government in that order. In other words, the federal government should step in only when the function to be performed is too big for the state or local government to undertake.

'The result of these somewhat complex constitutional formulas is greater protection and respect for the rights of the individual citizen. These rights are guaranteed by the Constitution, not only by the first ten amendments, which specifically refer to them, but even more by the system itself. Which is the most effective safeguard against arbitrary power ever devised by man.

'Yet the genius of the founding fathers is further demonstrated by the fact that while freedom for the individual was their primary objective they recognized that uncontrolled freedom for some would lead to the anarchy which would destroy freedom for all.

'Maintaining the delicate balance between freedom and order is, in my view, the greatest achievement of the American constitutional system. Inability to maintain that balance is the basic reason for the failure of regimes in Latin America, Africa, and Asia, which have tried to copy our system. They invariably go to one extreme or the other—too much emphasis the freedom of men to do anything they please or too much emphasis on controlling the excesses of freedom. Each of these approaches leads inevitably to dictatorship either of the right or of the left a tragedy which America will be able to avoid by continual dedication to the fundamental principles of our Constitution."

As the head of the law firm, Dick's year base salary was $220,000. Because of his ability and hard work and leadership, the firm grew and expanded. He negotiated with foreign governments for his law client's interests. Since Dick had given up his political base in California, I was wondering if he was planning to build another political base in New York. I was hoping this would be possible. It kept me in a watch-and-see—"Nixon" watching.

Also, Dick toured law school campuses across the country recruiting young new lawyers for his firm. One day while he was in Chicago on one of those recruiting tours, Dick suddenly paid a surprise visit to one of our United Republican Fund luncheons at the Palmer House. They're about 800 of us partaking of the delicious food. All of us present rose to our feet as Charles F. Carpentier, Illinois Secretary of State, guided Richard Nixon to the speaker's table.

Former Congressman Walter Judd was ready to speak to us on "American Needs a Realistic Foreign Policy" when Nixon walked in. Judd was a former medical missionary who served twenty years in Congress. He censured the Democratic administration for failure to recognize that Communism would not act like democracy or humanitarism.

After Judd had finished his speech, Nixon stepped forward and was welcomed by a standing ovation. I was pleased that Dick was still popular. He told us that Illinois would be an important state in 1964 because we must elect a Republican Governor as well as a vote for President.

Dick said, "There have been many rumors that I am supporting Gov. Rockefeller, rumors that I am to manage a draft campaign for Romney (Gov. George Romney of

Michigan), and rumors that am running a stop-Goldwater campaign."

The rumors are all wrong. I have not participated in any campaign. I have a high regard for all of these men, and one of the three or perhaps another one will be nominated. I will support the candidate who is nominated on the Republican ticket wholeheartedly.

Many asked what issues would Dick Nixon concentrate on if he were the candidate for President. Nixon replied that this, too, was untimely, but the principal issues today were high unemployment at home and foreign policy, specifically Communism in Cuba and the Americas.

I was delighted to see Dick Nixon once again. After hearing all the applause, I felt in my heart it would be a matter of time before we would see another presidential race. At the proper time I knew he would run again. We all had to bide our time and work to lay the groundwork for him.

President John F. Kennedy had committed 16,000 U.S. military advisers to Vietnam. The Democrat Party in Texas was having internal feuding among themselves. President Kennedy was concerned about what was going on there. He knew that Texas was an important electoral state for his re-election next year. Therefore, Kennedy was pondering what to do about the situation. He decided to go with Jackie and see what he could do to resolve the dispute in Texas.

However, Jean Dixon, a psychic, warned him to stay in Washington. Even, Rev. Billy Graham, the evangelist, called Kennedy and told him not to go to Dallas. It was not safe and he should stay. But Kennedy ignored the warnings and went to Dallas, Texas, anyway with Jackie and Vice President Lyndon Johnson. Then, I learned that Dick Nixon was to be in Dallas, Texas on law business in connection with the Pepsi-Cola Company. A few days later, I felt uneasy. Some how my premonition caused me to fervently pray about both the Nixon and Kennedy visits to Texas.

I remember that day—it was so intense and graphic. The television depicted that awful tragedy. The day before it, Texas newsmen were concerned about protest demonstrations against President Kennedy. When they heard Nixon was in town, the reporters asked him about it. Dick replied that President Kennedy and Vice President Lyndon Johnson should be treated respectfully. Strong disagreement on issues should not be a reason for being uncivil or rude. But, there were strong feelings being demonstrated in Dallas, Texas that day.

November 22,1963 Dick Nixon departed early in the morning for New York. There he hailed a taxicab. When his taxicab stopped at a Queens's stoplight, a man called out that President Kennedy had been shot. Dick didn't know if this information was gossip or reality. When arrived at his apartment complex, the doorman tearfully told him President Kennedy had been killed in Dallas.

Dick remembered when his brothers died and how he felt then. When anyone had passed on, he was always more than compassionate and wanted to help ease a family's sorrow. Although, they were friends as Senators, Dick had been critical of Kennedy's actions as President. Since the 1960 presidential race, there was no love lost between them. But now he was stunned and sorrowful.

That night Dick sat up until the wee hours of the morning meditating over the events which happened that day in Dallas. Then he wrote to Jacqueline Kennedy, The First Lady, a gracious letter expressing his help, prayers, and friendly thoughts.

In the commotion of that day reporters and the TV media surrounded the apartment complex where Nixon was living. When I saw that scene on television, I was curious why they were doing that. Dick was not in government work anymore. Were they confused? Or did they think Dick Nixon was heir apparent? One will never know what their reasoning was.

Pat and Dick flew to Washington for the Kennedy funeral Mass and the Arlington National Cemetery. Anyone who watched all these events on television did not forget it. It left such an impact on our memories.

Then, I learned later that Oswald, the man who was supposed to have shot Kennedy, wanted to murder Nixon, too. Oswald's wife managed to prevent him from killing Nixon.

Several weeks later, Richard Nixon received a letter from Jacqueline Kennedy thanking him for his thoughtful letter to her. She could not realize that this terrible thing could happen in this country. Jackie told Dick that he should be comforted that he had his life and family.

December 16, 1963 Dick sent me an announcement that as a member of the law firm of Mudge, Stern, Baldwin and Todd, the firm's name would be changed to Nixon, Mudge, Rose, Guthrie, and Alexander by January 1, 1964.

Dick's law practice permitted him to journey of considerable extent overseas to meet with some of his international clients. This way he made new friends, as well as visit with old friends from his administration days.

Pat said Dick was home more often for dinner. When he arrived home, she could hear the stereo playing one of the Strauss waltzes or a favorite Broadway musical recording. Of course, he liked to make a warm fire in the fireplace to relax by from the stress of work.

For the Christmas season Tricia and Julie were home from Chapin School, a private girl's school. Pat enjoyed having the family together. Their home was like Grand Central station, as young people were coming and going. There was much joy reigning there and many things to be thankful for. Dick would play the piano (always by ear in the key of G) and sing Christmas carols, as well as any other musical song requests.

It was a happy time with family and friends. Since I knew many people would be visiting at that time, I made candy for them to enjoy from my kitchen. The Nixon family always remembered others who were victims of circumstance at Christmas time. To see joy on the faces of others was their reward—the best present possible.

If 1963 was the start of a new beginning, I felt the year of 1964 would be the groundwork laid to help Dick Nixon someday to be a candidate for President.

Chapter 9

1964 TIME OF UNITY

The bitter feuding between President Lyndon Johnson and Robert Kennedy for the Democrat presidential nomination continued. Nixon was aware of the Democrat bloodletting between the two. At that time, the Republicans were the minority party in the country. Even they had internal disagreements of their own.

Nelson Rockefeller, the liberal New York Governor, and Barry Goldwater, the ultra conservative Senator from Arizona were debating and squabbling. Rockefeller was receiving unfavorable publicity regarding his nasty divorce. His liberalism and his divorce were being rejected by voters. Barry Goldwater did not want or pursue the office of President. However, the Young Republicans in the Grand Old Party (G.O.P.) persuaded him to run. The Goldwater movement was steamrolling along and picking up much support for his cause across the country. Division was brewing among the Republicans. This was not a good sign.

Dick surveyed carefully the situation. He was conscious of the fact that he might emerge as a Republican presidential nominee if the convention was deadlocked among the delegates. Dick would not actively seek the nomination but he left the door open and would be available. He felt it was his duty to be there for the Republican Party to protest and assist in anyway to mend the damage that a commotion would cause.

In January 1964, the former Governor Wesley Powell of New Hampshire publicized that he was starting a write-in campaign for Nixon. After Dick had spoke to a Republican fund-raising rally in New York, one of the reporters brought up the question of the New Hampshire write-in vote.

New Hampshire had its Presidential preference primary March 10. Dick commented that the voters in that state should consider write-ins their own decisions, and that he would do nothing to sway that decision one way or another.

When the New Hampshire presidential primary was over, there were a few surprises. Five Republicans on the ballot— Senator Barry Goldwater of Arizona, Governor Nelson Rockefeller of New York, Senator Margaret Chase Smith from Maine, Harold Stassen, a former Minnesota Governor, and a political unknown Norman LePage, a New Hampshire accountant. While two other Republicans, Henry Cabot Lodge and Richard Nixon drew their support from write-in votes. Lodge acquired 33,521 write-in votes, and Goldwater received 21,775 votes. Nixon who never campaigned there, the voters wrote in his name 15,812 times. Because Lodge obtained the most votes, all the Republican convention delegates went for Lodge.

Dick was determined to continue to be neutral. After the New Hampshire primary, he left on a business trip for his clients to the Far East, which included the countries of Vietnam, Philippines, Taiwan, Hong Kong and Japan. The press realized Richard Nixon was a newsworthy person, and they wanted his foreign affairs expertise.

Wherever Dick went, the various leaders of the countries he was visiting were discussing America's dwindling influence and wondered when the United States would demonstrate real leadership. In Vietnam, he discovered the Vietnam dilemma was quite different than what the Johnson administration was telling the people in our country. Because of this administration's marked indecision, our allies and friends were not sure whether we meant business to defeat the Communists.

The twisted media reporting was misrepresenting the situation in Vietnam, and so the people at home were getting a different view of Vietnam. The Vietnamese and American military wanted to fight to win. But the United States refused to support the military and give them permission to initiate air raids into North Vietnam and bomb the Vietcong arms supply line. What a way to try to win a war!

Henry Cabot Lodge (Jr.) had accepted the appointment as Ambassador to South Vietnam in 1963. For the life of me, I couldn't believe my eyes, when I read what the press reported what Lodge said about Vietnam in that we should feed them instead of shooting them, and no one should chase them behind the enemy lines. When Dick heard about that kind of thinking, he was as surprised as I was.

While Dick was on his trip to the Far East, Pat celebrated her fifty-second birthday with Tricia, Julie and friends. As the years went by, Pat had grown more beautiful and sweet. She was always kind and understanding of others.

I wanted Pat to come to Chicago for a luncheon party. However, she had other trips on her schedule, but none to Chicago. She thought they could come in the summer when Tricia and Julie were home for vacation. Pat knew by my letter there would be a lot of political friends of theirs at this party. She only wished the best of happiness for her many friends.

By April 15th, Dick returned home. No one, including the press, was not interested in Vietnam. It was the year of the 1964 election race, which was occupying the people's minds. Vietnam was across the ocean and far away from their thoughts. Hadn't President Johnson told us that we were not in war? So why think about it.

On May 12, 1964 Nebraska and West Virginia were holding their Presidential primaries. Fred Seaton had been organizing the voters In Nebraska to write-in Nixon's name on the ballot. The name of Senator Barry Goldwater was the only one listed on the Nebraska ballot. When the Nebraska primary was over, Goldwater had fell short of the fifty per cent of the vote, which was less than hoped for by his supporters. The rest of the votes went as write-ins to several other candidates. The Nebraska voters gave Nixon 42,800 write-in votes—about 31 per cent—and Henry Cabot Lodge, Jr. 16 per cent.

In West Virginia's presidential primary Governor Nelson Rockefeller of New York was the only one on the ballot. He attracted fewer votes than his workers had expected. A third of those voting chose not to favor Rockefeller In this primary.

Neither Rockefeller nor Goldwater won a full slate of delegates in these primaries. Both of them observed that Richard Nixon would be the man to beat for the Republican nomination at the convention in San Francisco next July. However, Dick was not running for the presidential office. He was tempted but cautious.

In Illinois two lawyers in Springfield, Illinois, wanted Nixon to run for President. I wanted Dick to run, too, but I wasn't sure if he would be committed to run in 1964. I took a pile of petitions for Chicago and passed them out to the various wards, churches, lodges, and veteran's organizations. If we could get a write-in vote as Nebraska did, we would be happy. Dick Nixon was aware of our endeavor, and at that time he didn't take any effort to stop us.

Our Illinois Nixon for President Committee State Headquarters was located at 125 North Fifth Street, Springfield, Illinois. The petitions that were given out read," I am proud to join the Illinois Nixon for President Committee.

I feel that Richard M. Nixon is the best qualified candidate for President of the United States, and I urge him to allow his name to be submitted as a candidate for that high office." We were to return all petitions no later than June 1,1964.

Polls continued to reflect that Nelson Rockefeller was doing real well with voters across the land. However, Rockefeller was having a problem in getting Republican convention delegates. Goldwater had most of the delegates locked up before the Republican convention. He eliminated Rockefeller in the California primary. Lodge ejected Rockefeller in the Oregon primary.

Therefore, Dick reassessed the situation and ordered our Illinois group to disband our efforts to get him to run. With dismay, we did. Again it was heart wrenching!

Dick determined to stay neutral. But he was pushed and pressured to assist candidates in their cause. Sometimes Nixon was caught in the middle of-the-tug-a-war, and we wondered how he could bring all the factions together. Dick decided he was the one who had to heal the wounds of the party split.

Nixon predicted Goldwater would be nominated on the first ballot, and he was right. Dick had asked if he could have the honor to introduce nominee Goldwater before his acceptance speech. His purpose was party unity.

This time I decided not to attend the Republican National Convention. My heart was not there, too many memories. Pat was not sure she should go to San Francisco for the convention. Instead, I watched it on television and would not be involved in any faction fireworks there. As the television cameras were roving around the convention auditorium, they suddenly focused on Pat and Dick sitting on the platform. Then, I was curious what made Pat change her mind to attend. Perhaps, Pat was more political-minded than we thought. Was it that Pat still wanted always to be with Dick wherever he goes?

The press was interested in what Nixon had to say.

Enroute to a visit to a California Republican delegation, they cornered Pat and Dick as they were leaving their San Francisco hotel lobby. Dick defended the 1964 Republican platform and emphasized the need for Republican unity.

Dick knew about the efforts of Governor George Romney of Michigan and Governor William Scranton of Pennsylvania to stop the Goldwater campaign in its tracks. Goldwater was nominated on the first ballot as Dick had predicted.

The convention speech by Nixon surpassed all his previous ones. As I listened, I knew he was a master of bringing people together. Dick emphasized that before the convention, we were split in different candidate groups—such as Goldwater, Scranton, Rockefeller, and Lodge—now we are Republicans period! He warned us not to sit this election out or take a walk, but to go to work to win in November.

However, Goldwater blew the whole thing and lost his chance to be President by what he said in his acceptance speech. His very words undermined what Nixon had said. "Anyone who joins us in all sincerity we welcome. Though those who don't care for our cause, we don't expect to enter our ranks in any case." Some cheered and others were shocked speechless. Why had Goldwater done this? To expel the other half of the Republican convention meant that he lost the only chance to win the presidency. Then, Goldwater added these divisive words, "Extremism in the defense of liberty is no vice! Moderation in the pursuit of justice is no virtue!"

I remember what I saw at that time. Pat didn't know whether to stand up or stay seated. When she saw Dick did not rise to applaud at what Goldwater said, she stopped and continued to sit with her husband and not to applaud as well.

Although electing a President was important, Dick's concern was with all those Republican candidates across the country. Now, they would be branded with the extremist label and doomed to failure at the polls.

In Dick's heart, he did not believe Goldwater had the stamina to beat President Johnson in this election. The Nelson Rockefeller and his supporters decided to sit this one out. Many party leaders found excuses to be inactive and not campaign for Goldwater. George Romney chose to concentrate on his own governor's race in Michigan. Even Eisenhower was angry with Goldwater. He wished that Goldwater would only think twice before he spoke and better yet to keep his mouth shut.

However, this time, Richard Nixon was the good soldier. Dick was not going to let the Republican Party lose the battle without a fight for the principles he believed in. So he pitched in and campaigned intensely for Goldwater.

Since Dick had decided to campaign for Republican candidates, Pat had other plans for the summer. She determined that she would take Julie and Tricia on a vacation trip with friends to Scotland, Ireland, Scandinavia, Holland, and Belgium before the school would start for the fall. It was a happy and lively trip. Politics were out of their minds. For once, they tried to be just plain ordinary people. When people over there heard the name of Mrs. Richard Nixon they became curious if Pat was who they thought she was. In some places, she caused quite a stir.

It was time to go home. Tricia would be attending nearby Finch College, and Julie would be returning to Chapin School in the fall. There were so many things to do and to get ready before classes started again.

Then, on September 6, "Checkers," the black and white cocker spaniel dog, died at Nixon's New York apartment. Checkers was the subject of nation-wide attention when Nixon divulged in a 1952 television radio speech that a man in Texas had given the dog to Tricia and Julie. Tricia had named the cocker spaniel" Checkers." Dick said they were going to keep the dog and denied that he had received sums of money improperly from supporters. On September 10, the

Nixon family buried "Checkers" in the Bide-A-Wee Pet cemetery In Long Island. Under a headstone marked "Checkers" 1952-1964 and two American flags, anyone could locate the cocker spaniel dog, which helped make Richard Nixon a celebrity. "Checkers" was the last Washington pet to have any political or cultural significance.

Vicky, a four-year-old gray poodle, had succeeded Checkers in the Nixon household. Julie thought the poodle was very exceptional sweet and very intelligent. Although, Vickie could never replace Checkers, but they all loved her as she was.

Then Tricia went out and brought Pasha, a Yorkshire terrier, without checking with Pat about it. Pat thought they shouldn't have two dogs in an apartment. Since Dick was such a "softie" pertaining to the girls, he urged Pat to let Tricia have the dog providing she would do the feeding and walking.

Six weeks before the election Nixon made more than 150 appearances In 36 states traveling over 50,000 miles for Goldwater and other Republican candidates. Dick knew Illinois was an important key electorate state. Therefore, he concentrated much of his time in the state of Illinois for Republican candidates.

From a speaking tour In Wisconsin Nixon arrived early at the Concord motel near O'Hare airport for some Illinois speaking engagements. After a press conference at the airport at 10:15 a.m., he went by charted airplane to Mattoon, Illinois. Dick was to speak at a fund-raising luncheon for Wayne Jones, a Republican nominee for Congress In the 23rd. District. Then, on to Springfield where Nixon and three Republican candidates, Elroy Sandquist, attorney general nominee, Charles Percy, candidate for Illinois governor, and John K. Kirby nominee for state auditor, rubbed the nose of Abraham Lincoln bust there for good luck. From there Dick's plane took him to the DuPage county airport for an Aurora rally at 4:15 p.m.

From there Nixon went by car to the Conrad Hilton hotel for his speech at a rally for our Cook County Republican precinct captains at 9 p.m.

I reported what had happened in my ward and precinct. I told my story of how voting machines were jammed and no votes were counted; registered voting machines already had 1,000 vote count on it before the election polls were opened. Many persons were threaten that they would lose their jobs for the city if they didn't vote the Democrat machine way. There Nixon talked to us about vote frauds in Chicago.

I remember the personal message that Richard Nixon left for all of us who were engaged in the drive against vote frauds. He referred to the drive to clean up the poll lists, which Sheriff Richard B. Ogilvie had been a leader in the skirmish against vote fraud and observed that "he is being obstructed at every turn."

"Obviously the Democrat officials of Chicago do not want honest elections," Nixon said, "They will resort to any trick or device to prevent decent citizens from cleaning up the mess which has stained Chicago's reputation for years and made it the symbol of crooked politics across the country."

Then Nixon mentioned some of the multifarious instances of ghost voters exposed in the 1960 election. Voting irregularities cost Nixon the Illinois electoral votes.

"These and literally hundreds upon hundreds of other cases of thievery and fraud were brought to light after that election," Nixon asserted, "They added up to a colossal contempt for the sanctity of the ballot, the foundation of this Republic."

Then, Dick left O'Hare field at 10:35 p.m. for New York City and home. Tricia, age 18, had attended so many high schools in her parents moves from Washington to California and then back to New York, she was not eager to move elsewhere. So Tricia chose New York's Finch College. Everyday she could commute from the Nixon apartment sixteen blocks to college. She selected history as her major. Julie, age 16, returned to Chapin School to finish her junior year there. However, when their studies permitted, they reported for campaign duties as honorary chairmen of the statewide New Yorkers for Goldwater and Miller organization.

At Dick's office, the mail kept rolling in and no one could keep up with the continued ringing of the telephone. As usual, Pat went down to the office and pitched in to help. Often she worked into the wee hours of the night for the campaign. Pat and Dick were dedicated in their efforts for the Republican Party. The prospects for Goldwater winning the presidential race looked dim, but they were working against hope that their aid to help other Republican candidates would endure the onslaught of the expected President Johnson's win.

The November 3rd. election day arrived. Johnson defeated Goldwater at the polls. It was a disaster for the Republicans. They lost 37 seats in the House, 2 Senate seats and 500 state legislature candidates. Republican candidates starting for their first bid for public office were crushed under the Johnson landslide.

But, we did find in Chicago some ballot boxes in an old store building when we were canvassing neighborhoods for ghost voters. The ballots were all for Richard Nixon, and were missing from the 1960 election.

I remembered when Nelson Rockefeller tried to twist the catastrophe election failure to his favor. He distributed a message pointed at Dick Nixon and the rest of us who supported Goldwater. Dick hadn't planned to say anything for months after the election, but Rockefeller's denunciation altered his intention.

Two days after the election, Nixon decided to hold a press conference. It took great courage for Dick to say what he did. He praised Goldwater for his valiant fight versus vast odds. Then he warned those who divide the Republican Party now cannot expect to unite it later. Dick called Rockefeller a divisive, poor sport. Of course, that press conference caused a commotion. But Dick said what was needed. If he hadn't done it, the Republican Party would have been split down the middle and there would not be any prospects of unity for the future. If he could work to keep the Republican Party from falling apart, Dick realized that this was a job only he should do for the good of country.

Nixon did not end the year alone in the public spotlight. His lovely daughter, Tricia, held it herself radiantly, too, as she bowed into society at the International Debutante Ball in New York's Astor Hotel. Tricia, now 18, led a parade of 53 daughters of wealthy and titled families around the world at the ball introducing them to society. Since Pat was honorary chairman of the charity event, Dick began the evening alone watching the dancers from a balcony box. Later he joined Pat and Tricia in posing proudly for family pictures.

Chapter 10

LAYING THE
PRESIDENTIAL
GROUNDWORK

If I believed what the press said, the Republican Party had sounded its death knell in 1964. But Dick was not convinced, and he predicted that the Party would rise again. He gave us hope when all others expected the worst possible outcome.

On January 9, 1965, Richard Nixon celebrated his fifty-second birthday. It was a time of reflection on the past as well as the future. I was sure he was re-thinking about his chances to run for the presidency again. Dick was not an impulsive person but one who thought and planned out things carefully before making a decision. For me, I never thought Richard Nixon was finished with public service, but when would he re-start again.

The Sales Executive Club of New York asked Dick Nixon to speak to their club. He emphasized that we were losing the war in Vietnam and that the war involved all of Southeast Asia. Do we surrender or win? Dick did not advocate a course of action that would be popular.

Then, Dick started to take more political speaking appointments. The law firm had grown to more than one hundred attorneys. His revived political activity with the required law firm obligations suppressed the time he had to spend with Pat and the girls.

One of his other speaking engagements was our 1965 Lincoln Day Dinner at the International Room at the Conrad Hilton Hotel in Chicago. It was sponsored by the United Republican Fund of Illinois, February 25,1965. Nixon was always a drawing card for raising money for the Republican Party in Illinois.

I was hoping that Pat could have come along on this trip. Afterwards, I talked to Dick. He said he failed to convince Pat to come along on short trips, even to Chicago. She thought she should be at home with Julie and Tricia to help them with their school study assignments. Since Pat had been a teacher, I could understand her reasoning for not coming with Dick on some of his political or legal assignments. Pat was a devoted mother. She was always there for her family and helping where she was needed.

After Dick left Chicago, he went to a party, February 27, for Rep. Gerald R. Ford of Michigan who had become the new Republican House leader. The party was given by the Chowder and Marching Club. At that party, one would have thought the Republicans had won a national election, but they hadn't. It was a happy crowd! Republicans in and out of Congress were expressing confidence about the future of the Republican Party. Our House Representatives from Illinois Charlotte Reid, Leslie Arends, and Robert Michel joined in song with Melvin Laird and Gerald Ford accompanied by Richard Nixon at the piano entertaining with his words and music.

Richard Nixon was the spark of the fire to liven up the Republican Party. Those, whom he had supported tireless, never forgot it. Now, Nixon was back in the middle of things.

The Republican Coordinating Committee was organized March 10,1965, and Nixon was invited to participate in Washington, D.C. at its first formal meeting there. They decided that by the 1966 election every American citizen should be assured of his constitutional right to vote without discrimination on account of race or color. Also, they attacked the Democrat belief that in Washington every problem in society required funds and federal supervision-and its costs-are unlimited and without boundaries. Should act only where state and local government cannot. Dick thought this concept of limited federal government was about to vanish.

Since Dick was traveling so much overseas and in the United States, Pat was staying at home with the girls and aiding them with their homework. She was also trying to help on some volunteer projects such as the Heart Fund or the Kidney Foundation. Without Dick being around, she became lonesome and restless.

Therefore, one of my Republican friends, Ardis Larson, from the 1960 Nixon campaign days, and I conspired we would plan a fairy-tale celebration for Pat's birthday, March 16⁻ one she would not forget! It really was a surprise box containing many beautiful wrapped packages. Then, we had the florist send a vase of exquisite sweetheart roses she adored.

Sitting down with her family with the roses decorating the coffee table, Pat unwrapped a photograph, which she added to her book of memories. Then, she sampled the black figs and delicious candy. Pat always loved her California figs and could not obtain them always in New York. Since she had so much leisure time on her hands, we chose a book she would look forward to read. Julie said her mother was so touched by the birthday gifts. She was glad to see her mother very happy. We were glad to see her so joyful on her fifty-third birthday, and that she had two good friends who never forgot her.

Nixon departed for Europe on business for his law firm in

April. He arrived in Moscow from Finland with Joseph Smallwood, Prime Minister of Newfoundland; they had reached an agreement with a company in Finland on building a paper pulp mill in Newfoundland.

As Dick was touring Moscow's skyscraper university on the Lenin hills, he intersected forceful debate with Nikolai Selyezor, pro-rector of the Moscow University. The pro-rector asked Dick how he should explain President Kennedy's assassination to his students. He said often had told them about the United States, but when his students asked, "How in this freedom-loving country a President can be killed? What should I tell them?" he asked.

Then this debate turned into an argument. It recalled to mind of what happened six years ago with Nixon's famous kitchen debate with Premier Nikita Khrushchev. Nixon responded that the United States was the first to admit its imperfections, but "We in turn could ask what happened to Beria. Why was he killed? Trotsky, what happened to him?"

Of course, the pro-rector roared back that Trotsky was killed on American territory. (Anyone who studied history would know that Leon Trotsky was assassinated in Mexico, 1940, by a Joseph Stalin's worker. Also, Lavrenti Beria, chief of Russia's secret police, was killed after Stalin's death.)

Nixon continued, "If you want to talk about force, then we should talk about force, then we should talk about soviet action against the freedom fighters in Hungary."

(You see the Russian army crushed an Hungarian anti-communist uprising in 1956.) Nixon told the pro-rector: "You can tell your students, we are trying to remove all vestiges of prejudice and hatred as evidenced by the Ku Klux Klan."

"We are trying to remove inequity and win the war against poverty in the United States. We have not succeeded as well as we would like and under our free system our failures are always advertised."

Now Nixon was on a popularity roller coaster. Everyone wanted him to come to speak and be involved with their group.

Our 13th. Annual Republican Women's Conference was held in April in Washington, D.C., and more women came than usual. It shattered all previous attendance records. In all, eight Senators and sixteen members of the House participated. After Ray C. Bliss, Chairman of the Republican National Committee spoke first; it was the speech by Richard Nixon, which made the difference. We went home with a store of vital information and guidance from Nixon who seemed to have the answers to spur us on. We all expressed our warm appreciation for his taking time from his busy schedule. I was sure that as women we would make a difference if Nixon should run sometime in the future.

Whittier College (Calif.) invited Richard Nixon, an alumnus to be their featured speaker at the commencement exercises. Bob Hope, the entertainer, was there also. Hope was to be awarded an honorary degree of humane letters for his dedicated service to our nation and his support of Southern California culture activities. Before the commencement exercises, Dick and Bob were kidding each other about their noses. It was a laughable time whenever those two would get together. Always thought they would have made a good comedy duo.

June 1, 1965, Republican Party leaders from across the country came to Washington to discuss G.O.P. policy in regards to foreign affairs and civil rights. It was a historic reunion for Richard Nixon. Three other living past presidential candidates—former New York Governor Thomas E. Dewey, former Senator Barry Goldwater, former President Dwight D. Eisenhower joined with former Vice-President Richard Nixon. At this meeting Senator Everett Dirksen (Illinois) was there and chatted with Nixon and Eisenhower about many issues pertaining to the country and world affairs abroad.

Nixon rejected any segregationist plank in the Republican platform. He emphasized that he would speak against it in any state, he would be campaigning. Dick warned the others not to use racial injustice but to do what was the right thing morally to do.

On June 21st, the Nixon family flew to Mexico City to celebrate their twenty-fifth wedding anniversary where they had a delightful time of reminiscencing.

Then, I remembered what happened in the summer of 1965. The Watts district of Los Angeles was burning and blacks rioted and looters were taking everything they could take away. I agreed with Nixon that the persons involved in the riots were due to blacks and whites who determined in their minds that they should obey only laws with which they agreed. This was the beginning of real change in our country and growth of permissiveness. Nixon thought we should not lament about it, but we should try to understand the problems and offer solutions for correcting it.

September rolled around and Dick was off to Vietnam. There had been a continual flow of congressmen flying into Saigon, departing on fact-finding journeys. Nixon's tour was more thorough than any of the congressmen. He talked to Vietnamese and Americans alike. Dick joked and kidded with newsmen, received gifts of Vietnamese military leaders and had a look at American military persons in some not-so-safe and remote areas.

Nixon looked down on the countryside from the observation post above the airfield from which Marine guards watched for Viet Cong infiltrators. Outside the Da Nang Vietnamese refugee center, he quizzed General Nguyen Chanh Thi, the Vietnamese 1st. Corps Commander as curious refugees watched both of them.

At the Chu Lai airfield, Nixon talked seriously with Marine pilots of the famed "Black Sheep Squadron" led by "Pappy" Boyington. As Nixon ate chicken noodle soup, marine pilots listened intently as they answered his questions. When Nixon completed his tour, General Thi gave him a Viet Cong assault rifle, which had been captured, manufactured, and supplied by the Red Chinese.

Nixon's fact gathering in Viet Nam became the basis of many speeches he made around the country. I was privileged to hear one of his speeches in Chicago, and to talk with him once more.

After Dick's intense whirlwind tour, October 5-6 through the state of Virginia for Lindwood Holton, Jr., a candidate for governor, he jetted into O'Hare airport at Chicago to speak to the Republicans there. The United Republican Fund of Illinois was in debt $50,000.00. They were hoping to wipe out this deficit and provide funds for a short period ahead. The Grand ballroom at the Conrad Hilton Hotel for a $100.00-a-plate dinner was jammed and packed. Above the speaker's table were enlarged pictures of Richard Nixon and Abraham Lincoln.

When Dick walked in, the crowd stood and applauded enthusiastically. As usual Richard Nixon did not use notes, and he had no copies of his speech. We were transfixed and hung on every word he said about foreign policy and our troops in Vietnam. Dick felt we should confine the war in Vietnam by using our air and sea power to shut off the intrusion of the Vietcong from Laos and North Vietnam to stop their terrorism against the South Vietnamese. It might involve Red China coming in the war, if the United States didn't do something to stop the interference, and all Southeast Asia in the Pacific would fall under the domain of the Communists.

When Dick finished, we all stood and applauded long and hard. It was a challenging and thought provoking speech. However, it brought to mind another sensational speech, Nixon made in April 1954, to the American Society of Newspaper Editors. On that afternoon Dick said the United States might have to send troops to Indo-China (which included Vietnam) if the French were unable to keep it out of Communist hands. That speech then aroused hostile comment, even in Congress. But Nixon was right and his prophetic announcement about Vietnam came true.

Later on, I wrote a letter to the Chicago Tribune regarding what Richard Nixon was trying to warn us about the other side of the Vietnam story. Many people responded to the letter. Then, I sent a copy of it to Richard Nixon with a letter asking him to re-think his position to run again for President. I knew how reluctant Pat and the girls felt about the intrusion of politics into their private lives. But, in my heart, I knew God had a plan and purpose for our country and that only he would work it out among his people.

Nixon's political mail, telephone calls, and more requests to speak tripled and poured into his office. Rosemary Woods, his secretary, could not keep up with the extra mail, since she was the only secretary in his office. Therefore, Pat had decided to come down and help Rose out. With all Dick's political journeys and his travels for his law firm, it was amazing how he was able to keep up with it all.

In the middle of one of the stacks of mail was my letter with the Tribune copy waiting to be opened. Dick was glad to get it and the newspaper clipping about his speech. I was hoping he would make the right decision about another presidential race. In all those other stacks of mail there, I was sure there were many who felt like I did.

Just before Christmas, I gave Pat and Dick a box of my homemade candy. My relatives and friends always enjoyed the breads and candy from my kitchen. Pat and I always exchanged recipes to sample one another's cooking. When Pat and Dick came back from their Christmas vacation at Key Biscayne, Florida, I received a thank you letter from Pat. She was pleased and happily surprised about my homemade candy. It was a big treat for all of them.

In that letter Pat gave me hope she would soon come

with Dick on his speaking political trips. I was convinced she had been thinking about it on her vacation trip. Pat wanted to help her husband, but she didn't want to go through the pressure of political life. I reminded her she was a special lady and people loved her as I did. It would be difficult for her to be under the scrutiny of the press and be on display as a public figure. Since she had been Second Lady and her husband as Vice President, there would be no return now to a normal private life.

Richard Nixon had been thinking about what people had discussed with him on his speaking tour for Republican candidates. He mulled over in his mind at Key Biscayne what should be the right decision to do. I reminded Dick that Abraham Lincoln had lost more elections than he had. Lincoln was called a "loser", too, but he never gave up. Would the Republican Party rise again from their defeat and make a come back? If all of us worked together, as Nixon had, wouldn't the prize be ours. I was never one of those who thought Nixon couldn't win. He was not a "loser" in my opinion.

By January 1966 Dick Nixon had assessed the risks and possibilities of another campaign and presidential race for 1968. Therefore, he hired Patrick J. Buchanan, a twenty-seven year old ultra-conservative editorial writer, from the St. Louis Globe-Democrat newspaper to assist him in research and political articulation.

Things began to change quickly. His office sounded more like a political campaign instead of a law firm. Dick called in William Safire, a thirty-six public relations consultant, to develop a program to project his public image, the possibilities and the overcoming of any difficult negatives.

Dick agreed to write articles for the North American Newspaper Alliance, a syndicate service. I remember reading the column each month in the Chicago Sun-Times newspaper. Some were about Vietnam and Communism here and abroad. Also, other articles were concerning racial injustice and what was right morally. Finally, Nixon was getting his message across for the Republican Party and what our role in the country should be.

January 19,1966, Dick spoke at the Alfalfa Club, the Capital dining organization in Washington, D.C. As usual Dick fired up the meeting with his sense of humor. When they introduced him as having graduated from Duke University, he said," Actually, I graduated from Whittier College, and then from Duke University Law School. I almost made it through Electoral College, but I flunked debating."

At that time, the nation was buzzing with conflict regarding the issue—"Should Children Pray In Schools." That issue still continues to this very day. However, Dick spoke there on this timely topic regarding our nation's faith in God. He emphasizes that American people are a deeply religious people who go to church and support the activities of the church. They pay taxes to provide a chaplain in Congress and the military. Every patriotic or public gathering should start first with a prayer of God's blessing. Our coins state that our trust is in God. Even, when we salute the flag and pledge allegiance to the flag of "one nation under God."

But than, I remembered another humorous saying Dick said regarding a school principal that came upon a group of six students on their knees during the lunch hour. "What's going on here?" he demanded in shocked tones. "We're only shooting craps," said one of the youths. "Thank goodness," the principal exclaimed, "For a moment I thought you were praying!"

At that time, Nixon said he favored a constitutional amendment legalizing non-sectarian prayers in public school. During the years that Nixon had spent in Washington, he had the advantage of hearing some of the prominent religious clergymen of his time. He thought many of them spoke about religion in generalizations rather than in the simple expressions he heard as a young man.

He summed up his speech by saying that there was a desperate need for moral and spiritual strength if we were to survive as a nation. What Nixon said then is just as true today—and much more. Our strength and character of the faith of our founding fathers is still relevant today.

Pat, Julie, and Tricia were proud of all Dick's many activities. But they had mixed feelings about politics. The 1960 campaign was still fresh in their minds. One thing they didn't like was the scrutiny of the press regarding everything they did.

My parents had a farm in nearby Knox, Indiana. I often escaped from the Chicago confusion to find peace and quiet there. Even, Pat said she was going to enjoy thinking of me there when the miracle of spring unfolded there. I felt that Pat wanted to get away to the outdoors, too. She enjoyed life in New York going to the theater, touring the museums—and just being out of the political public eye. Pat wanted to help Dick but disliked politics. I think Dick somehow knew she was in conflict. At times she felt guilty and that she was not pulling her fair share to help her husband. She finally realized that Dick's life was public service and most of all she wanted Dick to be happy.

Julie would be graduating from Chapin School soon. She felt that she should be home to help Julie with her homework every night. Last November, Julie was accepted at Smith College on the Early Decision Plan. Pat and Dick were proud of Julie's decision. They were glad that she chose to be close to New York so that Julie could be home often. Since Pat and Dick were a very "close" family, they would miss her greatly.

When Dick was Vice President his salary was $30,000 a year. But, in his law partnership earnings were more than $250,000, and that was not counting his royalties from his book, "Six Crises", and other writings. A few people asked me, "Does he really practice law? We haven't seen his name in any court cases."

However, on April 27,1966,those questions and doubts were laid to rest. Richard Nixon asked the Supreme Court to uphold a $30,000 damage award, against Time, Inc. in that "Time's Life magazine lied in 1955, linking a Broadway play, "The Desperate Hours" with the James J. Hill family 1952 experience who were held hostage by escaped convicts.

Time, Inc. attorney challenged the award made under the New York privacy law-saying the article published in connection with the Broadway play was basically true. The award should be set aside because the New York privacy law was unconstitutional and a violation of freedom of the press.

Speaking for the Hills, Nixon argued before the Supreme Court justices, "It is our contention in this case and it was argued, established, charged by the trial court found by the jury and held by the courts of New York on appeal that "Life" magazine knew that it lied."

Time's attorney pointed out that the play re-enacted was what had happened to the Hill's family. The play's cast pictures were taken at the Hill's home and newspaper headlines were reproduced dealing with incident was in the article.

Nixon said, "Life magazine was presented to its millions of readers the proposition that the Hill incident was the same as "The Desperate Hours" play. That was not true. The six pictures printed with the article presented six incidents which didn't happen to the Hills." Dick accused "Life" magazine of complete falsity on each of the incidents.

But the Supreme Court justices by a vote of 5-4 handed down a decision against the Hills. They based their decision on the First Amendment. The press was given constitutional protection, they said, even knowing or not knowing it.

However, the press, the New York Bar and the Supreme Court justices were impressed by Nixon's oral arguments before the court. However, Dick was more critical of his own self and wondered what he could have done better.

True, Dick had lost a court case and two elections, but in

his home Tricia and Julie, his daughters, were a couple of winners. Tricia, a honey colored blonde, with deep blue eyes and now twenty years old, was elected by her peers to be president of the junior class at Finch College (NYC.) When Dick heard Tricia had won her class election, he sent a note to congratulate her. How he won a few elections and lost two, but it was more fun to win than to lose.

But, the very same day Julie, a chestnut colored brunette, with dark brown eyes, won fifth place in a "Atlantic Monthly" essay contest. Her historical essay study on the Speaker of the House of Representatives was entered under a listed number and not her name. Julie felt she won the essay contest on merit and not on her famous last name. Just graduated from Chapin School, Julie would be headed for Smith College in the fall.

For the Fourth of July (1966) the Nixon family spent the holidays at Key Biscayne, Florida. It was one of their favorite places just to relax and get away from it all, swim, read, walk on the beach, and partake of steak and beans cookouts with friends. It was perfect for escaping from the invariable stress of life, which followed them wherever they went.

Dick left Florida early for a business trip in Europe. Pat and the girls would join him later in England. He was touching bases with all the political world leaders. Being a former Vice-President Richard Nixon discovered it opened many doors for him.

Pat and the girls chose to view designer Pierre Cardin's fall and winter collection in Paris, France, while they were there with their husband and father. Japanese model Iroko modeled hats with Julie and Tricia. Dick flew to Pakistan on business; and Pat and the girls departed for several other countries enroute to the beautiful Black Forest of Germany before returning home.

1966 was the year of change. Food prices under President Lyndon Johnson administration rose ten per cent. Women picketed grocery stores and started boycotts against food chains. Longhaired "hippies" folks sprouted up everywhere with their odd clothes. There were L.S.D. drug users, the free love and free sex, "Beatles" rock and roll music; and the miniskirt imported from Britain. The year of 1966 had barely begun when President Johnson announced 8,000 American solders had launched a gigantic attack on North Vietnam. In meeting with the leaders of South Vietnam, Johnson thought the war there would be victorious providing China did not decide to intervene.

President Johnson had said during the presidential race against Goldwater "We are not at war, I shall not send any American boy overseas to fight in Vietnam."

President John F. Kennedy had committed 16,000 troops to Vietnam. Now in 1966 President Johnson had sent 300,000 troops there, but in 2 years time that number would be expanded to more than 500,000.

Twenty-five thousand people protesting the Vietnam War paraded down Fifth Avenue in New York City. But there were demonstrators who disagreed with anti-Vietnam protestors and pelted them with eggs and other vegetables as they marched. Peace marchers and black civil right marchers took to the streets. It was the beginning of a turblent era.

September 12,1966 Richard Nixon met with former President Eisenhower at his office in Gettysburg, Pennsylvania about campaigning for Republican candidates. Also, both were concerned about the prolonging of the Vietnam War could bring Red China in conflict with the United States. They both thought that if the war would run five more years Communist China will have developed "nuclear capabilities". Nixon called for step-up in activity on the military and diplomatic fronts to shorten the war.

That fall Nixon went on the campaign trail for Republican candidates. He appeared in thirty-five states for eighty-six Republican nominees. Dick pepped up the local races with enthusiasm and inspired others to work for their individual candidates. He helped raise millions of dollars and publicity. The Nixon name was not dead and it aroused interest wherever he went.

Nixon chose carefully certain states to campaign for candidates. Illinois was one of them. Charles Percy was running for the U.S. Senate. I remember the large enthusiastic crowd gathered at Charles Percy's estate at Kenilworth to hear Richard Nixon speak. The reporters were there with their pens and cameras. I was fortunate to be there with my pen and notebook and camera. Illinois had not forgotten the close presidential race of 1960.

Nixon gave the Percy Senatorial race a shot in the arm. I was disappointed that Pat Nixon chose not to come along, but I understood why. It was good to see Dick again. I was hoping the 1966 campaigning by him once again would lead Dick back to the road to the White House. In my talks with him there, I felt more assured he was considering the next step in that direction.

Whenever Dick went on his campaign trips, he denounced President Lyndon Johnson for his policies- "Every time your wife goes into a food supermarket, she is encountered with Johnson's high prices . . . a business company can't create more jobs because interest rates on loans are too high because of Johnson . . . young married couples can't buy a house because Johnson has made the price of a new home out of their reach."

Nixon was aware of the Johnson policies of guns and butter and what inflation was doing to the country. Dick watched every move that President Johnson made. He knew that Johnson was capable of surprises at any time. Sure enough two weeks before the November election, Johnson met with President Nguyen Van Thieu of South Vietnam and other allied leaders in Manila (Philippines) to propose a mutual withdrawal from Vietnam. Nixon did not discuss the Vietnam

War issue in his newspaper column or on the campaign trail until President Johnson returned from the Manila Conference.

At that time I picked up the "Chicago Sun Times," I noticed Nixon's newspaper column he had wrote, "From diplomats in Tokyo to member of the President's own party in Washington, the question is being posed: Is this a quest for peace or a quest for votes?"

Dick received a copy of the Manila Communiqué and went over it point by point. Then 5 days before the election he issued his statement to the press. It was printed in every major newspaper. The New York Times" November 7, 1966 was the only newspaper which printed the statement in its entirety. Some of the pointed questions Dick asked in his statement "How many more American troops do we currently plan to send to fight in Vietnam in 1967? Are we really ready to stand aside and let he Vietcong Communist and the army of republic of Vietnam shoot it out? Will the draft quota be raised again to meet troop requirements? Shall we let the Vietcong intensify their communist aggression? How does the Johnson administration intend to pay for this war?"

I learned later from a Senate Congressional hearing President Johnson was using the Social Security Trust Fund to help finance the Vietnam War. Previously President Kennedy paid the United Nation past dues for the Soviet Union out of the same Social Security Trust Fund. I tried to inform certain people about that action I heard with my own ears at the U.S. Capitol—but nobody wanted to listen then.

A few hours later, President Johnson held his own press conference at the White House. He retorted sharply at Nixon, calling him "a chronic campaigner" who never really recognized and realized he had an official position. Nixon doesn't serve his country well."

I didn't know whether President Johnson's outburst was from being over tired from his long overseas trip or up to one of his nasty tricks. Nixon kept his temper under control. I was surprised at all the editorial writers defending Dick Nixon. Usually, it had been the opposite in the past.

Instead of helping the Democrat Party, Johnson had pushed Nixon out front as the top Republican leader and as an able political opponent for 1968. Then, on the other hand, perhaps Johnson had watched the polls and discovered that the pre-election polls were more favorable to Nixon and would be more painful for him and the Democrat Party. The outburst by Johnson was unjust because Dick Nixon had supported in March 1966. President Johnson's stated purpose in Vietnam when many Democrats had not.

Former President Eisenhower thought Johnson had gone too far on this one and issued a statement to the press that "Dick Nixon was one of the best informed, most capable, and most industrious Vice Presidents in the history of the United States."

Because of Dick's prominent national attention, the Republican Congressional Campaign Committee let him have a half hour network television time on NBC, Sunday afternoon, November 6, to answer President Johnson. I watched Nixon on television, it was one of his better speeches. Dick knew how to make the most of any opportunity allotted to him.

He opened up his talk, "I was subjected last week to one of the most savage personal assaults ever leveled by the President of the United States against one of his political opponents . . . I shall answer it not for myself but because of great principle that is at stake. It is the principle of the right to disagree, the right to dissent. That means the right to disagree with any government official even the President of the United States."

Dick used most of his speech to tell the people directly why the country needed a Republican Congress, governors, and state legislatures. He asked the people to make a difference and work for the cause of good government wherever they were. Dick criticized the Manila Communiqué and what was wrong about it. Then he reverted the last of his speech directly to Johnson violent outburst. It was not vindictive. (I think Dick was referring back when he lost the California governor's race).

"I think I understand how a man can be very very tired and how his temper then can be bone weary and tired, how much more tired would a President be after a journey like yours?"

Bill Lawrence of the ABC network asked Nixon to be a guest on "Issues and Answers, a TV interview which showed that same Sunday. Dick repeated what he had said on the NBC network arguing for a Republican Congress and against the Manila Communiqué.

Then, Bill Lawrence asked Dick, "When are you going to run for President yourself?" When I heard Dick say on this program, "After the election I am going to take a holiday from politics for at least 6 months with no political speeches scheduled whatever." I was shocked and surprised! Be assured I would find out what Dick Nixon had planned, and I did.

When I watched the election results on WGN (Chicago) television newscast, I discovered Nixon's hard work for Republican candidates really paid off for the Republican Party. The 1966 elections results were being enjoyed by Nixon too, and he wanted to celebrate the victory.

The big winners were George Romney as Governor of Michigan for a second term; Spiro T. Agnew for governor in Maryland;Ronald Reagan for governor of California; Nelson won a third term for Governor of New York; Winthrop Rockefeller won as the first conservative Republican governor of Arkansas; Edward Brooke, a black for Senator from Massachusetts, and Charles Percy for Senator from Illinois.

Nixon had forecasted that the Republicans would pick up 40 House seats and 3 additional Senate seats and 6 governorships. The actual election count was 47 House seats, 3 Senate seats, and 8 governorships. Dick knew in his heart that the G.O.P. victory would lay the groundwork for his run for the presidency. Republican knew that only one person—Richard Nixon—was responsible for their victorious comeback. Now he was the Leader of the Opposition.

In the fall Julie had entered Smith College, an all girls school, in Northampton, Massachusetts. Going off to college was a wrench for Julie. She missed her mother, father, and Tricia. To overcome her homesickness she became involved with many college activities. Julie became so popular on campus; she won an election, too. She was chosen by an upper-class student group, the Gold Key club, which showed guests around the Smith College campus.

Even though Julie had mixed feelings about politics, it was the Republican Women's Club of Hadley, Massachusetts political request that helped to change the direction of her life.

Seven miles from Smith College, David Eisenhower, the grandson of President Dwight Eisenhower, was attending Amherst College as a student. When the Hadley Republican Women discovered that David and Julie were in the same nearby vicinity, the women decided to invite both of them to speak at one of their luncheon meetings. At that time those Republican women didn't realize they would become matchmakers between a Nixon and an Eisenhower.

David decided to call Julie to see if she was planning to attend the meeting. They discussed it several times, both decided their first obligation was to their college studies, and they didn't think their speaking engagement would do the Republican Party much good. Julie and David declined the invitation.

At Julie's Baldwin House dorm, no boy friends were allowed in the girls' rooms. Only fathers and older people could go there. David had not seen her room. Then he paid an unannounced visit several nights later and waited to see her in the living room of the dorm. Julie and David liked each other from the start. From that moment, David wanted to see Julie more often.

On election night 1966 they watched the election returns. Julie knew that her father had been out on the campaign trail for Republican candidates nationwide. Therefore Julie celebrated with David that night knowing her father's campaign work paid off as he had predicted the outcome would be.

From then on they dated frequently. As soon as they did, the press followed them everywhere and were widely photographed. Julie considered her relationship with David only a "friendship." Every time one picked up a newspaper or magazine there were endless speculative tales about their affairs. It annoyed Julie; she wanted to choose to have dates without everyone in the country watching her. Privacy was important to her.

Shortly before Thanksgiving some men supporters wanted to organize a Nixon for President Club, even though Richard Nixon hadn't officially announced he would run. Dick authorized the campaign organization—only if it would be a low-key one—until he officially made up his mind about running for President.

Chicago winters were getting colder and colder. The extreme cold was getting to me. My doctor suggested that I should go West where it was warmer and drier to help my condition. Therefore I quit my position at Institute and stayed for a while at my parent's farm in Indiana until I had a chance to meditate what to do next.

It was almost Christmas time. My parents persuaded me to stay there for a while before making my move to the West. There I made several kinds of candy for my family, and so I mailed a package of candy to Pat in New York City for her family. It was thoroughly enjoyed by everyone.

Julie came home from Smith College. Even David came to visit for the holidays, too. Pat and Dick's home was like

Grand Central Station for young people who came to visit New York. Pat was joyful because Julie and Tricia were home. Both of them were thankful for so many things.

Instead of exchanging gifts with friends and family, the Nixons remembered others who are victims of circumstances. Their best present and reward for them was to see the joy on the other people's faces.

Then after Christmas Day, they all flew to their favorite spot in Florida—Key Biscayne to get a little sun, but the cold weather greeted them there, too. The weather didn't help their thoughts regarding an impending presidential race that Dick might decide to do. Would Pat and the girls give up their privacy if Dick once again entered public life? Surely all their privacy and independence would fly out the window. Pat made no secret that she couldn't face another defeat in another political race and to get hurt again.

The International Debutante Ball was held at Manhattan's Waldorf-Astoria hotel, December 29, 1966. Pat and Dick were watching from a pink-and-silver box high above the ballroom floor. The orchestra suddenly burst into "America the Beautiful" song. With that Julie Nixon stepped forward to make the first curtsy. Julie's mother and father were radiant with joy as their daughter came forward on the floor. Her sister had preceded her two years ago. This time Julie may have one-upped her sister Tricia in the escort department. At Julie's side David Eisenhower accompanied her. Everyone knew David by now, that he was former President Eisenhower's only grandson.

January 9, 1967 was Richard Nixon's birthday. Birthdays after fifty are not to be particularly enjoyable. Since I knew he was thinking about going overseas soon on a foreign trips I thought a "Moody Daily Reminder" booklet would be ideal for his notes. I was glad it helped to make his birthday a pleasant occasion.

Pat and Dick were distressed to learn that I was not

feeling "up to par," but they knew with my spirit I would feel better soon.

My parents put their farm up for sale to move later with me to Tucson Arizona. I had gone ahead and stayed with friends there.

Pat and Dick were surprised to learn that I had moved to Arizona. There only hope that the glorious sunshine plus the enchanting vistas would contribute to my return to good health.

Actually, they thought I couldn't be ill inasmuch as the Republican Party was counting on me as an enthusiastic able leader! I knew they were somewhat disappointed I wouldn't be there working in Illinois. But, I assured them I would be just as active in political affairs in Arizona as I was in Illinois.

To see if he had a chance, Dick had urged all his friends to get busy to work for his nomination at the Republican Convention. Apparently, only a few people in the Republican Party thought Richard Nixon could win the nomination for President. My step father and I thought he could. We started a letter writing campaign urging Republican headquarters nationwide to put Richard Nixon's name up for President at the Republican Convention. We received encouraging letters from most of them. Then, my stepfather and I obtained precinct lists and persuaded grass—root Republicans to send letters to delegates to draft Richard Nixon for President.

In my heart we knew Dick Nixon could win if we all started working now toward that end. Although, Dick had not come out officially to say he would run, I felt he was waiting for the proper time to make that statement.

However, in Pat's heart she was troubled about what to do. Also Pat realized that her girls were growing up and someday would be leaving home and making a life of their own.

On March 5, 1967 Dick Nixon left with Robert Ellsworth, a former congressman from my home state of Kansas, on a foreign policy fact-finding tour of Europe and Soviet Union. In England he conversed with Prime Minister Wilson and others; in France with Foreign Minister Couve de Murville; in West Germany with Chancellor Kiesinger and former Chancellor Konrad Adenauer; in Italy, with President Saragai and Foreign Minister Fanfai and Pope Paul VI; in Romania with Secretary-General Nicolae Ceausescu of the Communist Party and Foreign Minister Manescu; and in Czechoslovakia, with Foreign Trade Officer Bahacels and the Director of the Institute for International Politics and Economics. The Europeans told Nixon the Johnson administration did not consult with them or appreciate the importance of NATO. It worried them. There was concern about Vietnam, the non-proliferation treaty, the Soviets intentions and China.

In Russia the Communist Kremlin leaders snubbed Nixon and refused to meet with him. So Dick took the chance to visit with many of the Russian people. Wherever he went he was graciously and socially received.

For the first time, the Soviet news media covered Richard Nixon's activities there. In Alma Ata, in Soviet central Asia he discussed the Vietnam War with some factory workers. Dick knew little Russian, but he spoke in Spanish. The factory manager, a Cuban, translated for him.

Viktor Olmechenka, a disabled one-armed veteran of World War II asked Nixon, "Why don't you make peace in Vietnam?"

Nixon replied, "I am here as a private citizen and not as an official so it would be inappropriate for me to make political comments."

The factory workers objected, "We too are private citizens, and we have a perfect right and we are not afraid to express our personal opinions."

Nixon said, "It takes two to make peace." The workers then told him the United States should get out of Vietnam.

Then Nixon declared, "South Vietnam asked us for help

just as your country did against Hitler and we helped and are helping."

This exchange reminded me of Nixon's 1959 so called "kitchen debate" with Premier Nikita S. Khrushchev at a U.S. trade exhibition in Moscow.

The American position in Vietnam among the people in Europe was unpopular and not supportive. The Vietnam War had divided the United States, and many were protesting the war. Contradictory, however Nixon was able to talk about Vietnam in open and direct expressions without one antagonistic occurrence there with groups of Soviet Union natives.

April 1967 Dick with Raymond Price, previously an editorial writer for the New York Herald Tribune, traveled to countries in Asia. First he met with Prime Minister Sato of Japan and other Japanese political persons. Then, on to Taiwan to talk with Chiang Kai-shek. In Asia everyone supported our American place in Vietnam, but there was much concern about China and the direction that country was going. The last stop on this Asian trip was South Vietnam. They both landed at the Da Nang Air Base and were greeted by U.S. Marine Commander General Lewis B. Walt. After touring the air base with General Walt, Nixon was convinced after his seventh tour of Vietnam that the expectation for a negotiated completion of the Vietnam War was not very promising than it was a year ago.

His third trip in May was to Latin America. Dick took along Bebe Rebozo, his Latin friend. On the fourth one, Pat Buchanan from his New York office accompanied Nixon on his travels to Africa and Israel.

As I scanned several newspaper and magazines, I discovered the "New York Times" paper and the "Newsweek" news magazine had gone on attack why Nixon was making so many travels overseas. Once again the Eastern press media were pushing their denunciation against Nixon.

Ever since the Alger Hiss case, newspapers like the "Washington Post" and the "New York Times" used their barbed opinions against Nixon. Instead of giving both sides of a story, they only gave the public one side—their version.

June 21,1967 was Pat and Dick's twenty-seventh wedding anniversary. They had just returned from a recent trip when my anniversary card and note were discovered. The Nixons were glad I was enjoying my new home in the romantic West. Pat and Dick had enjoyed my "chosen country" Arizona with its clear air and spectacularly beautiful scenery and friendly people. They only wished that they could visit Arizona more often but the pressures of life kept them captive of city living.

Pat said "Parade" magazine would carry a cover story on Tricia and Julie on August 13. She didn't know how accurate it would be. Since the printed page often shocked Pat, but she was hoping for the best.

Then to my surprise, Pat gave me the address of the prospective organization for Nixon for President. Dr. Gaylord Parkinson was in charge. It was at P.O. Box 2500, 1726 Pennsylvania Ave, N.W.,Washington, D.C. 20013.

I wrote a letter to Dr. Parkinson about helping in the campaign for Dick Nixon. On June 26, 1967 I received a reply. They said Richard Nixon had not officially announced he was running for President, but Dr. Parkinson would keep my name on file for campaign work when and if Nixon made that announcement.

Apparently Pat had been doing some thinking. She had wrestled extensively with the decision about Dick running for President again. If she thought her husband would be happier out of public service, she found out now he wouldn't be. Public service was Dick's whole life. Pat knew in her heart that Dick had the ability to solve some of the other problems facing our country. So when I received that letter from her, I knew she had made up her mind to accept Dick's decision whatever it would be.

David Eisenhower had spent so much time with the Nixons, Pat and Dick put two and two together, and knowing Julie and David were in love. From the start of Julie's friendship with David, they loved him from the beginning. Since David was such a pleasant and wholesome person they thought he was the nicest fellow.

Julie and David were engaged June 12 and not in November. Pat was the only one who knew about it. David and Dick enjoyed being together watching ball games and the late newscasts. Often they would talk over political issues.

David was working at Sears Roebuck Company in Chicago, for the summer of 1967. When he left to return to his work in Chicago, David made an offer of marriage to Julie. They didn't want to tell anyone about it until David could afford to buy a ring for Julie. Julie and David corresponded with each other. He would tell her about his interesting experiences in the Sears complaint department that summer in Chicago.

When Dick arrived back to New York, he discovered that the political scene had changed in favor of him running for president. However, there was a few who thought Nixon had a "loser image," and others wanted "to wait and see," how Dick would do in the presidential primaries. However, not every state had presidential primaries. Republicans from every state chose their own candidates and sent their delegates to the Republican Convention to push for their candidate to be nominated. There, they would try to convince the other delegates their man was the best. Arizona was one of those states. (It wasn't until 1996 that Arizona had their first presidential primary). Many wanted to know what his plans were regarding his run again for the presidency.

The Gallup Poll showed Nixon a favorite candidate among independent voters as well among many active Republicans. My stepfather and I thought the pre-work, we had done for Republicans and others to support Nixon for President, was paying off. Even Congress finally got in the act and as well.

Leslie C. Arends, a Congressman from the 17ᵗʰ district of Illinois, wrote Richard M. Nixon a letter to his New York law office. It was also signed by 35 other Congressmen from across the country. Honorable Richard M. Nixon 20 Broad Street NY, NY 10005, "Dear Dick: In less than a year the nation must choose a new President. War in Vietnam; anarchy in our cities, collapsed farm policy, rising loss of confidence in National leadership—America's decision in 1968 will turn on these and other great issues.

'For us, even for the whole world this campaign will be a critical turning point.

"Your years of experience and leadership in the House, the Senate and the Vice Presidency, your wealth of knowledge accumulated from 20 years of painstaking study of our nation's most pressing domestic and foreign concerns; qualify you uniquely for President of the United States.

'The coming campaign is so crucial for our country that a forthright and vigorous Republican effort must begin now. We are convinced that many millions of Americans share this view. We urge you therefore to immediately announce your candidacy for President of the United States." Signed by Leslie C. Arends, IL 17ᵗʰ district.

Like any other political person, Nixon had both advantages and liabilities.

His strengths were:

He had the ability to speak directly on television or any place or occasion for political public speaking, without using a prepared written matter on a page or ghostwriters.

Dick had a record as a loyal and energetic Republican Party worker, causing him to be worthy of being accepted.

Over his 14 years time in Washington he had vast experience in the federal government on how it operated.

Dick gained expert knowledge of foreign affairs and national defense through his extensive travels around the world and participation in the cabinet meetings of the Eisenhower Administration.

His liabilities as I saw it were:

He was unable to eat properly because of high nervous tension on the campaign trail.

Occasionally a burst of bad temper due to overwork. Too much traveling and trying to do too much at one time caused stress.

Dick was always so polite, thoughtful and kind. I could never get over the press not showing what kind of a person Richard Nixon really was. Few of them ever gave him credit for anything.

On September 30, 1967, a telephone call interrupted his political concerns and his law firm meetings. Hannah Milhous Nixon, Dick's mother had died at the age of 82. She was born March 7, 1885 in Butlerville Indiana, and moved to Whittier California in 1897 with her father Franklin Milhous. In 1908 she married Francis Anthony "Frank" Nixon. Dick's father died at the age of 77, on September 4, 1956. His father had suffered a ruptured abdominal artery but he lived to see his son, Richard Nixon renominated for Vice President at the Republican Convention.

Two years ago before Hannah had suffered a stroke, Dick and his brother, Don, had to put their ailing mother in the Whitmar Convalescent Hospital in Whittier. Hannah needed constant attention, which Don and Dick could not provide in their home.

Dick adored his mother, but he did not show any emotion when he received the call about her death. It was all pent up inside. He felt guilty that he hadn't done more for his mother.

Then, he cancelled his plans for a speaking tour in Oregon. Pat and Dick and two daughters flew to Whittier for the funeral.

Billy Graham conducted the funeral for Nixon's mother at the Friends Church in east Whittier. Hannah had attended

Billy Graham's crusades in California. Both of Nixon's parents were devoutly Christians and poor, but honest hard working folks. They gave Dick a faith in God and taught him integrity and the desire to do any job well, to give more than was expected or demanded of him. Therefore, it was fitting for Billy Graham to be there with the local minister. It was there that Dick burst into tears. As usual I thought the press had no respect for the grieving families. They barged into church where they had no business to be. A funeral service is for families and friends of the deceased. Sometimes I think some reporters behavior showed rude manners in asking people how they felt. No wonder Pat and Dick resented the intrusion of the press in their private lives. I agreed with them.

Instead of conveying flowers for the funeral, I sent beautiful red carnations instead to their New York home with a note, "I am thinking of you." In Hannah's way that meant I'll be praying for you. It added a note of cheer and welcomed them when they arrived home from their sad journey. Pat and Dick were grateful they had dear friends who cared.

Since the Democrat party was now divided, perhaps a Republican would have the chance for the 1968 campaign race. The candidates were Governor George Romney, Michigan, Governor Ronald Reagan, California and liberal Governor Nelson Rockefeller of New York.

Governor George Romney made a campaign swing through Arizona. However, he did not go over well with the people of Arizona. Because of some of his inconsistent remarks about the Vietnam War, Romney turned off many undecided votes except the anti-war group. The Goldwater crowd was not impressed. Dick Nixon had not officially announced he was throwing his hat in the presidential ring. Therefore, they were looking at Governor Ronald Reagan the glamorous movie star as a possible presidential candidate.

But, my stepfather and I were getting restless from waiting so long for Dick to give the official announcement. The Arizona

Federation of Republican Women was having a state convention in Phoenix. Since I was a delegate from the Pantano Republican Women in Tucson, I drove to Phoenix for the convention.

In between session recesses I drove around Phoenix and made applications for employment at colleges and universities. After I had visited 4 colleges in Phoenix with no results. Then someone at the convention suggested Grand Canyon College (now a university). This was the last stop before going back to Tucson. That trip paid off. After my interview I signed a contract to be an assistant Registrar of computer services. They gave me several weeks for finding an apartment in Phoenix before reporting to work.

When I arrived back home in Tucson, I told my mother and stepfather my good news. Every weekend I commuted from Phoenix to Tucson, until they would sell the house later on to make a move to Phoenix.

In October 1967 Dick had two articles published. One was titled "Asia after Vietnam" published in Foreign Affairs. It involved China and how the United States could not leave it outside forever, that we must influence and persuade China to change.

The other article was "What Has Happened to America?" in the Reader's Digest. Nixon was wondering how our country became a blazing inferno of anarchy. If we as a nation enjoyed the abundance of freedom, why had we become the most violent and uncivilized? Dick had asked and answered many questions everyone was concerned about our society.

In this same month the Gallup Poll put Richard Nixon ahead of President Johnson 49 to 45 and for ahead of any Republican adversary. I said, "That should make Dick Nixon decide to run."

Then Nixon was off again to Illinois. At O'Hare airport, Chicago he was greeted by Thomas McKay to fly to McKay's Triple R ranch near Frankfort Illinois, for a fund-raising "roundup," for Joseph I. Woods as a Republican candidate for

Sheriff. Joe Woods was a brother to Rosemary Woods, Nixon's personal secretary. Rosemary was like family to the Nixons.

In November Joseph Woods, Cook County Sheriff was honored at a dinner in Chicago for his long service fighting crime. Senator Everett Dirksen led a group of politicians in a sing-a-long. Edward J. Barrett, Democrat County Clerk, and Richard Nixon were chosen to sing along with Ev and others. Illinois was a crucial electoral state and Dick was making the most of every opportunity there.

By Thanksgiving Julie and David decided to tell their families officially about their engagement to be married. When David told his family his grandmother, Mamie Eisenhower brought forth her mother's rings and offered it to David. This is the engagement ring, which Julie still wears.

The Eisenhowers and the Nixons were not surprised at the announcement; they all assumed that Julie and David were very much in love. When Julie told her father, she was disappointed because he did not get very excited about it. Julie went to talk to her mother about her father's reaction. Julie was really let down.

Pat approached Dick about Julie's feelings. Right away he wrote her a note and slid it under Julie's door.

I remembered part of Dick's note, "How lucky you both are to have found each other. Even though you must expect some ups and downs, I am sure you will have a wonderful life together. I am also sure you know just how much happiness I wish for you both."

That note from her father made Julie happy. Dick always made home life enjoyable and harmonious. The girls couldn't remember a harsh word by their father. They always wanted to be around him.

The year of 1967 was coming soon to a close. Dick had many decisions to make before the year of 1968 started. Our unofficial Nixon for President organization was waiting impatiently for Dick's announcement to run for President.

Three days before Christmas Dick had lunch with his law associates, and then convened with his campaign counselors in the afternoon. Then Pat and Dick had their annual Christmas party at their apartment for more than one hundred guests. Dick played Christmas carols on the piano and all joined in on the singing. Everyone enjoyed my homemade candy from the butterfly candy dish.

After all the party friends had left, Dick went to his library to think about whether he should run or not for the Presidency. He was depressed, Could he win? Losing would be a disaster again for his family. Would the media support his candidacy? He mulled over many questions until he was tired of it.

Pat told Dick on Christmas Day she would help out if he should decide to make another run for the presidency. Tricia and Julie were in on the family discussion. They both decided that whatever their father wanted to do, they were going to support him. All of them were completely happy with New York life, but they knew Dick would be miserable if he didn't try. Whatever he would decide they would be proud of him. Down in his heart Dick knew his wife and girls loved him. Now they perceived that public service was Richard Nixon's life.

When I arrived back in Tucson from my work in Phoenix, my stepfather and mother told me I had a large package from California. I was curious what it was. I couldn't recall about ordering anything from there. Finally I managed to get the package open. A beautiful Della Robbia wreath fashioned by the Boy's Republic in California was in the box. It had fruit and nuts and dried plants woven in this lovely creation that the boys had collected.

I told my stepfather and mother I did not order it. So I searched the package and discovered the card. It read from Mr. And Mrs. Richard Nixon. I was overwhelmed. Then I remembered Pat and Dick had one hanging on their library wall. The wood paneling blended with the subtle tones of the wreath there. Also, I had seen the same kind of wreath on the front door of the Eisenhower White House. Now I was privileged to have one too.

On December 28th Dick flew to Key Biscayne to relax and think about the decision he had to make. One side of him wanted to make the run for the presidency and the other side revolted against putting Pat and the girls, as well as himself, through the stress and strain of another campaign race.

To seek spiritual guidance, Richard Nixon called Rev. Billy Graham to come down to Key Biscayne. There Billy discussed scripture and politics with Dick. He told Dick you are the best-prepared person to be President and you should run in 1968. Problems facing our country are much more serious now. God has provided you another chance to lead our country.

Meanwhile in New York, Julie and David were discussing whether her father should make a race for the President or not. They thought political life was a thankless job. Also the liberal media distorted everything said or done or to follow persons around and pry. A family's privacy is sacrificed when one enters political life. Julie was more aware of that problem then David because he never experienced a most stressful political campaign or political life. David thought Dick had rare discernment and insight and could give guidance to the country. David felt he should tell Julie's father what he thought on the subject, and so he did.

After meditating on David's thoughts and Billy Graham's words of wisdom, Richard Nixon decided to run for the second time for President of the United States.

Pat told me about Dick's decision to campaign for President again. I was happy about his decision. The campaign ahead would be strenuous on all the family. This time Dick would win. My stepfather and I would keep on working, and the Nixons could count on our help wherever needed. Now I felt she had become reconciled to the fact that Dick was working for a cause, a generation of peace.

Chapter 11

THE 1968 ROAD TO
THE WHITE HOUSE

The year of 1968 was ushered in with violence and stress. The turmoil and venom, which had influenced our nation, finally erupted in a frenzy that shocked us for years to come. We were still at war in Vietnam. The anti-war dissenters, the defiant, lewd young people, race riots, and unfortunate political murders brought to surface a reaction by many who were perturbed by the absence of law and order. President Lyndon Johnson was withstood by angry protestors wherever he went. They kept singing and speaking in a monotone, "Hey, hey, LBJ, how many kids did you kill today?" Ho, Ho, Ho Chi Mink, the Viet Cong are going to win, one, two, three, four, we don't want your fucking war. Two, four, six, eight organize and smash the State." The demonstrators were viewed on TV everyday for all of us to see. Many were looking for some one to lead our country out of this jumbled disordered turmoil. As the year began I was convinced that Richard Nixon was the only man to guide us in a new direction.

On January 9th, Richard Nixon was fifty-five years old. Since I knew he would be hitting the campaign trail soon I gave him a pocket size "Moody Daily Reminder" booklet to keep track of his many date and events. It would prove to be most useful in the month ahead.

Dick had made up his mind to run for the presidency for the second time. He knew this time he would win the race. When Julie came home from college, Dick called the family together on January 15th to make an official announcement about his decision. Rosemary Woods, his personal secretary, and Fina and Manolo, their house servants, were included because all would be part of the campaign race ahead. It would be a difficult road to victory. The family was united with Richard Nixon, win or lose, to make this important step.

I continued as an active member of "The Nixon Network." All of the members played a key role in communicating Nixon's stand on issues pertaining to the country. Donald S. Whyte, the national director of the Nixon Network in New York, had a goal of having one active Network member in each of the 3,000 counties in the nation.

On January 23rd, North Korea apprehended the U.S.S. Pueblo, an intelligence gathering ship and held hostage the 83 men aboard. At a press conference Richard Nixon declared the Pueblo "incident an incredible blunder. The blunder was not that the Pueblo was there. The blunder was in our failure to have some protection for our ship. We should have had ships and air cover to protect it."

Dick said our first duty was to procure the release of the Pueblo 83 crewmembers held by the North Koreans. He urged that the Pueblo incident should be kept above politics and called the country to be united and support President Johnson.

It was the Tet Offensive on January 30th launched by the Viet Cong Communists troops in Vietnam which startled us as a nation. The television network coverage of the occupation of the U.S. Embassy in Saigon, by the Viet Cong appalled and depressed us at the same time. The government had told us we were winning the war in Vietnam. This escalation of the war dejected us as a people and unleashed the fury of the peace movement in America.

New Hampshire, the first in the nation presidential primary, was to be held March 12th. The Tet offensive dominated the news and the Vietnam War was on the minds of the voters of New Hampshire. However on January 31, 1968 Richard Nixon sent a letter to every registered voter in New Hampshire announcing his candidacy for President, saying, "The nation is in grave difficulties around the world and here at home. Peace and freedom in the world, and peace and progress here at home will depend on the decisions of the next President of the United States. For these critical years, American needs new leadership."

Dick came to Manchester, New Hampshire on February 2nd and had a press conference at the Holiday Inn. Representatives of the national media and the local press were there clamoring for a news story and photos. There Dick faced more cameras and microphones than anyone had ever seen before.

Pat and Dick always campaigned as a team. This time Julie and Tricia, their two-college age daughters joined the campaign team. Julie's fiancé, David Eisenhower, came along as well.

The presidential campaign race was now under way. I prayed that Pat and Dick would have the strength to go through all that. Campaigns are so exhausting! Pat and Dick would go from town to villages and the nights and days would blend into another. Sometimes one would wonder what day it was. There would be the continued chain of hotels and motels, automobiles, buses and airplanes. Anyone who campaigns gets up in the morning goes all-day and very late at night. Pat and Dick would be fortunate if they had time to change their clothes or take a shower. Dick would have to shave more often—three times. Pat would keep her hair combed and her face powdered. She wore dresses that would last all day and not appear to look wrinkled. She managed to maintain a beautiful, trim look wherever she went on the campaign trail.

Julie and David, age 19, and Tricia almost 22, would have their own timetables in this presidential race to visit many cities and towns. In Manchester, New Hampshire, Julie and David took part in a babysitting project to help free concerned voters for the March 12th primary.

Private polls of registered voters in New Hampshire implied that Richard Nixon would capture 50 percent of the total vote cast. Governor George Romney of Michigan was also on the ballot. Governor Nelson Rockefeller's supporters developed a write-in campaign for him. When Romney heard Rockefeller say he would accept a draft for the presidential nomination, that statement caused Romney to reconsider his plans. Then his pollster told him Nixon was far ahead in New Hampshire. Being realistic Romney withdrew his name from the race. The New Hampshire Secretary of State said the ballots had been printed and that Romney's name would remain on the presidential primary ballots in spite of Romney's last minute withdrawal.

Richard Nixon was disappointed by Romney's withdrawal. He wanted to defeat Romney as his opponent in the election. Pat and Dick wanted a definite unequivocal victory. However Romney's withdrawal didn't stop the Nixons from campaigning. They accelerated their visits to mills, shops, schools and factories, conducting many informal campaigns. Touring towns and villages, they made a special point of talking to young people. In turn the young people became Nixon workers. They liked what they heard and did something about it.

The Democrat Party was sharply divided over the Vietnam War. It caused a violent agitation in the Democrat New Hampshire primary. President Johnson decided to stay out of all primaries because he was too busy trying to bring the Vietnam War to a conclusion. Some liberal Democrats persuaded Senator Eugene McCarthy (Wisconsin) to run against Lyndon Johnson on "Stop the War in Vietnam," ticket in New Hampshire.

A week before the New Hampshire March 12th primary, Dick said in a speech at the American Legion Hall in Hampton, New Hampshire: " . . . I pledge to you that new leadership will end the war and win the peace in the Pacific, and that is what America wants."

All the newsmen immediately demanded how he would do it. They assumed he had a definite plan to accomplish it. Of course the Democrats jumped in and wrongly broadcasted that Nixon said he had a "secret plan" to end the war in Vietnam. This distortion had been repeated so often some people were taking it for a fact.

But Dick never, never said he had such a plan, secret or in other respects. If anyone was really listening he went out of his way repeatedly to say he did not. Dick hated war. He would have consulted with President Johnson if he had procured such a plan. It was gossiped around by those who did not care to know the facts. Dick Tuck, the Democrat Party's dirty trickster would pose as a news reporter. He loved to follow Nixon around and offer money to bands to play some funny tune to embarrass Dick when he appeared. This wasn't the first time the Democrats used nasty tricks.

When the New Hampshire primary results were in, it surprised many politicians and veteran analysts. The total vote-over 160,000 cast-was the largest in history for New Hampshire primary. The last big count of 129,100 was in 1952. This was a record.

What astonished everyone was that Nixon polled more voters than all candidates, Republican or Democrat-combined and-won the Republican contest with a 79 percent vote.

Nixon	84,000
(write in) Johnson	26,300
McCarthy	22,800
(write in) Rockefeller	11,700

Pat and Dick celebrated the victory in New York at the Nixon headquarters. It was one primary victory for the road to the White House. I was happy but there was still much work ahead.

On March 15th Robert F. Kennedy decided to challenge Johnson for the Democrat presidential nomination. Bitterness erupted in the Democrat Party and divided it once again. McCarthy and Kennedy were fighting one another and against Johnson too.

On March 21st Nelson Rockefeller called a press conference. All of us thought he would tell us he was a candidate too. However, he surprised us by saying he would not be a candidate for President and would not encourage a presidential draft either. Even Rockefeller signed a sworn statement to take his name out of the Oregon primary declaring he would not be a candidate now or in the future. This statement surprised and disappointed the Rockefeller's supporters. However I was still leery of anything that Rockefeller said or did because of his past actions.

The Vietnam War was making President Johnson physically and mentally exhausted. He was tired of that war. It was draining his energy and attention for the social programs he loved.

Then two days before the Wisconsin primary President Lyndon Johnson announced on the television networks, "I shall not seek, and I will not accept, the nomination of my party for another term as your President."

At that time I wondered how many others would drop out of the race. I sure thought the presidential race would be a contest between Lyndon B. Johnson and Richard M. Nixon.

Now the race for the White House had changed. Johnson's withdrawal meant that Nixon's primary object would be removed.

There was no love lost between Robert Kennedy and President Johnson. Johnson just regarded Kennedy as a nuisance. It was Bobby who wanted to do the feuding. The turmoil among the Democrats amplified. It did subside after Johnson's announcement.

But, the fear in my heart increased. I remembered the 1960 presidential race too well. Nixon's opponent would be Robert Kennedy now. We all would have to work harder. Bobby Kennedy would be more ruthless than his brother.

Many assumed that Lyndon Johnson disliked Richard Nixon, but that was not the case. Johnson concurred with Nixon's position on the Vietnam War and Communism. He actually appreciated Nixon's backing and support on those matters. If Nixon won the presidency he would not be upset about the election.

As I look back in time, the 1968 current circumstances reminded me of the situation in 1952, when the Eisenhower and Nixon ticket wrenched domination of the federal government from the Democrats for the first time since Franklin Delano Roosevelt's administration in 1933.

Then as it was in 1968, (President Harry Truman); a Democrat administration was entangled in elongated war in Asia. Our country had an epidemic of wartime inflation and public turmoil. Also, President Lyndon Johnson was under attack by members of his own Democrat party, just like President Harry Truman in 1952. If Nixon was speculating which Democrat opponent he might prefer to run against, he did not tell the press or any of us on the campaign trail.

The Nixon family was in Wisconsin campaigning and attended a party in Milwaukee. It was a great crowd and they enjoyed shaking hands and socializing with everyone. March

31st was also David Eisenhower's 20th birthday, and they relished his birthday cake.

Wisconsin primaries are usually a graveyard for presidential aspirations; Lyndon Johnson's name appeared for the first time on the election ballot in the 1968 campaign in Wisconsin, April 2nd. Eugene McCarthy, a Democrat "peace" challenger candidate and Richard Nixon were also on the ballot. Senator Robert F. Kennedy's name was not there because he jumped in the race too late.

Former Governor George C. Wallace of Alabama was deleted from the Democrat list of candidates, since he was running this time as an independent Democrat candidate for President.

Nixon had the organization and the money. If any Republican decided to enter the race at that time he would have difficulty in crushing the strength Nixon was establishing in the primaries.

In the Wisconsin primary Nixon did it again. He won 79 percent of the Republican total. On the Democrat side Eugene McCarthy sunk President Johnson 56% to his 34%. Robert Kennedy was not on the Wisconsin primary ballot. 46,500 Democrat voters wrote in his name. Johnson had no support in Wisconsin. The anti-Vietnam War candidates had won 64% of the Democrat vote.

Two days after Nixon's victory in Wisconsin, our nation was shocked by Martin Luther King Jr's assassination in Memphis, Tennessee by James Earl Ray, a lone gunman. Many thought the assassin did not work alone and conspiracy theories abounded for years.

The next week after King's death, black violence flared up in 125 cities in 29 states. As I viewed on television all the looting and burning, I wondered what was happening to my world.

In Chicago, Mayor Richard Daley Sr., ordered the police to "shoot to kill" the arsonists. Washington D.C. was struck more severely than the other cities. The fighting in the streets was at its worse. Bombs and bullets erupted just two blocks from the White House. Fifty million dollars property was damaged. All the rioting caused 46 persons killed, 2,600 injured and 21,00 arrested. We were worried about the many sudden changes taking place in our country. All the black violence and anti-war protesters was tearing our country apart and was leaving us troubled, confused and anxious.

Richard Nixon paid respects to King's widow and family and attended Martin Luther King, Jr's funeral. Then he refrained from any politicking for two weeks.

Dick decided to pay more attention to his campaign schedule in 1968. It was a complete reversal of the 1960 campaign where he exhausted himself. This time he took more weekends off and refreshed himself at Key Biscayne. In 1960 the Kennedy's outspent Nixon, but in 1968 many Nixon supporters donated more money than ever for him to win the nomination at the Republican Party and to fight for the presidential election.

Pat at age 56 had more energy for campaigning than I thought. Sometimes she outshone Dick on the campaign trail. I was surprised to receive a letter from her at home in New York. Apparently she was trying to catch up with her delayed stack of mail.

On April 19th Dick gave a speech in Washington D.C. at the American Society of Newspaper Editors. The speech was superb. The editors gave Nixon an active question-and-answer period after the speech. It was well received by the press. They were surprised by his sense of humor and observations.

Then Dick arrived in Minneapolis Minnesota on April 20th. Of course the press realized he was major news now and they were making the most of it. At a news conference Nixon answered their questions. Nixon said, "What we are talking about now is an immediate financial crisis. For any candidate or any political leader to come before the American people and tell a group of poor, a group of people living in poor housing, a group of people who want jobs, that right now the federal government is going to massively increase his spending program—that's dishonest and it's a cruel delusion to whom it's told. And I'm just not going to join that game, whether it costs the election or not."

Dick would rather lose the presidential election than mislead the American people.

While peace talks were underway Nixon suspended the Vietnam War as an issue in this primary campaign. Everyone was applauding Dick for his ideas on building a "New America" from within. He set forth sound new proposals for helping poor minorities. He then expanded his beliefs in some 30 personal campaign appearances throughout the Midwest and other mountain states.

On April 25th, over the CBS radio networks, Nixon called for us as Americans to build new "Bridges to Human Dignity."

Dick declared, "For too long, while America has sought to buy off the Negro—and to buy off its own sense of guilt—with ever more programs of welfare, of public housing, of payments to the poor—payments that perpetuated poverty and kept the endless, dismal cycle of dependency spending from generation to generation.

He emphasized, "Promises of increased federal spending are not the answer either. The reality of the economic situation is such that to talk of massively increasing the budget in order to pour additional billions into cities this year is a cruel delusion. He continued on, "What we do need is imaginative enlistment of private funds, private energies, and private talents, in order to develop opportunities that lie untapped in our own undeveloped urban heartland. We need new bridges between the developed and underdeveloped segments of our own society—human bridges, economic bridges, bridges of understanding help."

Almost ignored by the public and the press in the bustling campaign was Dick's impressive victory in Pennsylvania Presidential preference primary. April 25th Nixon outpolled Rockefeller, his nearest rival by a 3 to 1 margin, 105,991 to Rockefeller's 33,664. Pennsylvania's delegate votes were not binding for the convention in this election contest.

As I predicted on April 30th Rockefeller made a complete turn-a-round and again announced his candidacy for president on the day of Massachusetts's primary.

If Richard Nixon was irritated by Rockefeller's entrance again in the presidential race or winning the unexpected primary victory of 34 delegates in Massachusetts, he didn't show it in public. Dick seemed pleased to have an opponent at last and would carefully jab indirectly at Rockefeller for his refusal to enter primaries.

Then again Nixon on May 2nd gave a radio address on NBC radio entitled, "Bridges to Human Dignity! Part 11." Dick spelled out his suggestions in a 9-point plan.

Briefly they were:

1. Rural development and core city credits "Tax incentives—whether direct credits, accelerated depreciation or a combination of the two—should be provided to those businesses that locate branch offices or new plants in poverty areas, whether in core cities or in rural America."

2. New Capital-"If our urban ghettos are to be rebuilt from within one of they first requirements is the development of black owned and black run businesses. The need is more than economic. Black ownership of homes, land, and especially of productive enterprise is both symbol and evidence of opportunity and this is central to the spirit of independence on which orderly progress rests!

3. New Enterprises-"A new enterprise program should be established to serve the Negro in the central city, helping black employees to become employers."

4. Human Investment-"I urge immediate enactment of the Republican sponsored Human Investment Act, providing tax incentives to corporations which hire and train the skilled and upgrade the skills of those at the bottom of the employment ladder.

5. Computer Job Bank-"Under this plan, computers would be located in areas of high unemployment, both urban and rural—a jobless man could tell the computer operator his employment background, his skill, his job needs—and in minutes he could learn where to find the work or the training he seeks."

6. Student-Teacher Corps-"Young Americans have shown their idealism and their dedication in the Peace Corps and in Vista. To these now should be added a National Student Teacher Corps of high school and college students who would work at the tutoring of core-city children."

7. Extended Training-"I recommend Extended Training Programs in core-city schools in which classes in basic language and communications skills would be made available after regular school hours and during the summer months.

8. Teacher-Veterans-"Among the nation's greatest under utilized assets are the returning Negro veterans of Vietnam. Many of these would be superbly qualified for training as teachers. Universities and school should intensify their recruitment among these veterans. For its part, the Department of Defense should set up a special information program to make Vietnam veterans, black and white alike, aware of the opportunities and rewards of teaching."

9. Home ownership-"People who own their own home don't burn their neighborhoods: rather they turn to fixing up their communities and making them livable for themselves and their neighbors. Senator Percy's National Home Ownership Foundation Plan, for example would provide a private sector device for channeling mortgage capital into the slums and for enabling the poor to own their own homes and it would do so at only a minute fraction of the cost of packing them into public housing.

Nixon concluded, "The basis principle here is the same as in the job programs I outlined: imaginative investment of the private and the independent sectors encouragement of private ownership, development of the pride that can only come from independence."

May 7th Dick was eager to rack up a large vote in the Indiana primary to show Republican delegates that the people there were speaking the Nixon name. Wherever they went the crowds suggested they wanted Nixon.

At Gary Indiana 5,000 people waved and cheered. Nixon asked, "Do you want to go down a new road, or go down an old road with new faces?" Anyone present had no doubts that they wanted Nixon.

Later in Indianapolis 8,000 teenagers, adults and children clapped their hands and stamped their feet. The fervor was so great one would think the state of Indiana had won a sports championship. Dick was glad to be greeted by a warm reception from his mother's home state. Bumper stickers on Indiana cars now read "Feel Safer With Nixon."

Nixon had every reason to cheer at the election results in Indiana. In1960 he carried Indiana by nearly 225,000 votes. This time in 1968 he polled 508,000 votes. What was interesting in this Indiana election, Dick ran nearly 200,000 votes ahead of Robert Kennedy in the Democrat race.

Richard Nixon told citizens of Kearney Nebraska in an important farm address May 5th. "The problems of rural America have been relegated to the back of the bus by the Democratic Administration. It is because the power elite of the Democratic Party owes its political position to the urban voting blocks that rural America is being short-changed.

"I will not promise the farmers and ranchers rapid restoration of 100 percent of parity if I am elected. I will not say that every farm now operating will continue in existence under a new administration. I will not tell the farmer that Richard Nixon in the White House means Utopia in rural America. For no candidate can deliver on those kinds of promises. And the American farmer has more than his share of promissory notes defaulted on by political men."

Dick stressed, however, that while it is wrong to promise the impossible, there is much that can be accomplished.

Specifically he recommended:

"A new concern and a new interest in Washington. President Johnson described last year's plunge of 2 million dollars, or 11 percent in farm earnings as a dip in income. That was not a dip—it was a minor disaster.

"A new administration must commit itself to an increase of commercial exports of agriculture products-to an expanded effort to break down remaining barriers of the world to the sale of American produce.

"Diversification of rural America through the use of tax incentives to bring industry out of the city and a more concentrated research effort aimed at finding new uses for farm products.

"Careful exploration of means of increasing the farmer's leverage is bargaining for the prices of his goods.

"An end to inflation which has raised the cost of everything the farmer buys while the prices he receives for his products continue to fall.

Dick stated, "There are the modern dimensions of the

agriculture dilemma—one in which the more efficient and productive a worker the farmer becomes, the more he contributes to American prosperity, but the more difficult he finds it to live a prosperous life on the farm."

Nebraska had their primary election May 14th. This state was always considered Nixon territory. It gave Nixon his largest margin in 1960 against John F. Kennedy. This time Dick captured 70 percent of the vote in spite of Nelson Rockefeller's write in vote of 5 percent. Ronald Reagan had not encouraged his supporters in Nebraska and he did not campaign there personally. He received 22 percent of the vote. Dick was glad to have competition in a Republican primary because it made the race more of a contest.

Enroute along the campaign trail to Oregon, Richard Nixon, now the front-runner for the Republican nomination for President, stopped over at Sheraton Blackstone Hotel in Chicago, Illinois on May 16th. Pat and Dick had big smiles for the crowd there. They were searching for Illinois delegates to the Republican convention, and they found some for their efforts. The previous work by supporters were paying off. Illinois was beginning to look like Nixon territory in spite of Rockefeller's supporters to make a dent in it.

On May 17th, the United Citizens for Nixon was created to oversee and support volunteer organizations dedicated to the nomination and election of Richard M. Nixon for President. Our Nixon Network was now a part of the United Citizens for Nixon, and our new home was located in the World Center Building, 16th and K Street, NW in Washington, D.C.

At the opening of the news headquarters Joe Louis, a former heavyweight boxing black champion, gave the Nixon campaign an added punch and boost by appearing there.

The United Citizens for Nixon, first order for business would organize specialized volunteer support groups from many leading athletes, farmers, doctors, attorneys, veterans, and others whose mutual concern banded them together.

At a luncheon of Association of American Editorial Cartoonist, Nixon refused to spell out his views on Vietnam. He said, "An answer would give aid and comfort to the enemy and destroy chances for success in Paris, and that I will not do."

My heart jumped with joy when I heard the Nixons would be in Arizona before going on to the Oregon primary. So I dashed off a special letter to Pat, the New York campaign office asking them to make a stop at Grand Canyon College. My letter was forwarded to Pat along the campaign trail. Because the schedule was now committed, she would be unable to visit the college. She thanked me for thinking about them. Pat hoped she would be able to catch a glimpse of me at least in Phoenix.

Dick was to address the Trunk 'N' Tusk Club fund-raising dinner at the Townhouse in Phoenix. I was determined I would get to see them. There was a huge crowd of Republican well-wishers at the Sky Harbor airport. Pat and Dick's plane arrived about 2 pm that Wednesday. What a crowd! They pushed and shoved. All wanted to shake hands with Pat and Dick. Dick went down one side of the happy crowd and Pat went down the other side shaking hands and talking and visiting with those who waited.

I sized up the crowd and decided to stay at the end of the boisterous throng. The press was getting trampled trying to procure pictures. Then Pat spotted me and gave me a hug.

She hollered to Dick on the other side, "Dick, Helen is over here!"

Dick came over. They asked me if I was going to the dinner at the Townhouse. I said, "I had not planned on it because I wasn't sure I would be able to go." Then Pat said, "I'll be in touch with you before we go on to Oregon."

Dick went directly to the Arizona state house to confer with Governor Jack Williams as to governmental needs of

Western States. Pat departed to the hotel to rest and get ready for the dinner that night.

I arrived back at the college to make up time at work. It was difficult for me to concentrate on my work, but I became busy entering student grades on their course sheets. Sometime that afternoon the telephone rang at Dot Bickers, our receptionist and secretary desk. Dot was surprised by the voice on the other end of the phone line. It was Pat, and she startled Dot by telling her, "This is Mrs. Richard Nixon, I would like to talk to Helen Baughman."

Dot was so overwhelmed by the call, she almost forgot to tell me to pick up my phone for the message.

Pat told me, 'I wanted you to be our guest at the dinner this evening. I'll talk to you there. And so I was.

Dot didn't get over that call. She said why didn't you tell me you knew them personally. Of course, that news spread like wildfire around the college campus. My privacy suddenly went out the window, and I became instantly a celebrity. It was one thing to work in their campaigns, but it was another thing to be a personal friend of such a V.I.P.

At the dinner Richard Nixon addressed a crowd of 1,800 enthusiastic Arizona Republicans. Pat and Dick were first in their hearts. The audience cheered, applauded and even attempted a swing and sway "rock" song as Dick told them: "There is nothing wrong with America that new leadership and new instruments of peace can not repair." Nixon was the one!

Arizona Republican leaders at the dinner were impressed that a personal friend of the Nixons lived in Phoenix and was working for the Nixons here. They wanted to know more about my relationship and me to Pat and Dick.

Then Pat and Dick departed from the Sky Harbor Airport to Portland, Oregon campaign trip there. I said goodbye and wished I were going with them.

The election in Oregon May 28th loomed as the last major obstacle on Dick Nixon's primary journey and the last stand for any pre-convention "stop Nixon" ride. Dick decided to increase his campaign endeavors in Oregon knowing his Republican opponents, Rockefeller and Reagan, were spending thousands of dollars there. Neither Reagan or Rockefeller did not campaign personally in Oregon. Their supporters were trying to dream up backing for their candidacy in a last ditch effort. When the Oregon primary was over, Richard Nixon had received 73 percent of the primary vote. Reagan dragged in at 23 percent and Rockefeller' write in vote was only 4 percent.

On the Democrat side in Oregon, Eugene McCarthy clobbered Robert Kennedy, 45 percent to 39 percent. McCarthy had attacked everyone from J. Edgar Hoover to Robert Kennedy and everything from the environment to the Vietnam War. His snide remarks about Kennedy only enraged his opponent. For the first time Robert Kennedy lost a primary in a direct campaign contest. I was hoping they would continue fighting one another and that the Democrat Party would be more divided than ever.

After the Oregon primary Bob Haldeman joined the campaign team. Bob was a good organizer, but he thought he knew it all. If things were not done his way, he would be harshly curt and sometimes down right rude. I didn't like his attitude about Pat. Bob did not think Pat should be out front as part of the campaign team. Apparently he developed a complex about the worth of women in the political process. From then on I let Dick know when something occurred by Haldeman, I didn't appreciate or enjoy in the campaign.

The last primary was South Dakota on June 4th. Dick had strong organization support there and was expected to win all the 14 delegates in the uncontested primary there. Together the 6 primary states would send 112 delegates to the Republican National Convention—all pledged to Nixon who won the primary state elections. Six hundred sixty seven delegates were needed to win the nomination.

The work we had done on behalf of Richard Nixon was instrumental in achieving success beyond expectations. The Nixon primary victories were now history. From New Hampshire to Oregon, Dick had polled an average 74 percent of the vote—three times the vote of all his opposition combined!

Thousands of us as loyal supporters provided the dedicated service and finances which enabled Richard Nixon to successfully carry his message to the important primary states. This, we helped to create the clear opportunity that lie ahead.

The Republican Party can now elect a President who would return this country to its proper role as a world leader. Richard Nixon stood for law, order and progress. I knew he would end the Vietnam War with honor—bring back fiscal sanity—and reunite our nation.

Ours "Nixon Network" members were responsible for speaking out on the Nixon issues and for any getting additional funds to carry Richard Nixon up to and through the nomination at Miami in August—money to build his organization ready to move at once into the fall campaign. I know our dedication could result in the nomination of Dick Nixon—the one man who could defeat the Democrat candidate in November and give inspirational and dynamic new direction.

All of us watched the California Democrat primary on television, June 4th with great interest. Senator Robert Kennedy and Eugene McCarthy were running neck-to-neck.

This was the primary Kennedy wanted to win to stay in the race for the nomination at the Democrat convention.

When it was all over Robert Kennedy won 46 percent to McCarthy's 41 percent of the California primary vote.

I watched on TV Bobby Kennedy's victory statement at

the Ambassador Hotel. Then, he finished his speech. Someone suggested they take a short cut through the hotel kitchen. Then to my horror, Bobby Kennedy was gunned down by Sirhan Sirhan, a Palestinian, who objected to Kennedy's support for Israel. To this very day, I wondered how Sirhan knew that the Kennedy group was going through the hotel kitchen. I still think that Sirhan did not act alone because of that remark I heard watching the television news.

Pat and Dick attended Bobby Kennedy's funeral mass at St. Patrick Cathedral in New York. Even though Richard Nixon and Bobby Kennedy were political enemies and did not share the same beliefs, Nixon was appalled by the violent tragic shooting of a political opponent. This was one act Dick did not approve to cut down an opponent.

Afterwards there was no political campaigning for weeks by any candidate.

After Kennedy's tragic death President Lyndon Johnson ordered Secret Service protection June 5th, for all candidates and their wives. Because Julie and Tricia were busily engaged in their father's campaign, they were granted Secret Service protection as well. From then on, Pat and Dick and the girls had to let the agents know whom they saw and what they did. It was quite unnerving!

Tricia graduated from Finch College. Dick had consented to speak at the Finch College graduation ceremonies. Now the Secret Service was there as guests to watch the whole family present.

Wherever any of us went, there were crowds of demonstrators. Some would chant songs of peace and hold signs saying "Stop The War." It was a nervous and a strained time.

At Miami, Florida Julie celebrated her 20th birthday with David Eisenhower, her fiancé, at a private family party. Tricia, her sister, and Pat and Dick made it a happy occasion. It was good to just relax and get rid of campaign crowds for a while.

The month of July my stepfather and I were busy contacting delegates to support Richard Nixon for President. This would be the last month before the Republican convention, and we were not taking any chance with anyone connected to the convention. It was arduous work. After speaking to many Republican groups, we followed up with a letter for a reply. We even enlisted some Republican volunteers to pen individual letters to delegates urging them to nominate Richard Nixon for President on the first ballot. In turn, the volunteers gave us those replies from the delegates. It was going to be a tight race. But we didn't get much sleep as we kept up our increasing efforts.

July 15, Nixon was in Washington, D.C. visiting with about 30 Republican Senators at the Capitol. For two hours he discussed strategy and campaign issues.

At the same time there was some speculation why former President Dwight D. Eisenhower was scheduling a news conference. There were a limited number of reporters at the Walter Reed Army Hospital where Eisenhower was recuperating from a serious heart attack. It was Ike's standard practice to refrain from endorsing any candidate until that candidate had been nominated by the convention or primary.

Eisenhower said, "I think, however, that this year is an exceptional one. The issues are so great and confusing that I would like to break my own precedent. Most adult Americans have expressed themselves on this subject and so I feel entitled to do so myself.

Then, he added, "I endorse Richard M. Nixon for the Republican nomination for President. I am taking this step not merely because of Nixon's great service to his country during my administration but also because of his personal qualities—intelligence, decisiveness, and integrity."

Nixon said, after his two hour meeting with Senators at the Capitol, "The Eisenhower endorsement is a big boost to my candidacy. It's a great lift."

President Johnson suggested all the presidential candidates come to the White House for intelligence briefing. When Dick arrived there on July 26, President Johnson, Secretary of State Dick Rusk, and National Security Advisor Walt Rostow were present. Vietnam was discussed. Should United States withdraw without a fair peace conclusion, and would that withdrawal let communistic China be the only chief top force and authority in Asia.

President Johnson was worried about the Vietnam War. Dick was concerned about Nelson Rockefeller's pursuit of delegates prior to the Republican Convention, and Ronald Reagan, California Republican primary favorite son victory. Whatever Rockefeller and Reagan tried they could not break the state of Nixon being first in the Republican Party where Dick had worked so long for other candidates.

Senator Everett Dirksen (Illinois) reminded all of us that Richard Nixon would have to win on the first ballot at the convention. It looked at this point Dick had all the delegate votes needed. However, we worked and worked to stop any inroads by Rockefeller and Reagan workers. Reagan had not officially announced he was a candidate but I expected him to do at the right moment.

Richard Kleindest, a Phoenix Arizona attorney was in charge of responsibility for the delegation effort for Nixon. John Haugh, our Republican National committeeman for Arizona, Margie Braden, Arizona Republican National committeewoman, and Mary Dell Pritzlaff from Scottsdale were some of the delegates to the Republican convention. Nixon was the one in Arizona.

The Republican convention was in Miami Beach, Florida, August 5th-8th instead of Chicago where the Democrat Convention would be held.

All the Miami Beach skyscraper hotels were booked to the capacity for the convention. The hot sun and the humidity stupefied us. Some travelers wore very short short skirts and other sight seekers wore shirts that glittered in the sun. The sparkling blue water of the ocean gleamed back at us. Sometimes our air conditioners did not work—either was too cold or too warm. Invariably, we gobbled food on the run and gulped down hurriedly our java or soda pop between events.

Young voters for Nixon from Illinois voiced their welcome. Placard carrying youth surrounded them chanting, "Nixon's The One."

As I predicted on August 5th the first day of convention Reagan announced that he was a candidate. That was no surprise to any of us.

Pat and Dick arrived in Miami Beach for the convention the same day from Montauk Point, Long Island. A large excited and zealous crowd met them at the airport. It was an enthusiastic Pat Nixon who spoke to the crowd there.

"I feel different about this campaign, I truly do. I feel there's a spirit in the air, one I first knew in 1952 when Dick was first elected Vice President. You are really concerned instead of sitting back and complaining. You are doing something about it. Work for the principles you believe in."

Pat and Dick sped to their penthouse suite reserved for them at the Hilton Plaza Hotel. As soon as he arrived at the hotel, Dick got in touch with John Mitchell and Richard Kleindist on how things were going. Both of them assured Dick they had everything managed and checked. Dick was concerned about the delegate count at the convention. The press had reported that there were last minute defections from Nixon to Rockefeller and Reagan.

All of us had spent months of strenuous labor convincing delegates Nixon was the one. Senator John Tower (Texas) and Strom Thurmond, (South Carolina) helped us out in the South by telephoning and visiting delegates from all the Southern states. The very thin line held, and I was assured that Dick Nixon would be nominated for President.

Ted Agnew from Maryland placed Dick Nixon's name in

nomination. The balloting began. Alabama was first, Nixon-14 votes-Reagan-12 votes, Alaska-12 votes for Nixon. Arizona delivered all their votes for Nixon. When the Florida roll call came up Nixon received 32 out of the state's 34 votes. In Illinois, Dick won 50 out of 58 delegates.

When I learned that Charles "Chuck" Percy had switched the last minute his Illinois delegate vote to Rockefeller. It really upset me. Dick had campaigned long and hard for various candidates over the years. Charles "Chuck" Percy of Illinois, Clifford Case of New Jersey, and Ray Shafer of Pennsylvania were some of the candidates. Nixon had campaigned for in the past, and still they switched their votes to Rockefeller. Rockefeller had not worked for anyone except for himself.

I was so perturbed over this, I penned a note to Chuck on how I felt about his disloyalty to Richard Nixon. Chuck replied that he thought Rockefeller was more electable. He was sorry that I felt like I did.

Clifford Case had decided to run as a New Jersey favorite son and then switched his delegate vote to Rockefeller instead. The New Jersey delegation was divided over Nixon and Rockefeller. The fight became painful and bitter. All the delegation was polled individually. Out of the 40 New Jersey delegates, eighteen finally come out for Nixon.

New York gave Nixon four votes. Ohio held their ground for their favorite son, Jim Rhodes. Dick obtained 22 votes out of Pennsylvania's 64 delegate votes. When the final roll call of Wisconsin came in, Dick acquired his 692 votes, which put him as the top winner.

I jumped for joy—Nelson Rockefeller obtained 277 votes and Ronald Reagan managed to procure 182 votes. Our labor had paid off. With all my previous campaign experiences, I knew the road to the top of the mountain would be arduous and trying.

Ronald Reagan stepped forward and urged the convention

delegates to make Dick's nomination unanimous by acclamation. Rockefeller and Percy congratulated Dick on winning the nomination for the presidency.

If the press thought the Republican convention was boring and not exciting enough, they only had to wait awhile until the selection of the vice-presidential nominee. Nixon's first choice was Robert Finch, Lieutenant Governor of California. But Bob didn't want anything to do with that job as vice-president. He knew that his family would not have any privacy and would eventually destroy their family life. So he told Dick to take his name out of the running for vice-president.

Billy Graham, the evangelistic preacher and close Nixon friend, even suggested Mark Hatfield from Oregon as a good choice. However, Billy knew little about the political process and what it takes to win elections. If Mark Hatfield had been from the South and a conservative, instead of from Oregon and a liberal in the West, he would have been a very good selection.

But Dick was trying to build a bridge between the North and South. The South was very conservative and had no use for liberal candidates. The third party candidate, George Wallace, from the South, was a factor in the mulling over about Vice-President nominee considerations. It all came down to Spiro Agnew's name on Nixon's list. Spiro was from Maryland a border state to the South. He would be acceptable to all parts of the United States. Agnew record on law and order and civil rights appealed to Dick, as well as some of his campaign staff.

However, some of us were concerned about Spiro Agnew because we didn't know much about him. When Dick made the announcement to the convention about his vice president choice, boos and cries of "Spiro who" accosted him.

Suddenly, a small protest group came on the floor rebelling against the Agnew choice. They were suggesting Governor

Romney from Michigan as a substitute replacement. Dick was so angry and disturbed about this revolt,he ordered his staff to correct the problem. He did not want a replay of the 1964 debacle and was very concerned about the unity of the Republican Party. The rebellion was short lived. Romney received 186 votes to Agnew's 1,128 votes.Spiro Agnew now was the Vice President nominee.

When Richard Nixon was running for the Republican Party Presidential nomination, Pat was thought to be present at a notable Republican gathering, but the night before she sprained an ankle severely. From all over the country, prominent Republican women were waiting to see her. Her doctor ordered her to stay off her feet for several days. If anyone thought Pat Nixon would stay at home, they did not know this woman of great physical and moral courage. She showed up. She shook hands with every one of the 5,000 women attending. She stood there for three hours in unbelievable pain.

Pat believed in her husband and what he was trying to do. Most of us were excited, but Pat was overcomed.The 1960-year of defeat lingered in her heart. She was taking things one day at a time until the final election in November. Always Pat would be at her husband's side helping in any way she could.

Pat and Dick came near the convention hall lectern. The crowd stood to their feet and shouted, "Nixon's The One!" clapped their hands and stomped the floor. The whoop and holler was noisy.

Nixon's acceptance speech appealed to the heart of America. Dick described the problems of our country as he saw them and people were listening to every word spoken. To this very day I remembered what Nixon said. The conclusion of his speech was very dramatic and it went back to Dick's own personal roots.

"Tonight, I see a face of a child. He lives in a great city.

He is black or he is white. He is Mexican, Italian, Polish. None of that matters. What matters he is an American child. That child in that great city is more important than any politician's promise. He is America. He is a poet. He is a scientist, he is a great teacher, and he is a proud craftsman. He is everything we ever hoped to be and everything we dare to dream to be. He sleeps the sleep of a child and he dreams the dreams of a child, and yet when he awakens to a living nightmare of poverty, neglect, and despair. He fails in schools. He ends up on welfare.

For him the American system is one that feeds his stomach and starves his soul. It breaks his heart, and in the end it may take his life on some distance battlefield. To millions of children in this rich land, this is their prospect of the future.

But this is only part of what I see in America. I see another child tonight. He hears a train go by at night and he dreams of far away places where he'd like to go. It seems like an impossible dream. But he is helped on his journey through life.

A father, who had to go to work before he finished the sixth grade, sacrificed everything he had that his sons could go to college. A gentle Quaker mother, with a passionate concern for peace, quietly wept when he went to war but she understood why he had to go.

A great teacher, a remarkable football coach, an inspirational minister encouraged him on his way. A courageous wife and loyal children stood by him in victory and also defeat. And in his chosen profession of politics, first there were scores then hundreds, then thousands, and finally millions who worked for his success. And tonight he stands before you—nominated for President of the United States of America."

For the second time I saw Richard Nixon accept the Republican nomination for President. This time I was hoping and praying that the voters would choose Dick as their President in November.

We were all unaware of black rioting in Miami—cross Biscayne Bay—just afew miles from the convention, in Miami Beach. When I heard later of the looting, firebombing and sniping, I was wondering if this was an eruption of something more to come.

After the convention, I was so exhausted. My throat was scratchy. This "bug" hopped around from one worker to another until it decided to take up residence wherever it could. Even Julie was attacked by it and developed a high fever. All were concerned when Julie could not talk.

The Nixon's flew to San Diego California, the next morning for a rest. Since Julie did not get any better, Pat had to step in and complete Julie's campaign schedule of appearances in northern California. Pat was not comfortable with television interviews. Often the media would ask the same questions over and over until Pat would have difficulty to answer each one in refreshing, brisk way. Pat preferred to talk directly to people and encourage them to take their time to help one another.

She emphasized that men and women should get involved in their local political groups. She stated, "Make a difference—don't complain—go to work where you are. Work for a qualified candidate. Contact your Senator or Congressman. Let him know your opinion and feelings about issues."

While Dick was in San Diego California, August 14, 1968, he picked up the San Diego Union newspaper. Lo and behold, the Soviet Union decided once again to resume their attack on Richard Nixon. They said, "There is no new Nixon and no new line for the Republican Party." This was an article from the Soviet Union newspaper "Trud." "Nixon came in second to Barry M. Goldwater as the most non-favored American presidential candidate."

The Soviet paper added, "Selection of the tandem Nixon-Agnew ticket proclaims the fact that the bosses of big business stick to the old imperialist line and are content with the old political leaders. Anti communism remains the cornerstone of the Republican platform."

"Trud" then attacked Nixon as other newspapers have for advocating "negotiations from a policy of strength-a key phrase."

The Democrats held their convention August 26th in Chicago at the Stockyards Arena, where Dwight Eisenhower and Richard Nixon had been nominated in earlier presidential campaigns.

Hubert Humphrey was the candidate for the Democrat Convention. Even though Humphrey had not entered any primaries, apparently he had all the delegates wrapped up. What Democrat would come along to capture the Humphrey delegates? Some thought Edward "Ted" Kennedy was a better choice, but "Ted" Kennedy refused to be drafted.

What happened in Chicago that week on the night Humphrey, the Democrat presidential nominee, was chosen was not contrived to propose about peace. The Viet Cong obtained a military victory fighting against our American troops.

The television newspersons at that time shaped the news as a skirmish between young protestors for peace and ruthless uncaring police. If the television media had captured the gathering in Grant Park the public would have better understood what really happened. The demonstrators attacked the United States and its system of laws, oppression of minorities and its American history. The television media showed only one side of the story and never exposed the other side as it was.

The leaders of the march (The National Mobilization Committee to end the War in Vietnam) was denied a request for a permit to march to the Amphitheater to disrupt the Democrat Convention. The Chicago police passed out circulars and warned demonstrators through bullhorns that anyone who attempted to make an illegal march in congested streets would be arrested. Then, the police tried at another meeting of the leaders of the Communist Party and the Committee to End the War to stop the illegal march, but the leaders refused to listen.

The throng of demonstrators disrupted traffic. They shouted obscenities about President Johnson, called the police-"Pigs." Rocks and bottles were thrown, and they pushed and shoved the police. The protestors were disrupting and disregarding legal police orders not to take over the streets. No one wanted to be arrested by the police and so they resisted. The police had to use nightsticks to beat the demonstrators who resisted arrest. The police was vilified by most of the national television media. But the public supported their actions and said the responsibility for order in the streets was the responsibility of the police and not the crowd of rioters.

While the police and protestors were battling in the streets, the Democrat Convention nominated V.P. Hubert Humphrey (Minnesota) as their presidential nominee and Senator Edmund S. Muskie (Maine) as vice-president nominee. The divided Democrat Party became the party of violence. Television had associated the savage force of the demonstrators with the Democrat Party.

However, there was an aspect of Chicago police strategy during the Democrat Convention that went almost unnoticed until the violence in the streets was almost over. The Secret Service and the police had picked up reports that V.P. Hubert Humphrey and other top Democrats would be assassinated. Whether this was propaganda from Mayor Daley's machine or not, would the rumor mill feel better if any of the leading prominent Democrats had been blinded by acid or murdered by an assassin's bullet?

From then on, Humphrey was pursued by hecklers and had his speeches disrupted wherever he went on the campaign trail.

Just before Pat and Dick departed for Chicago, September 3rd, Julie and Tricia held champagne bottles and christened two commercial airline jets that the Nixons would use in campaigning. The ceremony took placed at La Guardia Field, New York.

Pat and Dick and daughters Tricia and Julie, with David Eisenhower and Senator Edward Brooke, (Massachusetts) descended from one of the campaign jets at Chicago's airport. It was Chicago where Richard Nixon launched his first fall campaign and the reception there was over whelming in the Chicago Loop. This was the first time in more than 30 years a Republican candidate for any office got such a tremendous welcome.

The noon crowds were estimated between 600,000 and 700,000. The size of crowds and warm reception of the people there stirred Pat and Dick's hearts. At the Board of Trade building at Jackson Boulevard and LaSalle, a blizzard of shredded newspaper and ticker tape began to swallow the Nixon motorcade.

People were packed neck to neck from rows of the buildings to the procession out in the street. Flanked by Secret Service men, Pat and Dick stood in an open car that inched along in the crowd. In another car Tricia and Julie sat with David Eisenhower in between them.

Tricia said, "This reception is just wonderful. I'm sure father can't be happier." And so he was.

The piles of confetti were from ankle deep and floated to knee deep in places. There were roars of applause and cheers from thousands. Once Dick got out to shake hands with people in a crowd and Pat was surrounded as well.

That night Dick kicked off his campaign by his first test of an arrangement utilizing a television panel of 8 persons. Television time on Chicago's channel 2 was paid for by Nixon supporters. The questioners—many not very friendly to Nixon—would enliven the television panel show and shoot questions at him for quick answers. This television method for Nixon would be used often in his special effort in the nine weeks before the November presidential election.

This time Nixon was more relaxed. He was not in pain from an injured knee as he was debating in the 1960 campaign. He seemed to enjoy this questioners skirmish.

Here is a partial text of Nixon's answers to the TV panel that I preserved for historical purposes for the election.

The first questioner asked:

"Some say there isn't a thin dime of difference between the two parties nor between the nominees of the parties. Would you recite what you think the difference between you and the nominee of the Democrat party are?"

'At the convention last week in Chicago, I think the American people received a picture of the choice they have and I think it is probably the most decisive choice—the greatest difference that you have between two candidates in this century—because the Democrat convention nominated a man who defends a man who helped to make, and a man who has been one of the architects of the policies of the past four years. He is a man who honestly believes in those policies. He believes those policies should be continued. I happen to disagree.

'I happen to think that as we look at those last four years we see that this nation has been at war with no end in sight; and see that this nation has seen respect for the United States fall to an all-time low; when we as far as the cost of living is concerned, it has gone up at record heights; that our taxes are the highest in history; interest rates are the highest in history; when we see that this nation is torn apart by disrespect for law; when we have not only no peace abroad, but no peace at home, I say that we cannot continue for four more years with the kind of leaders that we have had in the last four years.

'That is the difference, and I offer new leadership rather than a continuation of the old.

'In the area of domestic policy we need new policies with justice and progress; we need new policies to deal with the problems of the cities. All of this one will spell out during the course of the campaign.

'The question is this: Shall we continue simply with the extension of the old policies or renew them with fresh ideas or new leaders? That is a choice and that is why this campaign presents a real choice to the American people.

Another questioner inquired:

"Would you comment on the accusation which was made from time to time that your views have shifted and that they are based on expediencies?

Dick answered, "I suppose what you are referring to is: Is there a new Nixon or is there an old Nixon? I suppose I could counter by saying: Which Humphrey shall we listen today?

'I do want to say this: There certainly is a new Nixon. I realize, too, that as a man gets older he learns something I am not worth anything in public life.

'We live in a new world; half the nations in the world were born since World War II. Half the people living in the world today were born since World War II. The problems are different and I think I have had the good sense—I trust the intelligence—to travel the world since I left the office of Vice President and bring my views up to date to deal with the new world.

'I think my principles are consistent. I believe very deeply in the American system. I believe very deeply in what is needed to defend that system at home and abroad. I think I have some ideas as to how we can promote peace, ideas that were deficent from what they were eight years ago, not because I have changed because the problems has changed.

'My answer is, "Yes" there is a new Nixon, if you are talking terms of new ideas for the new world and the America we live in terms of what I believe the American view and the American dream, I think I am just what I was eight years ago.

Another panel questioner spoke up: In 1966 you were quoted as making a statement, "I don't believe any foreign aid should be used to subsidize socialism abroad. I have a two-part question. The first part is, "Would you name the nations today, if you agree with your statement in 1966, that should not receive any United States aid in this context, and what programs specifically do you have to withhold any United States aid or comfort to those who are not friendly to the United States today?"

Nixon stated, "United States aid should only be granted when we think it is going to work. It is my belief and also my experience as I look around the world, whenever we have used aid for the purpose of subsidizing basically a government-controlled socialistic enterprise, it has failed.

'I don't believe that the government of the United States and the people of the United States should be taxed for the purpose of sending money around the world for the purpose of perpetuating institutions that ought to be changed. I think we need a complete re-evaluation of foreign aid around the world in terms of the number of countries we are in. I think we should zero in on those countries where it would be in the interest of the United States of America to see that those countries were strongly economically."

Another panelist popped his question quickly: "In that connection would you comment on the relative importance and danger of the middle east and the N.A.T.O. situation together or separately as you see them?"

Nixon answered, "That's been one that our colleagues in the Senate have wrestled with—what to do with the U.A.R.

'Without the support of the Soviet Union for the U.A.R. and Syria and Algeria, there would be no danger to Israel today. We must see to it that Israel maintains a balance of power in its favor. If you want peace in the Mideast, be sure the balance of power does not get out of kilter. That is the short range.

'Second, what we need to do is to examine our policies towards Israel's neighbors as far as those moderate Arab states. Those that will have a live-and-let-live policy toward Israel should have an aid program to help strengthen their hand."

Then the same questioner added, "Would you make some comments about what you think the priorities of ending worthless spending, surtaxes, etc, would be if you are successful, if there is an end to the Viet Nam War?

Nixon was quick to reply, "Well, I have several ideas. First, I think that once the war is ended, we should get rid of a surtax.

'Secondly, I think that once Viet Nam is over, we should move to a volunteer armed force rather than the draft.

'It means that we will have a better armed force but it means that we will remove from hanging over the heads of millions of young Americans the fact that they are going to have to be drafted into the armed services at some future. And the third peace area that you move into is in the area of the cities. There is a lot of unfinished business, this unfinished business in terms of not only housing, education, and the rest but in this particular area I would put the primary part of the dividend in education to prepare men for jobs; education to prepare people to move up."

Quickly a previous questioner asked, "Aren't you talking about two-and-a-half years away from now?"

Nixon replied, "I could stand here and tell this great television audience: Look elect me and just as soon as that war is over we are going to take 30 billion dollars and all these things are going to happen.

'It isn't going to happen right then. I wish it were.

'Look, I would like to promise the American people: Elect me and I will spend 50 billion dollars. We don't have 50 billion dollars, you can spend next year because right at the present time we have had to cut the budget this year in order to save the dollar."

When asked, Dick commented on farmers in the agriculture area, "We have a situation where agriculture, at a time that it is producing more efficiently than ever in this nation, is being penalized because of efficiency. That's the important thing. It isn't just the fact that parity has gone down and prices have gone down but that costs have gone up. You need a new policy with regard to the stabilizing of cost of living in this country because you have got to stop the rise in the cost of everything that the farmer buys. His farm equipment and machinery have gone up 25-30 percent, whereas he receives have been staying even or gone down.

'And beyond that, of course we need to develop new uses within the United States, and we need also a complete re-evaluation of our parity system so that we can stop this cost-price squeeze which is driving many farmers away from the farm, and we need a program which will see that American agriculture remains strong and prosperous.

'I think one of the problems we had a Secretary of Agriculture who was not a farmer. I think we ought to have a secretary of agriculture who instead of speaking from the White House to the farmers, speaks for the farmers to the White House. And that is the man we are going to have."

Dick answered other pertinent questions about education, the U.S. Supreme Court and any other issued pushed at him. He refused to condemn Chicago officials for the force used to halt plans by protestors to take over Chicago streets.

After Dick's motorcade in Chicago and his question and answer of Chicago's television, everyone was remarking— "Nixon has united everyone for him." For the first time Democrat voters in Chicago decided Nixon was the one!

Hubert Humphrey could not match Nixon's rhetoric on law and order. Protestors trailed him, called him obscene names, disrupted his campaign speeches, and just made his life despicable and mean.

Humphrey was not alone in his battle for the presidency.

American organized labor leader were behind him. They never wavered in their support for Humphrey but the were worried about their labor members giving considerable support for Richard Nixon and George Wallace. Gallup Poll, September 11 showed a difference—among the union voters 35 percent said they preferred Nixon to Humphrey 42 percent. But George Wallace received 15 percent and 8 percent were undecided. Now, Humphrey knew he did not have all the union support, and it was worse in non-union voters—Nixon had 48 percent to Humphrey's 31 percent, Wallace had 14 percent and 7 percent undecided.

Many Democrats had voted for George Wallace in the primaries and so Humphrey recognized the handwriting on the wall. He changed his thoughts on the Vietnam War and departed from President Johnson's stand on the war.

When the labor unions and other liberal organizations realized that Nixon was far ahead in the polls, they decided to do something about it. They poured more money into Humphrey's campaign and agged on hecklers to disrupt the Nixon campaigns.

A block from the White House in Washington D.C. a small group of 18 anti-war protestors staged a demonstration outside the Nixon campaign headquarters. Splashed blood like material on storefront windows and even chained themselves to the front door.

They sat and stood in a circle in front of the headquarters and sang songs such as "All we are saying is give peace a chance." They chanted "one, two, three, four, sign the treaty, stop the war.

Although it was a peaceful demonstration, police were called to prevent things getting out of hand and to watch the situation. People had some difficulty in coming in and out of the headquarters until the police arrived. The protestors passed out literature signed by "Prisoners Strike for Peace." It said, "We are here today because we refuse to place hope and trust in an administration of deception, lies, and corruption.

They urged others to join them in acts of resistance until true freedom, justice, peace and self-determination are present in the lives of the people of Indochina and the United States.

Now, instead of focusing on Humphrey's campaign, the hecklers decided to follow Pat, Tricia, Julie and Dick around and shout filthy obscenities, carry signs and raise their fists in the air defying everything.

No part in politics was regarded as more difficult than that of Pat Nixon who actively participated in a political campaign for her husband. Even though she had heard a speech dozens of time, Pat must look interested and alert. Jokes that were not hilarious some of the time, she would laugh anyway—again and again. Pat had to attend endless teas and receptions. Nevertheless,she had to carefully hide any doubts and be ready to build confidence for her husband. This time Pat was enjoying the campaign and determined it would be a success.

All of us agreed that no one was going to vote Republican because Pat and Tricia were pretty or that Julie and David were the most engaging performers in the Nixon campaign. To be sure the 1968 Nixon campaign had a love ticket of Julie Nixon and David Eisenhower—that was lacking in 1960—a major asset that drew young and older voters to the Nixon camp.

So she could campaign full time for her father, Julie dropped out of Smith College in Massachusetts for one semester. David a junior at Amherst College in Massachusetts arranged his classes so he could be on the campaign trail with Julie.

With a twinkle in his eyes, Nixon would introduce David, his future son-in-law, "I always campaign better with an Eisenhower." David had inherited his grandfather's wonderful grin and name. His presence in the campaigns reminded voters of a quieter and calmer time when David's grandfather, President Dwight David Eisenhower, was in the White House.

Even though David's main responsibility was to help recruit college youth for the Nixon campaign, Julie and David's greatest impact was by parents and grandparents. These voters were angry at college students rebelling, the anti-war demonstrations, and the perplexed by marijuana drug use. Many older voters flocked to David and Julie as a star attraction. Everywhere they went they became the center of the crowd's attention. Unspoiled Tricia, 22, was petite blonde. Often people thought she resembled a Dresden doll princess. She beamed even when she remained quiet and reserved. On the other hand, Julie, 20, was taller and a chestnut brunette, bouncy, candid and outspoken. She was relaxed and would slip off her shoes sometimes during an interview. Out going, they were the good example—just like we would want our own children to be.

David, Julie and Tricia wrote their own speeches. They talked about the need for a change and appealed to students' common sense and constructive outlook. Sometimes they would be with Pat and Dick on the campaign trail. To them that was the most fun. Most of the time they would be on their own.

Both Julie and Tricia dressed modestly, didn't wear extreme dress styles and only wore a minimum of makeup. When both of the girls appeared together in the campaign, the crowd would burst suddenly in applause and voice their approval. Surely, Julie, David and Tricia were Dick's important chief political assets. I agreed.

The month before the election, all of us were working like we hadn't worked before. Pat and Dick speeded up their appearances in states, which had the highest amount of electoral votes.

Even though Humphrey was behind in the polls, we

realized that Governor George Wallace could siphon off votes from Dick by people who were disgusted with the policies of President Johnson. Dick was worried that Humphrey could get enough electoral votes to land the election in the House of Representatives and be decided there. George Wallace, as a third candidate could be responsible for that, in taking it away in a narrow victory election. The Democrats controlled the House and no one knew what they might do.

In the South the poll of popular vote for Wallace was substantially greater then that given to Humphrey or Nixon. Nixon and Humphrey were running even of 26 and 27 percent of the polled vote, while Wallace received 42 percent.

Humphrey faced a challenge to win back defectingDemocrats to the party fold and to overcome the problem of a lower voter turnout among the traditional regular Democrats.

Over all the country, the polls showed Nixon continued to hold a wide lead over Humphrey and Wallace. Nixon had 43 percent, Humphrey, 31 percent, and Wallace, 20 percent and the undecided 6 percent.

Even Senator Edward "Ted" Kennedy put in his "two-cents" worth at an October luncheon in Massachusetts sponsored by the Cape Cod Labor Council and the Joint Service Clubs of Greater New Bedford. Teddy expressed a fear that those who supported his assassinated brother, President John F. Kennedy and Senator Robert E. Kennedy, might vote for George Wallace "as a protest vote."

He stated, "My brothers believed in the dignity of men. How can those who stood with them support a man whose agents used cattle prods and dogs against beings in Alabama? George Wallace is in league with the extremists and stands for division and suppression. The Third Party is organized, directed by the extremist movement, which is using the party as a vehicle to power. Reject George Wallace, for the health of the country and our future as a nation."

One thing the Democrat Party doesn't like—when one

of their own "jumps ship" and runs against their ideas—is that person doesn't realize that their venom and poison floods against them in no uncertain terms. George Wallace, an defecting Democrat under attack, was soon to discover he was in the midst of the flood.

The radical, obscene, offensive demonstrators plagued the Humphrey campaign, as well as the Wallace team. Increasingly they made the Nixon campaign their main target. In Akron Ohio, "Students for Democrat Society" disrupted the meeting and yelled down Nixon in one of his speeches until he could not continue.

A major breakthrough came in the Nixon campaign when the National Baptist Convention (Negro) Political Action Committee endorsed Richard Nixon. It had 6 million members. It made an imminent impact.

At Hazelton, he stated, "Many Negroes are fed up with this administration, high flown oratory backed up with no action. No wonder Negroes are turning to the men ... who will provide bridges to human dignity instead of a system of permanent welfare with no light at the end of a long tunnel."

Dick and Pat were enroute in northeastern Pennsylvania on a 157-mile motorcade from Allentown to Reading to Pottsville to Hazelton.

Along the route, he leveled a steady flow of campaign indictments against Hubert Humphrey, his Democrat opponent. Nixon told a cheering crowd at Allentown, "I say it is time to reject the slap-happy economics of Hubert Humphrey."

Where thousands of people stood in Pennsylvania Square to hear Nixon speak, Dick prodded the Democrats for their television commercials. Nixon said the Democrat campaign managers were planning to eliminate Humphrey from television advertisements- "De-Humphrey-ization." Dick hoped they wouldn't go too far with it because he considered Humphrey their most practical salesman in the campaign.

HELEN M. MONTGOMERY

At Reading, fighting and violence broke out in the crowd. A state police sergeant was hit over the head with some object and ten college students were injured.

Meanwhile, Spiro T. Agnew was speaking at a rally in St. Louis and hinted that inside sources gave him information that the Vietnam War would be soon de-escalated. At the same time, President Johnson was telling us there was no break through in the peace talks.

Agnew praised Johnson for keeping the Vietnam War out of politics and for progress at the peace tables, which he hoped, would culminate, if all goes well, in some de-escalation of the bombing. Perhaps later today or tomorrow, it would be possibly a break through.

Then we received a report that the Better Government Association, a civic watchdog group, in Chicago, Illinois, had uncovered hundreds of ghost voters listed on Chicago election precinct poll sheets.

The fraudulent registrations were turning up official precinct voters lists in a ward, which surrounded district of cheap saloons frequented by vagrants and alcoholics and poor, low-priced hotels. Derelicts were paid to register. Transients without their knowledge were signed up. People were registered from vacant lots, and on the West Side of Chicago seven people were registered from a pile of rubble that once was a house. Even a man who had died the year before was listed on the precinct poll list. Shades of 1960!

The FBI was called into the investigation of fraudulent voters. Encouraging false registration or paying anyone to register to vote were violation of federal laws anyone convicted of this federal offense would be fined $10,000 and serve five years in prison.

I reminded Pat that it was very important to have a volunteer organization to fight vote fraud in Chicago, St. Louis, Missouri, and Gary, Indiana, Texas, Pennsylvania. Only Pat and Dick knew what the vote fraud in 1960 cost

180

them the election. So Dick decided to do something about it this time.

This was just the beginning of the battle against vote frauds. At the Nixon campaign headquarters in Washington, "Operation Integrity" was born. It would be an army of 100,000 Republican and Democrat volunteers to insure an honest vote count. All of us realized that States or areas where it expected to swing by narrow margins would be in danger of voting irregularities. We knew that we would face difficulties. When one party controls key precincts in "swing States, a few thousand votes in a close election could be stolen.

Of course, the Democrat National Committee attacked this operation. Their rhetoric betrayed their intent.

We determined that this presidential election on November 5th would be the cleanest and the most closely polled watched. This time we planned to have more, better trained watchers on the lookout for voting irregularities in all the 170,000 polling places. Thousands of polled watchers received special intensive training. Everyone had to know the State and federal laws, election judge duties, challengers and inspector's responsibilities, and the rights and obligations of poll watchers.

In turn, we had to instruct many thousand other poll watchers. More than half of the watchers would be allotted to big city precincts. In Chicago, five thousand were assigned to that city alone. In Texas, we focused on the rural counties of the southern section of that state. A small organized group of investigators and lawyers would cruise the cities in squad cars equipped by radio telephones to respond to poll watchers cry for help in just five minutes. Lawyers would take statements on the spot. This would prevent delays in assembling witnesses.

A local Chicago group, "Operation Eagle Eye" would send in their volunteers. This time we hoped vote frauds would be stamped out.

As the Election Day grew closer, Dick decided to initiate a fast intensive media campaign using $24 million to purchase TV and radio time. His subjects included NATO, Vietnam, problems of the cities, and the crusade against crime, the voluntary way, a new alignment for American unity, and a new direction for America's economy. Dick's addresses were so good they decided to put them all in booklet form to hand out to people on the campaign trail.

On October 25, 1968, Friday, Richard Nixon addressed the nation on CBS Radio Network on, "Where Government Should Be." If anyone were listening to that Nixon address today, they would swear they were hearing the words of the 1994-1996 Republican Congress.

Here are some excerpts from that speech that I remembered:

"Increasing centralization has siphoned top management talent from the state to Washington, handicapping the states in dealing with their pressing problems.

'Increasing centralization has created a situation of local fiscal poverty amid Federal fiscal plenty. Our states and cities have the problems;Washington has the money.

'Increasing centralization has removed decision-making from the local level and helped to breed an atmosphere of alienation, made people feel that they have no control over their destiny or the quality of their lives.

'The idea behind all this is that a few men in Washington know more about how to spend our money than we do— know more about it than state governments,more about it than local governments.

'I believe that we can find now approaches, more effective and more responsive to the needs of the people.

'The main reason for the growth of Federal power and the decline in home rule and self-government has been the proliferation of specialized Federal grants-in-aid. I believe that there is a better approach than such proliferation of programs at the Federal level. Instead we should begin to return tax revenue to states and the local communities in the form of bloc grants, and thus allow them, within the very broadest possible policy definitions to determine their own priorities in the allocation of resources.

'The initial distribution of funds should be to the states. However, the pressing needs of our cities and of other local governments require that any final plan must contain enforceable provisions to ensure that they receive a fair share.

'Revenue sharing will restore real partnership to American government. It will help to place decision-making in the right hands. For we do not believe that a man sitting in an office in Washington knows more about the needs of the people than our governors and our mayors, and our local leaders.

We must have a vital and effective Federal government in Washington. But one way to ensure that we do have one is to get the Federal government out of matters it is not competent to handle; and allow it to focus on its proper business."

'And so after 40 years of steady Federal expansion, the pendulum is beginning to swing. I believe that we are on the edge of great rebirth of state, local and independent vitality. Everywhere, the recognition is growing that this great nation, with it's diverse peoples and its complex needs cannot be run in every detail from Washington.

"This philosophy is right in the mainstream of the American tradition. The founders of this country, in the very beginning rebelled against rigid, remote government— government "from the top down."

They would not be ruled by kings and we will not be ruled by Federal bureaucrats."

Those ideas were not espoused by Ronald Reagan on the current Republican Congress, but in 1968 by Richard Nixon. It took along way for his ideas to come to fruition. Now they have arrived.

However, I was concerned about the liberal news media—
CBS-TV, ABC-TV, and NBC-TV, networks who employed
every technique in the book against Dick Nixon just to benefit
Humphrey.

It didn't sound good. Their bias was showing. Instead of
producing both sides of a story they twisted the facts and
misled the public.

Through the grapevine, stories were grinding out that
the Soviet Union was determined to stop Richard Nixon from
winning the presidential election. What was their plan, we
asked? Did it have a connection with the Vietnam War? Above
all they knew Dick was anti-communist and the Soviets would
fear him more if he became president.

Then, on October 31st we were stirred by President
Johnson's television announcement about his bombing halt
in Vietnam. If United States would stop their bombing, North
Vietnam had agreed to come to the peace talks and stop their
attacks.

But, this peace deal alarmed us politically. Since the
election was five days away, we were concerned what it would
do at the polls for the Nixon campaign. When the Harris poll
came out, our fears were confirmed—Nixon received 40
percent, Humphrey 43 percent, Wallace 13 percent and 4
percent had not made up their minds. To our dismay, Johnson's
announcement about the bombing halt boosted Humphrey's
chances.

Then we heard through the rumor mill that Mrs. Anna
Chennault, a Chinese widow of the "Flying Tigers," General
Claire Chennault, and also co-chairman of Republican Women
for Nixon, decided to do some back door unofficial diplomacy
of her own without Richard Nixon's authorization. This chatty
lady opposed the Vietnam peace deal and she was determined
not to leave any stone overturned to put stumbling blocks in
the process.

When the Democrats got wind of what this lady was doing

on her own, they instantly wanted to accuse Nixon of doing a hatchet job on the peace deal. After looking at the evidence, they came to the conclusion that Dick had no personal knowledge of Anna Chennault's enterprises and would have stopped her had he known.

Three days before the election, Saturday, November 2nd, President Nguyen Van Thieu of South Vietnam rejected Johnson's bombing halt and deeply regretted that it could not take any part in the peace talks. The South Vietnam government thought President Johnson had betrayed the South Vietnamese, and they condemned him for it.

The day before the election, Humphrey and Nixon were running neck to neck in the opinion polls. The suspense was killing us! Humphrey was counting on Hollywood movie stars, the wistful yearning for the Kennedy years, and for his strong civil rights record to keep the momentum ahead of Nixon.

But, Dick was busy, too. He appeared on television answering many, many questions in a 4-hour national telethon.

It was this answer—"If peace is at hand, how come the North Vietnamese are sending tremendous amount of supplies down the Ho Chi Mink trail? So far our military are unable to stop them,"—that caused a stir across the nation. The press jumped in and claimed Dick had invented it. The Democrats echoed the charge. But, when military photographic evidence came in, many were convinced that Nixon was right and peace would only come through a Republican President.

November 5th, Election Day, had arrived. Humphrey and Nixon's polls had been too close to call. However, I thought this time, in spite of the seesaw—Dick would be president in 1968. The suspense of the outcome made us all nervous and up tight. Pat and Dick had voted absentee, as well as the rest of us who were working in the campaign.

Nixon's presidential campaign headquarters was at the Waldorf-Astoria Hotel in New York City. Upstairs on the 35th floor was the Nixon family suite. Dick had the rest of his staff in contact with all the state Chairmen around the country. All campaign headquarters were linked together by a massive telephone system. Pat, Julie, Tricia, and David were watching the election returns on national television in their upstairs suite.

As I watched the election returns, it was agonizing. Some of my workers at headquarters were not sure of the outcome and they kept pestering me with questions whether we were going to win or lose.

At first Nixon was ahead. By 10:30 p.m., Humphrey and Nixon were even. By 11:30 p.m. Humphrey's lead was building. It kept seesawing back and forth. By midnight Humphrey was leading by 600,000 in the popular votes. But Nixon had already won 231 of the Electoral College votes out of 270 necessary to win the Presidency. I assured everyone around me that Richard Nixon would win.

It was a very nerve-racking restless night. No one wanted to go to bed. Sleep evaded us. Some did catnap or dozed by the television watching the late returns in the wee hours of the morning. Even, Pat dozed off and on as the morning hours arrived. David couldn't hold his eyes open either, and he was found down in staff headquarters, by the television terminal fast asleep. I was wondering if I could keep awake a few more hours for the outcome. Sometimes, I dozed off too, and had to drink coffee, or soda pop now and then to keep my eyes unglued.

This election in 1968 as in 1960, the states of Texas, California, Missouri, Ohio, and Illinois would decide the close election race. Ohio and California finally moved into the Nixon column. In Illinois, Dick was ahead by almost 100,000 votes but many Cook County precincts were still unreported.

When the television newscasters announced at 6:00 a.m. that Mayor Richard Daley Sr. (Chicago) was holding up some 135 Cook County Democrat precinct ballots. It was also reported that there was some Republican precincts from Lake

County were out too. We were wondering what was delaying their count. All of us who had worked in the 1960 campaign, our stomachs churned with nervous, uneasy tension when we heard the report. We said, "No, not again!" Pat was nauseated and squeamish. It made her ill. The memories of 1960 election engulfed us once again.

About 8:00 a.m. ABC News announced that Mayor Daley had released the Cook County votes in Illinois to be counted.

Nixon received 301 Electoral College votes compared to Humphrey's 191 and Wallace (American Independent Party) 46. The popular vote was real close. My fears of the election landing in the House of Representative because of Wallace intervention was finally laid to rest.

At 8:30 a.m., November 6, Illinois, was counted in the Nixon column. Richard Nixon had won the race and now would become President of United States.

Even, when Pat heard the Illinois election news, she still wasn't sure if it was true and real. Dick had to assure her over and over that he had won this election. When the truth finally broke through to her, Pat was overjoyed with tears of happiness. She now thought Dick could be of great usefulness to our nation and to the world.

The official vote canvas began in Cook County (Chicago) amid charges by the Republicans and the Democrats that there had been devious, dishonest methods or trickery in the election process.

As usual, Mayor Richard J. Daley, Sr., who was in charge of the Democrat party operation in Illinois was being accused again that his finagling with the returns caused a problem. I was sure the offered count would show some interesting and different figures.

There were 109 unreported precincts in predominately Democrat Chicago and 84 in suburbs. Even though those precincts contained 400-500 votes, none would be able to overcome Nixon's 135,502 Illinois vote lead over Hubert H.

Humphrey. The unreported precincts still remained a mystery beyond understanding.

In turn, Daley was hinting at possible vote irregularities by the Republicans. He asserted that 2 western suburbs where the returns were delayed and did not arrive on time. If the election was close, the returns were delayed to strengthen the Republican area.

Mayor Daley Sr. saw most of the state candidates go down to the wire of defeat. However, in Cook County, the Democrats retained their hold and control of Cook County offices. Daley was power hungry and this election caused him to lose his cool. He didn't want to explain how about 3,000 Republicans in the suburbs were refused ballots and were told their name were not on the voter rolls.

Julie surprised her father by giving him a gift, a crewelwork on the Great Seal of the United States; she had embroidered without Dick knowing about it. Dick was happy that his daughter, Julie, had faith he would win this election race. Dick was so proud of the presidential emblem; he showed it to the press after the triumphant election victory. All the world saw it on television at noon, and in newspapers. Hubert Humphrey, who had lost by half a million votes, called and conceded he had lost the presidential race to Nixon. Just before going down to the grand ballroom of the Waldorf Astoria Hotel, the Nixon family stood in a circle in the hallway and holding hands. Rev. Billy Graham was with them. Dick asked Billy to pray. "We all need prayer," he said, "Pray that God would help us to find a way out of the Vietnam War."

Then, they all went down to the ballroom of the Waldorf-Astoria Hotel, where 1,000 weary, buoyant supporters were assembled. The cheering and clapping was thunderous.

Even, though Dick's face showed fatigue, his voice was firm and his manner relaxed. He congratulated Humphrey for his gallant courageous, fight against all odds and that he never gave up. Dick said, "I know how it is to lose a close one, but "winning is a lot more fun." Cheers erupted.

Richard Nixon now the President-elect, pledged to lead an "open-door administration." He said, "We want to bridge the gap between races. We want to bring the American people together, and I am confident that this task in one in which we will be successful.

Nixon said his objectives were inspired by one sign he saw during his campaign that really touched him the most. It was held by a teen-ager at a campaign stop at Deshler, Ohio. The sign read, "Bring Us Together."

He divulged plans to fly Wednesday afternoon to Key Biscayne, Florida for a 3-5 day rest. Also, Dick said he would stop in Washington enroute to visit the ailing Eisenhower at the Walter Reed Army Medical Center. Then Dick thanked all those who worked for his campaign, and a special thanks to four people closes to him—Pat, Tricia, Julie, and David—who meant more to him than life itself. They were his life and kept him living and going. As Pat and Dick drove back to their apartment at 810 Fifth Avenue, they realized that they had not eaten for some time. Raiding the refrigerator then all of them realized they would have to eat what little food was there. No longer could they go out on the town for lunch. The Secret Service would always be with them wherever they would go. Now life would be different.

Dick retreated into his study and turned up the sound on his record player playing, "Victory at Sea." The sound was so deafening it could be heard all over the apartment building. Pat and the girls packed clothes for their trip to Key Biscayne, knowing at last their husband and father had achieved his goal for the presidency.

Pat Nixon on the campaign trail.

Richard Nixon playing the piano.

Nixon on the campaign trail for candidates.

Nixon giving the "thumbs up" Never Give Up sign.

Richard Nixon visits troops in Vietnam.

Pat Nixon—Ambassador of good will.

Nixon and Church Services in East Wing of White House.

Pat Nixon greeting people wherever she goes.

Dick and Pat at the beach.

Pat celebrating with women in Africa.

PUBLIC IS INVITED

SHOW YOUR SUPPORT FOR THE PRESIDENT OF THE UNITED STATES

6:30 P.M.
FRIDAY, MAY 3, 1974
MEMORIAL COLISEUM
(STATE FAIRGROUNDS — PHOENIX)

GALA ENTERTAINMENT SHOW

1974 support for Nixon around the country.

Richard Nixon Stamp issued in 1995 by Postal Services.

Chapter 12

I REMEMBER PAT AND RICHARD NIXON FROM ASSASSINATION PLOT TO PLEASURABLE WEDDING

The existing climax of the election finally dawned on me that Pat Nixon would be First Lady and Richard Nixon would be President. I stood in awe! What I had dreamed, worked, and prayed for had become a reality.

As their Air Force jet took off that November for Washington, D.C. enroute to Key Biscayne, Florida, I realized that Richard Nixon would have the dreaded task of bringing the Vietnam War to a conclusion. That would not be an easy, quick solution.

Pat and Dick and the girls stopped by to visit former President Eisenhower at Walter Reed Hospital. Eisenhower was happy with the result of the election and was glad the Nixon family came to pay their respects.

In Key Biscayne, the extreme weariness—the exhaustion from the campaign race—finally caught up with them. After nine hours of sleep, they felt better to enjoy the ocean and the sunny skies. Pat even lolled on the beach enjoying the sun. It was a special treat for her—no speeches to give—no rushing to meet planes—just to be with her family and the privacy she always yearned.

All was not rest and play. Pat had to appoint a press secretary and social secretary and the rest of their staff for her First Lady duties. Also, on her mind was Julie and David's wedding December 22nd and to decide what to do with all the New York apartment furniture. Some of it would go to the White House and the rest to equip and decorate the houses on the bay at Key Biscayne. She had to determine about the Christmas holidays and the upcoming presidential inauguration in January. As she sat on her deck chair watching the peaceful and quiet bay waters, Pat was praying and musing over what she could cope with and numerous things that were tumbling on her all at one time.

Already, Dick was planning his new administration. Most of the talk in Key Biscayne was concerning the filling of Cabinet positions and staffing the White House staff. Majority of the prime movers around Nixon during the campaign would find themselves in important jobs in Washington.

Nixon would fill his appointments in his administration with care. Caution was characteristic of Dick. He did not want to move to quickly in naming his Cabinet and White House staff.

Even though many people had worked in Nixon's political campaigns, it did not produce people who were the right ones for executing government correctly. When I heard crew-cut Bob Haldeman would oversee the White House staff, Pat and I had questions about this appointment. Haldeman had worked in key positions in three political campaigns and helped get Dick elected. However, I had qualms about it. In my heart, I felt uneasiness and the pang produced a fear that somewhere down the road it would lead to trouble. So I had to leave all of those fears and questions in God's hands.

Partners-in-Crisis: The Untold Story of Pat and Richard Nixon

Back in New York, the city police detectives and Secret Service agents broke up an assassination plot to kill Richard Nixon. The seized Ahmed Rogeh Namer and his two sons, Abdo Ahmed Namer and Hussin Namer and were charged in a conspiracy to murder Nixon. The three men lived in Brooklyn, New York and were from an Arab country of Yemen in the Middle East.

The investigation started by a phone tip to the police. The man told police the three Arabs had tried to recruit him and others in their murder plot and promised him a lot of money. The police traced the informer's telephone call to a Brooklyn bar. They decided to put him under protective custody, because they didn't know if there were any more men involved in the plot.

The informant, an expert marksman, had been with the three Arabs in their Brooklyn apartment and saw two automatic weapons and a M L rifle with sniper scopes. He stalled the three men and decided the police should know about it. After the police and the Secret Service agents questioned the informer, they decided to move in.

All three men were arrested. Hussin Namer, 20, tried to escape out of a window, but they caught him anyway. In the apartment, the police found the ML Army rifle and a carbine, 24, 30-caliber shells, two switchblade knives and a carving knife.

The police notified Nixon in Key Biscayne about the arrests and how the agents foiled the plot to kill him. Dick was not overly concerned because he knew the police were doing a good job in handling the situation in New York.

Between now and his Inauguration Day, Dick would work mainly in New York and then take opportunity for sporadic fun trips to Key Biscayne. His apartment at 810 Fifth Avenue, the Pierre Hotel, the campaign headquarters at 450 Park Avenue where the workers there were greeting telephone callers, "Offices of President-elect Nixon" would be his main bases.

After the assassination plot in New York, Nixon would still have his share of troubles and jeopardy. Then, he decided to stay mostly out of Washington until the Inaugural would take place. Without Nixon in view in Washington, the transition work between the Johnson administration and the new Nixon administration moved along never the less. Congress had allotted $900,000 to defray the transition expenses. When Dick had completed the appointments of the White House staff and his Cabinet, they could go on government compensation right away, and be briefed about what problems that might come along the way.

Enroute to New York, the Nixons stopped in Washington, D.C., for a luncheon with President Johnson. As they came down the airplane ramp, some members of the Young Republican Club at American University joined with the rest of the crowd applauding. Of course, the press was there and asking questions about his visit with President Johnson. Dick had not worn a topcoat. He forgot that November could produce a chill in the air in Washington.

While President Johnson and Dick were discussing problems of government, Pat and Lady Bird Johnson were talking about keeping house at the White House. Dick said he would go to Saigon or Paris if President Johnson would feel such travel would be helpful in ending the Vietnam War.

Although, Dick already thought about Cabinet choices, he said he would not make his choices known until December 5th. From Washington, Pat and Dick headed to New York where Dick would be conferring with his top workers about formation of a new administration.

It was Pat who gently nudged Dick to invite the Cabinet wives to sit in on the first meeting of the Nixon Cabinet, December 12th. She was listening and making friends among the wives there.

Pat would be busier than ever—planning Julies wedding to David Eisenhower for December 22nd, and helping Julie with their new apartment in Northampton, Massachusetts, the Christmas holidays, and the colossal transfer to the White House and the Inauguration ceremonies on January 20th.

Julie and David would be moving in a $95.00 a month apartment after their wedding and honeymoon. Furniture was no problem because Julie was allowed to choose furniture and rugs from her parent's New York home, to furnish their two-bedroom flat.

The wedding was the first series of concern. Pat and Julie accomplished in a few days what would have taken a few months. Moving through a wedding whirl with the same methodical orderliness. Pat was a sleek pro and coper. She could dress in 10 minutes. Pack her own luggage as well as Dick's. Often on 13 hours campaign day she would endure on the campaign trail on a coke or two cups of coffee and still make strangers at ease.

When Pat read the New York trade paper, "Women's Wear Daily," she was astonished that the front page news said, Julie and David's wedding would take place December 21st—the wrong date and the wrong church—Cathedral of St. John Divine. Pat promptly corrected the error.

After many bridal showers, Julie was ready to be married December 22nd, Sunday at Marble Collegiate Church, Fifth Avenue at 29th Street by Rev. Norman Vincent Peale. Julie wanted Billy Graham to officiate at her wedding but Billy was overseas in Vietnam. So she chose Peale to do the honors for the wedding ceremony.

Richard Nixon was acting like the father of the bride. And so he was. It was a crisis most pleasurable and very private of his long career. He considered December 22nd his most luckiest day and stated it had three good reasons for being very special. As a father, he would gain David as a son and not be losing a daughter. Most of all the North Koreans had freed the captured crew of the intelligent-gathering USS Pueblo ship. Then, the United States had launched a three-man Apollo astronaut team speeding into space and circling the moon ten times and reading from the book of Genesis.

Julie and David's fairy tale wedding marked a special niche in U.S. history by linking the Eisenhower presidential family with that of presidential-elect Richard Nixon 's family. David and Julie were popular out on the campaign trail, and now the eyes of the nation were once again captured by the glittering marriage of a special pair.

The setting was the Marble Collegiate Church, a 114 year-old Dutch Reformed Church, which was festively decorated with Christmas greenery and red and white poinsettias combined with pink and white theme of the wedding. Much of the wedding music was set in the Christmas mood, combined with old English wedding tunes, Christmas carols, and bits of Broadway hit tunes from, "The King and I," and "Man of La Mancha." The ceremony was broadcast by special closed circuit television to former President Dwight D. Eisenhower and his wife, Mamie, who both were in Walter Reed Army Hospital. Ike was recovering from series of heart attacks and Mamie ill with influenza.

Julie and David wanted their wedding to be a private and personal affair; another reason was their desire to have the wedding ceremony and the honeymoon trip over by the time they would have to return to college classes.

Pat looked stunning in her, "fashionably" short pale greenish-blue dress of woven lace over silk crepe, embroidered with aquamarines at the neckline, sleeves and hem. It had a fitted bodice and waist and a slightly flared skirt.

Tricia Nixon, Julie's older sister, was the maid of honor and Fred Grandy, David's former college roommate, was best man. Barbara Anne, David's married sister, and Anne Davis, Susan Harvin, Julie's Smith College classmates, were the bridesmaids.

Julie, as a bride-to-be, wanted a wedding dream dress. She combed all the available retail sources and bought the one she or Pat, wanted, regardless who made it. Julie fell in love with this special dress. It was made by Priscilla of Boston. The fashion reporters really perked up when they got wind of this news.

For Julie's bridal attendants, Priscilla used pink silk chiffon. Everyone there beheld the bridesmaids' beauty as they paraded down the church aisle. Suddenly, every mother and bride to be decided that Priscilla would be their source for wedding costumes and production of weddings.

As a bride, Julie, stole the show. Priscilla had made her gown so beautiful, it became a sight to behold. Julie, now 20, was radiant in an old fashioned Victorian type, full skirted, and with white silk pearl embroidered yoke d'ange dress with high collar neckline and short puffed sleeves. She held in her hand a small bouquet of lilies of the valley, sweetheart roses and narcissus. Her fancy veil was held with a garland of seed pearls.

Julie requested Dr. Norman Vincent Peale to read Psalm 121: "I will lift up mine eyes," and Psalm 100, which begins, "Make a joyful noise unto the Lord." In the 15-minute single ring ceremony the words "thee" and "thou" were used as requested by Julie. Reverend Peale, a Dutch Reformed minister, was marrying Julie Nixon, a Quaker, to David Eisenhower, an Episcopalian. That was really worldwide Christian unity!

Peale's advice to Julie and David, "Couples who pray together grow together—and stick together." Wouldn't it be wonderful today if all newlyweds would follow this advice?

What really surprised all who attended the wedding was the moment in the ceremony for Julie the bride, to be given away by her father, Richard Nixon, Julie turned suddenly and kissed her father.

With these sacred words, "To have and to hold from this day forward for better, for worse, for richer, for poorer, in sickness, and in health, to love and to cherish, till death do us part, according to God's ordinance, and there to I pledge myself truly with all my heart." Julie and David became husband and wife and pledged to each other, "What therefore God has joined together, let no man put asunder." David, the bridegroom, did not kiss Julie, the bride, when the marriage vows were formally sealed.

At their reception at the fashionable Plaza Hotel, the wedding cake was a six-tier, five-foot pound cake with lemon filling topped by a small basket of fresh white flowers. Also, the cake was decorated with silver bells and Lilies of the Valley made of spun sugar. The traditional bride and bridegroom figures on the cake were absent.

After the three hour reception where guests enjoyed cold and hot buffet food and dancing in the elegant "Louis XVI ballroom, Julie and David, attendants, and their parents went to the Plaza Hotel press room to pose for photographers and answered inquisitive news reporters questions. There, the newsmen wanted David to kiss Julie. They shouted "chicken" at David because he hesitated. Then, David kissed Julie soundly. Afterwards, Julie and David headed south for a secret honeymoon. We all suspected it was Florida because Julie only packed clothes for a warmer climate.

Even, though, Dick had a few problems with some of his out spoken new cabinet appointees at press conferences, he didn't let these occurrences mar Julie's wedding. Once the special day was behind him, Pat, Dick and Tricia headed for Key Biscayne, Florida, for a nine-day vacation. The Nixons had purchased a $127,800 waterfront home there and they didn't want to see no one else around. At last, they would have a few days of peace and relaxation away from the crowds, publicity and news hounds. Of course, they couldn't escape the Secret Service agents.

After Julie and David's honeymoon at North Palm Beach, Florida, they surprised Pat and Dick by coming home for Christmas. As usual, Dick lit a fire in the fireplace. But the fireplace wasn't working and smoke filled the living room. Everyone gasped and crepted out of the room until the fire was put out.

After their vacationing in Key Biscayne, the Nixons pulled up stakes and flew to the Rose Bowl game in California. Dick Nixon had never lost interest in football and often would tell stories of his Whittier College football days in his speeches. Inside Pasadena's huge Rose Bowl, he would leap to his feet when a player took off for an eighty-yard touchdown run. At half time, Dick changed from Ohio State's side to the Southern Cal seats. There he had a picture taken with Bob Hope, a comedian personality. The New York's Daily News printed it as a "tournament of noses."

Next day, Nixon received a "clean bill of health from his physician, Dr. John Lungren, regarding his annual physical check up in Long Beach.

The climax of their stay in California were several "Welcome Home," Pat and Dick parties in the towns where Nixon was born and raised. In Anaheim, 9,000 supporters came out to "Nixon-This Your Life" show. It was an evening of reflection by Dick's friends and neighbors of his youth and college days. Dick was not very good at football and sat out of most of the games. In whatever game—whether it was football or politics—he got knocked down and kept coming back again and again. This time Dick won at last in the game of presidential politics.

However, my greatest worry was how Dick would get along with certain elements of the national press in his administration. I remember how some of them were adversaries since the Alger Hiss spy case (1948-1950). Dick's struggle continued on in his vice-president days and climaxed with his 1962 California governor race with Dick's criticism of the press speech there.

Reporters who covered Nixon during the 1960 Presidential campaign were predominantly liberal in thinking.

In the reporting of news, I saw a trend toward more personal opinion and political partisanship. These intellectual liberals had an aversion against anyone who was not the John F. Kennedy type of politician. In their political reporting, they rejected objectivity and became involved too much in organized social and political activities and opposition. Leading this trend was, "The Washington Post" newspaper.

It was my prayer that Dick Nixon would be quoted directly rather than restating his views by giving the meaning in different words by TV commentators, and reporters. Dick wanted an "open administration" based on honesty, candid and shared respect. I was sure if we got back some of the credibility and confidence in Government, the communication problem would be solved.

Chapter 13

I REMEMBER PAT AND RICHARD NIXON INAUGURAL PROTESTORS AND FESTIVITIES

When the postman deposited a large envelope in my mailbox, December 1968, I never dreamed it would herald the most exciting, as well as the most embarrassing moment of my life. The white envelope was post-marked, Washington, D.C. My fingers trembled with excitement as I opened the envelope. It was my invitation as Pat had requested, to attend all the inaugural festivities of President Richard Nixon, of the United States. I realized that I held the honored distinction of being among the chosen few to participate.

There were many things to do before going . . . notifying the Dean of Education at Grand Canyon College (University), about the event, buying my airline ticket, and making clothes. The college administration was so delighted and pleased that I had received this distinction. They wanted me to represent Grand Canyon College at the inauguration. "Canyon Echoes," the student college newspaper, sent a reporter to interview regarding the Nixons. Then, the faculty had a reception for me before leaving for Washington, D.C. Two of the gifts I received were a pearled handkerchief and a pair of rhinestone earrings. As I packed my blue and silver brocade evening gown and the rhinestone ear rings in my suitcase, it did not dawn on me what exciting experience lay ahead.

Meanwhile the inaugural committee was wrestling with last-minute difficulties such as whether men were to wear white ties or to permit black ties, or hotels raising rates during the inaugural festivities. The Nixons journeyed to Northampton, Massachusetts to celebrate his fifty-sixth birthday, January 9th with Julie and David. Julie surprised her father and mother by making a delicious chicken casserole with cheese and broccoli for the birthday dinner.

When the Nixons arrived back in New York, Pat heard about the food drive for starving Biafrans that was organized by Senator Charles E. Goodell, Republican of New York and wanted to do something about it. After discussing it with Dick, she went to the St. Patrick's Cathedral and stood on the steps besides hundreds of boxes and shopping bags of donated food.

The Biafra Republic had seceded in 1967 from Nigeria, fearing they would not survive. More than one million had died of starvation. So Pat came and acknowledged her feeling of humanity and stood in the bitter cold until her nose turned pink. Starving people were of concern to Pat. She knew what it was to be poor and wanted to help with the food drive. More than any other political figure, Dick had taken a more vigorously pro-Biafran position to assist Biafra—the small territory in Africa—brought into conflict in a death skirmish with the Nigerian military government.

When I arrived in cold and rainy Washington, January 17th a government official met me at the airport. My heart skipped with excitement as a once in a lifetime schedule was outlined to me. I was glad to see Ardis Larson, a Nixon campaign worker from Chicago, who I had known since the 1960

Presidential race. We would be staying together at the centrally located Bellvue Hotel from which we could be in walking distance to the various functions.

I was ready for all the inaugural festivities, but I wasn't sure the city of Washington, D.C. was yet. Thousands and thousands were descending each day on the Nation's Capitol. The rainy weather caused taxi shortages and traffic snarls. The lack of parking cars caused a paramount problem. Even the police had trouble with people stealing special no parking signs. If anyone wanted to rent-a-car or a chauffeured limousine, none could be found. All hotels rooms were booked with no vacancy signs. Any latecomers were forced to look elsewhere outside the Capitol for rooms and parking cars.

Then, Ardis and I discovered that hundreds of young war protestors had erected a large tent near the Washington Monument for counter-inaugural festivities. They created a seething commotion of shrieking, shouting, discussions and arguments. The National Mobilization To The End (Vietnam) War sponsored the event. Many of the girls wore raccoon coats and the young men attired in combat jackets.

Some said they wanted "to give Nixon an exciting welcome he would never forget." Others shouted "Nixon is a bum Quaker" and "Government and society is very oppressive and is committing violence against everyone."

Outside, pro-Nixon young people exchanged words with the rowdy protestors. Police had to intervene and break up the demonstration. The protestor called the police, "Pigs" and moved on to different locations. Whenever they found an American flag it was stomped and mutilated. Even though blocks away, loud acid rock music assaulted our ears. Whenever anyone came to close to us we could smell marijuana wafting around us. What a nauseous day!

The next day, Saturday, January 18th, we attended the Distinguished Ladies Reception, which was held at the National Gallery of Art. This was the first official inaugural event. Enroute to the reception, Ardis and I encountered more unkempt anti-war demonstrators. We wondered if we would be allowed to cross the street to the other side. They were chanting, "Stop Your Husband's War," 'Be Somebody, Not Somebody's Wife," 'Don't Drink Tea While People Are Dying," "Women Are Oppressed." We managed to elude the protestors, but others were trapped among them and were late getting to the reception on time. The police finally came to their rescue.

Pat Nixon flew from New York to Washington and stood for three hours shaking hands and greeting the 10,000 ladies who attended the reception. The U.S. Marine Band provided us with music to spark up the long waiting lines. We didn't have any tea to drink because none was served. The long lines of enthusiastic ladies didn't dim Pat's smile or to tire her. We greeted Mamie Eisenhower and Judy Agnew, wife of the Vice President, in their reception lines too.

Pat said she would return to New York late that afternoon to spend their last night with her husband before he becomes President. Dick was in his Fifth Avenue New York apartment working on last minute changes on his Inaugural speech, and could not join Pat in all the social events commemorating the Inaugural. So Pat chose to come to the Distinguish Ladies reception and let Julie, Tricia, and David stand in for them at the All-American Gala extravaganza that evening.

When Pat left Washington shortly after 5 p.m., she discovered her right hand was all swollen and bruised with two red scratches on it. Here again, the real First Lady of the event was Pat Nixon. She loved meeting with people and so many ladies squeezed her hand wanting to greet her and exchange their love for her.

Ardis and I decided to skip the Gala and rest up in the hotel. We ordered dinner from Room Service and watched news on television. We found out from others we didn't miss much by not going to the Gala. Traffic tie-ups had delayed

Julie, David, and Tricia, as well as Vice President-Elect Agnew's family, from arriving on time. It was a state of disorder. Many of the entertainers scheduled to appear didn't show up. Some people didn't even have chairs to sit on—it was chair—less in some of the special boxes. Everything was late and so it ended at 1 a.m. in the morning. Whew! Was I glad we didn't go!

Sunday morning, January 19th, Pat and Dick attended Norman Vincent Peale's morning service at Marble Collegiate Church in New York. In Washington, D.C. Ardis and I attended the Capitol Hill Metropolitan Baptist Church. Rev. John R. Stuckey the pastor gave his message on "The Making of a President" which we thought was very inspirational and timely for the inaugural events.

We had to be at the Sheraton Park Hotel by 2:00 p.m. for the Reception for Governors and Special Distinguished Guests. It was crowded too. The U.S. Coast Guard Band was entertaining us as we paraded around the room. Ardis and I spotted Governor Ronald Reagan's reception line and we decided we would get in there first. Lo, and behold Bob Dole was standing in line in front of us. So we asked him to autograph our programs. When we met Ronald Reagan there he teasingly said, "Helen, are you trying to get everyone's autograph? It looks like you have a good start." As he autographed my program, I replied, "Ron, who knows some day you might be President, too." We both laughed.

Ardis and I rushed back to our hotel to get ready for the Vice President Spiro Agnew reception and to eat and relax. When we departed for Agnew's reception at the Smithsonian Museum of History and Technology, we were still tired from walking and shaking hands. The day was not over as yet.

Then, thousands of demonstrators surrounded us at the Smithsonian Museum and blocked the entrance. Some were throwing mud, rock and dirt at us. They cried for us to end the Vietnam War, capitalism, and racism. Club-swinging Park police on horseback waded into the crowd of hecklers. The protestors screamed filthy and lewd words at the police. Now, they were throwing, sticks and mud at the police and tossing firecrackers and burning cigarettes at the police's horses. Shouts of "Pigs" and Seig Heil" filled the air.

When we finally made it inside the museum, the music of U.S. Army Band welcomed us. The fruit punch, the elephant shaped cookies and the buffet of sandwiches helped settle our "tummies" and calm our nerves.

The floral decorations were beautiful and their beauty were out of this world. Some thought they were souvenirs and carried many of the flowers home with them. We took only our souvenir plastic glasses decorated with the Vice President seal, which we used at the reception. After talking and shaking hands with Vice President-Elect Spiro Agnew, we decided to go to our hotel room and collapse. We were weary and footsore, but we had the inaugural concert to attend to round out our splendid evening.

While we were fighting off demonstrators at the Smithsonian Museum, Pat and Dick arrived at the Andrews Air Force base from New York. Both were happy, relaxed, and excited. Thousands of people greeted them at the airport and to cheer them on. Along the way clusters of people waved their welcome.

The police escort drove the Nixons into the city round about way to avoid the noisy young demonstrators who tied up traffic downtown. Traffic was blocked and so the Nixon entourage had to be rerouted.

The protestors wore Nixon-type Halloween masks and the wildest, weird clothing and body paint. They carried signs, toy machine guns and coffins.

The men in charge of the protest said loudly, "We know why we are here—to stop THAT war. We are here to liberate the black man, Saigon, and Washington. Free enterprise only oppresses the weak. Down with American imperialism, racism and the military! Eradicate capitalism."

The Nixons traveled to the Statler Hilton Hotel, which is in sight of the White House. They had dinner there before going to the Inaugural Concert that evening at Constitutional Hall.

Sunday evening found us footsore, hand sore and blurry from lack of rest, but we carried on. We had to change to formal evening gowns and thought it would be good to sit down and enjoy the fine concert ;in spite of all we had gone through this today.

Ever since George Washington had been President, an evening of elegant music had been an Inaugural highlight.

Jane Beeson, Nixon's 79 years old, gray haired Aunt, arrived a little early. She forgot to wear her little white tag identifying her as part of the Nixon entourage. The Secret Service agent did not know her, and Aunt Jane's explanation of who she was, did not satisfy the agent. Aunt Jane, who arrived before Pat and Dick, refused to be moved from the presidential box because she didn't have a ticket for VIP seating. The Secret Service was convinced she had a forged ticket and escorted her to another orchestra seat. So Aunt Jane was evicted from the spot. She had to retrieve her white tag somehow.

When Dick Nixon came into the presidential box, he didn't see Aunt Jane there. He knew she loved music and was puzzled about it. Dick asked the Secret Service agent on guard, "Have you seen my Aunt Jane? She is a small lady with gray hair and loves music." Well, the Secret Service agent was embarrassed and apologetic. He managed to put out the word to find Aunt Jane. Very soon Aunt Jane was found and escorted back to the Nixon concert box. From then on Aunt Jane wore her white tag, after that incident.

We sang the "Star Spangled Banner" anthem as a huge American flag descended from the ceiling. It was very impressive. Then, the 375-voice Mormon Tabernacle Choir opened the program with "American Songs of Patriotism and

Brotherhood," in concert with the Washington National Symphony Orchestra. The Negro spiritual "Deep River" and Wagner's "This Is My Country" really put the zing into our evening.

Dick, who enjoys playing the piano himself, was entranced by the young black pianist, Andre Watts, rendition and brilliant piano techniques on Piano Concerto #2 in D-Minor.

After that pianist brilliant piano playing, Aunt Jane Beeson who gave Nixon his piano lessons when he was a boy, remarked, "If you had practiced more you'd be up there instead of here, "Richard."

But Dick was happy where he was. He had won what he wanted all along.

After the intermission, the orchestra played Dick's favorite music piece, Richard Rodger's "Victory at Sea." He was really enjoying his evening. However, Anna Moffo, the pretty soprano soloist stopped the show, singing "Climb Every Mountain," "Kiss Me Again," and the Italian Street Song from Victor Herbert's "Naughty Marietta." It had Pat and Dick and all of us cheering for more, but Moffo only bowed several times—no encores.

Then, the choir and the orchestra launched into the "Songs of Democracy" by Howard Hanson, which stirred the performance and us moved all of us to cheer.

Pat and Dick, game to the end, stood with the rest of the audience and sang, "America the Beautiful" with the choir. The entire program had given Pat and Dick the spiritual lift they needed. Dick was so moved by this inspiring performance, he left his presidential box at the close of the concert and walked on stage and shook hands with all the participants and thanking them for a lovely evening.

That ended the Inaugural Concert which Pat and Dick declared "wonderful impressive." We have been here many times before, but it was better than our stereo."

On January 20, 1969 Inauguration Day was gray and

forbidding. Despite the bunting and bright decorations and my feeling of excitement about the inaugural festivities, the city of Washington, was dismal, bleak and cold. The weather was threatening with rain. Dense gray clouds hung over the capitol for three days and had not departed. There was not a trace of sunshine and a cold wind swept across our faces.

Pat and Dick had woke up at 7:45 a.m. that day and had breakfast in their hotel room before attending an interdenominational prayer service at the State Department auditorium. Afterwards they drove to the White House to have rolls and coffee with President and Mrs. Johnson and Vice-President and Mrs. Humphrey.

At the White House the Nixons received an unexpected welcome at the door from their dogs, Vicky, a Poodle, and Pasha, a Yorkshire. The dogs had spent the night there at the White House.

Unlike former years, only persons with special invitations to the swearing in ceremony at the Capitol Plaza were admitted to the grounds of the Capitol. Right below the inaugural platform, I sat, with my camera in hand, in the stands for special invited guests.

Opposite the inaugural platform was a high tower alive with cameras and seething with news people. Surely, it was an important day for cameras and pictures to record this special event. I could see newsmen laughing and greeting one another and passing notes.

The, Nixon and President Johnson rode together with a pack of Secret Service agents to the Capitol for the inaugural ceremony. Pat and Lady Bird Johnson rode in a second car following the presidential wagon.

The inauguration was marked by pomp and ceremony. As President Lyndon Johnson and Richard Nixon emerged from the East entrance of the Capitol and proceeded to the front of the inaugural platform, the red-jacketed Marine band struck up "Hail to the Chief."

Nixon wanted Billy Graham to do all the prayers at the inauguration. But, Billy reminded him that he would be President of all the people and not just for one religious group. So Dick gave in and four nationally prominent clergymen offered prayers for the country, world, and for Richard Nixon as the new Chief Executive.

Just before the oath of office was administered to Richard Nixon, Billy Graham offered a prayer. In itself, it was an inaugural speech. I recorded here excerpts of that prayer as I remembered. "Our Father and our God, Thou has said, 'Blessed is the nation whose God is the Lord. Thou alone has given us our prosperity, our freedom and our power. This faith in God is our heritage and our foundation."

"As George Washington reminded us in his farewell address, 'Morality and faith are the pillars of our society.' We confess these pillars are being eroded in an increasingly materialistic and permissive society. The whole world is watching to see if the faith of our fathers will stand the trial and tests of the hour. Too long we have neglected Thy word and ignored Thy laws. Too long we have tried to solve our problems without reference to Thee. Too long we have tried to live by bread alone. We have sown to the wind and are now reaping a whirlwind of crime, division, and rebellion.

"Help us this day to turn from our sins and to turn by simple faith to the one who said, "Ye must be born again."

'We recognize, O Lord, that in Thy sovereignty Thou has permitted Richard Nixon to lead us at this momentous hour of our history.

'O God, our new President needs Thee as no man has ever needed Thee in leading a people! There will be times when he will be overwhelmed by the problems at home and abroad. Give him supernatural wisdom, courage, and strength. In the lonely moments of decision grant him an uncompromising courage to do what is morally right. We pray that Thou wilt so guide Richard Nixon in handling the affairs of state that the whole world will marvel and glorify Thee.

'We pray this humbly in the Name of the Prince of Peace who shed His blood on the cross that men might have eternal life."

I thought I was in a dream as I witnessed at first hand the inaugural ceremony itself of Richard Nixon being sworn into office. He chose a pair of family Bibles on which to swear his presidential oath of office. The Bible, dating back to 1828 and 1873, belonged to Nixon's Quaker family kinfolk. He had used them twice previously for oath taking, when he was sworn in as vice-president in 1953 and 1957.

For the inauguration ceremony, Pat wore a coat and dress costume of Anglo fleece in cyclamen pink. With it she wore a Russian sable tie and a two-skin, off-the-face sable beret.

Dick did not choose to wear a top hat or homburg. In fact, he did not have any on hand. He lost so many hats he couldn't find any in his clothes closet. Despite the chilly 35-degree weather of the ceremony day, he elected not to wear his dark gray double-breasted twill topcoat either for the ceremony.

The two Bibles were held by Pat one in each hand and above the other. All the time, Pat Nixon's eyes never left her husband's face. The Bibles were opened to Isaiah, second chapter, and fourth verse. "And He shall judge among the nations and shall rebuke many people, and they shall beat their swords into plowshares and their spears into pruning hooks. Nation shall not lift up sword against nation; neither shall they learn war anymore."

After the patriotic music and prayers, Richard Nixon faced Chief Justice Earl Warren and placed his hand on the two family Bibles and repeated the traditional 35-word oath to "preserve, protect and defend the Constitution of the United States as prescribed in Article II of the Constitution. After the oath, Richard Nixon vowed, "So help me God." Thus, my friend in an instant became transformed from a private lawyer to the awesome job of being, President.

As the cannons resounded out a 21-gun salute, the bright scarlet uniformed Marine band struck up "Hail to the Chief." Richard Nixon escorted Pat, his wife back to her seat-tenderly. The Nixons were not the kind of family to kiss in public. Just the opposite President Lyndon Johnson kissed everyone in sight.

Then, Nixon began his 17-minute address. He spoke reverential and with careful thought, calling for our country to go forward as a peacemaker and together, both blacks and whites.

As Nixon was speaking regarding the crisis of the Spirit, the dark cloudy sky parted above and a shaft of light came down over him. It was so impressive that many thought it was a good omen for the country.

He said, "Standing in this same place a third of a century ago, Franklin Delano Roosevelt addressed a nation ravaged by depression and gripped in fear. He could say in surveying the nation's troubles:" Their concern, thank God, only material things.

'Our crisis today is the reverse. We have found ourselves rich in goods, but ragged in spirit; reading with magnificent precision for the moon, but falling into raucous discord here on earth.

'We are caught in war, wanting peace; we are torn by division, wanting unity. We see around us empty lives, wanting fulfillment. We see tasks that need doing, waiting for hands to do them.

'To a crisis of the spirit, we need an answer of the spirit. To find that answer we need only look within ourselves."

But, Richard Nixon said, "We cannot learn from one another until we stop shouting at one another."

During his speech, we thumped our cold feet on the floor of the wooden stands in tune with our hands applauding him, nine times.

The band and choir began the National Anthem and then the inaugural ceremony was over with the benediction.

Newly sworn in, President Nixon and Pat with their family went immediately to the East Front Conference Room of the Senate for luncheon given for them by the Democrat and Republican leadership of Congress after the ceremony. Just before the luncheon, Nixon signed his first official papers, including the formal nominations of his 12-member cabinet. All were confirmed except Secretary of the Interior-designate Walter J. Hickel. There were reservations about Hickel's devotion to conservation, or strong enforcement of water pollution control. Hickel was the only controversial selection. Confirmation was expected very soon.

Pat remarked, "In a personal sense, I only wish Dick's mother and father could have been here—how proud they would have been."

At the luncheon, Nixon said, "The five invocations given today were all prayed to the same God, who is in this room, and each of the invocations will read well in history."

Besides Billy Graham, prayers were offered by a Roman Catholic bishop, a Rabbi, a Greek Orthodox Archbishop, an African Methodist Episcopal minister, and a Quaker California leader.

After the lunch we were off to the inaugural parade, which marches from the Capitol down Pennsylvania Avenue to the White House. Dignitaries from all over the country, beautiful, elaborate floats, elegant and best bands, and marching military groups would take part. For safety reasons, the Secret Service had put a bubble top on President Nixon's car before departing down Pennsylvania Avenue. They had information regarding noisy demonstrators organizing along the parade route.

Along most of the route, there were patriotic, friendly cheers for President and Mrs. Nixon. Happy crowds waved from the sidewalks. Some were huddled in blankets and trying to take pictures with their cameras.

At other points, protestors were agging the police on and calling the police, "PIGS." Police and cars were pelted with rocks. The demonstrators screamed obscene slogans and made lewd gestures. There was protest signs- "Nixon's The One- #1 War Criminal." Billionaires Profit off G.I. Blood!" American flags were burned. The police pushed and arrested demonstrators. It was so terrible, they had to call in the 82nd Airborne troops and the D.C. National Guardsmen to help quell the tense unruly demonstrators.

When the Nixon presidential car passed by, the demonstrators broke loose and concentrated a heavy barrage of rocks, sticks, beer cans, and cherry bombs on it. They screamed again and again, the most foul-mouth and dirty slogans about he Nixons I ever heard.

It was a national disgrace! I had witnessed first hand and never forgot to this day. After being in the middle of so many unruly shouting demonstrations, something bubbled up inside of me.

When the dissidents changed "Hey, hey, Ho Chi Minh the NLF is going to win, "the next war-revolution." and lifted a Viet Cong flag, it made Nixon angry. Ardis and I were disgusted and furious too. How could anyone be so mean and disrespectful?

The Nixon fighting spirit finally emerged. He was not going to let youthful rebellion ruin his achieving glorious day. Richard Nixon opened the bubble top and stood up to wave. He smiled and gave his V for victory sign. Pat came up by his side and the spectators' cheers erupted. Once President Nixon and Pat had made it to the Presidential reviewing stand, their anger and the protestors subsided.

Instead of finishing watching the rest of the parade from our reserved stand, Ardis and I chose to look at the TV view of the parade from Congressman John J. Rhodes, (Arizona) office in the Rayburn House Office Building. We were frozen cold to the bone. Betty and John Rhodes offered refreshments. The hot chocolate and coffee helped us get warm and thaw out our feet. It was better than sitting out in the intense cold. Also, we wouldn't have to put up with any more protestors. We had enough of that group to last for a lifetime.

The parade lasted until 5:25 p.m. It was late getting started and late finishing in the dark. A gentle rain started to fall, as President Nixon and Pat and family managed to walk to the White House. Several hundred Nixon and Ryan relatives greeted them there.

Neither of them had eaten anything. The Nixons had barely time to eat, but Pat was so excited she only wanted to a bowl of cottage cheese. The rest of the family ate prime-rib steaks. Pat's simple request for cottage cheese caused an uproar in the main kitchen. There was no cottage cheese to be found. One of the kitchen helpers volunteered to search the city for a deli, which might have cottage cheese available. Fortunately, a bucket of cottage cheese was located. It was no easy task in spite of the thousands of visitors attending all the inaugural celebrations. It wasn't until years later Pat discovered the truth about the cottage cheese incident.

The highlight of the inaugural evening was the six inaugural balls. The Presidential party would visit each ball at five downtown hotels and the Smithsonian Institution.

I was all "thumbs." If it hadn't been for one of the ladies helping me get in the gown, I might still be struggling with a zipper. As I put on my fur jacket to go to the ball, I glanced in the hall mirror and noticed my rhinestone earrings sparkling brightly in the light.

The ballroom at the Statler Hilton was decorated in white gold, and silver,which added color to the festivities. Many gentlemen in their bright and different colored tuxedos, and ladies in their beautiful gowns of various hues and styles caught the eye of each guest. Orchestras such as Bob Crosby and Les Brown played for the crowd. Soon floor space was at a premium for those who came to dance. The music was merry and lively and put everyone in high spirits.

I decided to walk in the hallway surrounding the ballroom to get a breath of fresh air. Apparently, many other people had the same idea, for it was crowded there too.

As I walked here and there shooting pictures of memories, I noticed the President's colorful marine guard had arrived with the band at the bottom of the circular stairway. Bending over the balcony rail to get a picture of the marine guards standing at rest by the front entrance, one of my rhinestone earrings fell off my ear. I looked and looked. Where did it go? The balcony hallway and the circular stairway were covered with a thick carpet. Therefore, I couldn't hear which way the earring had fallen. A wine velvet gate barred the stairway. I thought the earring had bounced over the gate down the circular stairway or on the main floor below.

I was feeling more desperate by the moment! The marine band would be soon playing, "Hail To The Chief." President Nixon would have to come up the stairway to the festivities. If the earring was on the stairway would he trip over it? I was panicky! Immediately, I was down on all "fours" and was crawling around searching for the missing earring.

"Did you lose something? Asked a gentleman from Connecticut, "or do you like to do this sort of thing?" He laughingly inquired. I explained to him what happened, along with my concern that it might cause President Nixon to fall if he should step on it. So my new friend from Connecticut joined me in my search on the floor. Television cameras and spotlights were moving around the room, but we were oblivious to anything except finding the lost earring.

A Secret Service man came up and asked us, "What are you doing? You should be in the ballroom. The President is coming up soon." I told him about the earring, and he joined us on the floor. The three of us felt over every inch of the floor and the stairway, but the elusive earring was not to be found. Suddenly, the marine band loudly proclaimed, "Hail To The Chief." The President was coming! All three of us jumped to our feet. My Connecticut friend and I rushed quickly to the ballroom.

As the Secret Service man walked away, I turned and looked toward the stairway once more. I put my hand on my chest. There to my embarrassment, I felt a small hard object. Was my face red! It was the missing earring. It had fallen inside the bra of my gown. Was I ever glad the Secret Service man hadn't decided to frisk me!

The Statler-Hilton was the last tour stop of the six inaugural balls President Nixon and Pat had to visit. He stood in front of the microphone and looked over the crowd. There, he saw a jam-packed dance floor—3,000—in fact—that all movement almost halted, he remarked, "I thought this was advertised as a dance."

We barely had room to breathe. The crowd was pressing closer to him. Then, he jokingly said, "Well, you know the theme of our campaign was "Bring Us Together." Well, we were brought very close together in a crushing way, all in one room.

In turn he brought forth Pat and said, "Pat has been the first lady in our house for 28 years. Now she is the First Lady in the White House." We all cheered.

Pat Nixon in her fluffy,silk ball gown with its embroidered beaded jacket was the most beautiful and decorative dressed First Lady. Even Julie and Tricia reminded us of two enchanting fairy princesses. Were we proud!

President Nixon continued on with his joking. He was happy and exuberant. I knew he was humorous, but that night Nixon stole the show. It was a night to remember.

He said, "Folks, I never had better seats for a parade than I did today. Of course I sent for my seats eight years ago."

Maybe Nixon's collar was getting to him, he kept

remarking, "Anybody out there who is able to invent a new, comfortable collar for a white tie—please let me know and I'll give them at medal from me."

We all laughed when he stated, "I understand all nine Supreme Justices are here at the balls . . . you know this is one way to get all nine of them to dance to the same tune."

Some called out, "What's your favorite song, Mr. President?"

Then he replied, "I never given it much thought, but after tonight, I've decided that my favorite song is "Hail To The Chief."

It was in the wee hours of the morning—in fact when I looked at my watch it was 1:20 a.m.—a very long day. Richard Nixon jokingly flubbed or he lost count of the many balls, "This is our seventh and last ball. I mean the last for this inauguration."

Then in departing from our party at the Statler Hilton, he said, "Thank you for your support and help. All of us will remember this day. It wouldn't have been possible without you. Now, they have given me the key to the White House, and I have to go home and see if it fits."

As my inaugural jubilation for Richard Nixon faded away, I realized that he, as a new President, would come face to face with many heavy burdens and awesome responsibilities, and to find a solution to the dreaded Vietnam War which was causing the death of so many of our American boys.

Before winging my way back to my Arizona home, I had promised Richard Nixon before leaving I would be his eyes and ears for him. He was inheriting a mess beyond any human understanding, and it was up to us to come to his aid. Without our help and prayers, he could not do his job alone.

Chapter 14

I REMEMBER PAT AND RICHARD NIXON FIRST YEAR FILLED WITH ACTIVITIES, PROTESTORS, BOMBINGS

As former President Eisenhower had said, "I can no longer call you Dick, but now it will be Mr. President." Since I was a personal friend of the family, I had to guard myself in public what to call him—now it would be Mr. President—before any public gathering. To me, they always would be Pat and Dick.

One of the kettles left stewing on the White House stove for President Nixon was an economy, which could either wither away or boil over. At the same time he inherited the Vietnam War, which was a full time fighting war for our country. Nixon was concerned about the inflation, the output of goods and services, and the climbing prices of food and other materials.

Nixon only wanted to give people pride and dignity. Give people the chance to own small businesses. Train men and women for jobs that existed and motivate them toward goals. Give Tax incentives.

For Pat—now First Lady—would mean taking on an unpaid toughest job for the country. She had-on-the-job-training as Second Lady. When Dick was Vice President in the Eisenhower Administration, the Eisenhowers called on both of them to fill in for them on various projects and events.

Being a very private and demure person, Pat realized that for her every word and action would be scrutinized and be the talk of every American household. Her first duty, as she saw it, was to make the White House a home for her husband and their unmarried older daughter, Tricia. Always she would be at Dick's side. She would never nag but only cheer them up.

Pat had more understanding of the average American grass roots citizen than any other First Lady entering the White House. Hadn't she been listening to the people for 20 years?

The first few days on the job as President were filled with staff and cabinet receptions. Three of the cabinet members—Walter Hickel, Alaska, George Romney, Michigan, and John Volpe, Massachusetts were Governors before their cabinet appointments. They had problems adapting to their new role as a cabinet member instead of being in charge as a Governor. Sometimes they talked out of turn and kept on talking and talking. It was an interesting sideshow.

Of course, reporters wanted to know if Pat Nixon had made any changes in the décor of the White House. She took the reporters on informal tour of the family private quarters on second and third floors.

Pat said, "We took out 50 phones out of the President's bedroom." She explained that Lyndon Johnson used two big telephone consoles with 25 push buttons to reach each one of his top aides. He kept one by his bed. But Nixon preferred only an ordinary white telephone by his bed.

Dick banished the large canopied four-poster bed that President Johnson had used. Pat had the room redecorated in red, blue and white and retrieved regular size bed from presidential storage for his bedroom.

The First Lady's bedroom had very few changes. Pat liked what Jacqueline Kennedy and Lady Bird Johnson had added to the room. But, she brought some art objects and paintings to cheer up her new room.

Since Dick liked strong bright colors, Pat had several rooms redecorated in vivid colors. The West Sitting Room became a cheerful yellow.

The President's Oval Office in the West Wing was brightened with prolific blue and gold rug and attractive gold curtains and sofas. Dick replaced the portrait of former President Franklin Delano Roosevelt over the mantel, with George Washington's portrait. Also, instead of the desk, which was there, he asked for his old desk from his Vice President's office at the Capitol to take its place.

On the second floor in the Lincoln sitting room, Dick brought his slightly faded, brown velvet easy chair from his study in the New York apartment. It was his favorite chair. Pat had asked him if he wanted it recovered, but he said no. After dinner he would sit and work at night. He would look out the window toward the Washington Monument and meditate. President Nixon had to have a crackling fire in the fireplace every working night and turn on the phonograph to play classical music.

Pat remembered when she made her own slipcovers. She liked to decorate and make things inviting to live in.

After that press tour, Pat found herself once again in the headlines. She had not commented about the wooden mantel, which was replaced by an antique marble one by Benjamin Latrobe. The old mantel had a plaque placed by Jacqueline Kennedy, commemorating Abraham Lincoln and President John F. Kennedy, her husband.

This caught the attention of the press. They implied that Pat was trying to erase the image of the Kennedys from the White House. It really frustrated Pat regarding this incident. However, to set the record straight, it was Lady Bird Johnson and the Committee on Preservation of the White House, which were responsible for the change. Since the press was not notified about the decision, they blamed the Nixons instead of first getting their facts straight.

In addition to his Oval Office in the West Wing—a 3 story office building—Nixon also had a working office in the old Executive Office Building where he like to work alone. The constant activity of the West Wing and the Oval Office often interrupted his thoughts. He always wanted to do the right thing. Mulling over the many decisions in private helped him come to the proper solutions. Nixon would then call in staff members for private meetings there.

Surrounded by his family photographs and mementoes, Nixon was more comfortable in those surroundings working and thinking. The Oval Office had a formal atmosphere, which Nixon could not get used to, even when he tried. Therefore, the Oval Office was chosen for official and formal meetings.

In the basement of the White House was the barbershop. Nixon often had to sign enormous stack of letters even when he was getting a haircut.

In Washington, D.C., it is the White House and the First Family who set the tone for social events and festivities. Pat started a social revolution when she became First Lady. The buzz around Washington in the social circles that white tie, formality and elegance once again would be the way of life at the White House. Whatever Pat revived, all the hostesses of social circles did likewise.

Just after the Nixon family moved into the White House, Pat was swamped with a gigantic deluge of letters from all over the country. Without asking Pat Nixon about it, Haldeman, Nixon's chief of staff, took over the operation of

Pat's incoming mail. He had opened and arranged each one. A form letter was developed for each one. A school child received a form letter different from a business wife, etc.

When Pat discovered what Haldeman was doing, she put an end to Haldeman's operation regarding her incoming mail. She had the big mail sacks brought to her bedroom on the second floor. Pat had brought in Bessie Newton, a Nixon secretary, to open each envelope. After that Pat answered everyone by her own hand. She did not use an autopen. From then on, Pat Nixon and H.R. Haldeman were in battle about various things around the White House.

The Nixons expelled the open liquor bar out of the East Wing of the White House that used to be in style for the Johnson and Kennedy's presidencies. Unspiked fruit punch and French wines were substituted for hard liquor.

Rock music was assigned to the teen-age groups. Now, the Marine Band played sedate waltzes and foxtrots.

Late hours no longer were the feature of the Nixon parties. When President Nixon and Pat retired to their living quarters upstairs, the party was over. In contrast, during his administration, President Johnson was up partying until 3 a.m. in the morning. He danced and kissed all the ladies. But, President Nixon hadn't danced at all. Neither did he give a presidential kiss on ladies cheeks. Suddenly, on the social scene, late parties were considered unfashionable.

Once a week, the Nixons held little black-tie dinner parties. Eight or ten people were invited, and so the invitations to those dinners were extremely valued.

When Nixon took out the bar in the East Wing and substituted non-denominational church services, the press and many other people made fun of President Nixon for this. But, he stood firm in his convictions to be an example.

When the newspapers reported about the White House worship services, some people criticized President Nixon for obscuring the separation of church and state. I thought those were silly remarks. The White House was their home. They were not establishing a state church. Even, Madelyn O'Hair, the atheist, got in the act and sued the Nixon White House, too.

President Nixon enjoyed the private services. He didn't want protestors defiling a church and demonstrating because he was in attendance. This way the Secret Service men did not have to get up early and look under church pews for bombs.

In spite of the criticism, many evangelical leaders came forward to participate. Church and college choirs clamored to be involved in the worship services at the White House. Several hundred people were invited. The social secretary at the White House was surprised by the volume of letters asking to come to the worship services. Somehow many persons prized this invitation more than any formal state dinner. The White House staff was overwhelmed by the response. I even had calls regarding how to get ministers and choirs to come to the White House services. It kept me busy trying to get some set up at the White House.

January 26, 1969 was the date of the first White House service in the East Wing. Billy Graham was the speaker. Nixon sat down at the piano and played hymns. George Beverly Shea sang. It was very impressive. Afterwards, coffee, juice and rolls were served and a brief reception was held in the dining room.

The services welcomed the children and teen-agers of cabinet members, Congressmen, and White House staffers. Billy Graham and Norman Vincent Peale spoke many times at the services. From all parts of the United States, ministers from the Catholic Church, rabbis from Jewish synagogues, and evangelical churches participated. Under this kind of leadership, Americans began to reassess themselves and to re-evaluate their recent history. Young people once again took an interest in religion.

His staff surprised President Nixon with a six-month-old

Irish setter as a gift. He decided to call it King Timahoe after a little village in Ireland where his mother's ancestors came from. Of course, the press decided to be there. Instantly, they were jokingly comparing Nixon's new dog to LBJ's beagle. President Johnson always picked up his beagle by the ears, and it caused uproar among animal lovers. Nixons had two other dogs—Vickie, a poodle, and Pasha, a Yorkshire terrier. It took a while for King Timahoe and Nixon to adapt to one another.

Pat said when the weather grew warmer, King Timahoe had a method for keeping cool. He would jump into the South Lawn fountain at the White House. Then, Tim would stand until he would get cool and come out of the fountain and shake off the water.

On January 30, 1969 President Nixon led a prayer breakfast at the White House. Only eighty congressional members out of five hundred showed up. Billy Graham stated that the only hope for America was to turn to God. That way we would have the only source needed to keep our country from ripping itself apart. Because of the lack of interest in prayer, showed the critical need for it in our land.

However, the same day at the annual Presidential Prayer Breakfast held in Washington, D.C. about three thousand persons attended it. For the first time in the history of annual Prayer Breakfast, all of the Nixon cabinet attended along with their wives at the head table.

President Nixon told us "that he and his cabinet" carry on our shoulders the hopes of millions of Americans and others. However, we are sustained and inspired by the prayers of the people of this nation and of this world. Our administration is dedicated to faith in God and to the spiritual principles upon which our nation was established."

President Nixon was concerned about all the people who worked at the White House. He appreciated each one and asked about their families. His friendly, courteous remarks touched their hearts. They were astonished by the differences in the two Presidents.

According to stories heard around the White House, President Lyndon Johnson wasn't well liked and was a regular pain to cope with. He would curse the people around him and thought they couldn't do anything right. The contrast between LBJ and Nixon was a real shocker for them.

On February 18, 1969, Pat had a luncheon for women reporters in the State Dining Room. All the reporters and Pat drew numbers for a seat at the table. Pat told them she wanted a volunteer recruitment program to enlist volunteers to help others around them—tutors, teacher aides, homecare for the aged and mental retarded, library book mobiles for aged and disability, and serving in hospitals, etc.

On February 23, 1969, Nixon took an eight-day working trip to Europe to visit Brussels, London, Bonn, Paris, Berlin and Rome. It was time for the U.S. allies to see the new world leader of the West. It was Nixon's first step on the road to peace. He was concerned and alarmed about the new ferocious assaults in Vietnam, and Dwight Eisenhower's recent illness, which troubled him. Nixon came to listen and pay attention to what others had to say on issues, which were troubling the world.

The first stop was in Brussels. Wherever President Nixon went, his Secret Service agents were there, too. He found out that kings have guards as well. There were many guards in regalia and rode on their beautiful horses escorting Nixon through the streets of Brussels.

At the NATO Council, Nixon told them no one country possessed the corner on truth and wisdom. He pledged to listen and consult with them on all major issues, which were disturbing all of Europe.

Then, off to London to visit with Prime Minister Wilson. There were threats and demonstrations there. But the British police contained them to a small square, except for their incessant yelling which went on and on.

Nixon became the first U.S. President to visit Westminster Abbey, and there he laid a wreath on the grave of Britain's Unknown Warrior. He had lunch at Buckingham Palace with Queen Elizabeth, Prince Philip, Princess Anne and Prince Charles. As a teachable traveler, Nixon took in the history and beauty of the statue-lined marble Hall and Westminster Abbey.

The German leader of Bonn and Berlin were pleased when President Nixon said he would renew U.S. commitment to them. In West Berlin, the crowds cheered Nixon along his tour there. He told them, "that Berlin shall be free and Berlin shall live."

The most important stop for Nixon was the visit with President Charles de Gaulle of France. De Gaulle had lost confidence in America's leadership that last few years and had become very hostile to the United Stares. Nixon had not come for pomp and ceremony, but to find a way to end the war in Vietnam. He knew France had political alliance with Vietnam and China. If Nixon could overcome de Gaulle's distrust of America, it would open up communication channels toward peace.

Wherever President Nixon went, the Soviet Union would come up in his conversation with the leaders. Charles de Gaulle was no exception. He raised it first concerning the Soviet Union threat to Europe. Also, China was not left out of their conversation. He told President not to isolate China but to open up communications with it before it grew into a powerful nuclear nation.

President de Gaulle was so impressed with Nixon's statesmanship; he accepted the invitation to come to the United States in 1970. In turn, Nixon filed his impressions and actualities in his brain. For that moment, sometime in the future, he would begin dialogue with the Soviet Union and China for his goal of peace.

On Nixon's last stop before going home was with Pope Paul VI at the Vatican. After talking over issues and problems, the Pope urged that the United States should continue our fight against Communism in South East Asia and make a stand for human rights wherever it was suppressed. While Nixon was in Rome, left-wing students used his visit as an excuse to demonstrate about the closing of the University of Rome. Nixon signs were everywhere.

March 16, 1969, another White House Worship Service. A buffet brunch followed the service in the State Dining Room. Pat had requested that her warm blueberry muffins would once again embellish the dining room table, along with sweet rolls and fresh-baked brioche rich in eggs and butter. The orange juice had been squeezed freshly for the occasion, and hot delicious coffee was served.

The same day, Tricia and Julie had arranged a surprise birthday party for their mother. Pat was now 57 years old. How they kept the party a secret from her was truly a miracle in itself. It was such a beautiful party, and was Pat surprised! She did not know the party was for her.

After the cake came in, President Nixon honored Pat with a toast. Then Pat blew out the candles on the cake. The beautiful roses I had given to Pat for her birthday was displayed and enjoyed by everyone there. Happy Birthday for the new First Lady. It was a party she remembered.

All through the country everyone was wondering if our new President Nixon would accomplish soon the ending of the Vietnam War, where others had failed. But the North Vietnamese tested Nixon by initiating in February a ferocious attack into South Vietnam. Nixon's intuition wanted him to repay the Communists right away. But the U.S. Commander in Vietnam, General Creighton Abrams, advised Nixon they should have B-52's bomb the Communist supply lines into neutral Cambodia.

But, the Secretary of State, Bill Rogers, did not agree. He said it would only bring down the wrath of the Democratic Congress and the press would denounce it. Nixon did not want any more anti-war demonstrations at home or abroad. Everyone wanted the Vietnam War to end—but how? He deferred his final decision what to do next. The media was speculating on what the Nixon Administration would be doing about the Vietnam War. However, President Nixon told General Abrams to plan to use B-52's but wait for his final endorsement later.

The Sunday afternoon after the church service and Pat's surprise party, President Nixon met with Secretary of State Rogers and other cabinet members and Chairman Wheeler of the Joint Chiefs to reexamine the situation in Vietnam. One thousand one hundred forty American boys had died according to the latest casualty figures given to President Nixon. To save the lives of more American boys, Nixon made the secret decision to bomb the Communists troops inside the Cambodia border. The North Vietnamese Communists had said officially they had no troops in Cambodia and so they did not protest the secret B-52 bombing on March 17, 1969. There were no protests from the anti-war demonstrators because they had no knowledge of it. This time there were no leaks to the public or any other outsiders. Because of President Nixon 's bold secret decision to bomb, many more American boys were not on a casuality list.

That week the Nixon hosted a White House reception for congressmen and their wives in the Blue Room. Hard liquor was not served, only punch and champagne. In the previous Johnson administration business suits were the approved attire at congressional receptions. Now it was different. The congressional wives were supposed to wear long formal gowns. The congressmen enjoyed primping in white or black ties.

However, when Joan Kennedy, Congressman Edward "Ted" Kennedy wife, walked into the room to join the reception. She horrified other guests because of her brilliant silver mini-dress. It was unusual to be the only one not like the other formal gowns. Others thought it was not in good taste. But Pat only stared at Joan. Anyone looking at Pat Nixon's face knew she was wondering how short Joan's mini-dress really was, and why she wore that kind of dress to a formal affair.

But, all of this informality didn't disturb President Nixon or any of the other congressmen. After all, Joan Kennedy was an attractive blonde and that dazzling dress really showed off her good looking legs. I'm sure all the other men noticed too.

Dick did notice. He said, not every woman has the figure to show off in mini-skirts. None of us should feel bad about wearing the longer length. Whenever he would go to their Florida retreat the women in bikinis were the most unattractive. Lots of women don't realize that to men they like what is feminine and have a mystery about them, and what is concealed to the eye.

March 24, 1969, the Nixons had their first state dinner in honor of Prime Minster Pierre Elliott Trudeau of Canada. He was a bachelor known for being a "swinger." That night, Trudeau arrived in the rain to the State Dining room with hundreds of other invited guests. The women wore long white gloves with their attractive formal gowns. The Prime Minister, like President Nixon and others, was in perfect formal attire. The music of the Marine Band was sedate.

Mr. Trudeau bid adieu by 11:00 p.m. The Nixons left at 11:30. Before President Nixon departed for the night, he encouraged the rest of guests to stay and dance. Many guests thought this was the first time a State dinner had come to an early conclusion.

Friday, March 28, 1969, President Eisenhower died at Walter Reed Hospital. He had been very ill for about a year. Everyone was praying that he would make a complete recovery but that was not to be.

I remembered his warm smile and his outgoing grandfather image but most of all his leadership. We were sad when he passed away. Many cried when Eisenhower died.

President Nixon was very tired and not feeling very well. When he was told of Eisenhower's death, Dick became very sorrowful and shed tears. In turn, everyone around him began sobbing. In his sorrow he forgot to tell any of his staff to notify Pat about Eisenhower's death. Before he decided to go to the hospital to see Mamie Eisenhower, Dick pulled himself together and called Pat and Tricia regarding the death of Eisenhower.

After visiting the hospital, President Nixon and family went to Camp David for the afternoon. Camp David is a beautiful country place hidden away in the Maryland Catoctin Mountains. It was there that Pat and Dick often retreated on weekends to work or relax. In quiet seclusion, President Nixon wanted to get away that day and work on his eulogy for the Eisenhower funeral. He was still under the weather and the emotional scene of Eisenhower's death affected him very much.

They decided that the Eisenhower funeral ceremonies would be held March 30 and 31, 1969 (Sunday and Monday). Former President Eisenhower had requested that he wanted to be buried in an $85.00 soldier's wooden coffin. The 21-gun salute and hymns made the ceremony splendid and remarkable. Nixon read his eulogy in the dome-covered large room of the Capitol. It was very impressive. But, Dick's goodbye to Eisenhower was very difficult and trying to him.

After he left the ceremony room, Dick broke down and sobbed. Quickly, he composed himself.

Since Monday was the official day for the Eisenhower funeral, foreign leaders and other diplomats came to show their respect and attend more services at the Cathedral and the White House reception for heads of State.

After the funeral ceremonies, President Nixon, Pat and the whole family flew to Key Biscayne, Easter weekend for a few days of rest. I took advantage of the Easter Break at the University to prepare for my trip to Washington, D.C. to attend the 17th Annual Republican Women's Conference, April 14-17th.

I was elected Vice-President of the Metropolitan Republican Women's Club. As an officer I had to attend many State, regional and national meetings. It was much more interesting since the Nixons were elected President and First Lady. So I attempted to be more knowledgeable in certain area of politics to help them out where I could.

The conference was held at the Sheraton Park Hotel. We had roll call by States. Soon the Arizona Republican delegates knew who I was. It was Margie Braden, our Arizona Republican National Committee woman, who let the "cat out of the bag." She was with Pat Nixon in Phoenix during the 1968 campaign and so my relationship to the Nixons became known. Margie was glad I came to Washington so she could know me better.

First Lady Pat Nixon often entertained with the tea parties at the White House. I was invited to come to this one in April with several other ladies. Pat greeted each one of us and showed all of us around the White House.

She served chocolate chip cookies and Sequoia Brownies with sparkling pink fruit punch. The punch was especially tasty, sweet and light. I found out later it was made with ginger ale combined with orange, pineapple, and cranberry juice.

Then, we were treated to a tour of National Arboretum—

a woodland with every type of bush, shrub and trees. The masses of brilliant flowering azaleas were so pretty. All around Washington the tulips, daffodils, and jonquils had come alive with beauty. The beautiful Japanese cherry trees along the Tidal Basin were in full bloom. Those lovely trees were a gift to Washington, D.C in 1912 by the Japanese in Tokyo.

Pat and Dick and all of us got out of our cars and strolled along the path at Jefferson Basin. The park police were really surprised that the President and First Lady were walking there. Suddenly we had more police surrounding us.

As we said goodbye to each other, I accidentally left my red umbrella in one of the cars and never was able to retrieve it. To this day I wonder where that umbrella went or was it stored somewhere in a White House storage room? Who knows!

On April 15, President Nixon was notified that one of our Navy EC 121 reconnaissance planes with 31 men aboard outside North Korean international territorial limit was shot down by Korean communists. This was an unexpected crisis that really tested the Nixon administration. Nixon agreed with others we should act dauntless, but he was not convinced this was the time to strike against Korean airfields. What would we do if we found ourselves in a Korean War while we were still at war in Vietnam? Dick knew we did not have the public support or the necessary manpower to fight two wars at the same time. He was angered and troubled by the situation.

Therefore, Nixon requested a irresolute protest to North Korea, April 18th about the murder of the 31 Navy airmen and to the right of United States to fly reconnaissance missions in international airspace, as we had done for 20 years. Despite his presidential order, the Pentagon did not cooperate. They postponed the public announcement three weeks and did not carry out the Nixon order. Also, the Pentagon had cancelled all the aerial reconnaissance in the Mediterranean and North Pacific without letting President Nixon know.

This was the beginning of the internal hostile clash within the Pentagon and U.S. intelligence to fight President Nixon and eventually remove him from office by any means necessary.

It troubled him that he had to keep on top of all things going on, and see that all orders were implemented. With his major goal of trying to end the Vietnam War, Nixon had an impossible job keeping tabs on people around him. He would find out later that not all people were doing what they were supposed to do.

What really disturbed President Nixon, was all those leaks to the newspapers regarding national security. Whoever was doing the leaks was seriously undermining the lives of our American boys overseas and negotiations to end the Vietnam War.

Nixon talked to J. Edgar Hoover, of the Federal Bureau of Investigation (FBI). Hoover reminded Nixon that every President since Franklin Delano Roosevelt (FDR) had used wire tapping on telephones. Even though, Nixon deplored wiretapping, he thought Hoover's advice the only chance to find out who was doing the leaking. But the leaking continued. Many articles appeared in the New York Times, Washington Star and Post papers.

As for me, I personally thought any leak of classified foreign policy information was treasonable matter. Any newspaper, which did this story, was more interested in the almighty dollar than working for the common good of the country and saving our fighting men overseas.

Tricia, the Nixon 's oldest daughter, received many invitations to be at various events. She was unmarried, 5'3" tall with long blonde hair and dark blue eyes. She captivated everyone around her with her radiant smile. The press tried to match her with any eligible bachelor. Although, Tricia did not attend every affair at the White House, she sponsored some events on her own. She also visited children's hospitals, did volunteer work with children and to research history when she could.

Tricia did not like the limelight. She cherished her privacy. Her father said Tricia is a strong-willed person. Whenever she had a date, Tricia told the Secret Service to stay out of sight. Dick told his daughter that she was taking a great risk with all the demonstrations going on around town.

At first her father and mother had to talk to Tricia about certain events. One of the events Tricia was unwilling to go to the Azalea Festival in Norfolk, Virginia. However after discussing it with her father she consented to go willingly.

April 23-27, 1969, there was one function in Norfolk Virginia that made Richard Nixon a proud father. Tricia Nixon was to be crowned Queen of the 16th Annual Azalea Festival. Tiny, trim Tricia went through many exhausting receptions and luncheons in an order of charming mini-dresses. Despite a strep throat, she managed a bright appearance, but gave the Norfolk town persons a surprising startle by showing up in her own coronation gown instead of the dress that the city had given her. President Nixon stole a few hours from his busy White House schedule and flew down for the festival. He had the honor to place the crown on his daughter's head as Queen of the Azalea Festival.

Tricia informed her father she was going to have a masked ball as her first official party at the White House. Pat Nixon departed from Tricia's party at an early hour and turned up her good music partly to drown out the rock music below. For her escort, she chose Barry Goldwater Jr., the newest congressmen from California. Young Barry was good looking and romantic. As they danced together Tricia and Barry made a handsome couple. It was only their first date and right away the press was buzzing about their relationship and prematurely putting a White House wedding on the calendar.

April 29th, Tuesday afternoon, Nixon spoke at Chamber of Commerce concerning student disorders. He said students should have the right to express dissent and all of us should listen to their side. However, they should not disrupt the campus with violence or use weapons to force their ideas on others. All college campus administrators must have the courage to combat this violence. Nixon caught the press off guard, and for once they gave him good coverage.

That night President Nixon proved to all of those present he could have a grand party. The occasion was a festive 70th birthday celebration for "Duke" Edward Kennedy Ellington. This was the first time, a black man had been so honored in the history of the White House. "Duke" Ellington was known over the world for the lyrics and songs he had composed and played on the piano. Even though Nixon was not a jazz fan he enjoyed music—especially classical. Old friends from New York gave Nixon the idea for the party. Since Dick was the first piano-playing president since Harry Truman, he welcomed the idea.

After the roast beef dinner in the State Dining Room, Dick went to the piano in the East Room and delighted everyone by playing "Happy Birthday." Even Vice President Spiro T. Agnew surprised the guests by playing two Ellington songs, "In a Sentimental Mood," and Sophisticated Lady."

President Nixon presented Ellington the Medal of Freedom—the highest civilian award; and said, "In the royalty of American music, no man swings more or stands higher than the Duke." Dick was surprised by the "Duke" kissing him twice on each cheek.

Then, the jazz program started beginning with the Duke Ellington's song "Take the A Train." This swinging night of jazz lasted for an hour and a half. Best of all the "Duke' played something soft, graceful, and gentle on the name of Patricia. Pat was charmed by the whole affair.

The Nixons retired by midnight. They reminded the crowd that the night is still young—inviting the guests to continue their night of fun, music, and dancing.

As soon as the Nixons left, the guests went out on the floor and danced. They continued the jam session until 2:15 a.m. Everyone—black and white—thought they never seen a party like this. The swinging jam session was only the icing on the cake! They were impressed that President Nixon honored an American Negro such as "Duke" Ellington.

Even though their home was upstairs and they were ready for sleep, the noise downstairs kept them awake. When the party was over, Pat and Dick heard the dull sound and grating of chairs being moved below in the East Room and the continuous vibrating sound of vacuum cleaners getting ready for the next day for visitors. It was not easy for either of them to get to sleep. This was the way it was after each party.

Pat Nixon had a busy schedule of meetings, receptions and dinners; answering her own mail, administer the decorating of the White House, and planning all the events that took place there. She had to keep track of which dresses worn, so she wouldn't wear one twice in a row.

May 7, 1969, she entertained some 80 chairmen of State and city commissions on the status of women.

Someone asked, "Mrs. Nixon, is there still discrimination against females in the United States?"

Pat said, "No, and that's the President's opinion, too. Women have equal rights if they want to excercise them. Women, who are really interested, should just go out and pitch. I just don't feel there's any discrimination. I know my husband feels that way. He feels there are well-qualified women, and he wants them to serve in Government. Also, I favor an appointment of a woman to the Supreme Court."

So far, President Nixon had named six women to high posts. Mrs. Patricia Hitt, Assistant Secretary of Health, Education, and Welfare; Mrs. Elizabeth Koontz, Director of the Women's Bureau in the Labor Department, and Mrs. Dorothy Elston, Treasurer of the United States were some of them.

But, outside the White House, women were picketing. They carried signs asking "equality for women now." Apparently, they didn't think Pat Nixon knew the facts of life and President Nixon should take women more seriously. The pickets hollered "Freedom!" They firmly disagreed with the First Lady.

All through the month of May her schedule was full-luncheon for the King and Queen of Belgians, tea with King Hussein of Jordan's wife, Princess Muna, the Senate Ladies luncheon, and a State dinner with the Australia prime minister.

Pat always believed that self-discipline and hard work was the key to a happy life. She found out she could do anything she put her mind to and adjust to anything she wanted to do. If people thing the world owes them a living, they will find out it doesn't. In her own lifetime she could verify that if anyone works, they can have what they want and achieve.

H.R. Haldeman, President Nixon's chief of staff, had some ideas about decorating the Oval Office. He knew Pat Nixon was in charge of this project, but Haldeman wanted to put in his two cents worth anyway. After much discussion regarding Pat's decorator, Mrs. Doyle, he decided not to go over Pat Nixon's head about the decorating of the Oval Office. I thought Haldeman was ruthless and he was trying again to put a wedge between Pat and Dick. I was glad he didn't win in this area for now.

May 14, 1969, I saw Nixon on television giving a big speech on the Vietnam War. He proposed the major part of all foreign troops—both U.S. and North Vietnamese—withdraw from South Vietnam within one year after a signed agreement. An international group would observe and watch the withdrawals and oversee unrestricted elections in South Vietnam. He admonished North Vietnam not to mistake our pliability with powerlessness. Dick said, "Reports from Hanoi indicate that the enemy has given up hope for a military victory in South Vietnam, but is counting on a collapse of will in the United States. There could be no greater error in judgment."

I knew President Nixon was trying to find a peaceful solution to end the Vietnam War with honor. Part of the peace plan was to train and equip the South Vietnamese and troop withdrawals. He knew peace would not come easily and as it looked now—maybe not at all.

May 21, 1969, President Nixon appointed Judge Warren Earl Burger as chief justice of the U.S. Supreme Court. Because of so many leaks, Dick had told no one about his decision to appoint Burger as Chief Justice. Therefore the press was kept guessing what was going to happen. If one doesn't want anyone to know about something, I guess "zip your lip" complete secret is the best way.

Justice Burger thought the Constitution should be interpreted as it was written. He was a "strict constructionist," as President Nixon wanted a judge on the Supreme Court to be, and Burger was well qualified for the job.

June 16, 1969, Pat Nixon set out on a trip to California and Oregon to show that ordinary people can make a difference and solve some problems better than government can. Since she had been a volunteer all her life, Pat wanted more people to get involved and help one another. Then things would change for the better.

Pat took her daughter, Julie Eisenhower, on this journey to the West Coast to inspect and observe and to gain public attention or support for volunteerism. No crowds or bands greeted them at the airport. Absent were politicians of any variety. No bouquet of roses were presented to her by any village or town Mayors. Why? Because she requested it not to be done.

In three days she visited grimy inner city places—often small and crowded—some with peeling plaster. Pat found a small-town church basement struggling to hold a day care nursery for migrant workers; a community vegetable garden project growing in an urban black slum area; and a make-shift arts center inspiring young artists to use their talents to brighten their community slum life. These were some of the sites visited.

About 40 reporters went along for that trip and they noticed Pat Nixon's promotion of volunteerism was "People First." Of course, some of the media did not think volunteerism was important and the ultra-extreme feminist women attacked the idea.

Pat's journey for volunteerism did meet some hostility in some places. Otherwise were friendly. They taunted her with banners and posters about the Vietnam War and hungry people and showered her with protest confetti in Oregon.

June 21, 1969, was the Nixon's twenty ninth wedding anniversary. Frank and Hannah Nixon, President Nixon's mother and father, used to receive regularly the "Moody Monthly" magazine. So I notified Bill Boyle, my old boss there, to send a subscription as an anniversary gift. Under separate cover I sent a box of California black figs. I knew Pat loved figs and it was a treat for the whole family. They were hoping their schedule would eventually bring them to Arizona and we both would have the pleasure visiting again soon. Dick had trouble sleeping the night before and so he stayed up late that night calling people about certain conferences of meetings and appointments.

While sister Tricia was overseas at Caernarvon Castle in Wales for Prince Charles investiture as Prince of Wales, July 1st, Julie was a volunteer for the summer as a White House guide. Julie was thrilled that Tricia could attend the investiture. By phone Tricia told Julie she would be in a selected spot near Queen Elizabeth and Prince Charles. Since the ceremony would be televised, all of us could see her there.

July 2nd, there were many tourists standing in line outside the gate of the White House for the customary public tours of the many staterooms. Julie chose 25 persons at random from the line for a special tour of sections of the White House and gardens that ordinarily visitors don't have the chance to see. Two or three groups each day were selected.

She showed them the grape arbor and a pretty little fountain in the First Ladies Garden. Julie had many stories to tell about the Diplomatic Reception Room. It is a charming oval shaped room with the Presidential Seal in the wall above the entrance door. This was the Presidential Seal, which was designed before Franklin Delano Roosevelt came in as President. He decided it should be changed. Julie explained that comparing seals one would notice the difference the way the eagle faced on the seal.

After showing them the Rose Garden where Presidential ceremonies are often held, Julie surprised everyone by taking them to the second floor private quarters to see the Treaty Room, Lincoln Bedroom, and the Queen's Bedroom. Just outside the Queen's Bedroom, she showed us a secret door to the third floor. To me, it looked like any ordinary wall. But, Julie just touched a spot beneath the picture on the wall and the door swung out and showed a stairway leading to the third floor. She had never done this before. I am sure all of those on this special tour would remember forever where the President resided.

July 5, 1969, Julie's birthday was Saturday. She was happy to be 21 because she could now vote. During the Presidential campaigns of 1960 and 1968, Julie thought all eighteen year olds should have the right to vote. She let her father know how she felt about this important issue.

Her husband, David, would be in Key Biscayne, Florida, for the Saturday birthday celebration. Tricia would be there two, arriving direct from London. As a close-knit family, they always celebrated birthdays and holidays together.

Julie said David liked his summer job working for the Senate Judiciary Committee. She also thought it was fun to do something special for people on tours at the White House.

We were still at war in Vietnam. Dick was concerned about all the leaks about the Vietnam War to the press. Leaks of classified information regarding the Vietnam War were treasonable as far as I was concerned. I was hoping President Nixon would get rid of the people in his administration who were doing this—giving encouragement to the enemies— endangering national security.

Of course, "The New York Times," "Washington Post," and "Washington Star," could care less about our country's security as long as they had a good story to sell papers. They didn't realize that they were selling out our American boys who were fighting and dying over there in Vietnam. It was the press and the media who gave the communist enemies exactly the information wanted.

I could never figure out why the press called President Nixon an irrational, secretive man. It was the behavior of the press and the national media, which prolonged the Vietnam War instead of ending it quicker. All the wiretaps arranged by the FBI, on individuals who had access to various information did not reveal who was leaking secret intelligence to the press. No wonder Dick was frustrated and angered regarding this matter.

Today, if anyone thought the recent Congress came up with the idea of work-for-welfare program, they were ignorant of the past and did not remember that it was Richard Nixon's original idea fostered July 14, 1969. He called it the Family Assistance Plan. Federal aid would be given to the unemployed and the working poor—only if each one would accept job training and work. When the bizarre news coverage broke loose on TV, regarding Sen. Edward "Ted" Kennedy's auto accident in Martha's Vineyard Pond, and one of the Kennedy's secretaries was left inside the car to drown, all of us became interested in this peculiar case. Dick thought Ted Kennedy was drunk that night and fled the scene leaving the girl trapped in the car. It was a very strange accident case that intrigued President Nixon. To this very day I had many unanswered questions what happened that night.

July 20, 1969, Sunday was a special worship service in the East Room. Colonel Frank Borman, an Apollo VIII astronaut, read again the first chapter of Genesis from the Holy Bible, as he had done before far out in space. Everyone sung the Navy hymn with intense feeling. Also, that night we all watched on TV, Neil Armstrong, an American Apollo XI astronaut, became the first man to walk on the moon.

President Eisenhower was the first President to advocate and approve for more increase in missile and space programs. As President Nixon continued Eisenhower's thoughts for more manned space vehicles and proceeded to expand and explore the unknown in space. But, the "New York Times" paper scolded Nixon harshly for participating in a televised phone conversation from the White House to the astronauts on the moon. Personally, they thought Nixon should give all the credit to Presidents Kennedy and Johnson. After that, Dick banned the "New York Times" from press activities. It was my opinion that some of the press was not happy unless they are attacking whoever is President.

On July 23, 1969, Pat and Dick departed on an eleven-day trip to Asia and Europe. Their first stop in the South Pacific was the Apollo XI astronauts' splashdown. Dick was excited as a little kid about welcoming the men back from the moon. It was one of his happiest moments.

The next stop was Guam, July 25, 1969. Lots of young people and children met them at the Guam airport. Pat and Dick had to shake hands as many as they could. Then, he spoke with the reporters who were covering their trip. It was there in Guam where he stated that he United States would keep all existing treaty commitments in the Pacific, but in the future all nations must provide their own troops to defend themselves. We would give arms to those countries, but we will not send our American boys to help them. There would be no more Vietnams! This came to be known as the Nixon doctrine.

By Saturday, Pat and Dick were on their flight to Manila, Philippines. That night the heavy winds and rain woke them up. They discovered they were in the throes of a typhoon.

Sunday morning, they were on their way to Djakarta, Indonesia. Smaller crowds met them here. There were many military troops around. The palace building was not air-conditioned. Pat said it was hot everywhere. Her clothes were dripping wet from the unbearable heat. Whoever had a fan used it to fan themselves all that evening.

Also, Pat toured a children's hospital in Indonesia. As she tried to talk with the children, the attending press persons surrounded her with cameras and flashing lights. It upset Pat to see this large press crowd around her. She only wanted to see the children and chat with each one. So, Pat calmed the frightened children in her motherly way and patted them on the head—telling them everything was all right.Never again did Pat want a large press following her everywhere.

Monday, monsoon rain greeted them at Bangkok, Thailand. As they stood for the ceremonies in the rain, they realized their clothes were being saturated to the bare skin. When the ceremony ended, the rain decided to stop. The King and Queen were very gracious. The beautiful palace and the delectable food were incredible, they said.

July 30, 1969, Wednesday, Pat and Dick departed for Saigon, South Vietnam. There were no airport ceremonies when they arrived. The humid heat was still with them. On arrival in a helicopter at Thieu's palace in Saigon, Nixon spoke with President Ngugen Van Thieu and decorated some Vietnamese soldiers. There were private strategy talks and commitments concerning the Vietnam War.

While Thieu and Nixon were talking strategy in the palace, Pat was entertained by Madam Thieu at a formal tea there. The palace in Saigon looked like a huge fortress with sand bags at every entrance door to keep down fires caused by bombing offenses.

Then, Pat and Dick took a helicopter for XiNam, the First Army base. President Nixon made a tour of the camp in an unprotected jeep. He moved among the troops and talked directly with each one.

Pat had a busy day too. She visited the Thuduc orphanage and a GI field hospital. Pat wanted to say hello to the troops who were doing so much for our country. She visited 39 sick and wounded soldiers at Long Binh hospital. Pat talked to each one and gave them warm encouraging words. Also she would send letters to their families to let them know about their sons.

I wondered how much persuasion Dick had to make Pat to go with him into Vietnam.

I remembered when First Lady Eleanor Roosevelt, wife of President Franklin Delano Roosevelt, made a tour of Pacific hospital during World War II. Now, Pat would be the second President's wife to visit troops in a war zone. Richard Nixon had remembered that incident as well, when he was a Navy lieutenant in South Pacific, regarding Mrs. Roosevelt's tour.

Pat and Dick were impressed with the American boys they saw in Vietnam. The soldiers there had different character than the peaceniks and protesters at home.

They made brief stops in New Delhi, India, and Lahore, Pakistan, where humid, hot weather of over 100 degrees accosted them once more. Then, everyone departed Lahore to Bucharest, Romania.

August 2, 1969, Saturday, Richard Nixon became the first American President and wife to make an official State visit to a communist country. In many trips before, it was their very first time they had visited this country. There were enthusiastic crowds of people everywhere, cheering and clapping. Some even threw flowers at them. Out in the streets,

President Nicolae Ceausescu and Richard Nixon were caught up in the dancing by the excitement and fervor of the Romanian people. Pat and Dick thought their trip to Romania was a historic visit.

Nixon in all his private talks to leaders of the various countries visited was trying desperately to find a solution to ending the Vietnam War. In Ceauescu he felt he had the opportunity for a break through in communicating to the Communist countries of Russia, China, and North Vietnam, which would help the Vietnam peace talks. President Nixon wanted peace in Vietnam, but not victory at any price.

Sunday evening, August 3rd, they arrived home in the rain. A huge crowd welcomed them back at Andrews Air force Base. We had to tell them the TV media did a good job covering their eleven-day trip abroad. Also, Pat had an interview on television August 10, 1969, Sunday. It was a Pat Nixon special concerning heartwarming experiences of their trip. She did a very good job articulating the meaningful parts of the trip. The public paid attention to what she had to say and loved her more for it. So did I.

Three places Pat and Dick liked to get-away to their residences—the Western White House in San Clemente, California and the Florida White House at Key Biscayne, and Camp David. Dick could get more work done in his California home than in one week at the Washington White House.

Richard Nixon named the San Clemente place—"La Casa Pacifica"—which meant the peaceful house. The press called it the Western White House. It was situated on a 75-foot steep cliff from which one could look down on the Pacific Ocean below. The ten room white adobe house with a red-tile roof was originally built by Hamilton Cotton, a Democrat Party Finance Chairman in 1926. The house was built around a patio in the Spanish tradition with a decorative fountain and tile walkways. The five acre scenery of lawns and gardens, had eucalyptus and palm trees bordering on the other three sides.

Inside La Casa Pacifica, I could see Pat's touch in decorating throughout the place. It was light and beautiful to see the splendid view of the blue Pacific Ocean from the window reminded me of Peace. And so it was. No wondered they wanted to visit there when they could.

It was always a "working vacation" for both of them when they came to San Clemente, California or to Key Biscayne, Florida. Erected on Coast Guard Station nearby were the offices of the President and his staff. Dick could take his golf cart and ride daily to his office in prefabricated buildings on the Coast Guard property. His office at Key Biscayne was not an elaborate as the ones at San Clemente. In Washington Pat and Dick made frequent use of Camp David in the Catoctin Mountains of nearby Maryland. This place was owned by the U.S. Government.

A few days after their eleven-day tour around the world, Pat and Dick once again visited La Casa Pacifica at San Clemente for three-week working vacation.

Dick would take time from his working schedule to swim in the ocean and to play golf with friends. When he flew from Washington, D.C. to San Clemente he had a difficult time readjusting to the changes in the time zone. It bothered him.

Pat and Dick knew not everyone would have the time and money to attend functions at the White House. Therefore, they had state dinners around the country. This way the people would have more of a chance to be involved in White House social affairs.

In Los Angeles, August 13th, they had an exciting, sensational dinner in honor of the Apollo 11 astronauts. Thousands attended that special dinner. Dick was master of ceremonies and did a superb job keeping all of us charged emotionally. The patriotism of that evening was more than I expected. Dick was so keyed up by the affair; he had trouble sleeping that night. The over excitement caused problems for two days until the doctor solved the dilemma.

Lyndon Baines Johnson's birthday was August 27, 1969, Wednesday. Dick invited LBJ to San Clemente for a special birthday party and planned every detail of it. Pat and Dick greeted LBJ and Lady Bird at the heliport with a mariachi band. As the mariachi band played Happy Birthday, everyone sang celebrating LBJ's birthday. LBJ seemed deeply pleased. Surely, LBJ and Nixon were more friendly and harmonious again. This was one of the kinds of gestures to others that Richard Nixon went out of his way to show.

Their vacation time was coming to a close. Julie and David had departed for home. Dick was getting restless, but Pat Nixon went to Artesia-Cerritos for the dedication of the Pat Nixon Park, September 5th. Her childhood home and four acreage were now annexed by the city. The old Ryan home would now become a community center. Pat spoke about her childhood, standing under a pepper tree in the backyard of her girlhood home. Pat remarked, "We had kind neighbors, all around us were open fields and we could ride horses bareback. We had fun playing run-sheep-run and all the other games one could have in our world. I am deeply pleased and hope children and young people will have a place to walk and ramble and dream. Out of all the home I have lived in I remember my childhood home the best. I took care of this house. My mother and father died here. I did the cooking, made the curtains and crocheted the "rag rugs" for the living room. Now the house will be carpeted throughout. "What she said touched hearts. All the people who heard her that September understood and related to their own lives. Pat was one of them!

Sunday, they attended church in San Clemente and took it easy the rest of the day. Then, a phone call interrupted their rest. Senator Everett Dirksen from Illinois had died. Now, Dick had to think about the Dirksen eulogy. He was wondering whom would Governor Ogilvie of Illinois appoint to take Dirksen's place in the Senate.

After they arrived back to the White House, Dick was concerned about confidential information being leaked out to the press or by the Defense Department or who? He was wondering if the White House or Camp David was bugged or tapped? Wanted everyone to be on their guard in their conversations until he could get to the bottom of how things were being leaked.

Before Pat departed on her trip in July, she had written an article for the "Ladies Home Journal" on volunteerism. It was published in the September 1969 issue. The title was "Power of a Woman." For payment Pat Nixon wanted it to go to the Girl Scouts of America for their work.

POWER OF A WOMAN

During a recent visit to a voluntary agency, which helps blind youngsters, the truth of an old adage— "The heart has reasons which reason knows nothing of"—came to me quite vividly.

Prior to my visit, I had read about the exceptional work done by the volunteers in helping blind children to become happy, self-sufficient human beings. I also had firm ideas concerning the great value of voluntary agencies in helping the needy and the afflicted.

All of this I knew. But it was not until I actually saw the happy faces of the blind children, listened to their laughter, felt the warm touch of their hands, and personally experienced the almost tangible force of love and concern which permeated the center that I fully grasped the essential truth of the matter.

What I experienced that day was a power that is known to all of us, but which, in the daily routine of our lives, often becomes forgotten or set aside. It is the power that comes when we direct our love and concern-our compassion, tenderness and deep strength—to the service of others, not because we thereby gain, but because we are helping those who need us.

There is in a woman's mind and heart the power to change the world—the dark world of a blind child; the despondent world of the unemployed, semi-literate teen-ager; the world of the lost and forgotten, the hopeless, the afflicted. She also has the power to inspire people of all ages and in all walks of life to join in this quest for a better world.

If I were able to speak personally to every woman in the United States, I would remind her of the many volunteer opportunities that ask, even beg, for her time and dedication—those small, splendid efforts that can turn the power of a woman into positive human values.

I would also say: Look. Look into your heart and mind. Then look at your community. Then, in your own way, bring to someone who needs help your power of love and concern; direct this power to a child, a neighbor, an invalid or simply some human being.

This is the true power. This is the power, which is never exhausted, because it is based on love. It is a power that can change a world—perhaps even yours.

Patricia Nixon

Our National Federation of Republican Women had our 15th biennial convention in Washington, D.C. at the Washington Hilton, September 25-27, 1969. So I took off from college work for a few days to attend the convention. I knew Pat Nixon would be there and that spurred my decision to come.

President Nixon and Pat entertained all 3000 of us on the South Lawn at the White House. It was wonderful. It was really a making of history and I was glad I was a part of it.

The last night of the convention we honored Pat Nixon and Mamie Eisenhower, our First Ladies. Julie Eisenhower and Tricia Nixon were also at the head table with David Eisenhower, (Julie's husband and Mamie's grandson).

Pat was given a document, praising her making a notable gift to international understanding through kindness and courtesy and friendliness. It was signed by all of the 50 state federations presidents.

Wearing a long sleeved turquoise and silver dress, Pat looked beautiful as she held up the red, white, blue-ribboned scroll for all of us to see.

Mamie Eisenhower, former President Dwight D. Eisenhower's widow, was named honorary Republican Woman of the Year. She had just come back from Abilene, Kansas, where her husband was buried. It was a sad journey for her satisfying but exhausting trip. Tears glistened in her eyes for a fleeting moment as she talked with us.

Since Mamie did not like flying on airplanes, she went to Abilene by train. However, Julie and David flew there and they were tired as well. Frankly, David was surprised to see his grandmother at tonight's dinner.

Dorothy Elston, former President of the Federation, paid tribute to Julie and Tricia as the best of young women in our nation. She greeted Julie and David as "that delightful happily married couple who depict the very best in our country and helped the President get elected and go to school the same time."

House Minority Leader, Gerald Ford, was one of the speakers on the platform, and he spoke out against some of those in Congress and elsewhere by their very actions were encouraging the enemy to think we will abandon the war and go home. He believed the majority of the American people backed President Nixon who thought South Vietnam should be settled through free elections and not giving in to Communist aggression. Pat smiled when our applause thundered all through the room.

It was good to see Pat and family once more. It was difficult to say goodbye, but both of us had jobs to do. It was an enjoyable visit; all of us women had much work to accomplish in getting Republican Congressmen elected to help President Nixon in his work. Therefore, we went home enthused in getting men and women elected.

Pat was determined to have her First Lady's office in the East Wing and do her own staffing there. Haldeman was trying once more to take over. This caused Pat to dislike Haldeman when he tried to interfere in the White House Preservation Committee's work. It was my opinion he wanted to control everything in the East Wing as well as the West Wing. Wasn't Haldeman Chief of Staff for the President? What made him think the First Lady should be under his thumb?

October 6, 1969 was the 100th anniversary for the U.S. Secret Service. James J. Rowley, Director of the Secret Service, and others awarded President Nixon a gold badge and a commemorative medal trophy to his delight. The Secret Service agents liked President Nixon very much, but they despised Haldeman. Haldeman tried to control the Secret Service agents, and they became unhappy with his arrogance. I was glad some others saw in Haldeman what I noticed first hand. He repeatedly was trying to exert his authority over every detail in the White House and did things without consulting President Nixon. I was sure there would be trouble somewhere down the road. Nixon told us he was planning to withdraw 35,000 troops by the middle of December from

Vietnam. He was urging all nations in the UN to do their best to persuade North Vietnam to negotiate to end the war.

Just before my departure to return to my work at Grand Canyon College, I was walking through Lafayette Park across from the White House. There were radical student protestors grouping together shouting violent rhetoric about the Vietnam War, the police, and everything in general. Many American flags were set on fire. I watched the flags go up in flames. As I stood nearby listening, their remarks about President Nixon grasped my attention. "We had one President killed! LBJ we drove you out of office. Now, we will see that Mr. Nixon will not survive!" Their rantings shocked and worried me at the same time.

That day, these anti-war demonstrators were planning a protest rally for October 15, 1969 nationwide against the Vietnam War in Washington, D.C. and other cities across the country. The two most radical groups were the Black Panthers and the Weather Underground. They thought revolutionary violence was the only way. The Weatherman was an offshoot of the Students for Democratic Society. There was no way of knowing where or when or how they were going to strike.

When I returned to Grand Canyon College, it was peaceful and quiet. Our students were not demonstrating but going about getting an education. But, outside my campus, the world was falling apart. The national television commentators were focusing on college campus unrest, bombings and brought the vivid scenes of the Vietnam War into our living rooms. No wonder we were shocked and disturbed by all the blood and violence thrown into our faces night after night by the television media.

My journal recorded that there were 174 major bombings and bombing attempts in the 1969-1970 school year on campuses. Cities became targets. Chicago police were killed and wounded. Even Detroit, Michigan, had bombs planted in their police stations. New York City had 400 bomb scares in one 24-hour period. Every time we picked up the newspaper or watched the news on TV, we watched 21 million properties destroyed. There were 40,000 bombings, attempted bombings and bombing threats. Many people killed and wounded. It kept everyone busy trying to locate who was doing all this. But, to no avail, the majority of the incidents the bombers could not be located or how to figure out their motives.

October 15th rolled around. Millions had come to demonstrate their protest against the Vietnam War. It was peaceful but their protest prolonged the war. The war did not end in 1969, as President Nixon wanted it. He even discussed with Billy Graham about having a Day of Prayer for peace. He was trying to end the Vietnam War with peace with honor, and not abandon South Vietnam to the Communists.

Pat was concerned about the millions of people protesting the war. She was hoping and praying that they were not blaming her husband, Dick, for the Vietnam War. In spite of the protestors, Pat wasn't rattled by their demonstrations. She kept up her usual timetable of award luncheons, teas for service clubs, and meetings with mayors here and abroad, and attending a national day of prayer.

The noisy protestors of the Vietnam moratorium overshadowed the "National Day of Prayer," that President Nixon proclaimed. Some of United States' largest newspapers did not carry one story about the special day. When some men and women were asked about it, they had not heard about Nixon's prayer proclamation. No wonder the vast majority of Americans failed to act when they were unaware of the President's request for prayer. The media neglected to tell the story because they thought prayer was not important.

However, Grand Canyon College and Moody Bible Institute and many other Christian colleges dismissed classes to pray for the nation. Some churches gave special emphasis on Wednesday night services, as Rev. Billy Graham led the nation in a time of prayer.

However, the protestors said October would not be the only time they would come out and demonstrate. They planned another one in November and it would not be as peaceful as the last one. President Nixon was concerned about the next moratorium day, and thought they should be preparing now or the November demonstration would be a disaster. Dick knew there would be some hard-core leftists organizing the demonstrations. There would be some men and women caught up in the fervor of the moment and go along and knowing not what it was really about. He could separate the two from each other. However, Nixon wanted the country to see what these demonstrators really were and let us decide who was right or wrong. The worse thing he could do was to make martyrs out of the marching demonstrators.

Then, Pat was to have accompanied her husband to a campaign rally in Roanoke-Salem, Virginia, October 27, on behalf of Linwood Holton who was a candidate for governor, but suddenly she felt nauseated and discovered she had a fever. Dr. Walter Tkach, the White House physician, advised her to cancel appearances for two days until the 24-hour virus disappeared. Pat was also to go with Dick to New Jersey the next day to boost William T. Cahill candidacy for governor. Therefore both of her appearances were nullified. At the same time, Julie Eisenhower, her daughter came down with the same virus bug in Massachusetts. Mother and daughter were feeling much better a few days later. However, Dick went on to Virginia and New Jersey to keep his promise to campaign for Republican candidates for Governor. There, he enjoyed the partisan journey. Large crowds followed him everywhere and were very jubilant. That pleased him tremendously. They roared their approval when he said government should be decentralized and that power should go back to the people at the local level. Until Richard Nixon became President, nobody had really done anything about it in the 50 years before him. He proposed legislation for revenue sharing with the states, welfare to work reforms, and job-training programs. This was just the beginning.

Tricia Nixon, the Nixon's oldest daughter, was busy being a hostess for various groups at the White House. She greeted 1,000 Boy Scouts who were her guests at a 3 p.m. reception on the South Lawn. These boys had cleaned up 200 miles of roadsides collecting tons of trash in North Carolina. The Freedom Foundation at Valley Forge, Pennsylvania honored the Boy Scouts for its project.

Then, Friday, she entertained 250 Washington children, ages 6 to 11, at a Halloween party at the White House. They kept her active posing for pictures with the children, fixing their Halloween masks and procuring more cookies.

Meanwhile, President Nixon was working feverishly on a speech about the Vietnam War. As usual, he retreated alone to Camp David working by his self. Dick Nixon was the only person I knew who had the ability to compose an important speech entirely on his own and give it without missing a word written. This speech was very important, and he did not want to rely on any presidential speechwriter.

Of course, the press was speculating about what Dick was to say to the nation. Some thought he would announce more troop withdrawals and others mentioned a cease-fire would be imminent. Because Nixon kept everything to himself regarding the material of the speech, the press didn't know what to do and just had to go through the guessing game.

I knew what the news media was doing all along. They didn't like Nixon at all. Since the Alger Hiss days, they were after his scalp to defeat him, no matter the cost. Pat and I felt that the best way for Dick to communicate his views to the public was by the direct questioning method. But, Dick detested to confront about 200 reporters and their bombastic ranking speech all at one time. Perhaps, that is why he didn't have as many press conferences as we liked. I could see his point. But, the other way whatever he did, they would constantly interpret his views or distort whatever points he tried to get across.

The night of November 3rd, I was one of the millions listening to Nixon's speech. He literally kept me glued to my television set. Nixon told us that we would stay in Vietnam until the South Vietnamese could defend themselves. He thought we should not destroy our allies. The obstruction to a peace settlement was Hanoi's refusal to join the United States in finding the right way to peace. More American boys could be brought home depending on the size in the scale of fighting. In no way, would Nixon be swayed by demonstrations in the streets about the Vietnam War policies. He assured us that the United States plan was not an easy way but the right thing to do.

Nixon concluded,

"And so tonight—to you the great silent majority of my fellow Americans—I ask for your support.

'I pledged in my campaign for the Presidency to end the war in a way that we could win the peace. I have initiated a plan of action, which will enable me to keep that pledge.

'The more support I can have from the American people, the sooner that the pledge can be redeemed; for the more divided we are at home the less likely the enemy is to negotiate at Paris.

'Let us be united for peace. Let us also be united against defeat. Because, let us understand: North Vietnam cannot defeat or humiliate the United States. Only Americans can do that."

After that I listened to the television network commentators, I was furious. They criticized Dick's motives and his very words. Personally, I thought they were talking about something else. It sure was biased in their talk and did not present impartial summaries about the speech. They just attacked President Nixon instead.

Pat said the White House switchboard lit up from the moment Dick concluded his speech. I sent a telegram congratulating him about not caving in to the protestors demonstrating violently out in the streets. The Silent Majority answered. More than 50 thousand telegrams and 30 thousand letters came in support of the President. I was happy to learn that this was the biggest response to a presidental speech. As the telegrams piled up on his desk, Dick was really pleased at the public's reaction. Last week he was down in the valley of discouragement, but this week he was on the mountaintop because of a public turn-around in attitude.

But, best of all the two men, Bill Cahill of New Jersey and Linwood Holton of Virginia, who Nixon had campaigned for Governor were winners in their races. To celebrate, Dick invited them to a victory lunch at the White House.

Some wanted all of our military troops out of Vietnam by the end of next year. It was Nixon's goal to move all of U.S. troops out of the combat zone before the November 1970 election. But, that was not to be. However, he said, "If it does succeed, what the critics say now won't matter. If it does not succeed anything I say then won't matter." With that viewpoint, we could all agree.

Pat and Dick flew to Key Biscayne, Florida, to relax a couple of days. While they were there, 150 militant anti Vietnam demonstrators picketed the Nixon's Florida home. Another group marched expressing their support of Nixon's plan in Vietnam. The Dade County deputy sheriffs came out to help the Secret Service agents.

The protestors signs read; "Love your enemies, Nixon is a cop-out," "Tricky Dick kills for peace," and "Nixon drinks in blood of American soldiers." They were identified with the group who would march in Washington, D.C. on November 15th. "Revolution" and the New Party of Florida.

The other side carried signs, too. It read—"Give Nixon a chance," Peace, yes; Surrender no,' "What will be left after the new left?"

One person was arrested for using foul-mouth profanity and assaulting a federal officer.

Just before the Nixons arrived in Florida, the Secret Service had moved into Miami and awaited a George W. Baker, until he came home from his Pan American World Airway job. Apparently, this man had wrote Nixon in May and said if his son was killed in the Vietnam War he would kill every federal official he could find—even the President of the United States. It contained a veiled threat to the President. So everyone at the White Hose noticed the statement.

The Secret Service agents went to his house. Inside this man got a drop on the agents with his high-powered rifle. He was captured without anybody killed or injured. Also, the agents seized the telescopic sight rifle along with 3 pistols and 3 other rifles.

November 11, Tuesday, was Veteran's Day. Nixon observed this day by going to the Veteran's hospital and visiting our American veteran military who were ill or wounded. He wanted no press coverage and no one to go with him. Just him alone except the Secret Service. Dick did not wish to gain by turning someone's unfortunate condition to his advantage. The boys thanked him personally for taking a tour for them outside his busy schedule of appointments.

Thursday evening, more people were walking around the White House carrying candles and posters listing the soldiers' names who had already died in the Vietnam War. So far it was peaceful and quiet. Mostly young kids parading, but there were a few kooky ones among their midst.

That same night V.P. Spiro Agnew attacked TV Network newscasters for their biased views. The public responded once again as they did for Nixon's November 3rd speech. It pleased both of them. But the media said the Nixon administration was assaulting the freedom of the press. That concerned Pat about the turn around of the media's focus.

Friday, November 14th, Pat and Dick departed early in the morning for Cape Kennedy for the start of the flight to the moon. When they arrived a rainstorm greeted them. After getting drenched, they had to take shelter under an umbrella watching the launch of Apollo 12. Three Apollo 12 astronauts in their space suits entered at the Saturn 5 rocket launching pad. The rocket disappeared in the low clouds and could not be seen anymore. Then, they went back to Washington, D.C.

That night the Vietnam protestors marched again. They were roaming the streets and smashing everything in their sight. As they arrived near the Vietnamese embassy, the police broke up the crowd with tear gas. No one wanted to go outside because of the irrational demonstrators in the streets.

November 15, 1969, Saturday the Vietnam Moratorium New Mobe Day arrived. It broke out in San Francisco and Washington, D.C. It was alarming to see 250,000 to 350,000 militant crowds descend on Washington, D.C. They were itching for violent confrontation with President Nixon. Also, some of them were out demonstrating and yelling, "We will kill Richard Nixon. We will kill anyone that stands in the way of our freedom." In Washington, Dick Gregory of the Black Panthers said, "The President says nothing that you kids do will have any effect on him, well I suggest he make one long distance call to the LBJ Ranch."

The White House was barricaded around a two-block and by huge buses. No one or anything else was able to get through. The police wore gas masks and helmets and stood by for action. The protestors knocked out windows along the streets as they passed by. That afternoon they besieged the Justice Department. The tear gas smell was really strong and bad in the U.S. Attorney General's office. An American flag was tore down, stomped on, and burned, and a Viet Cong flag hung in its place.

Since the Nixons private quarters were quite a ways from the street, Pat said she couldn't hear any special commotion or noise from the demonstrators. Although, she did read the newspapers about the dissenters and heard it on the television newscast. She advised that protestors should find ways to work through the system. Pat stated that the Nixon administration was always open to young people as well as others. Too bad our young people are lumped together and judged by the few in the streets. I am proud of the good work young people do. Glad to hear from them."

Pat and Dick had invited more than 200 older senior citizens to a big White House turkey dinner. November 27, 1969, Thursday, Julie and David Eisenhower came also for the special Thanksgiving dinner. After words of welcome and philosophy to the senior guests from the old-age homes, President Nixon asked whether anyone was 98 years old—no one answered, so Dick asked if anyone present was over 90. "We think of you as family, speak up."

There was an old, white-haired man, John W. Graves, from Missouri, who was slightly stooped, stood up and said, "I am 93, I was born August 7, 1876 in Neosho, Missouri, and I never had a sick day in my life."

Dick was especially pleased and grinned. "Lets give a hand to all our oldest guests. We are happy to have you. Did you know this state dining room has honored kings, emperors, prime-ministers and other presidents and now you are honored?" From the very heart of our country,—Missouri, we have this guest. I'm sure that President Truman is glad you are here. Also, I am going to tell my Secretary of Health, Education and Welfare to come to talk to you and get your formula for healthy living, so we can pass it around. May you have many happy birthdays in the future."

Afterwards, Pat and Dick left for Key Biscayne with Julie, Tricia, and David for peace and quiet away from the hustle and bustle of Washington.

The TV network reporters underestimated the public viewers response. The public became the vocal majority once again. Letters, petitions, and telegrams poured into Congressional offices for supporting President Nixon in his policy in the Vietnam War. The people had spoken. Therefore, Congress had to change their opinion. They co-sponsored a resolution backing on what Nixon had been saying. President Nixon had went to the people over the heads of the media and the protestors, and they rallied behind him. As far as I was concerned, Nixon's ability to reach out to people was a political masterpiece. He spoke to our hearts and encouraged us to do something about it.

As 1969 was drawing to a close, I remember that Richard Nixon was the first President in 120 years to begin his presidential term with the Senate and the House of Representatives in Congress controlled by the Democrats— the opposition party. In spite of his enthusiasm and determination, Nixon was resisted by Congress on many domestic programs he proposed, tax reform, reorganization of foreign aid, welfare-to-work, electoral reform, and drug and pornography and crime control. His tax bill and draft reform did pass. Surely Richard Nixon was being hit from all sides.

November 19, 1969, James J. Rowley, Director of U.S. Secret Service issued a memorandum to the White House Staff concerning food and beverage and Rosemary Woods sent me a copy.

Ardis Larson and I decided to go to Washington to see the lighting of the Yule tree before the Christmas holidays and the decorations at the White House. It was very cold and windy on Tuesday, December 16th, when President Nixon pushed the button to light the National Christmas tree. Five thousand red and white lights on the 65 foot high Norway spruce illuminated the whole area and was a beautiful sight to behold.

The ceremony was held on the Ellipse south of the White House. It marked the opening of the 1969 Christmas Pageant of Peace sponsored by the National Park Service. Among the crowd was a large group of peace demonstrators waving the Viet Cong flags. As soon as President Nixon began to speak, they started shouting and causing all kinds of disturbances. Personally, I didn't think no one should put up with that nonsense and spoil the true spirit of the moment. Dick did ignore them but I was sure he was angry inside. At least he didn't show it outwardly.

Then, we arrived back at the White House. Christmas is a family time for the Nixons. They always open their gifts on Christmas morning. Each member of the family, and the dogs, too, had red knit stockings hanging from the fireplace mantel. It was really beautiful and colorful. Pat had personally supervised the Christmas decorations. As we glanced around, it sure was going to be a red, green and gold Christmas at the Nixon White House.

The 19-foot fir tree in the lobby was decorated with large velvet and satin Christmas balls. We discovered that each of the 50 balls had the state flowers on it as well the name of the State. Large golden roping interlaced the tree.

Pat really made this Christmas at the White House aglow with glittering trees and an abundance of Della Robbia wreaths of fruits and pinecones. Much of the fruit was real and she hoped visitors wouldn't pick up any fruit. The apples, pears, grapes, lemons and limes sure looked appetizing.

Green wreaths and candles hung in the windows facing Pennsylvania Avenue. Red, blue and gold balls hung from the chandeliers and lighted wreaths in the windows as Pat had done in the past in their homes. All the fireplaces were lit, too. Red and white poinsettias were everywhere in tubs in the Green, Red and Blue Rooms.

In the East Room we viewed the 18th century Italian crèche with hand carved wooden Nativity figures surrounded by masses of red poinsettias. Even the State Dining Room had a freshly baked gingerbread house. We were thankful for the chance to see personally the Christmas decorations at the White House. Perhaps, we wouldn't have that privilege to do so in the future.

I didn't know how Pat and Dick could sleep in the White House. It was too noisy—parties breaking up, the sounds of moving chairs from the East Room and tourists making their rounds through the White House. It was worse than a hotel!

Chapter 15

I REMEMBER PAT AND RICHARD NIXON BOMBINGS, TERRORISTS, AND VISITS HERE AND ABROAD 1970

As the year of 1970 was ushered in, I was wondering if it would be for better or worse for our country. Would we have inflation or a recession, more crime or less, and would the Vietnam War be drawn to a close? There were many things, which occupied our minds. The Sixties were turbulent years—demonstrations seeking to change any perceived wrong or dissent about the Vietnam War—and it continued into 1970. Perhaps, We thought the beginning of the Seventies would be different from what we encountered in the Sixties.

For several days, President Nixon isolated himself at San Clemente to work on his budget and the State of the Union message. He would take a break and play a round of golf or take a scenic drive along the California coast. Before he was ready to leave for Washington, D.C., Pat, Tricia and Dick went to the Orange County Courthouse at Santa Ana to register for the 1970 California elections.

President Nixon was 57 years old on Friday, January 9, 1970. He was pleased that his White House staff had surprised him with a birthday party. Most of all, he was delighted with their birthday gift—a reproduction of the front page of the "The Washington Evening Star" edition of January 9, 1913 on it, "Future President Born," was headlined in the paper and listed under a Yorba Linda, California dateline.

That evening, the Nixons made a quick flight to Northampton, Massachusetts for a birthday celebration at Julie and David's apartment. Julie, now a 21-year-old senior at Smith College, personally prepared roast turkey, celery dressing, broccoli casserole and the rest of dinner. The White House chef sent a chocolate fudge cake—"Happy Birthday, Daddy"—long for the occasion.

After the meal, Pat gave Dick a pair of black house slippers. Julie presented a gold-frame photograph of her father and herself, taken the day of the wedding. Tricia gave a brown leather collar and leash for father's Irish setter—King Timahoe. I gave a "Moody Daily Reminder" book and a card and some news clippings about certain issues he was interested in. It was a very delightful and enthusiastic birthday party.

However, outside several hundred people had welcomed them to Northampton. But, now the crowd had taken on a differing shade.

The crowd chanted, "One, two, three, four, Richard Nixon stop the war." Some hollered "Tricky Dickie," instead for "Richard Nixon." Some of the chanters held white cardboard crosses as they chanted.

Richard Nixon ignored the chanters. But as he was ready to leave, he turned around and waved. The other part of the crowd cheered and drowned out the noise of the chanters.

Back in Washington, the budget proposal President Nixon had sent to Congress showed a surplus budget for fiscal 1971 by one billion dollars—providing Congress would approve four or five billion of new taxes. Nixon was opposed to any $1.2 billion added to the budget at the last minute by Labor and Health, Education and Welfare because it was "inflationary." It would be vetoed.

Dick relied on Haldeman too much. Somewhere down the road, the chickens would come home to roost. Haldeman was ruthless. No one wanted to argue or cross paths with him. Once again, he tried to interfere with Pat Nixon's approval of the personal family menus, in addition to the State Dinners and other official White House functions. It was a cause of friction between Pat and Haldeman. The First Lady's office staff in the East Wing became dissatisfied with Haldeman's interference.

Pat always liked healthful meals. She didn't have to count her calories because she was naturally slender. All I had to do was to smell good food and I put on pounds.

Dick Nixon avoided gaining weight by not snacking between meals, eating smaller portions at lunch or dinner. He really used a lot of discipline when it came to partaking of food. There were many evening dinners and receptions held at the White House, so their lunch at noontime had to be light—a fruit plate with cottage cheese or some other interesting salad plate with banana bread.

Everyone adored Pat's meat loaf. It had been a part of the Nixon household since they were married. No wonder it appeared on the White House menu at least once a month.

The Nixons enjoyed Chinese, Mexican, and Italian food. Spaghetti was one of their favorite dishes. When he was Senator and Vice President, Pat would always celebrate by making a pot of spaghetti and sauce, and serve it with meatballs and garlic bread. Dick would toss the salad and open the wine.

They usually would drink dry wines when guests would join them for dinner. Otherwise, they drank a lot of ice water.

Pat would approve all the menus for up-coming State Dinners, as well as their family meals; President Nixon selected the wines. If the menu was fish, Dick would select a German wine. With all meats, California red wine was served. Desserts usually had French Champagne provided. Sometimes American wines were supplied at special events.

President Nixon was concerned about the Republic of Biafra, a former African secessionist state, formed in 1967 in S W Nigeria. The IBOS, an ethnic group, who feared they could not survive within Nigeria. Fighting had erupted between Nigerian and Biafran forces. During the war more than one million Biafran civilians had died of starvation or were massacred. So Dick contacted Britain's Prime Minister Wilson on Sunday January 7, 1970 to discuss how food and medicine could be flown to Africa to help the people fleeing to safety.

Nixon was going over the final draft of his State of Union speech in the Lincoln sitting room. He liked to work alone there or at Camp David. As usual, Dick wanted a fire in the fireplace while he was making changes and additions in his speech. Pat said the smoke/fire alarm went off in the White House. Immediately the fire trucks rolled up in answer to the alarm. It was only Dick trying to light a fire. Everyone rushed in to discover a smoke filled room and an embarrassed frustrated President. The firemen had the delightful experience to instruct the President how to make a fire in the fireplace.

Now the White House police had new white and gold uniforms. As I looked at their military style hats with the fancy plumes, I was wondering what inspired Nixon to go European with the polices formal and military attire.

Then, I found out that Haldeman and the White House staff and the Secret Service approved the whole idea of uniforms. Of course, the press made fun of it. Every newspaper and television commentators mentioned it often, and the cartoonists had a field day about the uniforms. There was a huge flap. It was Pat who encouraged others that this was a bad idea. No wonder the uniforms were discarded!

Red Skelton, the popular comedian, was the first to perform at the "Evenings at the White House," January 29, 1970, He kept all of us in stitches with his good sense of humor. Pat and Dick had a really good time laughing at Skelton's jokes. We all wanted more and hoped every new program would be a smashing event as this one was.

At the White House church services black actress and gospel singer Ethel Waters brought tears to our eyes after her performance. Because of her generous size, she was provided a very large chair for her to sit on. Ethel sang three songs during the service. One was, "His Eye Is On The Sparrow," which touched my heart as well as the others guests.

Some several hundred friends and government officials joined Pat and Dick at the private worship services to hear the 74 year old black singer and Richard Nixon's Quaker minister, T. Eugene Coffin, from the Whittier Friends meeting in California. This was the first time there had been a minister from Nixon's home church in Whittier.

At the beginning Nixon's minister invoked a moment of silent prayer, which was typical of Quaker meetings. Dick recalled later that he and his parents would sometimes sit in total silence for 30 to 35 minutes. When we come in to a church service, do we babble to one another or do we take the time to talk to God and meditate on spiritual things? Perhaps, the Quaker Friends have something for us to think about.

The minister delivered his sermon on "The Evidence of Hope." At the end of the sermon, Coffin concluded, "It is a great hope in the hearts of millions that a just and lasting peace will be realized and that your dream, Mr. President, of a generation of peace will be a reality."

Before Ethel Waters departed, President Nixon told her, "You are the only one, I'll tell you."

Ethel Waters replied, "Oh, honey, anytime I get a chance to open my mouth and make a loud voice for my Savior—that's my thing." She kissed Pat Nixon and Richard Nixon goodbye as she left.

Prayer was important in Dick Nixon's life. It was center of his life. He attended Chapel at Duke University regularly. Hannah, his mother, wanted him to be a Quaker minister, but God had other plans. Even when his mother didn't want him to go into the armed services, he enlisted. While in the services in the South Pacific, he told us he read his Bible everyday. I knew Dick went off to pray alone during the 1960 campaign. In all his struggles and doubts, Richard Nixon consulted with God in a private personal way, "God's will be done, not mine."

When certain persons told me that they didn't think President Nixon was not active or progressive in domestic affairs of our country, I challenged them to look at his record. He wanted the power to go back to the people states, and cities—at the local level—where it should belong, working together to solve problems. Instead of talking about problems, Dick wanted to find solutions to correct whatever was wrong. He was trying to show others that he did care—not by words but by actions and deeds.

Therefore, President Nixon and Pat acted on their thoughts and words and decided to take the White House on tour early in February back to the people. Their first stop was Indianapolis, Indiana.

Dick explained the reason for their visit to a friendly crowd: "I want Washington to know the nation better than it does. We are bringing to Indianapolis and other cities. This is a theme I wish to emphasize. For a half a century, power has been flowing from the cities and states to Washington, D.C. It's about time the people at the local level has the power."

While there he conferred with nine mayors regarding crime problems. The mayors seemed pleased with the

President's visit. Most of the mayors did most of the talking, and Nixon did the listening. Dick thought government officials did talk too much.

Although Pat accompanied Dick and Cabinet officials and advisors, she had a travel agenda of her own. She visited the Noble Center for Retarded Children and listened to their music class. The children gave her a large box of Valentine's Day candy. Then, Pat toured the Christamore house, a social and recreational center to see what was being done about urban problems. She honored a volunteer worker there.

A huge reception line formed to meet Pat Nixon. She greeted 200 people shaking hands and chatting with them after all that hand shaking, Pat's smile was still radiant as ever.

After a tiring afternoon in Indianapolis, Pat and Dick headed for Chicago, Illinois. The smog over Chicago reminded them of Los Angeles. It obscured their view and filtered the sunshine to the residents below. They found out later Chicago had the second dirtiest air in the nation. There they attended another two hours of hand shaking at a reception held by Governor Ogilive in Sheraton Blackstone hotel that night. Pat looked lovely in her pink velveteen and silver sequins dress. Dick never stopped smiling for the guests in the reception line, once and awhile he spotted someone from years ago and they chatted amicably.

Some Democrats decided to attend and greet President Nixon at the reception. Why not? Wasn't he the President of all the people? Even though, Mayor Richard Daley Sr. met the Nixons at their arrival at Meigs Field with the Democrat Party faithful, apparently Daley and his party workers didn't have the heart and soul to show up at the reception. The greeting of a Republican President at the airport was enough for most of them.

Outside the hotel, anti-war demonstrators paraded peacefully in front of the hotel. Many carried posters—"Free The Panthers—Jail Nixon." The leader of the protest group was arrested for obstructing pedestrian traffic and not obeying police orders.

The nest day Pat's schedule was much more active and difficult than Dick's. While President Nixon met with the governors of the states bordering Lake Michigan to discuss the environmental crisis of pollution, she rose early to board a train for a 70-mile trip from Chicago to Commonwealth Edison's Company's Dresden nuclear power generation plant at the town of Morris.

Pat only wanted to emphasize the positive side in the fight against pollution. She sat patiently through the lectures explaining the construction and operation of nuclear plants and peaceful uses of atomic energy. As Pat looked down five floors down to the gurgling heart of the nuclear reactor, which had not been energized, she was struck with awe at the sight.

As she emerged from the plant, Pat decided to have a little fun with the crowd of newsmen. She held up a tiny round cylinder and told the press:

"Look out! It's radium. They gave it to me. Wasn't that nice?"

It was really funny to see the news persons jump back. Pat put the cylinder in her coat pocket and said:

"Oh, it was just a little piece of rubber tile I picked up. I thought I would have some fun with it."

For once, Pat got one back on the press. I bet some of the press never forgot that incident either. I didn't.

Because of her former X-ray work in hospitals, she understood quite a bit of the technical workings of the plant. The most important thing she learned there was that this plant did not cause pollution. Pat again boarded the train for a short tour through the Goose Lake State prairie area. Small groups of children with parents lined the track to wave and cheer. That delighted Pat.

Pat was particularly interested in the Goose Lake Prairie. It is virgin land that was saved. That meant a great treat to her. She always loved the outdoors. She was real pleased that he prairie would be conserved for the children of the future.

For Pat Nixon, she was having the best time she had in a long while.

She enjoyed her horse and farm wagon tour ride over frozen streams. It brought back memories of riding horses when she was a girl in Artesia, California.

Pat was having so much fun bouncing up and down in the horse drawn farm wagon she startled everyone by yelling, "Hi-Ho-Silver!" She even laughed at her Secret Service agent when he thought he was going to fall off the wagon during their fast ride.

Everyone was bone-chilled after the afternoon open wagon ride, but Pat's fingertips were cold. She was hoping to come back to visit in the spring. It would be a glorious time for her. Pat Nixon's trip was not designed for pleasure and fascination. The wind was raw and her brown eyes glistened with a little tears.

Her last big sight on the tour included the Peabody Coal Company's strip mines. Pat had never been so close to a coalmine before and found it fascinating. They showed her a large wheeled digging machine—a giant—that chewed up the earth to obtain coal. After the mining was finished, the Peabody Coal Company regraded the land. It brought in more topsoil and trees to form pastures, recreational areas and produce tree farms. Pat was pleased with their reclamation work. She assured them she would tell her husband, the President about it.

The Goose Lake Club ladies had prepared tiny cakes and finger sandwiches. But, Pat didn't have time for lunch. She grabbed a small cake on the run. Also, Pat was concerned about her daughter Tricia, ill with measles in Key Biscayne, Florida. Measles can be serious. Tricia already had them a week and now it may take another week to get over them. Pat planned to be with Tricia over the weekend.

While Pat was gone on her tour trip, Dick had his own agenda in place. First he motorcaded from the Sheraton Blackstone Hotel to Meigs field for a helicopter ride to Schaumburg airport. Before leaving to inspect Hanover Park sewage treatment plant, he slipped attempting to climb on the hood of auto at the Schaumburg Airport. Several aides came to his rescue and helped Nixon upon the car to address the crowd.

Noting that most of the crowd was young people Nixon said:

"Many of you have been let out of class to come here. So you had better get something to write about when you get back. I'd like to give you three new R's." So Dick named them out:

"Reform government institutions to bring them up to date to the 20th century.

"Restore the natural resources of this nation so the younger generation does not inherit a country where our air is filled with smog, our water polluted and our parks desolated because we didn't do the proper planning.

"Renewal of the spirit of America . . . . Sometimes you may get depressed because of foreign and domestic problems. But you've got to have faith in this country. My object for coming to Illinois was to bring Washington to the people instead of bringing more people to Washington. We want to see to it that you young people have a country like we inherited. We don't want natural history museums to be the only places to go to where you can see clean air and water. This part of the country has always been a can-do part of the country. We will bring back to Washington a spirit that says, "Yes, there are problems out here—there's a lake to be cleaned up—but we have the determination to do it.

The crowd cheered and bundled up spectators stretched forth their hands to shake the hands of Richard Nixon. Nixon enlisted the young people there in the war on pollution and they volunteered to do something about it.

Along the motorcade route to the Hanover Park plant, hundreds and hundreds of people were dispersed hoping to get a glimpse or a handshake from President Nixon. At the experimental Sanitary District facility in Hanover Park, Dick examined what was done there. The air there was odorless and the crowd friendly. Everything was going all right for Dick Nixon. The plant extracted 99% of the solid wastes from the sewage and then ran it through a third step treatment of wastewater emptying into the river.

Outside the plant on a table were four jars of water—one containing water of the three-step treatment at various stages. No one could tell the difference from the regular drinking water. Nixon didn't volunteer to drink a glass of water either. He thought the name of these plants should be changed from "sewage treatment" plants to "water reclamation" plants. Personally, I thought that was a good idea too—it sounded much better.

That morning at the Field Museum of Natural History in Chicago, President Nixon planned to let the governors of Illinois, Indiana, Wisconsin, and Michigan have the chance to tell what to do about pollution. It was the first U.S. Cabinet-level meeting held outside the White House. Eight Cabinet member and other government leaders beside Senator Charles Percy of Illinois, attended the conference meeting.

Outside the Field Museum, demonstrators paraded. Some held posters—"America's Air—Breathe It Or Leave It." Inside the only form of mild pollution was Illinois Governor Ogilvie's pipe smoking.

Nixon knew he could get more from the governors and wanted to hear the governors speak up. He knew what he was going to do about it. Governor Richard Ogilvie decided to challenge President Nixon about Illinois's problem concerning Lake Michigan "death" from water pollution. He wanted the President to supply new federal aid and controls to help Illinois. Of course, the governors from the other states chimed in their thoughts about saving Lake Michigan and the right to breathe clean air.

Before Dick had left on his tour, he had taken already an important step in solving the pollution problem. He issued a White House executive order requiring all federal agencies to comply with state water and air-standards by 1973. Military bases and other federal establishments had to eliminate pollution in the next three years.

President Nixon said there would be more visits like this one. It was his concept of the "New Federalism" with city and state governments working together on general problems. From Illinois Pat and Dick flew to Washington, D.C. and then to Key Biscayne to be with Tricia recovering from a bout of the measles.

Some of us in the Metropolitan Republican Women's club wanted to reactivate the Pueblo Grande Republican Women and pick up their charter. After the meeting, I was nominated and elected to be President of the new group. It was a challenge but our club grew quickly. I received an award for an increase in club membership. The news for the honor spread to the Nixon White House, and they were happy about it.

Tricia's birthday was February 21. She could not go out in public because she still had some skin discoloration from her long siege of measles. Therefore, the Nixon family flew by helicopter to Camp David to celebrate Tricia's twenty-fourth birthday. Pat had the pastry chef at the White House to bake a birthday cake that Tricia always liked—white cake with white icing and pink trim.

Julie and David flew back from college to help Tricia celebrate. Edward Cox from Yale, a frequent escort of Tricia's was invited as well as some family friends.

That night President and Mrs. Nixon were back in time to see the Broadway musical "1776" which was being put on in the East Room.

If President Nixon didn't have enough foreign problems overseas on February 24th he was having predicaments and demonstrations on the home front to exasperate him. French President Georges Pompidou was paying a State visit to the United States. But Pompidou encountered jostling, jeering demonstrations in Chicago, which did not represent the view of most Americans.

It only took a few people to make things look bad for the rest of us. The authorities there had not taken the necessary precautions to prevent the demonstrators from almost insulting Mr. and Mrs. Pompidou.

Jewish organizations and their political friends announced they had planned anti-Pompidou rallies during his stay in New York. Their protests were against the sale of 110 French mirage jets to the Arab state of Libya.

The Jews feared the jets might be used against the state of Israel.

Nixon was disgusted with Governor Nelson Rockefeller and Mayor John Lindsey who declined to meet Pompidou officially because of the Libya deal or attend the dinner at the Waldorf-Astoria in his honor. President Nixon always felt strongly that when a head of State was invited to our country and is our official guest, he or she should receive courteous treatment, even though, we might disagree with them on certain points.

Also he was annoyed with Senators in Congress who did nothing to save South Vietnam from communist domination but gave lip service to Israel. When the chips are down, their true colors will show. They cut and run. Nixon was for Israel in Middle East because they were pro-freedom. He never intended that Israel would go down the drain but at all times he would have an absolute commitment for them. However, he wouldn't tolerate behavior that was not right or just as uncontrolled by conscience toward any official guest of the United States.

When Dick heard that Mrs. Pompidou was so shook up by the incident in Chicago and wanted to go home because of it, he decided to do something about it. On Monday, March 2nd afternoon, he took Tricia his daughter, and Henry Kissinger with him to the Waldorf-Astoria in New York at the dinner to show Pompidou that the demonstrators did not represent the view of all the Americans.

Nixon apologized to Pompidou for the hostile demonstrations he faced in Chicago. Pompidou praised Nixon for flying to New York. Then and there, French and American relations were cemented because of Nixon's one moment of kindness and courtesy. Even Mayor John Lindsey saw the light and appealed to the New York citizenry to give Pompidou courteous treatment at all costs.

However, Nixon had assured Israel if a crisis would occur, the United States would always be on Israel's side. His decision to postpone delivery of the Phantom Jets to Israel at that time caused an uproar in Congress and the press. That very morning of March 2nd, Pat began her weeklong scheduled trip to visit student college volunteer programs in Michigan, Kentucky, Ohio, Colorado, and Missouri. Pat's big blue and white jet with the U.S. seal across it, landed at Capitol City Airport in Lansing Michigan.

It was wet drizzly and a cold wind that chilled the air, but the warm welcome cheered Pat Nixon's heart. Immediately, she was surrounded by a sea of students from elementary, junior and senior high schools. The Girl Scouts, the Sexton High School Band and many other people were also there. Pat was pleased to see a large crowd to come out in such bad weather. After shaking hand with Governor William G. Milliken and Mayor Gerald Graves, Pat received a legislative proclamation in her honor.

Michigan State University (MSU) volunteer services had the largest program of 10,000 students doing some volunteer work during the year. Thousands of volunteer students worked on a weekly basis. MSU was the first school in the United States to set up a separate office with full time coordinator dedicated to volunteer programs. The Volunteer Program director said, "There was no point for Pat Nixon to come on campus since all the projects are in the field—the town. There would be dialogue between the students and the First Lady.

When someone asked if she was avoiding college campus unrest, Pat said she would only go where the action was. She believed that protesting should be in a positive fashion. Neither did Pat accuse the news media coverage of campus demonstrators, but she suggested that they follow the other students around and see what they do for the communities.

Sitting an example, Pat Nixon set out to do just that. She sought college students in action—protesting a lack of concern for others—a peaceful volunteer commitment helping others. Pat was hoping volunteerism would become the thing to do with people in our communities.

Pat Nixon visited the Michigan School of the Blind, a state operated institution, where, 67 Michigan State University students regularly worked with 280 blind pupils at the school. Some of the children were deaf as well being blind. Many of the M.S.U. students worked four to five hours a week and received one credit in Education 484 by volunteering 30 hours of service. The activities Pat observed were swimming, basketball, wrestling, weight lifting and bowling. She reached out to touch, caress, and hold four and five years old deaf and blind youngsters. Some children "read" the face of Pat as she visited with them. She told them that she had two little girls but they are grown up ladies now.

Then, Pat stopped at the Beekman Center for Trainable Children (facility for the mentally retarded). Patients of all ages were treated there. Some of the older persons won Pat's attention by telling her that they voted for her husband. Pat told them she was glad they did. The younger children wanted Pat to watch them feed pet lambs.

While there she also observed children in a physical therapy room, gymnasium, and a replica community street area. Seventy-five students worked at the Center, which included 40 MSU women from the Gamma Sigma Sigma sorority.

The next stop was Holt Home, a private nursing home. Pat grabbed the stiffen fingers of aging men and women and introduced her self. It took a few seconds and smiles finally broke out on aged faces. Also, Pat learned that the Brownie Scout Troop 247 "adopt" grandmothers—a resident of Holt Home and pay regular visits to their "adopted" grandmothers at this elderly facility.

When Pat Nixon arrived at the Grand River School (a public elementary school) the school day had just ended. Some children who were outside the building and were trying to get a glimpse of Pat Nixon through the school windows. Pat was watching an alphabet game. Then, a youthful chorus sang "Put A Little Love In Your Heart—and the world will be a better place—"and Pat smiled. By the end of the day, she had made many friends and left her loving and caring imprint on all she met.

Since everyone were to refrain from giving presents or refreshments to Pat during her tour, Pat Nixon surprised everyone at each of her stops by leaving surprise gifts. Each was wrapped in white paper and gold ribbons with the Presidential Seal.

Pat wanted to see volunteers in action at the universities of Kentucky, Cincinnati, and Colorado, and the School of the Ozarks in Missouri. Her itinerary would not take her directly on any campus except the single one at Point Lookout in the Ozarks. Wherever the volunteer work was done, she visited mental hospitals, day care center, nursing home and community centers, schools in town.

At several of her stops, she ran into small groups of demonstrators shouting and protesting about everything under the sun. Some signs greeted Pat, but there were no massive outbreaks of violence during the trip.

However, at the University of Colorado at Boulder, there were some bombings. The police encountered someone who had heard several men contemplating plotting to kill Pat Nixon. But, she ignored the danger. Pat realized that she and her husband, in spite of the protection of the Secret Service, would be open to attack whenever they would appear in public.

Every time I picked up a newspaper or watched the late news on television, I came to the conclusion that the 1970's would be no better than the year of 1969. Across the land, students were protesting admission school policies on blacks, the Vietnam War, the ROTC, burning buildings on campus, and holding college administrators, and government officials hostage, and committing arson and bombings.

The New York Times reported that there were 174 major bombings and bombing attempts on college campus in the 1969-1970 school year. I was thankful this did not occur on my Grand Canyon College campus. The students were different and had more constructive things to do.

March 6-a large townhouse in New York's Greenwich Village exploded. They found three bodies and 56 sticks of dynamite and plumbing pipes stuffed with roofing nails and dynamite. Apparently, the members of the Weathermen Underground died when they were making explosives.

March 12-the Revolution Force 9 group set bombs in three Manhattan New York buildings and 15,000 people had to be evacuated. Bomb scares totaled more than 400 in New York City alone.

No wonder Nixon was concerned about terrorist bombings across the country. Dick expressed fears that he and his family and other government officials would be the target of such attacks. He asked the Secret Service and the FBI whether everything possible was being done to catch the terrorists and to use any means necessary to find the fugitives.

March 14-President Nixon and Vice President Agnew decided to arrange a piano duet at the Gridiron. It was amazing to have two political figures playing old classic songs. The audience loved it. The songs were old favorites everyone remembered. The last time we had a piano-playing President was Harry Truman. But, to have a President and a Vice President playing pianos was truly surprising!

Dick was surrounded by many problems. If he didn't have the Vietnam War to worry about, it was the bombings occurring around the country and the school-busing situation.

The Nixons supported desegregation but opposed busing. They thought it was better to have the school-busing problem solved at the local level and keep the involvement of the federal government out of it. Dick asked for Billy Graham's help in getting voluntary support for integration in the South and elsewhere. Nixon was convinced that forced integration of education or housing was just as wrong as legal official segregation. He thought that busing poor black children to affluent white schools did not help them to learn. The home environment by parents would encourage children to succeed in life. He believed in neighborhood schools and improving education where they lived.

President Nixon believed that segregation was a national problem. He worked with people instead of denouncing them. His solution to the problem led to the diminishing of the violence erupting in the Black communities.

Sixty five Black men and women were put in top Federal policy making and executive positions, such as State, and Treasury, and Defense, Justice, and Labor Department, Ambassadors and much more.

Then, on March 19, the postal workers called a wildcat strike in New York. It really irritated President Nixon. He was ready to fire all of them. Dick did not believe Federal employees should go on strike. As far as he was concerned, the postal workers were working for the taxpayers.

First, there was a settlement but then the workers refused to go back to work. The walkout had now spread to other major cities. Dick was worried that the postal workers strike would become nationwide and the need to call in troops to make certain the delivery of the mail. Also, this could spread to other groups, such as Air Traffic Controllers, etc, which would cripple the nation at once. He didn't want to over react, but he didn't want things to get worse either.

Then, on March 23, President Nixon ordered troops to take over essential mail services. I was glad he was firm and tough on the postal situation, and I wrote him regarding it. Dick responded thanking me for my encouraging comments. With the school busing and the postal strike on the people's minds, the Vietnam War for the moment slid to the back of our busy brains. However, the air controllers threatened to strike. It created just another problem to solve.

By April 2nd, the postal workers decided to go back to work. We were all glad about that, but the air controllers were still a problem. Dick threatened to fire each one if they went on strike. In spite of all these situations, President Nixon took time for the Duke and Duchess of Windsor and invited them for dinner.

He was still concerned about how things get leaked to the Press. Usually, Dick would go to Camp David or for a boat ride to get rid of the stress and resentment concerning the job. This would calm him down just to get-away-from it all.

Then, we learned in April that the Apollo XIII astronauts were having problems on their way to the moon. Fire and power failure caused an explosion in space. We wondered if the astronauts would make it back to earth. But they arrived safely in the splashdown. Pat and Dick greeted them in Hawaii. Everything went well, regardless of the press reactions.

Usually, President Nixon would get up as early as 5:00 a.m. to dictate his morning dictation if he could not sleep. He was very energetic in spite of little sleep. Otherwise, he would be in his office around 7:15 a.m. in the morning cranking his staff to go forward in high gear.

He was really bothered by how the communists had responded to his televised speech of troop withdrawal. Instead, they stepped up their attacks in all Indochina. I understood that President Nixon wanted to protect our U.S. troops in Vietnam and guarantee the success of the withdrawal.

As I watched on TV the map he was using, I came to the conclusion about the geographic, strategic importance of the communist Cambodian sanctuaries. It would be a joint effort of U.S. troops and South Vietnamese armies to go into Fishhook and Parrot's Beak where the Communists Vietnamese where already occupied in Cambodia. Nixon did not want to expand the war he had inherited. Neither did he want to abandon the millions of Vietnamese people to a horrible living death. I could see that the communists had already invaded Cambodia and he was making a painful decision to do something about it. The rest of our world did not utter one word of protest about that.

I could not believe they would condemn Richard Nixon for this action. But, some did. I knew that Dick thought President Johnson's bombing halt caused an escalation of the war. The biggest mistake our country made was we did not stay with it in 1968 and put the pressure on the communists Vietnamese then. However Nixon's action on the war led to more wide spread protests and fire bombings.

Every time I turned on the television news, I saw how violent our nation had become. The violence of April 1970 became etched in my mind. At my home state of Kansas, they set fire to the buildings of the University of Kansas. The most shocking incident occurred in California at Stanford University's behavioral studies center. The firebomb destroyed everything in sight. A lifetime of work and research went up in flames. Even, the Yale Law School did not escape the anger and fire of the radical protesters.

On May 1st, President Nixon announced that Sunday would be a national day of prayer for all American prisoners of wars and MIA—missing in action servicemen. He said the United States government was making every effort to relieve the anxiety of the P.O.W. families.

In his proclamation Nixon said, "One of the cruelest tactics of the war in Vietnam is the Communists' refusal to identify all prisoners of war, to provide information about them and to permit their families to communicate with them regularly. I urge all Americans to offer prayers on behalf of these men, to instill courage and perseverance in their hearts and the hearts of their loved ones and compassion in the hearts of their captors."

President Nixon took off for a Pentagon briefing. While there speaking off-the-cuff to a group of Pentagon workers, he compared the most savage campus demonstrators with U.S. soldiers in the Vietnam War.

Nixon said: "You see, these bums you know, blowing up campuses today are the luckiest people in the world going to the greatest universities, and here they are burning up books, storming around about this issue. You name it. Get rid of the war and there will be another issue."

"Then out there in Vietnam we have kinds who are just doing their duty. They stand tall and they are proud. I am sure they are scared. I was when I was there. But when it really comes down to it, they stand up and boys, you have to talk up to those men. They are going to do fine and we have to stand in back of them."

Of course, the remarks were leaked to the press. The media coverage and the misinterpretation of the spontaneous remarks caused much controversy. Many protestors used the "bums" remark as an excuse for propelling obscene harangues and violent pillage on campuses across our nation.

When everyone we clamoring to find out the reason for the "bum" remark, Richard Nixon explained:

"I received a letter from Professor M.N. Srinivas, an Indian anthropologist at Stanford University, who had worked 20 years compiling research notes on a subject he had hoped to write an important paper.

"He had written to me as President and told me how the Stanford building was broken in and set afire. His 20 years scholarly work went up in flames and was destroyed. It took only one person to do this."

"Then President Nixon said, "The guy who did that is a "bum." Personally, I agreed, but I would have called that person a worst name.

Whenever I hear Kent State mentioned it brings back many memories of what happened then. More than 400 colleges called for student boycott of classes on May 1, Friday. However, at Kent State there was no strike, but the students decided to bury the U.S. Constitution and claim that President Nixon had slaughtered it.

Crowds of drunken students spilled into downtown that evening. They were shouting anti-Nixon and Agnew slogans. The protestors built a trash bonfire and blocked off the streets with cars. The students smashed storefront windows. Theaters were closed. A curfew was ordered for the campus and the whole town. Gasoline could not be sold because everyone was afraid the radical protestors might make Molotov cocktails and use it against others.

Saturday night, two young men came on Kent State University and burned the R.O.T.C. building down while several hundred demonstrators watched. The National Guard was ordered in by Governor Rhodes to break up the demonstrations. He said, "Most of the students wanted the school to remain open, and the rest are the worse type of people in America."

Monday morning several hundred protestors confronted

the National Guardsmen who were armed with bayonets on their rifles. Then, the crowd of protestors gradually increased to about 2,000. The campus police ordered the student demonstrators to break up and go home.

But, they refused and answered them with sneers and jeers, of "Pigs—get off our campus" and "one, two, three, four, we don't want your fucking war."

They became more menacing and noisier. The Guard fired tear gas among the group. Instead, the students cast rocks and bottles back at the Guardsmen. The students broke up into two groups and had the Guardsmen retreating back up to the crest of the hill. Some of the young national Guardsmen panicked and fired into the crowd. Thirteen students were wounded or killed. Four dead, two girls killed were innocent bystanders on their way to class.

As the news of the Kent State deaths became known, hundreds of college campuses exploded in violent protest. Some faculties and students voted to go on strike. I recorded in my journal that there were over 200 incidents of burning and wrecking college property. Apparently, it was an insane dark hour for America. I remember it as if it happened yesterday.

All these terror and hatred disturbed Richard Nixon personally. He could not get the news pictures out of his mind and heart. He thought about the parents who suddenly had received news about their sons and daughters who were dead because of a campus demonstration. Dick wrote letters to each family, even though he knew that wouldn't help in their grief.

When he read in the newspaper that one of the dead girl's father said, "My child was not a bum." It caused a pain of anguish in Nixon's heart. Dick became discouraged and depressed. He could not sleep. Then he telephoned friends until wee hours of the morning.

It was now Saturday, May 9th. A National Day of Protest

was scheduled to occur. Dick had asked that the demonstrators be around the Ellipse, as well as the Washington Monument, so he could hear it. He wanted it to be a peaceful and non-violent as possible.

From his Lincoln Study Sitting Room, he gazed out of the window and noticed groups of young people had arrived on the Ellipse between the Washington Monument and the White House. Manolo Sanchez, his valet, came in to see if Dick would like some tea or coffee. As Nixon looked out the window, he thought the Lincoln Memorial at night was the most beautiful he had ever seen. Since Manolo had never seen the Lincoln Memorial at night, Nixon suggested that they go and look at it.

There were small groups already gathering around the Lincoln memorial. President Nixon surprised the students by shaking hands with them, asking them where they were from, how old they were, and what they were studying in school.

He understood their hatred of the Vietnam War, but he didn't want that bitterness to eat away their love of country and what the foundations stood for. Dick recalled that he was once a Quaker pacifist and going into the armed services was unthinkable. But, sometimes it takes courage to stand for the right thing, he said, even through it is unpopular. And so he went into the U.S. Navy because he loved his country and what it stood for.

The small group had become larger around President Nixon to listen. Richard Nixon realized that these young people were searching for answers to solve life's problems that surrounded all of us, as he did forty years ago. Material things do not satisfy us. Cleaning up the streets, the water, and the air and stopping the Vietnam War, would not solve the spiritual hunger inside of us. The spiritual things Nixon's mother had instilled in him as a young person came to the forefront, and Dick Nixon was witnessing to the crowd of what he believed in.

After his return to the White House, President Nixon was still too tired to sleep. Even though, he tried sleeping in his bed, Dick just tossed around. Got up and made phone calls and then back again to bed. Whenever Dick couldn't sleep, it affected his judgment and mood. Whenever his temper flared, we knew he didn't have his proper sleep. All the past few months of conflict had taken their toll.

Pat, Tricia, Julie, and David were at Camp David. Dick was concerned about their safety at the White House during the peace protest. But, Pat wanted to be with Dick. She decided that the rest of the family should be with him and not alone at this time of crisis. When Pat told the Secret Service about it, they were not pleased. However, they devised a plan to get the First Family back to the White House.

That morning men and women with long disheveled hair and ragged jeans carried Vietcong flags. This was the crowd of demonstrators, which greeted Pat as they entered the city. Outside the White House gate helmeted guards and policemen stood ready for any moves or actions by the protestors.

No lights were burning in the White House. It was very dark as they climbed the stairs to the second floor. All they heard was the synchronized incantations of the protestors and all the noisy rock and roll sounds outside, as they watched the demonstration on television or glanced carefully out of windows.

Outside the White House, the debris littered the streets. The gigantic peace demonstration didn't think about cleaning up the mess of trash they left. That was someone else's problem to take care of. Across the street a Lafayette Park, a small group was advocating a peace vigil.

Sunday, May 10th, was Mother's Day. As they walked through the White House Rose Garden with Mamie Eisenhower, Dick remarked that he slept better than before. However, we were not sure. How could he? Maybe, the quietness of the White House church services was to be more assuring. As usual there were reporters covering the church services. The reporters were told that they should limit questions they asked "to Mother's Day" and the church services, and not to anything which happened last night or in the future.

The American Legion, Chaplain, from Ohio gave the sermon on Mother's Day. He spoke along the timely theme.

He said, "We can get along without well-dressed ladies, but we can't go along without Mothers. It was a Mother who carried us in her womb, who taught us to talk, who taught how to pray, and who taught us to love with her own love. Everything that is beautiful, loving and kind—Mothers had something to do with it."

Then, he cited the story of Jesus Christ's mother—the Virgin Mary—and what Alexander the Great and General Ulysses S. Grant said about their mothers. We all agreed that trust in the Lord and love of our family would able us to find true joy.

President Nixon was pleased by the Gallup Poll, which came out in the middle of May. It showed 65% of those polled approved of his handling the presidency, and 50% approved of the troops sent into Cambodia. Fifty-Eight percent blamed demonstrating students at Kent State University for the deaths of four students. The poll only showed 11% blamed the National Guard for the foray.

Then, on May 26th, "Sixty Minutes," the CBS television news magazine, delighted the audience with a personal tour of the White House guided by Tricia Nixon through the First Family's living quarters—which was rarely seen by others. I was so surprised to see Tricia doing this tour. She was a gracious little princess. Tricia is usually the introvert. She does not like limelight and loves her privacy, but here she handled her public appearance with great flamboyances.

This was the first TV tour since Jacqueline Kennedy's CBS 1962 special. But, this time was different. Mrs. Kennedy showed only the first floor of the White House historic rooms. Tricia took us, as viewers to the second floor of the White House—which is not open to the public—only to those who are invited by the Nixons.

Harry Reasoner and Mike Wallace, CBS newsmen, accompanied Tricia Nixon on her tour. They started their tour in the West Wing visiting the living and dining rooms, and Pat Nixon's sitting room and the state guest rooms in the East Wing. Many distinguished women, such as Queen Elizabeth II and Dutch Queen Juliana, stayed in the Queen's Bedroom. The Lincoln Bedroom, which was the Cabinet Room during the Abraham Lincoln's administration. The Truman Balcony was another point of interest. David and Julie Eisenhower welcomed them there.

I'm sure Reasoner and Wallace found out it was a nice place to visit, but would they like to live there? They asked many spontaneous questions and Tricia shared a personal fascinating side of the White House for us.

Billy Graham had his evangelistic crusades May 22-31 at the University of Tennessee Neyland Stadium, Knoxville. President and Mrs. Nixon knew what the Crusades were about. The appreciated the work which Graham was doing. Before the 1968 election, the Nixons came to the Billy Graham Crusade in Pittsburgh, Pennsylvania. They attended many of his crusade meetings as they could. However, even though Nixon believed the Bible from cover to cover, he had to be careful he didn't alienate others who didn't believe as he did.

When people got wind that President and Mrs. Nixon would be there on May 28th more than 100,000 people came and welcomed them. President Nixon shared the platform with Billy Graham. He spoke for 13 minutes and said, "I can tell you America would not be what it is today, the greatest nation in the world, if this were not a nation which has made progress under God." He also quoted spiritual needs for young people and urged them with these words,"If our young people today are going to have a fulfillment beyond those material things, they must turn to those great spiritual resources that have made America the great country it is."

It was the first in history that a President of the United States addressed an evangelistic crusade. Nixon's appearance helped attract the largest Tennessee crowd for any event held.

Throughout the east section of the stadium several hundred anti-war protestors carried signs, "Thou shalt not kill" and chanted "Peace now—Peace now—when Nixon was talking. They kept this up through most of the service. Several people were arrested.

Western singer Johnny Cash and his television show cast also was there. Cash told us about how he accepted Jesus Christ when he was a 12-year-old boy at an Arkansas Baptist Church, and now he was putting more emphasis on spiritual things of his life.

Pat Nixon shared honors with Mamie Eisenhower at he Congressional Club's annual First Lady breakfast at the Shoreham Hotel. They both received a standing ovation from the thousands of Congressional wives and guests.

Mamie looked slimmer than before. She had lost so many pounds. Her grief for Ike, her husband, helped her to lose weight without her trying to do so. Mamie told us that Ike did not want her grieve but to live for the living.

Pat looked beautiful in her pink linen jacket with her silk floral print dress. We all noticed that the hemline of her dress was about 3 inches below her knees. That was the nearest thing to a midi-dress I had ever seen.

Several weeks before Julie and David's graduation from Smith and Amherst Colleges, the officials at the college warned them that no one could guarantee their safety at graduation time. If they or their mothers and fathers would attend the graduation ceremonies, there would be more than 200,000 protestors, which would disrupt the graduation ceremonies. Classes were already dismissed because of the strike on campus.

Pat looked forward attending Julie and David's graduation ceremonies. She could not forget what the protestors had done to spoil the special event she longed to see. Everything was affecting both of them personally. The Secret Service had warned him that he would be assaulted by thousands of demonstrators at the Smith and Amherst. There would be no way they could protect him unless he wanted to call out the National Guard. Dick was so humiliated when he had to cancel his visit to Julie and David's graduation ceremonies.

For the first time, Pat and Dick realized that they were being confined as hostages in the White House unless they met the demands of the radical demonstrators. It was painful and horrifying. Everywhere they went, the demonstrators were chanting, "One, two three, four, we don't want your fuckin' war," "Hell, no we won't go." "Fuck Julie, fuck David" Peace now"

I could see why they retreated to Camp David, Key Biscayne and beautiful San Clemente. It was there they could be blessed with peace and quiet away from the noisy protestors.

It was at Camp David, Saturday, June 6, the Nixon's celebrated David and Julie's graduation. It was suppose to be a fun time and to relax, but no one was very enthusiastic at the party. They could not get in the mood when their minds were at the graduation ceremonies.

Julie was very appreciative of my graduation message and remembrance to them. Both Julie and David invited me to visit the White House soon! Which I was planning to do as soon as I could take leave of my work at Grand Canyon College.

It was 95 degrees hot outside, but very cool inside the White House. On June 19th, Friday, Pat stopped outside to welcome a huge crowd of children for the "Summer in the Parks" White House carnival. It was preview of Expo '70, which was to bring all the planned activities for "Summer in the Parks" program at Rock Creek Park starting Sunday.

The children and reporters followed her everywhere as she visited the different exhibits. Pat plunged into the sea of children and smiled and hugged, held hands and chatted with the children, as they watched each note-worthy happening.

Even the reporters were having a difficult time keeping up with Pat, and they were wondering how she could do it in all that humid heat. But, Pat never thinks about whether it is hot or cold, she just keeps doing what is necessary.

Many of the children wanted to know where President Nixon was and how he was getting along. Pat told them "the President would like to be here, but he had to work today."

A rock band played nearby and the music could be heard inside the White House and the people heard it across the street in Lafayette Park. Near the East Gate, Pat, visited a karate exhibit. Karate students in their white pajama outfits showed how to ward off knifers, muggers, and purse-snatchers. She was interested in learning about karate. However, Pat didn't think she would be able to find the time, and wasn't sure her bones could take it with all that bouncing around.

The Catoctin Cultural Arts Camp folk singers entertained everyone with their singing and musical renditions on violin, guitars, and jazzy flutes. Pat looked at some of the wood sculptures and attempted some of the techniques in wood sculpturing herself. It did look like a totem pole. She even praised the young boy's next to her for his carving. His nervousness disappeared and he enjoyed Mrs. Nixon being around him.

After the basketball game and tumbling tricks, Pat painted her name on a 10-foot balloon and watched Merlin the Magician. Everyone wondered how he did some of his magical tricks. They asked Pat Nixon if she knew. Then all the children and Pat had their hot dogs to eat. As the day ended, Pat departed once again inside the cool air-conditioned White House leaving hundreds of happy children to remember the fun-filled day.

June 21st, the Nixon's 30th wedding anniversary was quietly observed at Camp David. I remembered them with some delicious treat of California figs, which they always enjoyed. They were looking forward to seeing me again when both of our schedules permitted.

Julie had a punch and cookie party in the Jacqueline Kennedy Garden at the White House of neighborhood children who had participated in the "Summer in the Parks" program. The children had taken a tour of the White House and then enjoyed the cookies and punch after the tour.

David's summer job was working with the Washington Senator's Baseball Club. Julie and David would be watching the Senator's play ball in Washington every night except one night when the Japanese ambassador honored them at a dinner.

Then, they planned to leave June 30th by military plane to participate in the Expo 70 in Osaka, Japan and return to Washington July 5th. Julie showed her wristwatch which David's grandfather, General Dwight D. Eisenhower had ordered for her prior to his death in 1969. On the face of the watch at each quarter hour instead of numerals were pictures of David, Pat, Dick, and Tricia. The watch arrived a month after Eisenhower had died.

Ever since the devastating earthquake of May 31that hit the Huiascaran Mountains in Peru, Pat Nixon was troubled and concerned. The television media gave us the reports of 50,000 dead and many thousands of villagers homeless due to the mass of snow, icy rock, and earth sliding down the mountainside.

As she watched the news, Pat wanted to do something to help. She realized that our country had strained relations with Peru because the seizure of U.S. oil fields and plantations there by the revolutionary Velasco government. But, she wanted to do more than the aid our government had sent. In her heart she knew what was the morally right things to do.

She talked it over with Dick and he told her to go. Right away Dick made telephone calls to see if Pat would be welcomed in Peru with supplies. President Nixon discussed it with Haldeman to set up the humanitarian mercy project. It would be from the people of the United States and not from the government. Tons of supplies were to be raised by private donations.

On June 28, Sunday, Pat Nixon flew to Lima, Peru. After landing there President Velasco's wife welcomed her to Peru. Nine tons of relief supplies were loaded on a C-135 cargo plane, which took Pat Nixon, Mrs. Velasco and some American journalists. The cargo plane did not have any passenger seats. The American journalists had to sit on the floor of the plane. Mrs. Velasco had to sit in the co-pilot's seat. A make shift chair was bolted on the floor for Pat to sit on. None of the American press and Pat had a seat belt to wear.

All were making a very hazardous trip into the snow-covered Andes Mountains. The valley was very narrow. The dirt landing strip was inadequate and abrupt. No jets could ever land there, but the cargo plane managed to do so. If anyone else was worried about the situation, Pat didn't look bothered or show concern.

From there, Pat, Mrs. Velasco and the news media flew in a helicopter to tour the regions of the worst ruins. The destruction there from the earthquake and avalanche reminded everyone of what was bombed in Germany at the end of the World War II. It was difficult to tell the difference. It was horrible!

Pat was touched by all the suffering and calamity. Children, women and men gathered around her. Many had bandages around their injured heads and legs. They were very fortunate to get out alive in time. Others did not. So Pat gave everyone a hug as she felt their pain and need. Those people knew she really cared.

The American press had been told by Pat not to mention anything about the difficult relations between the U.S. Government and Peru. This was a mercy effort and not a political difference. She would not allow it to be otherwise.

By the end of the day, Pat had won over this revolutionary, Peruvian President Velasco. He invited Pat Nixon to dinner that evening in the beautiful, affluent Presidential Palace and awarded her with the Grand Cross of the Order of the Sun. He thanked her for helping in such a trying time in his country. Velasco appreciated very much her efforts in behalf of the Peruvian people.

Sometimes more things can be achieved through small kindnesses in helping others instead of evil words and deeds. Pat Nixon practiced what she preached by focusing on helping others in their suffering and tragedy. Her life was an example all should follow. As far as I could remember, no other First Lady ever tried what Pat Nixon did—a courageous diplomatic goodwill mission of concern—which accomplished more than all the official negotiations.

The Whittier College class of 1934 scheduled their 36th class reunion July 13th at the White House. They made a special tour of the White House, which included a look in President Nixon's Oval Office. Just ordinary tourists didn't have that privilege to do so.

As each one went through the White House receiving line, President Nixon remembered the names of many of his college classmates, except one. He didn't recognize his college sweetheart, Ola-Florence Walch. She looked different than when they were romantically involved during their college days. Her hair was short and curly when she was going to college in the thirties. Now she had long straight hair, pulled back in a braid for the seventies.

When someone introduced Ola-Florence to Dick Nixon, everyone laughed when he asked her if she still lived in Vista, California. She told him she had moved to Sedona, Arizona. Pat leaned over and said to Dick, "If you had been reading the newspapers you would have known she lived in Arizona."

Pictures of each classmate with her husband or his wife and the President were taken along with a class picture on the front portico of the White House.

July 16th, Thursday, was an exciting day. Prince Charles, the 21st Prince of Wales and heir apparent to the British throne and his sister Princess Anne, 19, came to visit the White House. Last year President Nixon invited them to come to visit during his trip to England. Pat made most of the arrangements for the royal pair to come. From there, Tricia, Julie and David took over the most important plans for the royal visit.

The Nixons wanted the visit to be informal and to emphasize on youth. This offered Prince Charles and Princess Anne an off hand impression of what young Americans of their own age were like here. When Tricia had invited Prince Charles as her houseguest, the silly news media were manufacturing a love affair. The press was dreaming up a perfect match about Tricia Nixon and Prince Charles to hatch up more fanciful stories that were not true. The only thing Tricia and Charles had jointly shared were their repugnance for the publicity the new media constantly was spouting around each of them.

It bothered Princess Anne more. She had not been told about the actions of the U.S. Press corps. They swarmed around her in their over enthusiastic bid for a story and picture. Finally, nineteen-year-old Princess Anne told the press, "I cannot stand having 10 million reporters on my heels. I do not give interviews or talk to any of the press."

Even the Prince Charles had an aversion toward the publicity that ensued; he had the ability to be polite and tactful and made many friends for Britain.

President Nixon welcomed the royal pair with his famous smile and a handshake. But, he had trumpets heralding their arrival and urged thousands of people to be admitted to the White House grounds for this special event. He promised Prince Charles and Princess Anne all the adults would stay out of sight the three days they were here.

Prince Charles acknowledged that they always wanted to come to the United States to visit. Tricia showed the royal guests their rooms: Anne to the Queens Bedroom where Elizabeth II, her mother, had slept, Charles to the Lincoln Bedroom where the mattress was still lumpy.

Foreign guests usually didn't sleep at the White House. Blair House was usually used for guests at the White House.

It was revealed that Charles and Anne did not drink hard liquor. But, Anne said she preferred Coco-Cola. They said they would appreciate by each of their beds a bottle of Vichy water.

All the aides and staff were brushing up for special etiquette courses for what was proper thing to do for royalty. However, Julie and Tricia had manners and dignity, which would have charmed any royal court. They made Americans proud.

Julie, Tricia, and David were the tri-hosts. Prince Charles and Princess Anne took off in a helicopter with them and others several young people to Camp David in the Maryland Mountains for a picnic and cookout. They bicycled to the skeet-range and participated in whom would be the best in breaking clay pigeons. There was swimming and watching baseball.

The evening was not over and young people noticed that Prince Charles was just plain "Charles." The royal protocol had been dispensed with. He had captured the hearts of young Americans with his calmness, exuberance, sportsmanship and interest in everything he saw and heard. Anne was still reserved and somewhat bored with the protocol. She did listen but said little around others for fear the press would misquote her. At home in Britain she liked to take wild horseback rides and dashing around the countryside in trucks.

All the partygoers returned to Washington and took a moonlight tour of the nation's monuments and memorials—the Lincoln Memorial, the Iwo Jima Statute, and the Washington Monument. Wherever the five young people went there was much laughter and joyfulness. If only the press would have stayed away, so they could enjoy their youthful events in privacy without the press snooping into their gaiety. Wouldn't that be wonderful?

At the top of the Washington Monument, Charles suggested that they all dash down the 898 steps of the stairway to the bottom. David was the only one who took him on. But, the girls—Tricia, Julie, and Anne chickened out and took the elevator down to the ground.

On the second day of their visit they sauntered through the U.S. Capitol. Of course Princess Anne gave handsome Senator Mark Hatfield, Republican from Oregon a very long admiring look. Also, they had a difficult time understanding the syrupy Southern drawl of Senator Strom Thurmond from South Carolina.

Charles showered everyone with many questions such as why the eagle was America's symbol and how the congressional leaders were elected. Then, the leaders of both political parties escorted them on the Senate floor before the opening of the Senate session. Several Senators greeted them on the floor which was very unusual before any session starts.

Then, Tricia, Julie, and David brought them to the

Smithsonian Institute to meet Neil Armstrong who became the first man to arrive on the moon. Frank Borman, a retired astronaut, discovered that Prince Charles had much understanding and information about the rocket capsules, which were on exhibit at the museum. From there, they took a cruise in the Sequoia yacht down the Potomac river to Mt. Vernon where George Washington lived and was buried.

President Nixon and Pat, and special friends watched from the darkened Truman balcony the formal dinner-dance, overlooking the big, lighted pavilion set up on the lawn behind the White House. The Marine Band played more romantic fox trots. The two rock bands provided more music and sound, which the young people enjoyed through the wee hours of the morning.

Prince Charles was dancing with Tricia and spent much of the evening with her. David whirled Princess Anne around the dance floor, as well as some other young women. By 2:30 a.m. they called it a night to remember. Soon the royal pair's visit was coming to an end and shortly they would have to say goodbye and return to London.

Julie told me they would probably be in San Clemente in August, but be sure to let them know about when my travel plans again were firm.

Pat Nixon's White House schedule was the most pressing requirement. The news media made sure the public knew most everything they could find out about the President, Pat and his family. Even his administration didn't escape the onslaught of their bloody search for a news story. In checking, out old history stories in books and archives, I discovered the Presidential families of those earlier years were never subjected to the mass media attack the Nixons were. They wanted the Nixons to have an answer on any subject and be questioned at the end of a reception line, before any dinner or at any photographing of any event. No wonder they relished their privacy—just to get away. Finally, Pat evaded many personal and private questions. She knew how some quip would be taken out of context and manufactured in a fantastic story.

After I double dutied through the summer registration and counseling at the College, I managed to get away to Washington, too. I got in touch with Pat just before they were to go to Camp David and told her I would be there to see her around August 10th.

Because the Nixon's were away at Camp David I decided to stay at the nearby Claridge Hotel this time. The hotel was near the White House and I could walk over there.

I received a call from the White House that the Nixons were expecting me to visit at 10:30 a.m. the morning of August tenth. My heart was fluttering excitably. Walking through Lafayette Park, I could view the White House, a simple, not showy or ornate, dwelling place. This time I didn't run into any radical protestors on my way to the White House.

I arrived at the gate and showed my card I.D. picture to the guard. He called and I was cleared to go in-"They are expecting you."

Pat gave me a hug and we settled down on the sofa talking about various women things. She wanted to know what I had been doing. That made her happy. Then, Pat told me about what was happening to her since she became First Lady at the White House.

"Helen, I feel so isolated. I can't go out and see any of my friends. One is so ill. If I decided to visit her, the Secret Service men has to go along, too. Then, the press would be in there as well. There is no privacy.

"As you may know when Dick was Vice-President, we could go to our home, go shopping, and also we could relax and unwind in a friend's house. It is so different now."

Being First Lady and President, we discovered everything we say or do is news and open to criticism and speculation. If

I look at Dick differently, my whole life becomes fair game for comment by the press."

I enjoyed the nutritious salad luncheon, which was served in the dining room. The healthful plate of julienne chicken strips and avocado arranged on a bed of escarole was surrounded by wedges of tomatoes and quartered hard-boiled eggs. It looked too beautiful to eat. I enjoyed the tasty poppy seed dressing. The hot biscuits hit the spot!

After lunch Pat and I prowled around the second and third floors. As we looked at the windows, I discovered how thick the window glass was. Pat explained it was all bulletproof glass. Then, we went up to the Solarium for a view of the Ellipse. The various paintings around the White House were a joy to behold. Pat knew I did painting pictures myself, so she asked my opinion, what I thought of each one.

Best of all, Pat showed the Lincoln Sitting Room to me where Dick did his private studying and working. I recognized his brown velvet easy chair. This was his favorite chair to relax by a crackling fire in the fireplace.

I asked Pat, "Does he still like to have a fire going anytime of the year?" Pat laughed. "Yes, he has to have a fire going in the fireplace, and then we hear classical music playing, too."

In the Queen's Bedroom, Pat and I discovered a bobby pin Princess Anne had left behind. Pat gave it to me in a glass case as a souvenir of my visit.

Family dinners were always special to Pat and Dick. It was the only time where they could relax and enjoy the meal. Not at any time I never did see Pat Nixon in slacks around the White House. Dick Nixon always wore a shirt and tie. They knew there was a time and place for everything. They loved beautiful and elegant things and wanted others to appreciate beauty.

Dick said whenever visitors come by his office, he always showed his silver cigar case, which his staff had given him.

As it sat on his desk it would play "Hail to the Chief." He delighted in passing pens, Presidential Seal pins, cuff links, and golf balls to those who came by.

I think Dick Nixon was the person who relished being at the White House the most. If his cheerful little whistle was quiet everyone knew he was worried and disturbed. But, he wanted everyone to remember the historical beauty of the White House, and so he did his level best to be optimistic and cheerful.

The next day I departed from the White House. Pat warned me to go out a certain door to escape the swarms of the press, which were gathered in the other direction. She didn't want the news media to pursue me everywhere if they got wind that I was a personal friend. Well, I escaped that onslaught.

I took a taxi to the Capitol and attended a congressional committee conference on drug abuse. While I was there, I discussed with Arizona Congressmen not to pass the Equal Rights Amendment for Women. I told Congressman John Rhodes what I thought about the amendment and also my visit with the Nixons.

It was time for me to get back to work at the college. Vacation time was over.

After many negotiations with the union and congress, President Nixon signed the postal reform bill on August 12th, which completely restructured the nation's postal service. This independent postal service was to replace the U.S. Post Office, which we have today.

August 13th, Pat flew by helicopter to Bainbridge, Maryland and Scotland, Maryland to visit two programs that showed how the Navy was using its personnel and resources to help communities in need and remedy the plight of underprivileged children.

She went first to Camp Concern, a day camp at U.S. Naval Training Station in Bainbridge. It was sponsored by the U.S.

Navy Department and the City of Baltimore. About 500 inner city children participated. There would be a different group—between 10 and19 years of age—each week Navy officers and enlisted men to serve as volunteers and counselors.

Pat Nixon watched several hundred young persons—many who never had the opportunity before to be out of their city neighborhoods—to enjoy camping, even though it was just for a week. Many of the youngsters wrestled, played basketball and were swimming. The WAVES taught the girl campers knitting and dancing.

Pat had hugged, patted heads and shaken hands and answered many questions. Some questions she politely ignored. She has a way with kids. Each one clung to her and talked to her as though they had known her forever. In return, the kids received a smile from Pat and a lively hello. Many camp personnel lined up wherever she went to capture a peek of her.

Pat carried her own lunch tray. She lunched with six young people in the Camp's Concern. As she ate the food on her tin tray, Pat had her young companions talking incessantly.

After her lunch at Camp Concern, Pat took-an hour-long flight to D.C. Recreational Summer Camp at Cornfield Harbor where she observed campers playing golf, practicing archery, and working on tents and construction.

She had trouble driving a nail at the campsite. One of the young fellows suggested Pat should have a bigger hammer, so she wouldn't miss the nail all the time. Finally, she drove the nail into the wood and went on to observe the archery range. There was some good-natured joking about her skill at hammering. They were wondering how her aim with a bow would be. Smilingly, Pat declined this time to try her hand at the archery sport.

Pat wound up her tour by watching young boys crabbing. Some of the boys had never been fishing before—in fact they didn't know what a fish was. She saw the delight on their faces when each one caught one. It reminded Pat when she took her daughters fishing on a New Jersey vacation. Seafood was one of her favorite foods.

Just before she left the camp, she asked why the boys had more weeks at the camp than the girls. The officials responded that in District of Columbia they had more problems with boys than the girls. Pat saw that girls were much nicer than the boys.

August 14th President Nixon flew with Pat the next morning to New Orleans. While Dick was meeting with public officials Pat had a full agenda of sightseeing of her own. She visited the French Quarter or Garain District of this old historic city and spent a longer time at the first American dwelling there.

The Trinity Episcopal Church in 1894 built Kingsley House, a children's neighborhood settlement home. Pat wanted to visit their day-care center and recreation program for children of working mothers. Her White House schedule was so demanding, no wonder she wanted to get away from it all.

August 23, Sunday, I appeared on a panel discussion program, "Editorial U.S.A," KTVK, Channel 3, Phoenix with three college graduate students at 2:30 p.m., on the proposed constitutional changes for women rights. I discussed why we shouldn't adopt the amendment as it was written.

The year 1970 also marked the fiftieth anniversary of the Nineteenth Amendment granting women the right to vote. The radical women's liberation movement ("women lib") took advantage of the anniversary moment. On August 26th, ten thousand women marched down Fifth Avenue in New York City. Carrying posters demanding that the Equal Rights amendment be passed, to strike out sexist language even in the Bible, and asked for day care centers. The only thing I agreed with these women was their advocate of equal pay if they were doing the same like job the men were working. Neither did I think we were oppressed.

At the beginning of September, the Federal Commission on Obscenity and Pornography recommended the elimination of all lawful deterrents on mature adults who wished to purchase sexually explicit films, books, or pictures. They concluded that pornography did not contribute to emotional disturbances, sexual erotic stimulation, or crime. Five member of the eighteen member disagreed with the rest of the commission's report. They called it a declaration of moral bankruptcy and manipulation of insufficient evidence. I knew as long as Richard Nixon was President, every Main Street in the U.S.A would not turn into porno alley of smut. Even today this is still a hot topic everywhere.

September 12, 1970 the radical (P.L.O) Palestinians Palestine Liberation organization Commandos hijacked four commercial airliners in Amman, Jordan, and held forty passengers as hostages. Most of these were Americans. When President Nixon learnt about the incident, he cancelled his first Israel decree and sent more jet planes and military aid.

He wanted to develop administration plans about the hijackings. Dick pushed hard for adding restrictions on any nation that gave haven to hijackers. Some thought this would impede peace negotiations. He would have to determine a way to do it without jeopardizing the fragile negotiations.

With the Vietnam War cooking on the front burners, September 16 a full-blown civil war in Jordan was brewing on the back burner for Richard Nixon. Dick did not want Israel driven out of existence. He was aware that the United States could confront the Soviets who had inspired the rebel action. If the Syrians, Egyptians, Iroquois moved their armies against King Hussein, Nixon warned that the United States would have to act. He told them to "Keep Out". Apparently the Soviets got the message and discouraged any intervention by anyone else.

Working through diplomatic channels Dick warned all involved to pull back armed forces from Jordan. We would support any air strikes by Israel on them if they didn't comply. This tough Nixon diplomacy put out the fire on the back burner. Surely, President Nixon had enough to handle without this other civil war complicating the negotiations to end the Vietnam War in Asia. Surely, we were being tested as a nation. What else could pop up?

Pat was disgusted with Haldeman. When it came to scheduling trips, Haldeman didn't always inform her until the last minute what the agenda was. His unconcern angered Pat, but she didn't show this in public around her office staff. I know how she felt because Haldeman was capable of anything trying to put a wedge between Pat and Dick. She only raised her criticism when Haldeman and her husband were together alone. That was the best-planned idea.

Sunday, September 27, 1970, President Nixon and Pat departed on an eight-day trip to Europe. Dick talked with Italian leader and Pope Paul VI in Rome and assured them he would do all he could for peace.

Before departing to review the U.S. 6th Fleet in the Mediterranean, President Nixon made a trip to Rome's Fiumicino Airport to greet 31 freed American skyjack hostages from their Jordan hardship experience. While there in Rome, Pat and Dick were greeted by thousands of Italians who gave them a cheering, tumultuous welcome. During the boisterous scene, Dick climbed up on the roof of his car waving his arms and giving the V-for victory peace sign. The enthusiastic crowd loved it!

On her own in Rome, Pat aroused enthusiastic approval from the Italian newswomen with her fashionable manner of speaking and her ability to answer tough questions about everything in her family. School children poured into the street giving her a gift of gladiolas. They also gave her a note for herself and President Nixon.

It read:

"To Mrs. Richard Nixon, First Lady of America: Please

believe that the entire Italian 'silent great majority' stand by President Nixon and by America with deep gratitude, high admiration and every heartfelt good wish." Signed, "from all true Italians."

Dick had met Monsignor John Carroll-Abbing, the Roman Catholic prelate, in the late 1940's when he was a member of Congress, and so he asked Pat to make a special call on him at Rome's Boys Town. The monsignor had started his work in a basement near the railroad station caring for homeless boys—mostly shoeshine boys.

As Pat bid farewell to the students at the Santa Rosa School for Retarded children, she was surrounded with children waving little paper Italian flags and chanting "che bella"- "how pretty she is" and giving her more flowers.

Then, she flew to Naples to rejoin Dick for their trip to Yugoslavia.

When they arrived at the Belgrade airport, there were no cheering crowds to greet them—just strictly protocol courtesy of President Tito. After the many respectful and graciousness at President Tito's palace, President Nixon laid a wreath at the Tomb of The Unknown Soldier. Wherever he went the enthusiastic crowd engulfed his car. Sometimes Dick had to get upon the hood of the car to the delight of the crowd.

Even though the European trip for Pat Nixon was planned at the last minute, she managed to have a full schedule and it was successful. With all the Yugoslavian and American news correspondents around her, Pat caught them off guard by asking them questions of her own. She charmed all the reporters around her. Now, they knew that Pat Nixon was very knowledgeable about the governmental affairs of the world.

The next day, Oct 1st, President Tito and his wife took Pat and Dick for a tour of the countryside and his birthplace. It was pouring rain. People were jammed in the streets in spite of the rain. This time Tito did not stop the motorcade for President Nixon to visit with the people.

When they got back to Belgrade for the State Dinner, Pat found out President Josip Tito's wife Jovanka, really liked her very much. Whenever Jovanka felt moved with affection, she would wrap her strong muscular arms around Pat and give her a crushing hug several times.

Friday, October 2, 1970, they stopped in Madrid to see President Fransisco. The people enroute were crammed together for miles hoping to get a glimpse of President and Pat Nixon. Because of the clamor of the excited pushy crowd the horse guards had to barricade and obstruct the scene.

Pat said the Royal Monclea Palace was truly beautiful—especially the unbelievable gardens and crystal chandeliers. After their white-tie dinner at the Palace, they went outside and the crowds caught up with them and swarmed around to shake hands. And then on to England. They stayed at Prime Minister Edward Heath's country estate at Aylesbury. Queen Elizabeth came and welcomed them both there.

Dick and Pat stopped over in Ireland heading home to United States from their tour through Europe. The Irish-American millionaire, John Mulcahy, was Pat and Dick's host at his Limerick County country estate at Kilfrush. The 6-course dinner lasted an hour and half. The Irish entertainment was excellent, but it lasted more than an hour. By that time Pat and Dick and the other guests were very weary and ready to turn in for a good nights sleep.

Unbeknownst to Pat Nixon, she discovered Haldeman had arranged for her to meet distant Irish cousin relatives she had never known. It made her feel uneasy. She was disturbed that no one had failed to notify her earlier about meeting her Irish relatives.

Even though Pat had not made the arrangements, she did not disappoint those who had waited to meet her. On Sunday, October 4 she met several Ryan relatives and talked to many before the arranged luncheon. The uneasiness and anxiety finally disappeared and the occasion became a happy one for Pat and her distant Irish cousins.

In Ireland, there are two villages called Timahoe—one other in County Kildare and the other one in County Laois. Both villages were vying one another which one had the Nixon connection.

On Monday, October 5th, President Nixon visited the Kildare's now disappeared Quaker community where a Johan Millhouse was buried. Hannah, Nixon's mother had a different spelling of Milhous. They uncovered the foundations of the old meetinghouse behind the graveyard. Only fragmented head stones were left. Others were taken and made into a road. Brier bushes and saplings had taken over the graveyard. In looking at it one thought it was just a woodland corner.

Many village churches that lie in ruins for lack of a congregation or a minister. Therefore the Quaker derelict cemetery gave testimony to Irish Republic's Protestant community decline.

The rival Timahoe in Laois was a neat picturesque village of 60 people and 3 pubs. It had a round tower, which was built by monks of the church to protect the residents from Viking invaders. But this Timahoe claimed the Nixon connection which was President Nixon's fathers name of Frank Nixon.

The villagers dug into the village historical archives and discovered there was a student listed as Robert Nixon in 1779. Also, a church of Ireland minister by the name of Harper Nixon lived there once upon a time. Since President Nixon had names of Bates and Porter listed on his family tree, the villagers claimed those families lived there about 50 years ago.

After visiting with crowds of people around the countryside, Nixon headed for a meeting and luncheon with the Irish Prime Minister in Dublin. Dick was not aware of what kind of anti-demonstration the Irish leftists had planned. But he knew something might happen.

The lawless Irish Republican Army charged President Nixon of tying Ireland to the Anglo-American camp and negotiating to establish NATO or American bases there. They made themselves clear that the Irish people would not agree to it.

The Maoist Communists in Dublin denounced President Nixon and accused him all kinds of misdeeds in Vietnam, the Middle East and Latin America. In spite of all the garbage thrown at him—Nixon survived. For the most part the crowds were very good and respectable. It only took a few to spoil the festivities for others. They took Air Force One and made the long trip back to the United States.

While Pat and Dick were on their tour of Europe, David Eisenhower was receiving many invitations to campaign for Republican candidates across the country. Before the Nixons left on their European tour, David and Julie had discussed with them about the congressional campaigning. President Nixon approved David's idea.

David was "an original" in politics. He visited schools and fairs in Illinois, Ohio, and Florida and planned to have six other states added to his schedule. David became the most sought after speaker in the 1970's congressional election campaign.

Pat's staff handled David and Julie's scheduling of their trips. Julie restricted her campaigning because she was taking courses for her teaching classes. However David would be entering Naval Officer Candidate School in Newport, Rhode Island, October 24th and so he hit the campaign trail early for Republican candidates.

Dick had decided not to do any campaigning in the 1970 congressional elections. Thought Vice President Ted Agnew could reach the silent majority of citizens out there in the heartland. However, when Nixon returned from his European tour, he discovered Republican races were in deep trouble.

I was working on Senator Paul Fannin's campaign in Arizona and I knew about the problems that lay ahead. We knew as it looked we would lose 30 seats in the House and maybe all but one in Senate races. I wanted to be sure Senator Fannin would not lose his Senate race. I always saved a lot of my vacation and special personal time to work where necessary on campaigning and speaking. The Nixons knew they could count on me whenever they needed me to work.

Julie, Tricia and David were furnishing glitter for the ho-drum campaign election year.

Clean looking, sparkling, genuine, they attracted many people to their side and was less controversial, too. Candidates were fortunate to have these young people campaigning for them in a close gubernatorial or senatorial races.

Reporters, cameras and crowds followed them everywhere. Even the voters appeared to be apathetic; they were intrigued by attractive Tricia, dazzling Julie and lanky David. The qualities they portrayed packed a powerful impact on the crowd of middle-aged voters. Tricia resembled a little princess. People wanted to be near her. Anyone looking could see the effect she was having on the people. Tricia had a dislike for campaigning. This year she appeared to be enjoying herself on the campaign trail.

Thousand of requests for their appearances continued to pour into the White House. Some of the presidential assistants screened each request for assistance in the campaign, but Julie, David, and Tricia chose which one they like to go. In states, which were too close to call, Julie and David turned on their "spell charm" and captivated potential voters wherever they campaigned.

President Nixon was really charged up to hit the campaign trail. Just 3 weeks before congressional election, Dick spent one whole week to campaign personally for candidates in 22 states.

On October 24, 1970 Nixon denounced the conclusion of the Commission which was appointed by Democrats had turned in a "morally bankrupt" report, Nixon said.

Nixon stated the panel had concluded, "that the proliferation of filthy books and plays has no lasting harmful effects on a man's character. But the history of civilization and plain common sense indicate otherwise."

"The commission calls for repeal of laws controlling smut for adults-while recommending continuing restrictions on smut for children. In an open society this proposal is untenable.

"If the level of filth rises in the adult community, the young people in our society cannot help but also be inundated by the flood.

"Pornography can corrupt a society and a civilization. The people's elected representatives have the right and obligation to prevent that corruption.

"The pollution of our culture, the pollution of our civilization with a smut and filth is as serious a situation for the American-people as the pollution of our once-pure air and water.

"Smut should not be simply contained at its present level; it should be outlawed in every state of the union and the legislature and courts at every level of American government should act in unison to achieve the goal.

"I am aware of the importance of protecting free expression "but pornography is to freedom of expression what anarchy is to liberty. As free men willingly restrain a measure of their freedom to prevent anarchy so we must draw the line against pornography to protect the freedom of expression.

"The Supreme Court has long held and recently reaffirmed that obscenity is not within the area of protected speech or press.

"Moreover, if an attitude of permissiveness were to be

adopted regarding pornography, this would contribute to a atmosphere condoning anarchy in every field-and would increase the threat to our social order as well as to our moral principles.

"We all hold the responsibility for keeping America a great country—by keeping America a good country. American morality is not to be trifled with. The commission on Pornography and Obscenity has performed a disservice and I totally reject its report, Nixon said."

Wherever he went there were enthusiastic crowds. There were demonstrators, too who badgered Nixon with sneering taunting words and threw rocks and vegetables. Dick did not want Pat, Julie, Tricia or anyone else to see the angry repulsive confrontation. He emphasized that the Silent Majority should stand up and be counted. Don't be like those who shout obscenities and throw rocks. Vote at the ballot box-that would carry more weight than all the four letter bad words.

After making campaign stops in Chicago and Omaha, October 29th Thursday, Nixon proceeded to San Jose, California. Thousands of supporters greeted him inside the San Jose Municipal Auditorium. When Dick was speaking inside several thousand anti-war demonstrators outside where pounding on all the doors around the building and shouting, "One, two, three, four—we don't want your "fucking war."

After his speech, Nixon went outside to his car. He heard the rantings of the protestors and decided to stand once again on the hood of the car and give them his V sign. That infuriated them! There were jeers and boos. They threw rocks, vegetables and eggs at President Nixon. This incident shook up the Secret service who was protecting the life of the President. They were use to facing anti-war protestor wherever the president went, but this was the first time the demonstrators had directly assaulted and threatened the President of the United States.

The staff car and press bus was not so lucky. When the

car and bus stalled, the demonstrators surrounded them throwing more rocks and smashing bus windows. Fortunately, none of the staff and press were hurt by this incident in San Jose.

After the San Jose speech, Nixon flew to San Clemente to the Western White House. It was cold and damp that night. The weather was not exactly what the California tourist bureau had advertised. So, Manalo Sanchez Dick's valet built a fire in the study's fireplace. Everyone knew that President Nixon liked having a roaring fire burning in the fireplace when he was studying or working. Often he would turn on the air conditioning just so he could have a fire. Nixon's study room was above the dining room and could only he reached by the outside staircase in the Spanish style interior courtyard.

In July 31, 1970 the Pentagon order made it easier to obtain abortions in 163 military hospitals throughout the country. When President Nixon got wind regarding it, he made a special statement from the San Clemente Western White House to rescind the Pentagon order. He did not believe government should be involved in the abortion business.

"From personal and religious beliefs, I consider abortion an unacceptable form of population control. Further, unrestricted abortion policies, or abortion on demand, I cannot square it with my personal belief in the sanctity of human life, including the life of the yet unborn. A good and generous people will not opt, in my view, for this kind of alternative to its social dilemmas. Rather, it will open its hearts and homes to the unwanted children of its own, as it has done for the unwanted millions of other lands."

After working on another speech, Nixon retired early to his bedroom on the other side of the courtyard. Pat was not there. She wouldn't return until the next day from a campaign tour of her own.

The buzzing of the dining room smoke alarm beneath the study kept ringing. Then another alarm sounded off.

Manolo and Fina screamed, "The house is full of smoke! Call the fire department." They notified all the Secret Service agents on duty.

The Secret Service agents woke up Dick in his bedroom and got him away from the fire to a safe place. It was not their duty to be firefighters, but they trained the fire hose directly on the burning wall to keep it spreading to the rest of the house.

When the San Clemente volunteer fireman arrived, they thanked the agents for taking quick action or the Nixon home might have been quickly destroyed. After the fireman cleaned up the mess, Nixon thanked each one of them for coming. As he looked around, Dick knew Pat would be exasperated when she sees what had happened.

Even today, Billy Graham the evangelist, appealed for the introduction of tougher measures in the United States to deal with demonstrators violent outbursts. He arrived from New York to Lisbon, Portugal for a 4-day visit. Billy said, "Throwing stones and shouting obscenities at the President of U.S. is disgraceful and un-American. These events have hurt the American image abroad and should not be tolerated."

Following a rally Friday at Anaheim California, Nixon flew to Phoenix, Arizona October 1, 1970 to help support Senator Paul Fannin and Congressman John Rhodes reelection candidacies. I was at Sky Harbor Airport with my Dean of Education, Dr. Robert Sutherland, to welcome President Nixon. Thousands and thousands of cheering Sky Harbor crowds greeted him and were packed like sardines in the hanger to hear him speak.

Dick told us in his most toughest and blunt statement:

"It is time to quit making heroes out of those who protest and brand them as the same thugs and hoodlums that have always plagued a good people.

"It's about time we cut out this nonsense about repression being the cause of violence. As long as I am President, no band of violent thugs is going to keep me from going out and speaking with the American people wherever they want to hear me and wherever I want to go.

"If a man chooses to dress differently or wear his hair differently or talk in a way that repels decent people—that's his business. But, when he picks up a rock or a bottle or throws a bomb they are the super hypocrite of our time.

"The permissiveness in our legislatures, court, family life and universities have eroded the strength of the American society and called on "the great silent majority of Americans "of all ages and of every political persuasion to stand up and be counted against appeasement of the rock throwers and obscenity shouters."

"There were many who somehow forgot that tyranny is wrong, whatever its form—whether the tyranny of government, or the tyranny of terrorists or the tyranny of those who shout down speakers, or the tyranny of those who shut down colleges or blockade streets in an effort to impose their own views on others."

Referring to those who attacked his automobile in San Jose, Nixon said, "It is time to draw the line against them and their congressional defense. It is time for us to recognize that candidates for the Senate and the House who have either condoned this, defended it, excused it, or failed to speak up against it, do not have the qualifications to take the strong stand that needs to be taken against this kind of lawlessness and violence.

"No protest for peace justifies violence, justifies shouting down speakers, justifies lawlessness of any kind.

"This is a free country and I fully intend to share that freedom with my fellow Americans. This President is not going to be cooped up in the White House."

Applause interrupted Nixon 25 times. When he mentioned the San Jose incident, the applause really thundered and shook the Sky Harbor terminal hanger.

It was Nixon's greatest ovation received. The crowd waved their posters and cheered and stamped the floor with approval. Nixon just smiled and was enjoying the crowd's applause. Surely, Arizona was not the same as San Jose.

After his address at the National Guard hanger at Sky Harbor Airport thousands of enthusiastic young people gave President Nixon a warm greeting and crowded in during his hand-shaking short pleasure trip. He was reveling in the enthusiasm for all the Arizonians who swarmed around him. The crowd pushed and touched the President and for a few worrisome seconds, I thought we were going to lose him in the mass of humanity. When Nixon finally got back to the top of the ramp of Air Force ramp, he turned and waved at us for the last time.

But, getting home was a different matter. It was the biggest traffic jam in Phoenix history. There were cars still trying to reach the terminal to hear Nixon and were backed up three miles, and the rest of us in the mass of 10,000 people trying to leave to go home. All that traffic snarl didn't dampen their enthusiasm. Some parked their cars and stopped for refreshments until the right time to leave. After listening to our car radio for a while, we managed to get back to the college a few hours before closing time.

The Nixon staff videotaped the Phoenix speech for his television night the next day. The huge airport hanger caused the audio sound to bounce around and was garbled and shrilled. It was really terrible!

After I heard it on NBC network, I couldn't believe my eyes and ears. The technical quality of the tape was very poor and granular. Many of my Republican friends thought someone had damaged the tape to get even with President Nixon. Ever since that time, everyone wanted to be assured that any videotape purchased would be the very best quality. All of us complained about it, including President Nixon. After that TV disastrous incident, I felt the Nixon staff would not make that mistake again.

November 3rd, Tuesday, was election day. The Republicans gained two in the Senate but lost nine in the House. However, Dick was glad some of the extreme liberals were withdrawn from circulation by the voters across the country. Whenever unemployment was on the rise, usually the political party controlling the White House lost by forty-six. Overall this was a very good showing at the time. Nixon was disappointed that we lost eleven governor races, and we only had 21 Republican governors to work with.

Now we had to work harder. Nixon told us no candidate in the future should run for any office if he or she was involved in some personal ethical conduct, which was suspicious. At all times, we should be on our guard against getting involved in any political scandal.

After the election on their way back to Washington, Pat waited until Haldeman and her husband were alone on Air Force One. Then, she let Haldeman know in-no-uncertain terms she did not want any interference in the East Wing social operations by the West Wing of the White House. Felt it complicated things for her staff and the decisions that have to be made. So, on this point, Pat won and overrode Haldeman once again.

When some wanted Veteran's Day (once called Armistice Day) to be switched from its original date of November 11th, marking the end of World War I, to the fourth Monday of October, the Veterans of Foreign Wars and American Legion opposed the change. They let the President know about it and held programs on November 11th throughout the country.

Observing the 50th Anniversary of the burial of the Unknown Soldier at the Arlington National Cemetery, President Nixon conducted wreath-laying ceremonies at the Tomb of the Unknown and greeted the V.F.W. Commander-in-chief. There was a moment of prayer and a salute.

For Thanksgiving the Nixons invited 100 military men and women from nearby hospitals who were unable to be with their families for the holidays. They came on crutches and in wheel chairs. The sight of those crippled from the war touched all who saw them. Most of all Pat was affected by their guests who were most grateful to be invited to the White House for Thanksgiving dinner.

On Thanksgiving Day President Nixon issued a proclamation:

He said: "Despite problems facing our nation today we are indeed, a most fortunate people. Giving thanks today, we express gratitude for past bounty and we also confidently face the challenges confronting our own nation and the world because we know we can rely on a strength greater than ourselves.

"This year, let us especially seek to rekindle in our respective hearts and minds the spirit of our first settlers who valued freedom above all else, and who found much for which to be thankful when material comforts were meager.

"President Abraham Lincoln asked Americans on October 3, 1863 to set apart and observe the last Thursday of November as a day of Thanksgiving. This was the year of the Battle of Gettysburg and other major battles between Americans on American soil. To many, this call for a national day of Thanksgiving must have seemed strange, coming as it did at a time of war and bitterness.

"Yet Lincoln knew that the act of thanksgiving should not be limited to times of peace the serenity. He knew that it is precisely at those times of hardship when men most need to recognize that the source of all good constantly bestows His blessings on mankind."

December 1970, our Pueblo Grande Republican Women's Club held a Christmas Party for 70 youths at the Maricopa County Juvenile Detention Center. The Phoenix Gazette newspaper was there and published a photo of the affair, as I was helping the young people decorate the tree, which we had given to the detention center. All youths were presented a Christmas gift.

Margie Braden, the Arizona Republican committeewoman, saw the photo and the story. It was just the sort of Republican action she had been trying to push since 1962. Our club was the one of the clubs in the state to do this kind of community action. It was good public relations for Republicans and I was glad we could do this.

President and Pat Nixon always encouraged this kind of program. So Margie wanted to take this picture and let the Nixons know about it. She knew Pat would enjoy it and would love to hear what I was doing from someone else, too.

As the year of 1970 was winding down, Ardis and I spent another Christmas time visiting the White House. Pat showed us a list of items—furnishings and antiques—that they would like to acquire for the White House. After all when millions of tourists tramp through White House rooms for nine years, it can deteriorate and become a little shabby.

Pat had been busy replacing worn furniture and creating new living space. She led the hunt for persons who would be willing to donate antique pieces, which would be too expensive for their budget. Pat would like to see the day when a complete duplicate set of all the antique furnishings would be available. Otherwise, when a single piece needed repair, there was nothing available to take its place.

I thought the big evergreen wreaths loaded with pinecones and bright red berries, and the red candles in the center brighten all the windows facing Pennsylvania Avenue. The Blue Room will have blue walls again, Pat said. A nineteen-foot Christmas tree stood there against the white wall with blue draperies and valances. The chandelier had to be taken down to adjust it in the Blue Room. The monster center table had to go as well. I noticed that Pat had the wonderful portraits of Monroe and Jefferson moved to the right and left of the Blue Room windows.

The Red Room magenta walls were streaked and soiled. This time Pat said the walls would be redone a true red. We were showed a Gilbert Stuart painting of Dolly Madison which she was able to obtain for this room.

The State Dining Room had the most inviting ginger bread house I ever seen. In the East Room, on raised platforms in the shape of a pyramid tree, were many poinsettias that were very beautiful to look at.

I was glad Pat left in place in the China Room my favorite portrait of Mrs. Calvin Coolidge in a red dress. There is something about that picture that really intrigued me. As we wondered around the China Room, I could tell it was still unfinished. The China Room houses a collection of presidential china used by past Presidents. Pat was able to get the new draperies, rugs, and chandelier donated for the China Room. She was hoping she would be able to obtain a portrait of John Adams to match the quality of the other seven Presidents on the wall.

Fires were burning in the fireplaces in the Blue, Green, and Red rooms. We enjoyed the Christmas Carols being played. Sometimes we stopped and sang and swayed to the beautiful music. The shimmering candles gave each of us a magical glow. As we departed the White House, we turned around and looked at it glowing in the night and the lighted American flag waving in the breeze.

Then we recalled what Pat had arranged. This was the year she began lighting the White House. She took great care that the illumination would be indirect lighting and enhance the beauty of the White House. Ever since that time, I remembered it was Pat Nixon who had the White House's beauty brighten at night for all of us to enjoy. Whenever I see a lighted flag day or night, I think of Pat and Richard Nixon who gave us so much.

Chapter 16

1971
BOMBING OF U.S. CAPITOL
TRICIA WEDDING,
AND PAT'S TOURS

Every time I went shopping I discovered that prices were slowly creeping up and inflation had exceeded the 5.7 percent. Five million people in the United States were unemployed. I remembered when we had experienced unemployment and inflation before, but not at the same time. This really baffled everyone.

Tremendous ant-war rallies persisted in Washington, D.C. and around the country. In 1969 there was 534,000 U.S. troops in Vietnam, but by 1971 that number was reduced to 230,000.

Many problems still existed for President Nixon. He felt overwhelmed with all that confronted him day by day. I was wondering if he would survive the daily onslaught for the next election.

On January 15, 1971 President and Mrs. Nixon attended the opening of Dwight D. Eisenhower National Republican

Center in Capitol Hill. Mamie Eisenhower former First Lady had the honor in cutting the ribbon for the grand opening.

On Monday, January 18, 1971 President Nixon ordered the military to cut the Ho Chi Minh trail by attacking the Communist forces in Laos. The United States would provide air power cover and artillery support, helicopter supplies, guns, troops, and B-52 raids.

February 8th, The South Vietnamese wanted this operation to be theirs. However, the American military did not anticipate how strong the Communists North Vietnamese were and did not provide the necessary air cover. Casualties were massive. But they fought back courageously and deprived the Communists the ability to initiate an attack against our American forces.

The Vietnam War persisted to control the national news. Many of President Nixon's programs were kept on the back burner because of the war. There were leaks from the State and Defense departments regarding the Laos build up to the press and television coverage. President Nixon was about to lose hope in controlling the bureaucracy where leaks were concerned.

The Fashion Foundation of America on January 28, 1971 named President Nixon as the best-dressed statesman of 1971, Vice President Spiro Agnew won the honor in 1970.

February 4, 1971 the White House got wind of the work of my Pueblo Grande Republican Women's Club in Phoenix was doing. We had received an award for increased membership. Pat was happy to send their very own words of congratulations. Pat and Dick were deeply grateful for my enthusiastic and dedicated efforts, which inspired success in attaining their mutual goals. They both appreciated for the major contribution I was making along with other club members.

On February 9, Tuesday, 1971, the Nixon family agreed to ban two women reporters form the Washington Post from any social affairs at the White House. If Judith Martin and Isabel Shelton were allowed in, Dick said he would fire anyone whoever is responsible for letting them come in. That was a presidential order and wanted it carried out.

February 24, 1971 Wednesday the Democrats were attacking President Nixon about the Vietnam War and his handling of it. They wanted us to get out of the war now, which they had started, in the beginning under President John F. Kennedy and Lyndon B. Johnson. But the question of P.O.W.'s never seemed to be part of anyone's solutions. What do we do with the P.O.W.'s and how would we get them out of Vietnam? It is easy to complain but they overlooked this one problem. As far as I was concerned, anyone should "zip their lip" if they didn't come up with a solution how to do this. When President Nixon came into office in 1969, forty thousand American boys had died out of two hundred thousand injured. But they didn't realize Nixon was trying to get our troops home and end the war. However, there were small minorities of Democrats who agreed with Nixon 's war policies and supported him.

When Dick first came to the White House he ordered the Lyndon Johnson's taping system removed in 1969. All presidents, such as John F. Kennedy, Franklin Roosevelt, Dwight Eisenhower and Lyndon B. Johnson had taped or recorded their phone calls and various meetings or conversations. But, the year of 1971, he decided to install a voice-activated tape recording system to be personally used only for his memoirs he would write after he left office. Wherever Dick would spend much of his time, recording devices were put in place. The rest of the Nixon family and close friends were not aware of the devices until later.

Anyone who knew Dick Nixon knew he only let off steam and blocked most of his frustration in the privacy of his presidential office to close trusted aides. He never would do it in public. It was private. However being so involved in closing down the Vietnam War, he forgot the taping system was there. In listening to the tapes, at times Nixon would appear wavering and indecisive. But, that was his way to draw persons out and to incite them to explain their personal beliefs opposite to his own views. Thus, Dick could partake of their opinions and concepts.

If anyone wants to keep something secret don't tell anyone about it. Pat thought the viewing of the official John F. Kennedy portraits to be hung in the White House should be viewed privately by Jacqueline Kennedy Onassis. No one knew about it, but it finally leaked out to one of the reporters. It is amazing how some reporters find a way to get a story by one way or other, regardless of someone's feelings for privacy.

Jackie appreciated Pat Nixon's kindness and thought the dinner, the portrait viewing and the White House tour was one of her precious moments spent with her children, ten-year-old John and thirteen year old Caroline.

However, Pat was unhappy how Jackie's visit was leaked to the press and told that one reporter so. She may have not liked what the media wrote about certain White House events, but she understood they were doing their job in getting a story.

On March 1, 1971, Richard Nixon flew to Des Moines, Iowa to speak to the Iowa State legislators. The legislators enjoyed his speech and honored him many times. But outside the Iowa capitol many militant demonstrators of the Students for Democratic Society, SDS, were chanting some foul mouth obscenities and holding signs, which were bad, too. These college age protestors threw rocks and vegetables and anything else they could get hold of to show their protest.

But, on this same day back in Washington, D.C. thousands of protestors besieged our U.S. National Capitol and disrupted the federal government in a massive demonstration. On the Senate office side of the U.S. Capitol the Weathermen terrorist group bombed it. They threatened to do it and made good on their promise. It was a really chaotic time. Many were arrested. But this was just a beginning leading up to future demonstrations in April and May as they planned. It was a headache.

Nixon wanted more intelligence reports how the Students for Democrat Society and the Weathermen had organized and how they arrived in Des Moines and Washington, D.C. Apparently, our intelligence group did not brief President Nixon on these demonstrators.

On March 11, 1971, President Nixon called in a group of women newsmen into the Oval Office to pay tribute to Pat Nixon his wife. This was an unusual special time for the month of March for them.

He told the reporters that Pat always helped and complement him by supporting him in whatever he did. He said Pat was the strongest partner. Her greatest asset was sensitivity about people. Neither did she blow easily under stress.

Pat like her privacy and dislike letting everyone know about her activities. What she missed most of all was to walk alone, window shop, and move alone along on the beach. She would never run for any political office or seek it. But she did like being First Lady. It was Pat who brought peace and calmness and made a difference.

David Eisenhower, Julies husband, was graduating from Naval Officers Candidate School at Newport Rhode Island on March 11, 1971. They flew up to Newport for the commencement exercises that morning. President Nixon delivered the commencement address and gave David his naval commission as Ensign. The only thing that marred the graduation exercises was the protest gathering of Catholics and hundreds of hard hats there. The CBS TV news made us aware of the disturbance. It made Dick upset as the rest of us.

March 16, 1971 was Pat Nixon's 59th birthday. On the

eve of St. Patrick's a state dinner was held. Irish Prime Minister, John Lynch, was the guest of honor. However, Tricia Nixon stole the show when she arrived in her white satin gown trimmed in ostrich feathers. Speculation once again abounded whether Tricia was planning to be engaged to Ed Cox. The deep dark secret was they were already engaged. Ed had asked President Nixon's permission to marry Tricia in November 1970. Tricia and Pat decided June 12th would be the perfect date for the wedding. But, they kept the press guessing when the engagement would take place. Now Tricia and Ed announced their official engagement at Pat's birthday party.

Pat was glad to get my birthday gift. She treasured my special remembrance and the expression of friendship it represented. Also, when I told her about Robert McConnell, one of Grand Canyon College graduates and also on the White House staff for his beautiful singing voice, she became interested in him.

Howard K. Smith interviewed President Nixon on ABC, Monday March 22, 1971 at 9:30 p.m. On TV he sounded extremely well. However, I was wondering what the reaction around the country was . . . Dick and family were wondering, too.

By the end of March at San Clemente President Nixon was concerned with more withdrawal from the Vietnam War. He told the Democratic Congress not to tie his hands in anyway and let the Vietnam government fall to the Communists. That would leave him no choice and go directly to the people and let them know the truth. On the home front he discussed wage problems with industrial leaders and the drug problems with religious leaders. Dick wanted Julie and Tricia to use government planes rather than commercial planes for their personal trips and to charge him for the commercial airline fares.

An all-time Gallup poll indicated Nixon at 50%—the

lowest ever. The Harris poll showed he dropped to a low of 41% on the handling of the war. In spite of this, the President seemed to be in good spirits and in a positive optimistic attitude. Perhaps, the press and the people out there took a pessimistic viewpoint because they didn't have all the facts. The economy was gradually advancing into a strong situation. Weren't we getting out of the war and honorably? Also, to get our P.O.W.'s-prisoners-released.

President Nixon had proposed a revenue sharing plan. This 16 billion dollar program would include 5 billion in new funds, state and local governments unrestricted use and 11 billion for Federal revenue sharing funds for urban and rural development, education transportation, law enforcement and manpower training. It would mean that once again the government would be placing their trust in people.

Local communities would have a better chance to solve their own problems and get directly at the problem of rising local taxes. States and cities were confronted with financial crisis. Some were cutting back on essential services such as trash collections. Others were caught between bankruptcy and a heavy tax burden. So President Nixon said, "we must put the money where the needs are and put the power to spend it where the people are."

At the same time, he urged, "Congress to resist expenditures that would go beyond the limit of the budget— for as we wage a campaign to bring about a widely shared prosperity, we must not permit a rapidly rising cost of living to undermine that prosperity. The present welfare system is a national disgrace. We must start getting people off welfare rolls and onto payrolls. Let us provide the means, which more can help themselves. But let us stop helping those who are able to help themselves and refuse to do so."

On March 29, 1971, the public had a strong reaction against the Army Court Martial of 1st Lt. William Calley Jr. who was found guilty of killing 22 South Vietnamese civilians.

The North and South Vietnamese people looked alike. No one could tell who was the enemy in My Lai. This small village was a Vietcong fortified place. Our American boys had suffered many wounded and dead trying to clear out the North Vietnamese. Calley had ordered his platoon to kill all the villagers on sight.

The press and certain congressmen expressed violent excessive insults against the Vietnam War and President Nixon. They were ignoring what the atrocities the North Vietnamese Communists were committing and down played this side of murder and horror. Reports of the massacres trickled out and were not reported by the national media.

Over 5,000 telegrams against Calley's conviction arrived at the White House. Emotions were continuing to run strong in support for Dick to intervene in this case.

On April 1, 1971 President Nixon ordered that Calley be confined to his apartment on the base and removed from the stockade. Everyone applauded Nixon's decision except the anti war people. The polls showed 96% of Americans thought this was the right things to do. After that President Nixon reviewed the Calley case it was determined that Calley's sentence should be reduced and would be eligible for parole later on.

Wednesday, April 7, 1971, all last week Richard Nixon worked on his latest speech about the withdrawal of 100,000 American troops from Vietnam. When it was given, there was a common reaction among the people that it was good. Afterwards the poll showed Nixon's approval rate once again shot up from 41 to 54.

Friday, April 9, 1971, Pat and Dick decided to attend Good Friday church services at St. John's Episcopal Church across from Lafayette Park. This church is called "the Church of the Presidents" because many have worshiped there. A pew is always reserved for the President and his family. Some how someone got wind of their attendance and a dozen demonstrators had gathered there in front of the church and chanting "Peace now." They went in for the 30-minute service and departed out of a different door. But the church was surrounded by demonstrators. Any trip announced where the Nixons would attend, the anti war protestors were always there. No wonder they couldn't enjoy Easter church services elsewhere, so they would often have to cancel.

On television news, it was announced that our American table tennis team was competing in a world championship contest in Japan. China had asked our team to play a few matches in China. This became known as the "Ping-Pong diplomacy." Also, it was the beginning of the termination of our Chinese trade embargo.

Friday, April 16, 1971, Pat Nixon became very ill. She couldn't breathe. After examination by the White House doctor, he recommended she be taken to the hospital for x-rays to see what was really wrong. We feared for the worse but the doctor said she had pleurisy. This was an inflammation of the membrane that lines the chest and covers the lung. A few days rest and medication should rectify the condition.

That month of April I was driving to work at Grand Canyon College early in the morning. I had to drive 25 miles to get to the College. Traffic was heavy as usual that morning. Half way through the intersection of Bell Road and 7th Street, Phoenix, a drunk driver slammed into my car and swung it around and around and almost toppled it over. He had been late for work at Sperry Rand and ran through the red light. I was bruised and shaken up quite badly. The policeman said if I hadn't been wearing my seat belt, I would have crashed through my front car window and died.

Pat was relieved I wasn't seriously hurt and in time I would be recovered from the auto accident. She said she would be in Arizona in July, but the First Lady official schedule had not been finalized. She was hoping it would include a stop at Grand Canyon College to visit me.

One of Nixon 's greatest achievements was regarding the school segregation problem. He believed segregation was a national problem. When the Supreme Court decision struck down his neighborhood school concept and defended busing for the intention of desegregation, Nixon became the conciliator and used the art of persuasion toward the South and elsewhere. Whether it was compulsory segregation or racial balancing, he felt it was wrong and the deadlines set were unrealistic and difficult to meet. Instead he focused on education not race. Enforced the law and upheld the Constitution. Encouraged reform by offering financial assistance.

All the Presidents before him could not solve the problem, but he did. It was his willingness to work with people on the segregation issue instead of censuring them. By the time Nixon left office, others discovered his plan had worked in dissolving the situation of desegregation of schools.

Nixon believed the character of children was being destroyed by too much permissiveness. He believed young people should take responsibility for their acts themselves and don't blame others or things for their problems. Also, they should come to their conclusion, the problem is—ME—not something else or some one.

Pat supported equal rights for women. All her life she worked. She thought that women in employment should merit equal pay and treatment as men in the same type of job. Many times she discussed this with her husband.

April 22, 1971, Therefore, Barbara Franklin a staff assistant to the President was given the obligation to create a job bank for eligible competent women and to bring more women into federal government for policy-making and middle management positions. This had not been done before by any president. It all happened because of Pat Nixon's urging that it should be done.

April 24th was the big day for peace demonstrators in

Washington, D.C. Probably around 200,000 in the crowd. They marched to the Capitol and sang and made speeches. Tore down more American flags, threw bottles and rocks at police, stopped traffic and burned some things on the way. Otherwise they were not as violent as they were before.

They promised a more anti-war demonstration. On Monday, May 3rd, it happened. They wanted to block roads and bridges that had access into Washington, D.C. This way no government worker could get to his job. President Nixon debated whether to call out the National Guard. Everywhere demonstrators were running about the city. When the crowd marched to the Justice Department the police arrested several thousand. The others decided to pack up and go home to everyone's relief about the situation.

As First Lady Pat Nixon presented a plaque Tuesday in the White House diplomatic reception room, to Kate Frank, a retired 82-year-old schoolteacher from Muskogee, Oklahoma. The remarkable woman's teaching career extended for 47 years. Even though, this teacher retired in 1956, she continued to be active in community activities for teachers and senior citizens.

Pat congratulated this National Retired Teacher of the Year and cited her for her "outstanding achievements in public service activities at the community, state, and national levels which have contributed to a better life for retired teachers and for all Americans." As one teacher to another, Pat Nixon and Kate Frank exchanged stories from their teacher years and fascinated one another.

Just before her wedding to Eddie Cox, sweet Tricia Nixon was named "one of the best dressed children in America." A group of children's wear manufacturers awarded her the 1971 "Goody Two-Shoes" award.

Tricia never liked those kooky far out modern fashions. She dressed, as children should. No wonder she was the best-dressed sub-teens in the country.

By spring of 1971 Nixon moved that the production of nuclear energy to begin. He directed the first breeder reactor proposal to commence.

On June 4, 1971, his study of the threatening energy dilemma caused him to be the first President in our country to give an energy message. Nixon urged formulation of a plan to transform coal into clean fuels and to speed up gas and oil contracts to lease on property on the external shallow submarine plains of our country. Nixon recommended that all fifteen energy programs be brought together under the creation of a new Department of Energy. He wanted to find new sources of energy that would not pollute the environment and air.

One day early in June the postal carrier handed me my mail. He remarked, "You have something important in that stack of mail. I noticed it was from the White House."

Sure enough it was. In the upper left hand the words on the envelope were embossed in gold. I noticed the special American flag stamp. Inside was a second envelope. The folded white paper inside had a gold-embossed presidential coat of arms centered at the top underneath it read:

"The President and Mrs. Nixon request the honor of your presence at the marriage of their daughter Patricia to Mr. Edward Finch Cox on Saturday, the twelfth of June, one thousand nine hundred and seventy-one at four o'clock in the afternoon, The White House."

Also, a smaller card was also enclosed inviting all guests to the reception and as acceptance card for the social secretary. I had never been invited to a White House wedding before and so I was very excited to attend this one.

Edward Finch Cox, 24, was a handsome, romantic, socialite, rich, law student. Tricia and Eddie had met at a Senior High School dance. They like each other a lot, even though both were strong willed and opinionated and disagreed politically many times over many issues.

When the day of the wedding began, it was very cloudy. Periodically, a fine misty rain developed off and on all morning. The wedding was to be in the Rose Garden. President and Mrs. Nixon kept looking out the window to see if it was going to rain any more.

Since it was Tricia's wedding, it would be her decision to move it inside. However, after she consulted with her father, they both decided late in the afternoon to still have it outside. Now, the wedding ceremony would start at 4:30 p.m.

At first, Tricia hoped the wedding ceremony would be private. After thinking it over, Tricia and Eddie thought it would be proper to share with the American people their wedding via the television. All the wedding occurrences would be covered except the 10-minute ceremony. Personally, I thought Tricia would be the last person to turn her wedding ceremony for the whole public to see. To our surprise, she did.

The rain finally stopped. Pat went downstairs to the West Hall to wait with Julie. Both looked so beautiful waiting for Tricia to come. Julie, the matron of honor and the bridesmaids dressed in mint green and lilac dresses began the procession down the long staircase into the Rose Garden. The gazebo was an elaborate spectacle of breath taking beauty of flowers intertwined with one another around a wooden altar.

Then Dick Nixon escorted Tricia, his daughter, along the path to the Rose Garden. He had a happy look on his face as he led Tricia down the center aisle. For Tricia, it was her day with Eddie.

Tricia was a storybook princess doll, and she looked radiant in her exquisite, white silk organdy-wedding gown. Embroidered white lilies of the valley beaded with miniature pearls patterned the dress. She carried a small bouquet of white roses, lilies of the valley and baby's breath.

The marriage service was written by Tricia herself. The service consisted of prayers and the exchange of vows. The ceremony was performed by Rev. Edward G. Latch, chaplain of the House of Representatives, and former pastor of Washington's Metropolitan Memorial Methodist Church. He was Nixon's minister during his Vice President days and Tricia's childhood. Latch was the only clergyman to perform the ceremony.

Rev. Latch, a white-haired minister admonished Tricia and Eddie that marriage will bring pleasures and sadness, successes as well as failures.

He told them: "And so, unaware of what definitely is before you, you accept one another. To love is to appreciate and cherish our beloved as a unique person, deep, extraordinary, exceptional. It is to visualize him or her as an equal, yet complementing individual.

"Love each other, but do not make a bond of your love. Stand together but not to near together just as the pillars of a temple stand apart yet stand together."

Then Rev Latch asked the old but new question:

"Who giveth Patricia to be married to Edward?"

That was President Nixon's signal to impart his one-line consent and surrender his beloved daughter to Edward Cox's care.

The vows exchanged in this double-ring ceremony were an adaption from the Episcopalian Book of common prayer- Edward took Patricia, and Patricia took Edward, "to have and to hold, to honor and comfort, in sickness and in health in sorrow and in joy, to love and to cherish from this day forth." (Tricia had changed the last part from "until death to us part" to "from this day forth."

After Tricia and Ed were pronounced man and wife, they knelt in prayer at the altar. At the end of the ceremony, they returned to the Blue Room for photos and a reception line.

Then everyone moved into the East Room for the dancing. When the band began playing, Dick Nixon danced with Tricia and Pat with Ed. This was the first time Pat and

Dick had danced at the White House. Then he cut in and danced with Pat, and whirled Julie around the floor to everyone's pleasure and applause. During his Vice-President days no one had ever seen Nixon dance in public and so this was a surprise to everyone.

Then, we all went into the Entrance Hall. There we saw the most tallest and widest giant Lady Baltimore cake. I was sure the bottom layer of the cake could have fed all of us. This huge cake was topped with a sugary gazebo filled with eatable cherry blossoms. Figurines of a bride and groom were not included on the top of the cake either. Adorning the cake were sugar decorations of flowers, wedding rings and lovebirds. It looked almost too beautiful to eat. Each guest took home a slice of cake in a special tiny decorative box for a memento of the occasion.

Afterwards Tricia tossed her bridal bouquet from the staircase. Then Tricia and Ed departed out the back door of the North Portico onto Pennsylvania Avenue. She was still wearing her wedding dress. Everyone threw rice and cheered, as they departed for Camp David for their honeymoon.

Julie, Pat and Dick went upstairs to talk things over and watch TV specials about Tricia's wedding. They enjoyed it and were proud that Tricia had chosen Eddie for her husband.

However, they were saddened by the knowledge that Tricia and Julie were now married. This would remind them they would not have their daughters around. Henceforth Pat and Dick would live alone in the White House.

Julie would have to leave Sunday to join David. Pat helped her to pack and took her to the airport the next day.

On Sunday morning, June 13th, after church I picked up several national newspapers to see how the papers treated Tricia's wedding. When I picked up the "New York Times" from the stack, I recognized the picture of President Nixon and Tricia in the Rose Garden on the front page. The headline above it read "Tricia Nixon Takes Vows." However, the next headline next to the picture said, "Vietnam Archive: Pentagon Study Traces 3 Decades of Growing U.S. Involvement."

I was wondering why the New York Times put this Vietnam U.S. story on the front page opposite Tricia's wedding. It described American involvement in Vietnam from World War II through 1968, which Robert McNamara, Secretary of Defense under President Lyndon B. Johnson, had commissioned the study. The New York Times failed to tell their nationwide readers that they had obtained illegally top secret documents. It blasted President John F. Kennedy and President Lyndon B. Johnson administrations for their involvement in South East Asia.

It was the biggest leak of secret classified documents in U.S. history. President Nixon was concerned about foreign policy and staff leakage in every department of government.

Of course before the publication, the New York Times did not inquire at the White House if this would endanger the American boys lives in Vietnam or threaten national security. All they thought about was a story or the money received from the articles published. Personally, I thought they were irresponsible journalists and were not working for the good of the country. This information the New York Times published was profitable to the Soviet Union and the North Vietnamese Communists. Apparently someone there didn't have their thinking cap on straight!

What was President Nixon to do? Should he move toward the New York Times? He was certain the publication-"The Pentagon Papers" would hinder the effort to bring the Vietnam War to an honorable conclusion. Even though, Nixon did not start the war, it did reveal in 1963 President John F. Kennedy's involvement in the coup that caused Vietnam President Diem's death. President Lyndon Johnson saying he would not increase the number of men in the Vietnam War, but in secret he was calling up about 185,000 American boys instead.

The New York Times and the Washington Post had done

a complete flip-flop about the publication of the "Pentagon Papers." In the 1960's as I remember, Otto Otepka from the State Department showed classified documents to the Senator's committee about lax security pertaining to governmental affairs.

How about the Cuban missile crisis when Stewart Alsop, a columnist for "Newsweek" magazine wrote about the plans of the National Security Council Members? Why did this newspaper fume that this was a breach of security?

Those two newspapers at that time were outraged and indignant that anyone would do such a thing. Now they were doing the same, as the man they accused years before.

The attorney general ordered The New York Times to cease publication. The Washington Post, St. Louis Post Dispatch, and Boston Globe decided they wanted a piece of the action and obtained copies too. However, the New York Times refused.

When a Federal Court temporarily barred the Times publication of the documents, what did they do? They peddled the papers to other Anti-Vietnam War newspapers. Eventually, it went to anti-war congressman to force a quick withdrawal date of our forces in Southeast Asia. They forgot who would want to exchange their views if the next day it would be published worldwide? If a negotiated peace is in the United States interest for Vietnam, the New York Times did not help in this matter. These tactics would eventually lead to a destruction of the freedom of press.

President Nixon ordered that no one should be interviewed by the New York Times unless he granted that request. President Nixon believed in the security of government secret documents and what the New York Times did was a violation of Top Secret classifications. He did not want to be connected to it since it was a deception practiced by the Kennedy and Johnson Democrat Administrations.

Then, President Nixon got "wind" of information the

Soviet Union had obtained a copy of the Pentagon Papers long before the New York Times did. He discovered Daniel Ellsberg was the man who was responsible for the leaking of the papers. By this time Nixon was frustrated and furious, and he was determined that the Democrats would not make the Vietnam War an election issue. After all, all of the things achieved were done by Democrat administrations, and he was not going to take the blame for their "misbaubles" and mistakes.

Saturday, June 19th Pat and Dick flew to Key Biscayne, Florida to relax if they could. They were still President and First Lady and the country's business went with them-even there. He was still disturbed about the New York Times case and how David Ellsburg stole the papers and how the Times printed them. They both did something wrong and violated the law.

Sunday June 20th they went to Key Biscayne Community Church, and also celebrating their 31st wedding anniversary at the Florida White House. They were still happy about Tricia's wedding and held precious memories of the occasion, which became all the more cherished when friends shared their warm sentiments about it.

One Wednesday in June, President Nixon surprised everyone when he dumped the Pentagon Papers case in the laps of the Democrat Senators, Mike Mansfield and Carl Albert. He wanted to see how they would handle it. This way it would put the fire under them instead of the Nixon administration. Also Nixon reminded Senator Mansfield about his amendment in setting a definite date to end the Vietnam War in 9 months. He told this Democrat Senator in-no-uncertain terms, if the Nixon administration failed in its negotiations to end the war, it would be the action of the Senate that wrecked the peace with honor. If so, President Nixon would have to go to the people and tell them what happened.

The next day Dick went to Indiana to a dedication ceremony for a historical marker to serve as a memorial for his mother's home. The whole community came out and they sang with the band. It was a very enthusiastic crowd.

Then, President Nixon journeyed to Chicago from Indianapolis. Mayor Richard Daley Sr. met the President's plane at Meigs Field. It was unusual for a Democrat Mayor like Daley to go out of his way to pull out all the welcome stops for Richard Nixon. He had his bagpipe band playing and fireboats spraying the water red, white, and blue.

The parade route was changed enroute because the police shot a man in Grant Park in a gun battle. Everyone was excited about this and didn't know if the person was waiting for President Nixon or not.

Dick Nixon was perturbed what was going on around him in his administration. He was tired of all of his decisions finding its way on the front of every newspaper or moved around by the TV media. Nixon realized that most of the bureaucy was against him, and that his administration was open like a sieve. Everything around him was unraveling daily and getting out.

Departments were fighting another. He expected that would happen. But, why in the world why were they letting the press know about all the bloodletting? Nixon made it perfectly clear he was the one who would make the decisions. Don't take it on their authority but clear it with him. After all he only wanted a little discipline. Anyone who violated national interest, Dick Nixon was going after anyone who leaked about it.

President Nixon was determined that Daniel Ellsberg be prosecuted for what he did. When he heard Ellsberg say he did it for the sake of the country, it brought up memories of Alger Hiss. He said the same thing. Definitely, Dick thought it was some kind of conspiracy, and that Daniel Ellsberg did not act alone.

July 5, 1971, Nixon thought if 18-year-old boys were old

enough to be drafted in the military, they should have the right to vote. On this date, Nixon signed into law this legislation. It was under the Nixon administration the draft of young men law was also cancelled and annulled.

Pat Nixon came to Arizona and visited Williams Air Force Base to observe the summer youth program, July 12, for under privileged children. Two hundred Arizona children would participate in the summer program conducted by Williams Base, which is the largest of all the 10 undergraduate pilot training bases in the United States.

There would be 45 young people employed. There would be many supervised activities, athletics, tournaments, instruction classes, and contests. Also, there would be career seminars for senior teen in nursing, medicine, dentistry, flight training, engineering and law.

The young people were hired in jointly with the Arizona State employment office and Bureau of Indian Affairs. Their employment would include work on maintenance on roads and grounds.

Pat Nixon in her one day there thought this was a worthwhile program the Air Force personnel had produced. She reported her observations to the Air Force officials in Washington.

Because her schedule was so tight, she couldn't come to Grand Canyon College as planned to visit. She hoped the students would not be too disappointed and their hopes dashed.

In late July, Pat became the First Patroness of the American Rose society. She politely received the honor at the White House.

American beauty rose "Garden Party. The roses were so beautiful and life-like. It was so difficult to know that the roses were not the real thing. One had to touch them to discover that.

Pat said, "Because I share in the universal response of

admiration for the rose, it will be an honor and pleasure for me to be associated with the Rose Society in this capacity."

All rosarians across the land voiced their hopes that Pat Nixon could attend the grand opening of the hundred-acre site of American Roses Center in Shreveport, Louisiana. As First Lady she could participate in every Rose Society's national function. All the Rose Societies were clamoring for her attention and wanted her to attend any of their lavish, spectacular rose shows or events.

1972 would be an election year. Dick was concerned that the Vietnam War would be a big issue. He wanted all the ammunition he could get against the Vietnam War critics. Truly, Dick was being battered from both sides. He was really from all the pressure and stress put on him. Wanted to get-a way on a real vacation.

Richard Nixon believed in open public communication administration regardless of how many people around him were attacking him on many issues. He felt that our country was in a deep moral and character crisis and needed patriotic leadership from the churches, labor and education. Where were the leaders to come out strong on issues? No one wanted to stand for what was right and speak out. One side would tell him he didn't care and the other side said you didn't go far enough and was too soft. At that time Dick was discouraged and overwhelmed. Who could he turn to when he needed them?

President Nixon made the announcement on July 15; he would be going to China. There was a lot of talk about the Soviet Union reaction, but 3 months later, the Russians agreed to a Soviet U.S. summit.

July 23, 1971, the Roper poll showed President Nixon how the people were feeling about how things were going in the country. When 23% of the population felt we were going in the right direction, this got his immediate attention. The people thought the cause of the problems were: 31 % forgot about God, 27% economic and jobs, 33% racial tension, 40% Vietnam, and 47% said drugs were the problem. If everyone was discouraged and dissatisfied, it was time for him to act to change this discouraging direction of the country.

So he got busy on the various issues the people were interested in-drugs, veterans, agriculture, education, crime, pollution of the environment, and Senior Citizens. At that time, Dick Nixon favored a voucher plan and tax credits for education as also being proposed today. It was Richard Nixon who thought of it first. He was concerned that teenagers were committing over half of the savage and forcible crimes. How to stop it was another thing on his mind. Dick felt that the veterans and farmers had been forgotten. Since he was a veteran he wanted to move things forward to help them. If prices went up for the farmer, he realized that the cost of living would go up too. All he wanted was peace without war and economical prosperity for his country.

Pat Nixon thought people should help people. As First Lady, she chose volunteer service as her special concern. She realized that there are many serious problems in our inner cities, in education and in health. Many individuals can accomplish things that government alone cannot do. This is where she could help and encourage others to make life better for those around them.

Pat had grown up during the Depression years as I had. She knew what it was like to be without a job. During those years, it was terrible. Many people did not have food and jobs were scarce. It was a time for people helping one another because we all were in the "same boat." By helping one person, she accomplished something by bringing joy to other people.

Because what was in her heart, many remembered Pat Nixon what she did. All her lifetime she was a volunteer helping others. Many families she adopted and helped them to supply their needs. Never did she do this for publicity.

Whenever she went on trips overseas, she would visit hospitals and non-profit organizations and take books, candy, and medical supplies.

She felt that if everyone would spend 30 minutes or more helping others and demonstrate to them we care as a nation. Just to show a little bit of kindness and love to someone else. Love does matter. Letting that person know you really do care and that in any difficulty you were there to help. She taught me to give of myself, which was one of the greatest things I could do. I found joy, fulfillment and a challenge what I did.

Pat encouraged everyone to volunteer their service in every sphere of activity, because it would improve life everywhere. A smile or a friendly word doesn't take very much time. If everyone takes the time and tries volunteering, it could change life around us, she thought. Most of all working with children is most important. What we do, will improve their chances in the future.

She believed everyone should join the political party of their choice and then work to get people elected to public office. Pat thought it was important to write letter or phone elected officials and tell them what you think. Letters to the Editor was a good thing to reach others with your opinion. Like anything else, Pat said that's how you get good government and anything else in the community.

Time was flying by and it was July already. The 1972 election would be here sooner than we think. My Pueblo Grande Republican Women's Club decided to have a fund-raiser luncheon, August 7th using Pat Nixon's personal recipes.

Even though we found out what was cooking in Washington, Pat gave us assistance right from the White House. She gave us full support by supplying the Nixon family cuisine favorites for our Saturday luncheon.

Pat Nixon's personal recipes for hot chicken salad was supplanted with cool melon surprise and delectable blueberry dessert. It was all arranged around a star-spangled, Pat's photo centerpiece on the buffet. Even the Phoenix Gazette newspaper came out and took a picture of this affair. It really drummed up some grass roots support through kitchen politics. One thing Pat was a very good cook and everyone enjoyed the First Lady's recipes.

Pat could not have the pleasure to be there and the opportunity to personally appraise my culinary expertise with her recipes, she wished me well. Also, she included the address of the 1972 campaign re-election headquarters. She remarked it was thoughtful of me to look that far ahead and offering my assistance for Dick's Presidential re-election.

In mid-August in a five-state cross-country trip, Pat Nixon journeyed for the President in Legacy of Parks mission. She was returning eleven million dollars worth of Federal real estate of 4,249 acres to the American people for parklands. This program placed special emphasis on the growth of recreational and park areas that would be easily accessible to city dwellers.

Pat turned over a $3.5 million, 230-acre parcel to the National Park Service Director at McLean, Virginia. The land would be used for a baseball park, bicycle paths, walking trials, and picnic area.

Then following the McLean ceremony, Pat flew to Battle Creek, Michigan to deliver the deed for a 4,000-acre package of old Ft. Custer to Michigan's Lt. Governor James Brickley. While there she tramped the lakeshore trails, tasted franks and coffee of Boy Scouts camping and inspected their tents and hit hard a volleyball over a net.

Tuesday, she went to Ft. Snelling in the Minneapolis-St. Paul area to transfer 141 acres from the federal government to the state of Minnesota. This way no federal bureaucy could take this beautiful place for any other kind of building. Pat sat on the Parade Grounds platform with many dignitaries in the scorching sun while many were remarking about the transfer of the property.

During Pat Nixon's speech, several member of the American Indian Movement (AIM) protested the transfer of land. They held up signs, "Nixon Speaks with Forked Tongue," No Free Giveaways Today." "Another Tricky Dick Land theft," and yelled and yelled, "Indian land, give us back our land!"

The Indians claimed that Zebulon Pike in 1809 stole the land in an illegal treaty. The land was taken many years ago long before any of us were born. Pat had never seen any protest like this one at Ft. Snelling. Some people heckled the Indian demonstrators and the Indians yelled back at the hecklers.

When she left the platform, she watched four men on polo ponies demonstrating how polo was played. Pat stopped to see the three men exhibit putting on a beautiful golf green. She tried several times herself and missing all three. She joined an outing of Senior Citizens and cheered a Little League ball game. Pat signed baseball gloves for little leaguers and any thing else for those who were fortunate not to have gloves. Wherever she trekked, the Secret Service, FBI agents and local sheriff's deputies followed her.

After Ft. Snelling, Pat flew from Minnesota to Oregon. A cheering crowd of thousands awaited her arrival. The Oregon region of 500 acres included Camp White, a novel reserve training station and Adair Air Force Station.

Pat said Camp White was the best of fans she had in a long time. She rode in a Conestoga old-style covered wagon over a bumpy trail. Stood for more than an hour in hot, blinding sun, watching sky diving exhibitions, dune-riding motorcyclists racing and Labrador dogs retrieving.

Her tour's final ceremony in burning heat at the Mexican border on August 18th in which Pat Nixon turned over a 6,000-foot ocean-front military tract, Border Field to the California Treasurer. It marked the 39th transfer of federal government-held properties to state and local governments.

Democrats and Republicans alike could take a lesson from Pat Nixon. She was deeply moved by the hundreds of Mexicans behind the barbed wire fence peeking at her. She thought this border fence separated the people of two friendly countries. The official White House plan was to cut a part of the fence and let an authorized Mexican delegation come into the United States to greet Mrs. Nixon. But, Pat had a different plan. She asked if the barbed wire fence could be cut so she could go over the border and greet thousands of Mexicans on the other side.

Then, she walked right through the hole in the fence followed by a crowd of cheering Americans and mingled with the Mexican crowd. They besieged Pat Nixon just to touch her and say thank you for coming. In turn, Pat held a child from Mexico and an United States child in her arms. If there was any hostility that day, Pat erased it by one single ladylike courtesy. Her sudden move worked wonders.

Pat Nixon found lots of enthusiasm for her husband on her cross-country trip. People were telling her personally that they were for Richard Nixon's re-election. They liked what he was doing, and that Nixon was doing a good job for the country.

While Pat was finishing up her "Legacy of Parks" trip cross-country. Dick was starting a cross-country trip of his own in New York City, addressing the Knights of Columbus Catholic organization the evening of August 17th that would eventually end at the San Clemente Western White House, in California.

After staying overnight in New York, President Nixon took a plane to Springfield, Illinois, to sign a bill establishing Abraham Lincoln's home as a national historical site.

There were immense crowds everywhere along the motorcade routes to the Illinois Capitol and at the Illinois State Fair. At the State Fair he was virtually swamped and squeezed by the people there. The reaction from the crowd caused Dick Nixon to be more encouraged that things were much better for him in the heartland.

On August 18,1971, President Nixon left for Idaho Falls, Idaho. A very good crowd met him at the airport. He stayed overnight in a pretty cabin by the lake at the Grand Teton National Park at Jackson Hole, Wyoming. The trout dinner was so delicious; Dick had some for every meal. After taking a boat tour around the lake and taking in the beautiful scenery, he departed for Dallas, Texas to speak at the Veterans of Foreign Wars. Since he helicopter from the airport to the stadium Dick avoided crowds of demonstrators waiting for him outside.

His trip ended in San Clemente where Pat and Dick would begin their second summer working vacation. In July, they had spent 12 days there.

By August 28, 1971, the residents of Cerritos, California were so enthused about Pat Nixon, they decided to make plans to dedicate a museum in her honor. It was the first time a museum would be built for a First Lady—a wife of a President. It would dwell in a white three-room house where Pat had lived as a child—now located on the Pat Nixon Park. The Cerritos Chamber of Commerce endorsed the project as well as the blessing came from the President himself.

Across the country, people knew that Pat Nixon cared and listened to their problems and needs. Thousands of letters poured in each week. Pat read each letter and saw to-it that response was given. When she could not help personally, Pat referred that person's cry for help to a government agency, which could assist and remedy the situation. Every letter was signed by her personally. She wouldn't let anyone do that for her.

Pat always did her personal laundry, undressed herself and hung up her own clothes. When she went on trips she did packing and unpacking of her own luggage. Never late. Always ready with a warm smile and handshake. Although, independent she put others before herself.

President Nixon had problems in 1971 on the domestic home fronts as well in the foreign affairs. The inflation rate had diminished and the stock market took a sharp turn down. The Democrat Congress was concerned. In 1970 they issued legislation to give President Nixon authority to issue wage and price controls. Nixon resisted making compulsory government controls on wages and prices. He thought that the controls would interfere with the free market and dictate regulations for business and labor.

The National Commission on Productivity and the Council of Economic Advisors, Nixon had appointed to look into the situation were ineffective. With a Democrat Congress at the front door and a lack of confidant public at the back door, Nixon was caught in between a rock and hard place. What was he suppose to do? If he did not do some action, would the economy recover?

All though the year of 1971, the economy was still sluggish. Nixon finally acted on wage and price controls after consulting with others about it. He was still against any form of price and wage controls, but he was forced to do it against his better judgment. On the short term, it was immensely popular with the public and the Democrat Congress. After it was all over, Nixon was right that wage and price controls were not the answer. As a country we paid a high price for monk eying with the mechanisms of economics.

Personally, I thought America was at the crossroads. When all taxes took about 50% of our income, we would be working for the government than for ourselves.

Another young man, John Dean, was appointed by Haldeman in 1970. I didn't like Dean's attitude either. He had "hippie" style with long blonde hair and drove a Porsche sport car. He loved digging up dirt on anyone who opposed President Nixon and spread that gossipy dirt around. Haldeman and Dean made a good pair together, as far as I was concerned. They were the same in their tactics.

In July,1971, Dorothy A. Kabis,Treasurer of the United States, her untimely tragic death occurred. This position had always been filled by a woman. Her duty was to sign currency.

On September 19th, President Nixon nominated Romana A. Banuelos, a native Mexican-American from Miami, Arizona to be the new treasurer of the United States. She would be the first Latin-American background to be appointed to a government high position with Senate approval. Nixon had searched the country for a woman who was qualified and had the ability to be treasurer. President Nixon asked for a pen so Mrs. Banuelos could give him a sample of her signature that would ultimately be on our nation's paper money. All he wanted to see how that signature would look on the currency. And, when he did look at it, Nixon thought it was much more neater than his own writing.

October 2, 1971, President Nixon appointed Governor Ronald Reagan of California for a tour of six Asian Nations. He was to be the president's personal emissary.

When Pat Nixon gave me the address of the Re-election of President Nixon, I wrote to them offering my assistance in helping with the campaign. Robert C. Odle, Jr. replied on October 4, 1971 to my letter. At their particular point in time they were just beginning to plan their activities in the area in which I expressed an interest and develop their thinking as what should be done in the forth coming campaign. They decided to put my name in an active file, so that my assistance offer can be acted upon at the appropriate time.

However, this concerned me because I knew in the1968 campaign we had planned political activities away ahead. Perhaps, a new bunch had different ideas or there was an exclusion of those who had worked in all Nixon campaigns.

The 3-day biennial conventions of the National Federation of Republican Women were held in Washington, D.C. October 21, 1971. Dodie Londen, one of the club presidents decided we would be roommates at the hotel. We had a delightful time with over two thousand women and munching on tasty fish and lobster at a restaurant by the bay.

At no time did Dodie and others know I was a personal friend of the Nixons. I kept that secret to myself until we all went to the White House for a reception.

Pat was shaking hands with hundreds of ladies. She couldn't miss our "Nixon '72" pins that sparkled on our dresses and purses. Some she posed for photographers and autographed pieces of papers.

Then when I came next in line, Pat made a fuss over me to Dodie's surprise. Of course, Pat brought me over to the Chicago Tribune reporters and told all about me. Dodie couldn't get over that I was a personal friend of the Nixons, and I was her roommate for the convention. Now, my secret was out of the bag! I wasn't quite sure at that time I could cope with all the instant spotlight. Then, my life took a certain turn-a-round, and my life changed from private to public. Everyone would know. Pat gave a warm hug. That was one of the most precious moments of my life.

November 4, 1971, Prime Minister Indira Gandhi, India, paid a visit. Pat and Indira had shared many mutual things since Pat was Second Lady. Indira Gandhi was a national Indian leader willing to fight for the power to govern where she lived. Pat desired no power for herself even though, she was in the thick of power things herself.

Overlooking the south lawn of the White House, President Nixon and Pat, with Indira Gandhi from the balcony, pointed toward the welcoming ceremony. As usual Nixon gave his welcoming speech without any notes. He made the point that India and the United States were not bound by a treaty but a special relationship. Urged Indira to not seize the opportunity to intervene in the East Pakistan's independence from Pakistan.

Nixon was aware of India's alignment with the Soviets in Moscow and China's interest in East Pakistan. Mrs. Gandhi expressed words of peace but did not offer any suggestions or commitment to decrease the dangerous peril. As time passed President Nixon expressed that Indira Gandhi had deceived him at their meeting in November. She talked peace, but Gandhi didn't practice what she preached. She said one thing and did the opposite. As the American Indians would say-she talked with a "forked tongue."

President Nixon used a diplomatic signs and compulsion to save West Pakistan from being invaded by India armies. The presence of cautious Chinese armies on the border of discouraged the India armies from acting. A cease-fire was arranged to everyone's relief.

When I picked up "The Washington Post" newspaper, Jack Anderson, a syndicated columnist, had published word for word what had gone on in the meetings. Everyone was wondering who had leaked the information. This action by a newspaper journalist disturbed and surprised me that members of the Joint Chief of Staff were spying on Richard Nixon and leaking secret information to the media.

In the middle of the Vietnam War, there was no excuse by journalists or anyone else for this kind of behavior. It was distressing for all of us to hear and see day after day, listening to all the bombasting ranting speech of lectures against Nixon. We could reply, but he could not. At that point, I determined to be an advocate and defend Richard Nixon. If someone disagrees with the administration policies, no one should take secret information to a newspaper journalist and put the country in jeopardy.

In November, President Nixon conferred with Pat regarding her potential trip to Africa. Pat agreed to the plans, as well as Julie's it was suggested that only one television network would have the exclusive right for her trip. President Nixon wanted Pat to talk with each President in the countries she would visit.

We were all keeping our eyes on Julie Nixon Eisenhower comings and goings. She popped up in New York, Ohio, New Jersey, and recently in Illinois. We knew the 1972 re-election campaign was now on the way. Her husband, Ensign David Eisenhower, was on current duty on the U.S.S. Albany, a missile cruiser, and so Julie was campaigning for her father's programs while David was on sea duty.

Since her father can't be everywhere, Julie was glad to represent him. Dick would like to meet each one on a one-to-one basis to convince them he really did care about them. It was always a joy to see how Julie in her youthful political style won over each one on her various campaign trips.

When the Turkey Growers Association presented a 35-pound turkey to President Nixon and family, Pat was chosen to accept the turkey in the Rose Garden ceremony. But Pat granted the turkey a reprieve and sent it to a children's farm to live. When the press didn't believe the Nixons were not going to eat the turkey, they sent a reporter out to the farm to check if the turkey was alive, active and lively. Wasn't that something?

Pat was glad I remembered them at Thanksgiving time and all about the interesting account of my recent activities. My friendship and support was a constant source of encouragement for which they were grateful.

After Thanksgiving the public usually starts their Christmas shopping. Pat was not exception and took advantage of that time of year. Pat and Julie went to stores like Sears Roebuck in Washington, which were cooperating with President Nixon to keep the lid on prices. She looked over a selection of neckties and decided on a red, white and blue striped tie, a pair of blue sneakers and an electric popcorn popper.

On December 6, 1971, it was a delight to see NBC "Day in the Life of the President" on television. It was interesting to see that the NBC TV persons were elated how the day went and how President Nixon gave them more time in his office.

President Nixon wanted Julie to do a Christmas TV special. Pat wasn't sure it was the right thing to do. So it was off and on thing with Julie and Pat. After discussing it, Pat decided that Julie could do the Christmas Eve televised tour of the White House.

Before the Christmas Eve event, President Nixon promised Pat and Julie to go to New York City for a family trip for dinner and theater. While they were there, they would be able to attend Sunday services at Dr. Norman Vincent Peale's Reformed Church. Dick was concerned that everyone should know the true meaning of Christmas and that one-day we would be able to live in peace without war.

The White House emphasized the spirit of Christmas this year. Christmas decorations, trees and lights were put in place earlier than usual. The biggest attraction in the Blue Room was a 20-foot Fraser fir tree from North Carolina. It glowed with thousands of gold and white lights. The eight-inch satin and velvet ornaments were bedecked with miniature flowers or gems of our 50 states and District of Columbia.

In the Cross Hall the huge chandelier was decorated with cardinals, pinecones and graduated wreaths. Outside south of the White House the "National Christmas Tree, a 65 foot fir tree was set up on the Ellipse for all of us to see. Pat saw that the 18th century Italian Nativity scene was in place. It was the fifth year that the crèche had been part of the Christmas season at the White House.

Christmas 1971 was a happy busy time for the Nixon family. Many parties echoed with joyful laughter in the White House. In the East Room 60 children from the Los Angeles Foundation for the Junior Blind were welcomed by Pat and Julie. There everyone was delighted with their marvelous singing of beautiful songs from "The Sound of Music."

Pat and Dick were happy that Tricia, Julie, David, and Ed could be with them this Christmas Eve. It was a perfect evening with family and the dogs enjoying their Christmas doggy stockings.

Everyone was laughing as "Jingle Bells" was sung in different versions, especially the ones where dogs were barking. Every time I heard that barking dog song at Christmas time, it reminded me of so many memories of a very happy time long ago. None of us realized at that time what was going to happen in 1972 to menace happier times.

Chapter 17

CHINA AND RUSSIAN TRIPS AND THE 1972 CAMPAIGN

The year of 1972 was an exciting one with sad and unusual happenings. The Vietnam War was not over and persisted in the news forever and ever. The media was manufacturing stories, which weren't true about the Nixon administration. It was difficult to defend the credibility of each news story which came out.

Since November 1971, Pat Nixon's seven-day trip to Africa, as a diplomat, had been planned. On January 1, 1972, she flew to Liberia, West Africa, to attend the inauguration of the new 19th. President William Tolbert. Pat led the official delegation, which included Billy Graham, the evangelist and the Grambling College marching band from Ruston, Louisiana. The crowd was enthusiastic about the college band's abilities and performance. Everyone was fanning themselves in the over a hundred degree heat. Because of the extreme humidity, the clothes of those attending were saturated to the bone.

We were delighted with CBS television coverage of Pat Nixon's African trip. We heard the music of unshaped sunken timber drums and watched tribal women dance. Pat was wrapped in floor-length bright blue cloth from head to toe, and the happy African women covered her head with a bright cheerful turban of 3 yards of cloth. She was surprised and joined the troupe leader in a few African dance steps.

In Ghana, Pat spoke at the National Assembly and she was welcomed with cheers. She renewed a friendship with a Ghana African tribal chief who they both knew when she was Second Lady.

The press corps, who accompanied Pat Nixon on her African trip, marveled at her ability to work with leaders of countries she visited. Even though, neither one of them couldn't understand a word of what the other was saying, Pat was getting along gloriously. Also, they were surprised the way she directed any meetings or conference with the press.

Pat arrived back to Washington in time for Dick's fifty-ninth birthday, January 9. Dick was pleased with my photo cube displaying snapshots of one of Julie's birthday parties and my "1972 Moody Daily Reminder" pocket diary for his birthday party.

I thought Pat looked very tired after her strenuous African trip. Not one of President Nixon's staff gave credit personally to Pat for her accomplishments on the trip as First Lady. Of course, Haldeman would never mention what Pat had done to win the approval of the people in the country. That would hurt his ego and pride to tell her personally. In spite of this, Dick showed his approval of everything Pat did. Pat would always be first in his heart, and he let everyone know it around him.

The 1972 Campaign was on its way. Just one block from the White House a "Citizens Committee" opened a campaign office to re-elect President Nixon. The White House staff said President Nixon was aware of the efforts of the publisher of the "Cincinnati Enquirer" had done. But no one had encouraged the promotion by the group. It was just a grass roots campaign movement.

On January 14th, Dick addressed the students and faculty

of the University of Nebraska. Before thousands of students he said,

"There can be no generation gap in America. The destiny of this nation is not divided into yours and ours—it is one destiny. We share it together. We are responsible for it together. There has been too much emphasis on the differences between the generations in America. There has been too much of a tendency of many of my generation to blame all of your generation for the excesses of a violent few. So let us forge an alliances of the generations. Let us work together to seek out those ways by which the commitments and the compassion of one generation can be linked to the will and the experience of another, so that together we can serve America better, and American can better serve mankind."

"I will ask Congress to combine the Peace Corps, Vista and related agencies into a "new volunteer service corps that will give young people an expanded opportunity for service you want to give. This new agency will permit millions to contribute time, talents and your hearts to building better communities, a better country, and a better world.

"How will you do this? By dedicating yourselves to clean up the environment, combating illiteracy, malnutrition and suffering at home or abroad."

Shouts of "Peace now" and few boos interrupted Nixon, but the lively students crowd's applause drowned out their expressions. As the Nixons went outside after the Nebraska speech, some one tossed a snowball at Dick. To everyone's amusement, he stopped and picked it up. Then, he hurled it back at the students.

The greatest story of 1972 campaign year was the depth and breadth of public confidence and trust in President Nixon, based purely on his record as President. He did no campaigning in the primary elections and received in the Republican primaries astounding majorities. He had unified the Republican Party and the country. The majority of people would vote for him and not just against Senator McGovern, his opponent.

Nixon's most important job was to identify the positive voters and make sure they would get out to vote. We were determined that all the people would actually vote and not for or against each man. Many 18 year-old youth could now vote for the first time. Nixon wanted to improve his image among our youth in America.

After his western trip to Alaska to communicate with Emperor Hirohito of Japan, President Nixon took a long plane ride back to Washington in time in honor of Mamie Eisenhower's 75th birthday party. She was always Nixon's favorite celebrated person. Pat always wanted the White House to be Mamie's second home.

Even though Mamie's real birthday was on November 14th, the birthday party was held in advance of that date, because of national love and high esteem held by our country. Everyone who came to Mamie's party received an American flag brooch.

President Nixon went to the stage at the Washington Hilton Hotel to play "Happy Birthday" twice on the piano. A thousand voices sang that birthday tune. Then, the West Point Cadets chimed in to sing, "Army Blue," Mamie had to burst into tears as her husband, "Ike" had loved this song as his favorite.

The five-tier pink birthday cake was a sight to behold. It even matched Mamie's lovely pink dress. Three gifts of a diamond tree-of-life pin, a "Military Wife of the Century" plaque, and a music box overwhelmed Mamie again with tears of gratitude.

Ray Bolger, from "Wizard of Oz" fame, stole the show by rising to sing "Once in Love with Mamie." Then, the Marine Band played "Ruffles and Flourishes" to let President Nixon say a few closing remarks.

He said, "Mamie is the most heartwarming example of the kind of wife a man needs, the kind of wife who remains strong in the background while her husband is out there in the arena fighting."

Pat remarked, "We love Mamie and wish she would be with us more often. She really is my ideal. When I am asked which First Lady I would like to be like, I think of her. The Queen's Room will always be ready and waiting for her to stay as often as she wants."

Even though, Pat Nixon thought Mamie Eisenhower was her ideal of a First Lady, I considered Pat, as an example of what a First Lady, should be.

She always liked her job as First Lady despite there wasn't enough hours in the day to complete her busy schedule. Pat really worked! Somehow, she kept herself above controversy throughout her husband's politically defeats, victories and crisis. Pat viewed her role as a supporting one and trained herself to avoid any controversial public issue or matter.

I was glad Pat Nixon was her self and not trying to imitate First Ladies as Eleanor Roosevelt or today as Hillary Rodman Clinton. As First Lady, she encouraged communities to start self-help projects, volunteer and education programs and inspired worthwhile goals for young people.

When Pat moved into the White House she thought that women already had equal rights. As American women became touchy on the subject she let others know that she supported the equal rights amendment. I knew this position apparently was taken reluctantly and unwillingly under protest.

Many people do not know that Congress holds Congressional prayer breakfasts. It has been the tradition since the time of World War II. The Senators hold their prayer meetings on Wednesday in the Capitol's Vandenberg Room and then on Thursdays the Representatives have their prayer meeting group. This is the time when congressional leaders forget their differences to express their belief in the power of prayer.

In 1952, prayer breakfast leaders of Congress approached President-elect Eisenhower about the idea of an annual prayer breakfast, which the President could attend with them. Eisenhower endorsed the idea. Most reporters and television cameras were barred from covering the prayer event.

On February 1st, more than 3,000 persons attended with President and Mrs. Nixon at this annual National Prayer Breakfast. Many religious leaders were invited to attend. This was the largest group participating in a presidential prayer breakfast.

President Nixon told Americans that we should all engage in silent prayer in order to hear the instruction of God. In his 15-minute speech, he said, "Try to listen more to what God wants rather than telling God what we want. That as a child I use to ask my grandmother why Quakers prayed silently, and I was told that the purpose of prayer is not to tell God what thee wants but to find out from God what he wants from thee. What this nation needs to do now is pray in silence and listen to God and find out what He wants for us and then we'll all do the right thing."

The prayer breakfast and the Nixon white House worship services had aroused so much attention and interest that many people had written congressmen and President Nixon for invitations.

Pat and the cabinet wives got together and worked on needlepoint replicas of presidential seals, which she had created. When they finished with their needlework project, the beautiful seals were displayed in the Blair House in Washington, D.C. She was awarded ribbons with scissor and pincushions attached for the needlepoint creation.

A few days before Pat and President Nixon went on their China trip, I received word at 2:30 a.m. that my brother Howard, in Dodge City, Kansas suffered a heart attack and was in the hospital there. I didn't know what to do. The airline pilots were on strike, and I was in the middle of spring college registration and getting it ready for the computer. It was difficult to keep my mind on my work. After talking to Dr. Sutherland our Dean of Education, it was decided my trained student assistant would take over until I could get back from Kansas. We piled into the car and drove as fast as the legal limits allowed on the Arizona highways.

When we arrived in Liberal, Kansas, I phoned the hospital in Dodge City. I was saddened when I found he had passed away at 7:30 p.m. We couldn't make it into Dodge City, so we decided to stay in the motel in Liberal.

There, I turned on the TV news and discovered that this was the day (February 17) that Pat and Dick was departing for the Middle East. There I saw President Nixon waving from the steps of the presidential helicopter before departing to Andrews Air Force Base where they were to board the Spirit of 76. I thought Pat looked very fatigued and bothered. No wonder after her African trip, Pat had to bone up and do her home work for this special journey to China. Surely, Pat would see more of China than her husband.

After stopping enroute in cold and rainy Hawaii and a brief stop in Guam, the Nixons then went on to China. The day there was frigid and wintry but shiny when they arrived at the Peking airport. After the airport ceremony with Premier Chou En-Lai, they were whisked away in a car through town to the official guesthouse. No crowds of Chinese people were allowed at the airport or along the motorcade to wave or cheer.

While President Nixon and Premier Chou En-Lai talked shop for three and half hours, Pat Nixon was adhering to her own rigorous schedule of diplomacy activity. Her enthusiasm surprised her Chinese hosts. She made an effort to mingle with the children, peasants, and ordinary people such as technicians and workers. Since the press corps were shut out from the diplomatic talks they followed Pat Nixon and recorded every activity she was engaged in.

Nixon was engaged in formal discussions with Chou En-Lai and Communist Party Chairman Mao Tse-tung. But Pat was doing important work, too. She visited a hospital and eye witness surgery with acupuncture as the only anesthetic used; talked with men and women in a commune who worked side by side in the fields; became the center of attention when Pat set out for a shopping trip; applauded children performing in a skit at Evergreen People's Commune School.

She was delighted with the five pandas at the Peking Zoo. Pat was more thrilled when Premier Chou En-Lai decided to trade two giant black and white pandas for two musk oxen from the San Francisco Zoo. The antics of the white and black bears with pointed ears and black-circled eyes amused Pat. She thought the bears were beautiful and learned what they like to eat.

The Chinese smiled and laughed as Pat used chopsticks to sample Chinese luscious food while touring the kitchen of the Peking Hotel. They told her it took ten years to be a good cook of Chinese food.

At the Monday night banquet, Nixon toasted several hundred (700) guests. He said, "We have at times in the past been enemies, we have great differences today. What brings us together is that we have common interest which transcend differences." But, while we cannot close the gulf between us, we can try to bridge it so that we may be able to talk across it.

"So let us in these next five days start a long march together, not in lock step, but on different roads leading to the same goal, the goal of building a world structure of peace and justice in which each nation, large or small, has a right to determine its own form of government free of outside interference or domination."

President Nixon and Pat had planned to do some sight seeing in China, but their first priority was the "talks" with the Chinese leaders. I was glad that the TV networks made a special effort to film their tour for all of us to see. Not many of us would have the chance to see the interesting sights of China otherwise.

On February 24th, they visited the Great Wall of China, which was 2,200 years old. Nixon remarked, "We do not want walls of any kind between peoples. It was truly a wonder of the world. From one spot on the wall, one could see a striking view of the mountains and the valleys below all the way to Russian and Outer Mongolia borders.

In the Ming Tombs, the Nixons found the other side of China. Thirteen Ming Emperors and their wives were buried there. They discovered among the stone animals depicted there—lions, camels, and mythical creatures—an elephant! Pat and Dick laughed that the symbol of the Republican Party was everywhere. It was taller than them and they were fascinated with the stone elephant.

President Nixon announced in July 1971 he was going to China, but he had not made his decision hastily. It was a move he had been meditating on since 1967. For years American Chinese Christians had been praying that God would open the door once again in China. Nixon brought in Christian leaders and counseled with them. The week he went to the Republic of China had been bathed in prayers. The way to peace was lined with many pitfalls and President Nixon did not fall into any of them. Chou En-Lai and Nixon discussed their differences without compromising their principles. There were still major differences and they still existed. His historic trip to China opened the door for negotiation instead of fighting about it.

When President Nixon landed on American soil at Andrews Air Force Base, Maryland. February 28, 1972, he remarked, "When I announced this trip last July, I described it as a journey for peace. In the last 30 years, Americans have in three different wars gone off by the hundred of thousands to fight, and some to die, in Asia and in the Pacific. One of the central motives behind my journey to China was to prevent that from happening a fourth time to another generation of Americans."

"As I have often said, peace more than the mere absence of war. In a technical sense, we were at peace with the People's Republic of China before this trip, but a gulf of almost 12,000 miles and 22 years of non-communication and hostility separated the United States of America from the 750 million people who live in the People's Republic of China and that is one fourth of all of the people in the world."

"As a result of this trip, we have started the long process of building a bridge across that gulf, and even now we have something better than the mere absence of war. Not only have we completed a week of intensive talks at the highest levels, we have set up a procedure whereby we can continue to have discussion in the future. We have demonstrated that nations with very big and fundamental differences calmly, rationally and frankly, with out compromising their principles. This is the basis of a structure for peace, where we can talk about differences rather than fight about them."

Nixon felt the most important thing that the United States and China had was a new relationship and both agreed not to use force in relation with one another. Would we able to live with our differences or to die for them, time will tell.

I welcomed Pat back from her exciting trip to the People's Republic of China. She had many interesting things to say about what she had been doing there. When I told her about my brother, Howard, dying so suddenly from a heart attack, Pat was really distressed by the news. She knew how saddened I was by this untimely loss, but she knew fond memories of my brother would long be a source of comfort.

With all President Nixon had on his mind, Pat Buchanan his communications man, couldn't decide whether to resign his administration job or not. Apparently, he couldn't support the Chinese communiqué. After thinking it over Buchanan realized his leaving would create a stir of hullabaloo and that would shatter confidence in the Chinese trip developments. Therefore, he decided this is where he should be. President Nixon abhorred communism but he only wanted people to see there was another alternative to it.

The week after Pat and Dick arrived back from China, the newspapers were full of Jack Anderson's syndicated column concerning ITT (International Telephone and Telegraph Corporation). He charged that he discovered a scandal in Nixon administration. His information was based on a memo allegedly from Dita Beard, an ITT lobbyist. Anderson insinuated that the government anti-trust settlement with ITT had been influenced by ITT contribution to the upcoming Republican convention.

The charge by Anderson was not true. In fact the contribution had been made to the city of San Diego, so the city could bid to be the location of the 1972 Republican National Convention. The ITT Sheraton division was opening a new hotel in San Diego and thought the contribution was a good investment promotion.

When the Justice Department persisted in their pursuit of ITT, President was so angry that his phone became a very hot line. He felt that the Justice Department suits were a clear violation of his own anti-trust policies. In cabinet and staff meetings, Nixon made his position perfectly clear. He was convinced that big and strong American businesses should be able to compete in the international market; and businesses shouldn't be broken up unless they violated the laws of fair competition.

Then, the so called-memo was declared a forgery by Beard. The Democrat committee had played this situation to the utmost in the press. Then Nixon realized that he had played right into the Democrats hands.

The damage was done and he knew it. To me, the press had a double standard. Fair procedure should be followed, but they did not. Even the public did not know exactly what had been involved. At the beginning of the problem it should have been laid to rest—so to-speak—the whole record of events on the table—and left there.

Friday, March 17th Pat was another year older. At her birthday party I gave her a charming remembrance—a lovely sachet I created especially for her. After viewing a movie, Pat thanked us all for our confidence and support and friendship. It was a lovely time with a charming First Lady.

Then, toward the last of March, information trickled through the grapevine news. Sources from Ross Perot and Henry Kissinger that the North Vietnamese would release a certain amount of sick and wounded prisoners for a million dollars. Everyone was listening and that this was a ray of hope pertaining to P.O.W.'s. But we did not have our hopes up too high because we had been disappointed before.

Enroute to Phoenix, Pat was selected to be "The 1972 Woman in the News" by the Los Angeles Chapter of Theta Sigma, a professional journalism and communication organization. At the same time Helen Thomas, a UPI, White House Correspondent, was to receive "The Woman behind the News" award.

Excitement mounted for me as I learned Pat Nixon would be in Phoenix for the 18th National Republican Women's Conference, April 6,7, and 8. Pat would be there guest of honor at the banquet. Thursday evening would be a reception. Then, we would have a fashion show of historic inaugural ball gowns entitled "First Ladies on Parade." This conference at the Towne House was one of the four in the nation bringing Washington, D.C. to the regions. Our theme was "Party of the Open Door."

Pat Nixon arrived in Phoenix on Air Force Jet Star and was greeted by the steady tom-tom beat of Apache Indian drums. Bouquet of roses and boos from farm workers protestors also welcomed her. Fifth grade children unfurled a paper banner that said, "Welcome to Phoenix, Mrs. Nixon." But the Arizona farm workers had a banner which said," Give our families our human rights and defeat Arizona House 2134, a measure would limit the activities of farm labor organizations.

Pat shook hands with all the well-wishers she could at the Sky Harbor airport. She was presented with two Pima Indian paintings by Alden Altivine, a Ute Indian and student body president of Phoenix Indian School.

Then, she spoke briefly, "I have visited here often and always enjoyed it here in your great city. I have enjoyed the last four years in the White House and I am going to enjoy the next four. My husband must win re-election so his policies can be completed."

I was so happy to see her again. In both of our busy schedules, we always wanted to see each other to chat and find out what each of us was doing. Pat told me that she stopped briefly in Tucson, Arizona to attend the dedication of the restored John C. Fremont house, which was occupied in the 1860's by the territorial governor. She said, "General Fremont explored and mapped the West. You know he was famous in California as well as Arizona. Truly Arizona is one of the last true frontier states."

Pat delighted all the Republican women at the conference. She told us that "women of all ages and races everywhere should take a more active leadership role in all levels of politics."

When Pat left for the airport she gave me a big hug and remarked, "Helen, be good and take care of yourself! Keep in touch." Everyone around me was surprised at the First

Lady's admiration. They were not aware of our personal friendship.

Outside the Towne House demonstrators were once again picketing and shouting "Down with Nixon and Republicans!" Carrying posters and the black eagle red flag, the United Farm Workers chanted and marched back and forth all around the Towne House. Most of the chant was in Spanish. Thank goodness Pat escaped the second protest similar to the one at her arrival at the airport.

Back in Washington, D.C., President Nixon was busy, too, at a ceremony congratulation Police Chief Jerry V. Wilson for making the capitol city one of the safest cities in the country. The last 3 years the crime rate there had been cut in half. But, Mr. Wilson said the credit belonged to Nixon for his backing and other steps, such as brighter streetlights, the reorganization of the courts and doubling the number of prosecutors.

Nixon walked into the White House amid a group of tourists from Arizona taking a tour of the White House mansion. There were 30 in the group. Their guide had told them he was guiding them through the White House on his birthday. So the crowd burst out singing "Happy Birthday" to him.

When President Nixon heard the singing, he walked toward them and shook hands with each one. He looked at one man and noticed his Hopi sun god emblem on his boli tie, and said, "You must be from Arizona." Everyone was completely flabbergasted and speechless. They couldn't utter a word when he wished them well and shook their hands. It was a thrill-of a lifetime for seeing President Nixon in person.

On April 23rd, Pat flew to Lincoln, Nebraska to commemorate the 100th anniversary of Arbor Day. Young Billie Szalarwiga, a freckle-faced 10 year old boy would help Pat plant a tree next week on the White House lawn. Young Billie stood by the Nebraska Governor Exon and Pat and explained his job as National poster boy.

"I want to help Nebraska and Americans plant more trees. We need more tree houses."

This red-blooded American Nebraska boy was taking part in Arbor Day centennial celebrations and national promotions across the country to encourage the planting of trees for the environment and the wise use of natural reserves. Arbor Day was first celebrated in 1872 at Nebraska City and this year would be motivating a yearlong ecology efforts in many communities.

Pat Nixon accepted the honorary chairmanship of the board of trustees of the Arbor Day Centennial Foundation. But it was young Billie who won Pat's heart. She described him as "an all American boy if I ever seen one-freckles and all." Whenever he talked about trees, he couldn't help grinning or smiling. He was a delight!"

President Nixon had a lot on his mind concerning ways to end the Vietnam War with honor. The North Vietnamese was continuing their offensive in the South. Nixon was prepared to use all our military and naval strength against military targets throughout North Vietnam. He would hunt them now and in the future. The Soviets were not helping to restrain the North Vietnamese. The South Vietnamese had lost their will to continue fighting, and Nixon thought the thing may be lost. He did not want that to happen.

Being a war president was not easy. To complicate matters at home, J. Edgar Hoover, Director of The Federal Bureau of Investigation (FBI) died in his sleep at the age of 77 on May 2, 1972. As long as I could remember, he was always there on the national scene. He was a member of the National Presbyterian Church, and he thought every child should be in Sunday School and learn not to get into trouble. Many judges took his advice and sentenced many young people to attend. Sunday School and report back each week what each one had learned. What good advice! To many Americans, Hoover was a hero because of his tough anti-crime legislation, pro-American, and against anything that threatened the security of our country.

Now he was gone. From then on the FBI has never been the same. Things happening today would never happen under the Hoover FBI administration. President Nixon had to find a new FBI director to replace him. Just one more thing to think about.

Nixon believed it was essential to cripple the North Vietnamese invasion into South Vietnam by mining Haiphong Harbor and for bombing railroad lines for transporting military supplies, fuel, and equipment. So many people were disillusioned with the Vietnam War but what would be the right thing to do? He felt that United States should not lose in Vietnam, even though we would lose some battles.

This was a difficult time for the Nixon family and friends. We had to encourage one another, especially the President who was carrying a heavy load trying to settle the out come of this detested war.

That evening I watched President Nixon on TV give his speech. It was forthright and to the point. His new peace proposal emphatically said all American prisoners of war should be returned; and that there should be an internationally supervised cease-fire; and after all acts of force are stopped then there should be a complete withdrawal of American troops in 4 months.

The Democrat Congress and the liberal media criticized Nixon for his decision. The Democrats started the beginning of the Vietnam War, but they did very little to give help in solving how to end it. It took political courage for Nixon to say what he had to say. The military were sitting on their backsides and not saying how to accomplish the ending of the war. The Democrats were talking big and acting very little. That was the weakness of the Kennedy and Johnson administration and how we got in the Vietnam War in the first place. If Nixon failed, it would be the result of the efforts of bureaucrats in the bureaucracy, the Defense Department, and Democrats in Congress that would erode the action Nixon had taken. He had the will power to act and destroy the enemy's war capacity.

To everyone's amazement after Nixon's speech the Soviets backed down regarding the mining and blockade in Vietnam and agreed to a Summit meeting in Moscow. The Democrats had predicted disaster. When it didn't happen, they switched tactics and said Nixon was bombing civilian targets. They were not doing a thing to help win the war.

Neither was the media. The media thought Nixon had put the summit in jeopardy and they didn't know what to say when it didn't happen. Were they surprised when the White House was deluged with thousands of telegrams praising Nixon's actions.

Pat told her husband, "Don't worry about a thing." She thought that Dick should always go on television and reassure the people what is the truth—that is different what the media was trying to tell.

Truly, I thought Nixon would win re-election. However, Governor George Wallace, the independent Democrat third party candidate, and the Vietnam War worried all of us regarding the presidential election race. President Nixon's foreign policy with China achieved him popularity among the people. The stock market had rose to an all-time high; the economy was good, inflation was down and federal taxes were down 20 percent. Peace and prosperity was an unbeatable combination. If Nixon would fail in Vietnam could he survive politically?

I knew that a third party candidate like Wallace could deny him the Electoral College votes needed to win re-election. The shades of the 1968 election campaign haunted me! Then we got word on May 15th that Governor George Wallace was shot by a lunatic, Arthur Bremer, at a political rally in Laurel, Maryland. The bullet paralyzed him from the waist down and caused him to think about withdrawing from the presidential race.

Bremer had stalked the Nixon motorcade in Ottawa Canada, but he was unable to accomplish his mission to kill President Nixon in April there. It forced me to have the horror of flash backs of the Kennedy assassination. Where would this violence stop? Our country was locked into a climate of fear and Nixon didn't want that to happen. Now I knew that the Democrats were the only political group Nixon had to fear.

President Nixon did not like violence of any kind. His mother drilled that into his head when he was a young boy. Even, though George Wallace was his political opponent he went out of his way to visit Wallace at the hospital to see how he was doing. Wallace was disgusted with the other Democrats because they were blaming Richard Nixon for the Vietnam War they had engineered in the beginning. He didn't like their criticism of Nixon because he was trying to get us out of the war. Wallace was a strong American patriot, even though he was a person who appealed to the emotions and prejudices of certain people in order to advance his own political ends.

On Saturday, May 20th, Julie and Tricia said goodbye to their parents, as they were about to board The Spirit of '76 jet at Andrews Air Force Base for Salzburg, Austria, enroute to Moscow, Soviet Union. It was raining when the Nixons departed. The Democrats and the media were predicting this summit trip would not be, and now they were on their way, believe it or not.

Rain welcomed them once more when they arrived in Moscow. After the Russian officials greeted them at the airport, they were whisked away to the Kremlin. No crowds were allowed on the streets where the motorcade raced. Any crowds of people were kept blocks away just like in the China visit.

The Soviets did not understand the role of American press,

why they had to be so involved in the activities of the President and the First Lady. It was a horrendous problem. Our American press did not get into the room where President Nixon and Brezhnev were discussing about Vietnam and arms limitations, joint space flights, environment, medicine and health, and science technology.

Pat Nixon had her own independent schedule in Moscow. Her friendliness captivated the Russian people wherever she went. The American press who went with her were jostled and pushed away from her by the husky KJB women. They formed such a human shield, one could hardly breathe.

Guided by wives of Gromyko and Brezhnev, Pat managed to mix sight seeing with a visit of foremost Russian shops. She visited a school and listened attentively where a Russian youth recited a poem in Pat's honor. Pat donned a set of headphones in Moscow's secondary school with the aid of one of the Russian students. She viewed students practicing ballet at the Baloshoi School; and then at a Moscow style center, the Russian modeled gowns, which held her interest.

Apparently, the Russians were determined to tighten security around Pat Nixon. They pushed away news journalists from Pat, so they couldn't hear any conversations. At the GUM department store security became excessive. Pat had to interfere with the guards tackling an American Associate Press journalist and roughing him up. Our journalists shouted protests and pushed back. Pat, in the middle of the jostling became bruised in all the pushing events.

Russians didn't want any women at the signing of the ABM anti ballistic missile treaty, by President Nixon and Brezhnev. However, Pat waited until all the officials entered and then hid behind one of the pillars and witnessed the signing of the ABM treaty, by Soviet Party Chief Leonid Brezhnev and President Nixon.

The next day they visited the Piskaryev Cemetery of Lenigrad where thousands were buried when the German

Nazis had attacked the Russians. There, Pat and Dick heard the sad story about Tanya losing all her family in the war and how she was killed. They were so moved that they hoped that his tragedy would never happen again.

In Kiev, in their summit trip to Russia, Pat also visited a state-run playroom and loved every minute with the children there. On their arrival in Minsk, Pat and President Nixon were engulfed in crowd of Soviets waving Byelorussian and American flags and were trying to shake their hands. It was a glorious day for them.

They flew back to Moscow and attended on Sunday, Church services at only Moscow's Baptist Church, the all-union council of Evangelical Christian Baptists. To their surprise, they didn't know why the church should have so many young people in attendance. Then, they learned the KGB agents had displaced the older people with the Russia KGB young ones. Not many young people attended the church regularly. Most of the other young people attended the underground evangelical church where the communistic government officials could not interfere.

On May 30th, President Nixon and Pat stopped over in Iran visiting Shah Mohammed Riza Pahlevic in Teheran. Our country had ties with this strategic country. While the Nixons were there, their brief visit was marred by terrorist bombs explosions. The Nixon entourage was not in any danger from the bomb blasts. Friendly throngs of Iranians greeted Pat and the President.

Enroute to Washington, May 31st, the Nixons stopped over in Warsaw, Poland. Hundreds of thousands turned out to cheer and applaud the Nixon's arrival. Their visit there resulted in a consular treaty and move to stronger trade connections. As they boarded the presidential jet at the Warsaw Airport, the Nixons were given an armful of roses. They smiled and were satisfied that their international mission was accomplished.

President Nixon was an effective forceful president who was doing some courageous things that many other presidents weren't able to do. His recent trips to China and Russia had upset all predictions, which persons had said at the beginning of his office term.

While I was a personal friend, I hadn't always agreed with everything that was going on in the administration. If I did have criticism I would tell them in private and not announce it to the world in public.

I favored Nixon's trip to Red China and Soviet Russia because we are living in a brand new world and one the United States could not longer dominate. I knew President Nixon's goal was to keep the peace. His plan was to get out of Vietnam. When the North Vietnamese crossed the DMZ, Nixon had to act fast to save our troops from another Dunkirk.

Pat Nixon was in Los Angeles. She flew from there to Rapid City, South Dakota to attend an ecumenical memorial service for the victims of the South Dakota floods.

The service was planned at 6:00 p.m. Sunday at the Stevens High School gymnasium in Rapid City. Pat returned to Los Angeles for a dinner to be held in her honor.

About the same time, some one stole a replica of the presidential seal displayed in a stained glass window in the "Mission Inn's" presidential suite at Riverside, California. The 12-inch diameter seal was put in the window in 1903. Several presidents have stayed at the Mission Inn, but President Nixon and Pat were married there.

By June, none of us, who had been on Richard Nixon's previous presidential campaigns, had not been contacted. This was so unusual! Well, I decided as well as others, to go to work on our own for the President's re-election.

There was a new tribe of political people heading the show now in Washington. There were nasty remarks and rudeness toward local campaign workers and the field organizations were careless and sluggish in their attitudes.

When I couldn't stand it any longer I called Rosemary Woods, President Nixon's secretary at the White House, to let them know what was going on. I followed up with a letter to the President. I knew Dick couldn't know all what his staff at "Committee to Re-Elect the President" in Washington were doing. That pesky Vietnam War was taking up his time in solving the situation.

On the Democrat side, Hubert Humphrey and George McGovern were battling it out in the Democrat primaries. By June 6th George McGovern had won the California primary.

The Democrats were in disarray. Here they were divided on McGovern's views and could not stomach what he proposed. He favored amnesty for draft dodgers; and unilateral withdrawal from South Vietnam; no concern for POW's, increasing foreign aid; bussing children was essential for integration and he would give $1,000 to everyone on welfare.

No one could decide what McGovern was going to do when anyone hears extreme statements. Many of the press agreed with the positions McGovern stated. However a few of the press saw through his ideas on the campaign and tried to warn their readers about his stand on drugs, abortion, amnesty for draft dodgers, and welfare.

I thought McGovern was very clever and would say or do anything to win the campaign race. McGovern even named his cabinet selections before he was nominated by the Democratic Convention. There was much more to do in the election campaign this summer to awaken the people and arouse them to action.

On the Friday afternoon President Nixon left for a Bahamas island to spend a weekend there with friends and to relax and swim. Pat had gone to the West coast setting a schedule of fast pace of public appearances there.

The drama and excitement of the re-election campaign

was heating up. Julie and Tricia were out there too, on the campaign trail and generating warm interest. They were most willing to take on the challenge of an election campaign once again and were definitely assets for their father.

Pat was now known as a world traveler. Request for her to say a few words at many places were piling up every week. Whenever Pat, Julie and Tricia traveled for the campaign appearances they journeyed on Government planes. The Secret Service didn't want them to be in jeopardy if there was a hijacking event. None of this was at taxpayer's expense. All the travel expenses and maintenance of the aircraft were paid by the Republican Party.

Pat projected her personal warmth and interest in the people she met. The elderly, the handicapped and the children responded to her sunny smile and kindness. They knew she was a special First Lady.

In Chicago, she made a four-hour stop at the annual Lithuanian Folk Dance Festival, at the International amphitheater. When Pat arrived there 14,000 people greeted her with a warm welcome. She received such a boisterous, yelling, standing acclamation, it made an impression on us all. If the Cubs or the White Sox had won the pennant, it couldn't have been noisier.

June 18th, the story on the front page of the "Miami Herald" caught Nixon 's eye. "Miamians Held in D.C. Try to Bug Democrat Headquarters." Five Cuban men were arrested wearing rubber gloves bugging the Democrat National Committee headquarters at the Watergate Hotel in Washington. Right away President Nixon thought it was a prank of some kind and dismissed it from his mind. There were important things to think about such as food prices increasing and George Wallace as a 3rd party candidate and his schedule of events for the week.

The three days of rest, fresh air, and swimming gave Nixon a sharper mind and bigger lift to do the job, which lie ahead of him. He was determined to get more exercise to help him for good effects for the work he knew he had to do.

On his way back to Washington, Bob Haldeman told him about the break-in of the Democrat headquarters and that someone in the Committee to Re-Elect the President was involved. Nixon thought it was foolish and irresponsible to bug the Democrat committee headquarters. As far as I was concerned, I agreed with Nixon, that it was useless to find any information on the Democrat headquarters. Then Nixon found out that the Democrats had bugged the White House committee rooms too.

Ever since the 1960 campaign, I knew about the vote fraud and the dirty tricks, which the Democrats had pulled. It was common for Democrat candidates to bug one another and the Republicans had done the same. It was just plain stupid and senseless.

The more President Nixon thought about the Democrat break-in, it really bothered him and was very concerned if anyone at the White House was involved.

Then, President Nixon informed all campaign organizations that all members should be above reproach in their conduct. No booze or fancy restaurants or hotels. Never give the other side or anyone else ammunition to use against us.

Martha Mitchell, wife of John Mitchell, the Nixon campaign director, tongue was loosen with liquor and saying all kinds of silly and absurd things. Anyone who knew Martha knew she was very outspoken when drinking. One had to be careful what one would say around her or she would twist it around to her advantage. She would blow her stack and report it to the FBI or the Washington Post paper.

When she found about the Watergate break-in, Martha really lashed out at her husband. Wanted John Mitchell to get out of politics, and she caused trouble for everyone around him. She even felt Pat Nixon had snubbed her at every reception, which was held. Martha would go into a tantrum and throw things and demolish everything in sight. John said he was going to quit as campaign director and move to New York. He would work only as a consultant and help otherwise with the campaign. The whole thing was a nightmare!

There were many stories about the Watergate break-in and bugging. Haldeman remembered all of them and he told every story to President Nixon. Still, Nixon was baffled by all the so-called stories given to him. He saw no reason to bug the Democrat committee headquarters. Haldeman assured him no one at the White House was involved.

Nixon thought nothing was being done about settling the Watergate break-in case and removing it from the eye of the public. Otherwise, the media and the Democrats would continue to hammer them with it. He wanted the people involved to plead guilty so that he could forget about it and get on with more important things. Nixon did nothing to discourage stories explaining about the break-in. Many thought his inactions during this time appeared to many as a cover up. However, he perceived the Watergate problem as pure politics, and he was looking for every way to lessen the damage to his staff, his friends and the presidential campaign. All I could do was to pray and stand by for the Nixon family. If Nixon hadn't been so involved in the winding down of the Vietnam War, he would have spent more time in solving the problem of the break-in.

Pat scarcely noticed the news about the Watergate break-in. By June she was focused on the long 1972 presidential campaign ahead of her. She was very proud of the record her husband was pursuing regarding the federal revenue sharing program of funds back to the states and cities to diffuse power at the federal level, and the crime rate was down; wages were up and taxes had been cut. There were many other issues she was concerned about and thought Congress should pursue it.

On July 1st, Pat and President Nixon went to San Clemente—the Western White House—for a couple of weeks stay. There they would rest and watch the Democrat Convention on television. But, Nixon took his work with him. Since John Mitchell resigned as campaign director he had to discuss campaign activities with Minnesota Congressman Clark MacGregor to take over the campaign. MacGregor agreed. There were many questions about the Watergate thing. Would it have happened if the Martha Mitchell affair hadn't bobbed to the surface? No once really knows.

By executive order, Nixon set up the National Narcotics Intelligence Office in the Justice Department as a necessary step in his crusade against the illegal business of buying and selling drugs. He requested $135.2 million in drug abuse treatment funds and for prevention and law enforcement endeavors. Heroin addiction statistics had shown an increase more than anyone was aware of. Also, Nixon asked Congress to impose a $250 billion ceiling on federal spending and he promised to veto any measure he considered excessive.

As we watched in July the Democrat Convention held in Miami, we discovered the Democrats had collapsed in political shambles. They had cleansed the party and adopted reforms, which included blacks, homosexuals, migrant workers, and welfare mothers. George McGovern had sponsored the delegate reforms. He chose Senator Thomas Eagleton of Missouri as his Vice President candidate.

As far as I was concerned the radical left are always willing to compromise principle until they get in power. Then when they get in office they smash their opponent and do what they like on the issues. Those on the right would rather lose standing for principle and that is why the extremist left people beat them.

McGovern was off and on regarding his Vice Presidential nominee, Thomas Eagleton's disclosure about his hospital treatment of mental depression. First he was on the Democrat ticket and then dropped him from the ticket. The press persisted in their outrageous stories about the incident.

The McGovern nomination forsook the conservative and moderate Democrats. Therefore, the defections of Democrats to Richard Nixon created the New Majority Nixon had dreamt about. Of course, the organized labor and George Wallace as a third party candidate remained uncertain.

In the middle of July, Frank Fitzsimmons and the Teamsters Union voted to endorse Richard Nixon's re-election. Also, George Wallace from his hospital bed announced officially to not run for the presidency as a 3rd party candidate.

When President Nixon arrived back in Washington, he asked his staff regarding the news update on the Watergate break in. It troubled him. Jeb Magruder was involved some how and may be indicted. In discussing it with Bob Haldeman, John Dean, and John Ehrlichman. Nixon was concerned about the potential political damage and how it could be contained or minimized. It was a powder keg about to explode!

As we prepared to open the Republican National convention in excited Miami Beach, President Nixon toiled in the wooded Camp David in seclusion Sunday on his nomination acceptance speech for re-election of his second term. He conferred with Henry Kissinger on his Vietnam mission. There had been many speculations regarding a possible Vietnam negotiations break-through. I was wondering if Nixon would disclose any new developments in his acceptance speech at the convention.

As the Republicans convened Sunday evening for their first sessions, several thousand peaceful protestors gathered in the rain in front of the Convention Hall to listen to Jane Fonda, Black Panther Bobby Seale and all-woman rock band.

Monday evening, Pat arrived with Julie and Tricia with their husbands, David and Edward. Two young female protestors shouted insults at Pat Nixon, and called her "Miss

Pig." About 150 protestors and Nixon young supporters exchanged jeers outside the Fontainaebleau Hotel-the conventions headquarter where the women of the achievement Nixon entourage were to attend a brunch held by the National Federation of Republican Women.

Dozens of police stood by to keep the picketing protestors and the Young Voters for President Nixon apart as they staged their rally outside the hotel. The Young Voters members cheered and shouted "Four more years, four more years!"

The protestors from Students for a Democratic Society counteracted with cries to end the Vietnam War and racism, "Famous lady, fascist lackey. One, two, three, four, we don't want your sexist war."

The Young Voters yelled, "Nixon now, Nixon now." The opposers chanted, "Racist, sexist, we say no. Richard Nixon's got to go." Delegates and Nixonettes clad in red, white, and blue uniforms were jostled by some of the demonstrators. About 10 members of the Gay Liberation Front taunted the Nixon Young Voters, and finally the police persuaded them to move to a different location.

I was sure the peaceful tranquility would not prevail as the convention continued. The police agreed with my thoughts. They said it would be more militant as it progressed. These people are trying to work out in their heads whether they want to be arrested in action.

An invigorated Pat reacted to the opening of the special film tribute the GOP convention gave her. It was a documentary film of her activities in the White House and her travels on the road. When she was brought to the podium at the end of the film, Pat told us it would be a night she would always remember. She waved the gavel at the delegates and the crowd went wild and gave her cheers and applause. They really loved Pat as First Lady.

Twenty-five million young people were eligible to vote for the first time in November and many of these were college students. Nixon wanted everyone to have an absentee ballot if they needed one.

At the youth rally at the convention, every one of the young ones agreed to support President Nixon. Most of the youthful supporters had paid their own way to Miami to work at the convention. Their achievement within the party remained for the young persons the most important reason behind their elections to delegate and alternate posts. They expressed the desire to participate more effectively in the coming campaign for President Nixon. The 3,000 young people were really excited to go to work of the cause they believed in.

The youth rally was the highlight for President Nixon. Their chant of "Four more years! Four more years!" was music to his ears. When Sammy Davis, the black entertainer, surprised Nixon by hugging him. We roared our approval and he remembered it, too.

Pat saluted the Republican women who were running for political office. She hoped they would all be elected. She admired each woman who ran for an office. It was all very exciting for Pat and that kept her going. The convention provided happiness in meeting old friends.

That night Richard Nixon was re-nominated for a second term by a vote of 1,347 to 1. I was very happy! All our work paid off. Outside protestors tried to set fire to the delegates buses. They threw rocks and eggs and were frustrating everyone. The chant of "Four more years! Four more years!" from the delegates rang in my ears. He never forgot that night and neither did I.

Richard Nixon reminded us that his administration would continue his strong efforts to open equal opportunities for women, clearly recognizing that women are often denied such opportunities. While every woman may not want a career outside the home, he believed every woman should have the freedom to choose whatever career she wants and an equal chance to pursue it.

President Nixon said, "In the United States today we have got to have the best people in positions of leadership. If a woman has that capacity, we want her. We want women in the House. We want them in the Senate. We want them in government positions. We want them in elected positions everywhere. The full and equal participation of women is crucial to the strength of the country."

Therefore, he set an example to government and business by more than fourfold the top-level policy-making women appointees of any administration before him. Half of these appointees held positions never before held by women. Nixon was the first President ever to appoint a woman to be the leading force to expand a recruitment program for bringing more qualified women into high-level government posts.

His natural inclination was to respond to people as human beings, regardless of whether they were men and women. No wonder women came out to work for his presidency.

Pat and President Nixon bid farewell to the 82nd Airborne Division at the Homestead AFB, Florida. The troops were sent to Miami Beach area to help quell any convention disorders but they were not needed. Enroute to the Western White House at San Clemente, Nixon stopped at Chicago and Utica, Michigan to make a couple of speeches. The excited crowd at the San Diego stopover boosted Nixon's tired spirit too.

At San Clemente, a surprise party had been planned. There were more Hollywood stars than there would have been at any award ceremony. Most of them had campaigned for Democrat candidates in the past, such as Frank Sinatra, Jimmy Durante and Charlton Heston. Of course, the Republicans valiants were there—John Wayne, Glen Campbell, Jimmy Stewart and Clint Eastwood. Mingling with them who had their feet in both world—the Hollywood movies and politics—Governor Ronald and Nancy Reagan. Even sisters, Zsa Zsa and Eva Gabor were talking with another—which was unusual.

There must have been a lot of closet Republicans or many Democrats dissatisfied with the McGovern choice. But, when Tricia Cox, Pat and Dick's daughter, arrived she outshone and charmed most of the Hollywood stars there. Also, there was Billy Graham, the evangelist, who was a personal friend of the Nixons, wandering among the guests. By the time the party was over, President Nixon was really bushed, but pleased and Pat was happy but tired.

On Wednesday, August 30, I was excited when I read the latest Gallup poll—Nixon had 64% of the public poll opinion and McGovern—30%, 6% were undecided. It was the largest post-election poll favor of any Republican candidate in the history of Gallup's polling.

Pat's schedule became very busy and hectic. There were so many places set up for her to visit as First Lady. At a White House ceremony she was made an honorary Army Community Service Volunteer. She even modeled an ACS uniform which was given to her by the Fort Sill, Oklahoma, ACS chapter members. Pat looked wonderful, and the uniform fit her perfectly. Then, she visited the NASA-Ames Research Center at Mountain View, California for medical applications of space technology demonstrations. Pat seated with her arm in a metal sleeve and demonstrated a remotely controlled operated robot arm that moved another metal sleeve following her every move, which was just five feet away. The press followed Pat Nixon wherever she went. She was news and the public loved her as First Lady.

Since the Alger Hiss case, President Nixon fought a war battle with the press. Most of it was political and reporting was not objective. When Nixon came to the White House, he collided with the period of anti-government rancor in the big national papers such as the Washington Post and the New York Times. The voices of conservatism among the smaller papers were heard but they were often drowned out by the cries of liberalism. To help Nixon out, I wrote individual letters to the Letters To The Editor to get his point across to the public.

In turn, Dick did try to build bridges to the press. All his efforts to do so went down in failure. Major leaks continued and 45 stories came out concerning national security were a serious violation. It was difficult for President Nixon to ignore this large discharge of secret information regarding the Vietnam War. I was not surprised when Nixon took measures to find who was causing the leaks. The press then did not have any concern for our men fighting in the Vietnam War but to bring down Nixon at any cost. He was their targeted goal.

By September I started the fall semester at Grand Canyon College with out our Academic Dean, Dr. Robert L. Sutherland. He resigned and transferred to a college in St. Louis, Missouri. He really was the one who made the wheels on campus go around. We really missed him on campus. The work had doubled for us when he left.

The Presidential Campaign for 1972 was in progress. Then I received a notice from the White House that President Nixon wanted me to work on some special assignment for him. He also spoke of concern regarding Pat suffering from a constant earache, but she would not slow down her First Lady duties and campaign schedule appearances.

Sept 11th, Nixon was concerned about everyone's campaign schedule. The Watergate affair bothered him. In spite of his virus, which caused him to do a lot of coughing and sneezing, it caused him to feel discouraged and distressed. He took much medicine to keep the virus cold down to a minimum. There were many political planning sessions. Concerns about poll results in key states and those who were in doubtful ones. Richard Nixon wanted to beat McGovern in all 50 states.

The sixteenth day of September Pat set out on a 6-day campaign schedule of her own. She was nervous about any encounter with the press and the questions they would throw at her. However, she handled every question the press asked of her—abortion, childcare, and the Vietnam War. Pat loved to talk with persons one-on-one. But, too much public speaking caused her to be uncomfortable and substantial anguish.

Also, this day was the official kick-off of the Nixon Presidential campaign. The Republican Party and the Committee for the Re-Election of President were combining forces to bring the campaign to the people. Volunteers would be out in every city across the country ringing doorbells. Members of the Cabinet, Congressmen, and Senators, Julie, Tricia and Ed Cox would have their different assignments in certain cities they visit.

On the night of September 27th, some one fire bombed the Nixon for President headquarters in Phoenix, Arizona. I was going down there to work the next morning. It happened when Julie Nixon Eisenhower was here for a visit. The arson fire destroyed a lot of literature and money. My hands were black with sorting papers that were scorched in the fire.

Paul Harvey, the newscaster on the radio, was the only one who reported that other Nixon headquarters in California, Ohio, Texas, and Minnesota had been bombed, burned, or broken into. The Democrats for Nixon headquarters in Washington, D.C. were trashed and office supplies were stolen, destroyed campaign posters and office equipment. He also told us about the break-in at President Nixon's personal physician's office, Dr. John Lungren at Long Beach, California. Dick's medical files were removed and scattered around the floor of the doctor's office. Nothing else was taken.

The rest of the press didn't publish it or make a fuss about it as they did the bugging of the Democrat headquarters. Nothing was stolen or burned in the Democrat headquarters, but why didn't they arrest the ones who did all this? That is a good question no one has yet to answer for me. I only believed that those persons hated Richard Nixon and wanted to drive him out of office one way or another.

Pat was still out on the campaign trail. She liked people and enjoyed herself. Some of the people were surprised how real she was and didn't expect her to do so much campaigning. After all she had been doing this since 1946. She was a real pro! She had visited Indianapolis, San Diego, San Francisco and now to Ft. Meyers, Florida.

In Ft. Meyers, she was welcomed by a crowd of 2,000 people. Even, the Mayor proclaimed that day "Pat Nixon Day" and gave her the key to the city. Pat enjoyed the warm welcome and shook hands wherever she went. She smiled, patted hands and hugged the children. They responded in kind. Pat's right hand was all dented up with fingernail scratches. However, these little things didn't bother her.

She loved people and to have a word or two with them and a word with the children. Pat completely captivated the crowd.

Then, on to Morristown, New Jersey Pat entered the world of the blind. She donned a mask and let "Winnie," a German Shepherd dog, be her guide. The supervisor of dog training told Pat how to hold the dog's leash for her seeing-eye dog.

In Philadelphia, Pat was honored by the fashion group there as the "best in taste" and most feminine women of the year. When she accepted their award she was almost speechless. On the campaign trail, Pat had developed a slight case of laryngitis and so she could only manage to whisper a hoarse "thank you." The award was a crystal form of soft curved pair of wings ascending from the compact crystal foundation.

All though President Nixon hadn't been seen much in the public eye this campaign season, Julie, Tricia, Pat and Ed Cox (Tricia's husband) were becoming more visible to the delight of the crowds along the way, all were active in the campaign-except for David Eisenhower. As a Navy lieutenant junior grade, he could not make any speeches at any political rallies. However, he deported recently on a sea duty for six months, on the cruiser, "Albany." David could appear in civilian dress at a rally whenever his ship would dock periodically at Mayport, Florida—but no speeches!

It was Julie who won the travel honors among the Nixon family. She logged 38,234 miles and visited 22 states. Julie did take one week off to fly to Spain to see David, her husband. As long s the Democrat Congress was meeting in the congressional chambers, Nixon would remain in Washington for the most of the sessions. That would mean Nixon would be there about 75% of the time and to see that his legislative recommendations sent to Capitol Hill would be passed. He would put his presidential job first and the campaign second. Nixon did not intend to get more involved in campaigning until shortly before the November election. Then, it would only be selected, short trips.

Pat Nixon was nervous about press conference encounters. She enjoyed meeting people and talking to people one on one. However, she found that making lots of speeches made it difficult for her. When Nixon ran for the congressional seats and Vice-President, Pat didn't have to give speeches. He spoke for himself.

Now the press was following her everywhere and writing down every word she said. The 1972 campaign was wearing her down as well as others. She worried about the campaign group of men who chose to make decisions without revealing their plans to her husband. Richard Nixon was so busy with winding down the Vietnam War; he secluded himself from others in his cabinet and most of the staff and left major decisions with Haldeman and Dean.

Pat had her busy schedule as First Lady, and on some other things she didn't want to bother him about it. After her visit to Rochester, Minnesota she attended several events in

Chicago. Following a parade with Mayor Richard Daley, (Sr.) who surprised Pat with his friendliness. Then she attended a tea in her honor at McCormick Place. For a few hours Pat shook hands with several thousand women.

The press related that two thousand others were turned away and couldn't get in. I always wondered how she was able to stand in line that long. But Pat did! She believed in her husband—not for attention or publicity for her self. Now many loved her as I did—a real First Lady of courage.

Pat was troubled by the stories about Watergate the press was rolling out. She wondered who would be next on the list. The Washington Post exaggerated stories, which Pat knew were not true, about White House practice of spying. Pat wished the media would concentrate on how to end the Vietnam War instead of continuing to stir up apathy concerning it.

For years, the Democrat National Committee had employed Dick Tuck who carried out so called "pranks" against Nixon and other Republican candidates. So President Nixon's appointment secretary, Dwight Chapin, hired Donald Segretti, a young Vietnam veteran and attorney, to counteract Tuck's actions. Segretti duplicated Tuck's tricks, but on one instance he went too far on one of his pranks. The Washington Post got wind of what he was doing and accused Segretti of sending out forged Democratic letters on the Democrat candidates and leaking other false items—a political spy and sabotager for the White House. This didn't help the Nixon administration and the accusations were damaging.

President Nixon finally got the word that his personal friends and workers were not working or just plain left out of the 1972 campaign. Although, I was volunteering at the Arizona campaign office on my own, I was delighted to hear from Clark MacGregor, the National Campaign Director, in behalf of President Nixon, to participate in a special way in the President's re-election. Nixon wanted all campaign workers to make their personal responsibility to see that his personal friends—which I was one—would be contacted and see that they would be offered a specific assignment which would help assure victory in each state. He wanted to be advised of method and the results of the follow-up to his request. I decided to take the assignment on "Get Out The Vote."

President Nixon became the target for the most nasty and vicious campaign against him more than any other President of the United States. The Washington Post and New York Times were praising the ones who were secretly watching others to obtain illegal information for their own side. They gave President Nixon's opponent—McGovern—ammunition to fuel the name-calling, the heckling, and the violence. McGovern called Nixon another Hitler and the Republican Party a duplicate of the Ku Klux Klan. The issues were being bypassed.

The McGovern campaign had a group of religious peoples called "Religious Leaders for McGovern. "It included William Sloane Coffin, Harvey Cox, John Bennett, and Robert McAfee Brown, Rabbi Abraham Heschell and other liberal clergy who supported the McGovern's cause. The only prominent black clergyman who did not sign on McGovern's campaign was Joseph Jackson.

Any politician must form a wide group of associations. That was what the McGovern camp did with the RELIGI-MAC—the White liberal constituents. Michael McIntyre took over the religious part of the McGovern campaign. He ran one of the most candid, wide-sweeping zealous entreaties ever prepared, which included regional association and assemblies. At that time, he didn't have one evangelical clergyman on his side.

McGovern was calling the Nixon administration the most corrupt in the history of the United States. But in turn, he uttered suddenly and impulsively a few profane exclamations in the last reckless days of his campaign and lost many points with the people he was trying to reach with his viewpoint.

Although little reported in the media, evangelical and moral persons met at McGovern's appearance at Wheaton College in Illinois in mid-October. Their strategy was the art of meeting McGovern under condition advantageous to their one's own force and a careful plan for achieving their end. McGovern's original speech date was cancelled by Wheaton College and so he rescheduled again in his bid for the Protestant right vote. It was unusual and unique.

However, at the same time Billy Graham was in San Diego, California and was being interviewed by "The San Diego Union." Billy rebuffed McGovern charges that the Nixon administration was corrupt and immoral.

He stated that he voted for President Nixon by absentee ballot and described Richard Nixon as "a man with a deep religious commitment." I know the President as well as anyone outside his immediate family. I have known him since 1950, and I have great confidence in his personal honesty. I voted for him because I know what he is made of."

Billy Graham made this statement to the press just a week before the election. As we all know, the 1972 election was one of the biggest landslide triumphs in our American history for Richard Nixon. It had been predicted by the pollsters it would happen. But, Billy had to speak up. Since he was the most admired leader of the evangelicals, the few words from him dismissed McGovern's corruption issue. Henry Kissinger had announced that peace was at hand in the Vietnam War. The only issue McGovern could dream up was the corruption issue.

I remembered that in 1968 George Wallace wanted his candidacy to cut into the southern states, which were exceedingly Protestant. This would have denied Nixon or Humphrey an Electoral College majority. Then, Billy Graham put in a word to the press he had voted for Nixon. Following the Tuesday election, the Southern States of North and South Carolina, Kentucky, Florida, and Tennessee moved over into the Nixon column. Without those States, Richard Nixon would have lost the majority of the vote. Sometimes a word to another person or persons does make a difference in an election outcome.

Anti-Vietnam war demonstrators were actively protesting during the campaign. Usually they left Pat Nixon alone. However, on November first in Boston, Massachusetts, thousands broke windows outside the hotel where Pat was attending a Republican fund raising dinner. They over turned and burned cars, collided with police and caused much violence. However, Pat had left by a side entrance and escaped the demonstrators.

The last two days of the campaign Pat and President Nixon traveled together to Illinois. There were a lot of harassment and obscenity along the way. One could tell it was deliberate to keep President Nixon from talking to the people.

In Tulsa, Oklahoma, it was better but there were still some hecklers, too. When they went to Rhode Island they ran into more of the same. The mass meetings in North Carolina caused large crowds to break across a sloping roadway connecting different levels. They were happy that the rallies went well there. New Mexico went naturally without trouble or difficulty. Their final step was Ontario, California. At he end of the airport runway, a bleacher structure with tiers of seats was set up for those who came to see the President and First Lady. It would be the last time Nixon would speak as a candidate. He thanked everyone for coming to make it the most wonderful rally that they ever had.

On Election Day, the Nixons voted at Concordia Elementary School in San Clemente, California. Julie and David voted in Gettysburg, Pennsylvania and Tricia and Ed voted in New York. Then, the family had dinner at the White House waiting for the early voting returns to come in.

At the Phoenix headquarters, we had dinner catered in, as we watched more details of the election come in. We were happy for the results for President Nixon. However, we were dismayed that we did not pick up enough congressional seats to provide legislative support for President Nixon's programs. The Republicans had gained 12 seats in the House, but in the Senate we lost 2 seats. In the State House line up for governors, the 31 Democrats out ranked our 19 Republicans. We had lost 1 state house in this election.

I was happy that Nixon received 47,169,841 votes to McGovern obtained 29,172,767 (60% to 37.5%). Nixon only lost Massachusetts and Washington D.C. It was the second largest percent of popular vote in our history and the greatest ever given a Republican. Nixon received the largest number of popular votes ever cast for a presidential candidate and the second largest number of electoral votes. Nixon as a candidate for President became they first to win so many states. In checking Gallup polling, he won a majority of every key population group except the Democrats and the blacks. Many had never voted for a Republican candidate before. Surely, this wasa personal victory for Richard Nixon. Also, one for me,too. My work and prayers paid off along with thousands of campaign workers who really worked and worked to see Nixon become President for a second term.

Shortly, after his election eve dinner Nixon lost an old bridge or cap on one of his front teeth. It caused a lot of pain and had emergency dental work done that night and more to be done the next day. This muted his enjoyment of his victorious night. Perhaps, it was the failure to bring in more Republicans in Congress or he hadn't been able to end the Vietnam War or the Watergate affair.

The election came and was gone but still the Vietnam War was on our minds.

All Americans wanted the Vietnam War to end. It was President Nixon's top priority to bring and honorable end to the war. He was hoping both sides would sit down and sign the October agreement to end the war. No one knew what the communist North Vietnam would do next. They played a frustrating guessing game. Would there be a cease-fire before Christmas? Le Duc Tho of the North Vietnamese were still stonewalling negotiations. Nguyen Van Thieu (South Vietnam) was in deliberate stalling form until the Vietnamese people would accept any agreement that was offered.

President Nixon sent a message to the North Vietnamese after the November meeting that the U.S. would return later for more talks with the desire to reach a settlement. He also had a reduction in the bombing of the North until he could get them to take the final step to sign to end the war.

The next meeting would be on December 4th, Monday. Kissinger blamed his self for the early statement of "peace at hand," and wanted to resign because he felt he had blew the situation. President Nixon didn't want to hear about Kissinger's discouraging resignation remarks. He just wanted him to keep trying to get an agreement between the two Vietnamese leaders and to work our way out of the war.

Nixon knew the Congress would cut off money by January if there were no peace negotiations on the table. What would happen to our P.O.W. American men? Did they care?

Richard Nixon tried to "Bring Us Together" when he was first elected in 1968. The political violence, the rebellion of our youth, racial hatred and the Vietnam War infected and contaminated us. The Vietnam War was the principal ingredient. As all of this was stewed together and formed harmful morals which exhausted the strength of our country and warned us about our crumbling foundation. The hard rock, drugs and the hippie life style and many intemperate orgies were arrayed as an organized public demonstration of disapproval against our communities and nation.

The news media and Congress were affected by this rebellion. The press shifted from objectivity to oppositions.

No longer was the Presidency to be honored and respected but it became the target to be criticized and assaulted. In my opinion, "The Washington Post" was the first paper to lead the attack. Richard Nixon was their foe since the beginning of Alger Hiss spy days. That paper could not see any wrong in Alger Hiss—a spy and a traitor. They could not forgive Nixon for his part in exposing Hiss who sold his country out.

President Nixon always complained about the federal bureaucracy. Some people get elected and others appointed but for the rest he wondered how they got that job. He regretted he had not reorganized the executive branch of his administration. The day after the election, Nixon ordered Haldeman to announce to the White House staff and the Cabinet had to submit their resignations. Everyone was stunned. Haldeman did not make himself clear about what the President wanted-"Do you want to leave government service or go working for a private employer? Or stay in government and change your job or stay where you have always been. "Of course, Haldeman's ruthlessness didn't help the situation at hand. All thought the President was not grateful for their loyal services. Later, Nixon admitted this was a mistake. So what was needed that Richard Nixon should have done a little peace-making himself. Again, he left all things to Haldeman instead of carrying this one out himself. The Nixons decided to have Thanksgiving at Camp David. After the holidays they determined to go to New York with the family to do Christmas shopping, go to the theater and visit Tricia and Ed's home in Brooklyn.

By December 13th, negotiations were going nowhere with the communist North Vietnamese. It was hopelessly deadlocked. So President Nixon decided to take strong action on Sunday, December 17th, he ordered our airplanes to re-seed the mines in Haiphong Harbor and authorized B-52's to raid North Vietnam. It was a difficult decision but necessary. America would no longer accept a stalemate.

That same day President Nixon and Pat attended the 36th White House worship services. Two hundred fifty people attended the half hour service in the East Wing. Roman Catholic archbishop, John Cardinal Krol of Philadelphia offered prayer for all prisoners of war and those who died or were injured in the war, for those missing in action and all of the families, "May they all be special objects of God's love and our continued concern."

The Obernkirchen Children's Choir from Germany sang three Christmas songs in German. If we didn't understand the words we knew the familiar music. There was 36 members of the choir. Their ages ranged from 7 to 18. After the church service Nixon chatted with the children.

Among those who attended were Mamie Eisenhower, widow of President Eisenhower, and present and past Cabinet member, some Democrats who supported President Nixon 's re-election, and White House guests who were entertained by the Nixons last night at a White House dinner. Then later, the Nixons and Julie flew to Camp David retreat in the Maryland mountains.

Pat Nixon was busy with her daily December schedule. Anyone who played a role in the Nixon re-election was entertained at the White House. But, the Vietnam War persisted to dampen the Christmas party's merriment. We all realized that this was the fourth Christmas for the Nixons and us that the war in Vietnam continued on and was not settled so our American boys could come home.

The media called it the "Christmas bombing" and that President Nixon had started a huge terror bombing and was killing civilians in Hanoi. The newspapers and TV media were exaggerating the whole thing.

December 23rd, Pat and President Nixon went to Key Biscayne, Florida for Christmas. This would be the first Christmas without Julie and Tricia. Tricia and Ed were traveling in Europe and had delayed that trip until after the campaign. Julie's husband David Eisenhower was aboard the U.S.S. Albany and would meet Julie in Athens, Greece when it docked in port for the holidays. Tricia and Ed joined them in Athens.

However, this Christmas was very lonely for the Nixons. They didn't have the heart to even open Christmas gifts in Key Biscayne. The season was not the same as previous years. They really missed the girls and the very few friends around them.

On Christmas Eve, December 24th, a twenty-four hour Christmas truce was approved in Vietnam. For this day we were at peace. However, December 26th over a hundred B-52's bombed Hanoi-Haiphong area. On December 28th, the North Vietnamese decided they had enough and agreed to sign the agreement January 2nd and 8th dates.

Harry Truman (former President) died December 26th. On December 27th, Pat and President Nixon flew to Independence, Missouri for the funeral and to pay their respects to Bess Truman.

Richard Nixon was going to look forward to the days forward with great enthusiasm and joy and rise to the challenge. He recognized that God's help would be required for the task ahead, as well as the help of loyal staff, family, and friends.

Chapter 18

1973
THE ENERGY PROBLEMS
AND THE WATERGATE
TURMOIL

The year of 1973 began with great rejoicing and achievement to celebrate the re-election victory of President Nixon. His inauguration pomp and ceremony was to begin on January 20th. After a lonely Christmas without the girls, Tricia and Julie, Nixon didn't think he should arrange any plans to celebrate his 60th birthday, January 9th. The Vietnam peace negotiations were still on his mind.

Nixon was in good health the doctor said after his annual physical examination. However, his doctor advised him to walk more and relax. How was that to be, when the Vietnam War mess he inherited was predominate as his duty to win the Vietnam War at any cost to save military men's lives and bring P.O.W.'s home?

However, the afternoon of President Nixon's birthday, Kissinger called him that there was an important change in the peace negotiations with the North and South Vietnam.

The Viet Cong agreed to sign the peace agreement in Paris, France, instead of Hanoi. Nixon was elated and hoped that both sides would not change their minds. It was the best birthday news ever!

Now Nixon wished some birthday celebration had been planned. Instead of being down in the dumps, he was on the top of the mountain of joy! Un-be-knownst to him, Pat helped Julie and Tricia plan a surprise birthday night dinner. Pat kept the secret from Dick. Was Nixon surprised and astonished! When Nixon walked into the Blue Room, fifteen dinner guests greeted him, as well as all his family members. Six candles crowned his birthday cake—one for each ten periods of his life. The cake itself had coconut icing and pineapple filling which was one of President Nixon's favorite cakes. It said, "Happy Birthday RN" on the cake.

Nixon told us that most important element for keeping young in spirit was to have young people around, the ability to avoid boredom and look always to the future. Curtailing activities and slowing down as older persons is a terrible mistake. "Never slow down the spiritual heart; then age is not going to pull you down."

"Boredom, rather than the burdens of the presidency is more likely to cause a breakdown in health. I expect the next four years I will be serving my second term to be very interesting and I hope to do great things."

Some gave him funny gifts to cheer him up. After the dinner someone arranged a boisterous merry birthday skit intertwined with the showing of Humphrey Bogart's movie, "The Maltese Falcon." It pleased Pat someone would do that for her husband whom she loved so much.

I congratulated President Nixon for his re-election and gave him a Moody "Daily Pocket Diary" and also my article about him, "A Portrait of a Christian Statesman." He was grateful for my thoughts in writing and giving it to him.

After Congress convened, the Senate Democrat Caucus

voted, January 11th, to scrutinize any examine any 1972 Republican election misconducts and transgressions and the break-in at the Democrat headquarters at the Watergate Hotel.

On January 15th, all bombing and mining of North Vietnam stopped. Everyone was overjoyed and elated. I was happy. President Nixon has done the right thing.

The "Washington Post" were churning out stories that the Watergate bugging was the result of political spying on the behalf of the Nixon's re-election campaign for the presidency. But William Loeb, publisher of the "Union Leader" paper in New Hampshire accused the "Washington Post" of fabricating the whole incident to discredit the White House. I agreed with him that this was one of the dirtiest pieces of political pool I had ever seen.

The trial for the five men, who were arrested for the Watergate break-in, continued. James W. McCord, Jr. and Gordon Liddy were the only two still on trial charged for doing political espionage against the Democrats. Five other men pleaded guilty to the break-in and wiretapping.

McCord, who was chief of security for Nixon's re-election campaign organization, believed that he broke into the Democrat headquarters to prevent violence against President Nixon and other Republican Party officials. It was his notion that acting like he did would not be illegal because he only wanted to prevent harm to others.

There were some violent groups supporting George McGovern, the Democratic presidential candidate, such as the National Peace Action Coalition and Veterans Against the War. I only hoped the evidence would show McCord had a reason to believe that. But, I wasn't sure what else those men were looking for during that Watergate break-in. At that time I didn't know what was the truth.

The Gallup Poll polled Pat Nixon as the world's most admired woman. Now, she was a shining, happy, confident

First Lady. She accomplished much by helping her husband win a landslide re-election and finally achieved a unique life's fulfillment. As his wife, Pat tasted especially her husband's victory exultation and experienced his many set backs during his long political career.

Pat longed to be rid of the incredulity of the political life. Now she realized that he next four years would be last time around, much to her relief.

However, she enjoyed being the First Lady of the White House and making it a more readily receptive place. Pat never had been known to disagree with President Nixon on policy matters, but she had a way of getting her point of view across. In her own politics, Pat was a conservative and a firm believer in self-reliance and the work ethic as her husband did. She was happy and she believed and supported her husband. Neither one was bored and both thought each other was the greatest.

Skies were overcast and the cool temperature was in the mid 40's as President Nixon stood coatless renewing his presidential oath for his second term. The flags at the Capitol moved quickly in the cold air at half-staff because of the mourning period for former President Harry Truman's funeral.

Pat was at President Nixon's side in a double-breasted green wool coachman coat with a sable collar. She held two family Bibles, which her husband had used, in other oath-takings when Nixon was Vice President and for the first term as President. Pat had shared in her husband's triumphs from his congressional 1946 race, the journey to China and Soviet Union.

Nixon said in his second inaugural address, "Our nation was not built by government, but by people—not by welfare, but by work—not by shirking responsibility, but by seeking responsibility. Above all else, the time has come for us to renew our faith in ourselves and in America. We are embarking here today on an era that presents challenges as great as those

of any nation or any generation has ever faced. We shall answer
to God, to history, and to our conscience for the way in which
we will use these years. Let us go forward from here confident
in hope, strong in our faith, and in one another, sustained by
God who created us, and striving always to serve His purpose."

"In our own lives," he continued, "let each of us ask—
not just what will government do for me, but what I can do
for myself. In the challenges we face together, let each of us
ask—not just how can government help, but how can I help."

This was one of Dick's better speeches. It spoke to the
heart and that we should stand for something and not let
government do everything.

Even though, a peace agreement in Vietnam was near,
the war demonstrators hurled eggs and rocks and derision at
Pat and President Nixon as they passed by.

Than National Peace Action Coalition, the People's
Coalition for Peace and Justice, the Students for a Democratic
Society, the Progressive Labor Party, the Youth International
Party Yippies, and the Vietnam Veterans against the war—all
avowed to have thousands there to demonstrate. And they
did. They appeared and the police and National Guards were
on hand to avoid any clashes or to violent disturbances. What
a crowd!

At the close of weekend celebrations of concerts, balls,
and receptions, we were invited to the religious service,
Sunday morning at the White House. That pace was difficult
in keeping up to attend everything possible.

Pat and I were disturbed and surprised about Nixon calling
for the resignation of every professional government
employee at the White House. This was a stunning blow to
the cabinet and other aides who had worked so arduous for
Nixon's election.

President Nixon said later that calling for their resignation
was his mistake. It was only symbolic of a new beginning for
his new four-year administration.

He told us that when he took office as President, he had failed to fill all department and agencies with directors who were loyal to him as President. More than half of the bureaucrats were hostile to him and his programs. With this kind of environment in the White House, it was a wonder how anything was done.

Of course, if Bob Haldeman had left for unknown parts, that would have been all right with Pat and me. Haldeman was taking more and more time and responsibility to shut out Nixon's original aides and supporters from contacting the President. It disturbed us that Nixon was solely depending on Haldeman for everything.

The Vietnam War was on Nixon's mind and how to end the war honorably. Therefore he was oblivious to Haldeman's exceeding trespasses on the President's authority.

On January 22nd, President Thieu of South Vietnam agreed with the United States to sign the peace agreement. At the same time, former President Lyndon Johnson, at the age of sixty-four, died of a heart attack. He did not live to see the signing of the peace treaty. His plans for a "Great Society" had been curtailed by the Vietnam War which had drove him from office.

The Nixons paid their respects to Lady Bird Johnson and accompanied her to the Rotunda of the Capitol where her husband, President Lyndon Johnson lay in state. Pat was not very good in speaking-one-to-one-person who was grieving at the loss of their loved ones. She dreaded it because she always became a part of their strong tearfully feelings face to face.

On January 23rd, Richard Nixon announced on television that he dreaded Vietnam War would soon be over. The nation rejoiced, but a terrible price had taken their toll on Pat and Richard Nixon who only wanted to end the war with peace with honor.

On January 27th, envoys from the United States, the North

and South Vietnam and all the Vietcong signed the cease-fire peace agreement in Paris.

No sooner than the Vietnam peace agreement had been signed, Congress decided to fight with President Nixon about the budget cuts, the Vietnam War bombings, and any thing else President Nixon proposed. Congressional Democrats complained that Nixon stole power from them, and they decided to act. Also, they were frustrated by the Gallup poll, which showed that Congress had fallen in respect in the people's opinion to 26 percent low. When the same poll gave President Nixon a 68 percent high, Congress became more irritated.

The battle lines were drawn. The Senate Democratic Caucus voted to limit Nixon's Presidential authority to invoke executive privilege. Then, they introduced legislation to limit Nixon's war powers as President. No other President had been treated that way.

The real battle in the Democrat Congress was over Nixon's impoundment of funds. Every President since Thomas Jefferson had used this action of withholding funds for congressionally appropriated funds for pet projects that were considered unnecessary. The Democrats didn't object when President John Kennedy and Lyndon Johnson did the impounding of certain funds. But when Nixon urged Congress to have some fiscal restraint in their spending, he was talking to a blank wall. The Democrat Congress was not listening. The opposition woke up and realized how Nixon effectively attacked them for their for their irresponsibility. They were not going to have a conservative Republican President tell them what to do. The war was on!

On February 5th, with all this confrontation between Congress and President Nixon, the Senate Democrats called for an investigation of the 1972 Republican campaign practices and the Watergate break-in. Mike Mansfield chose Senator Sam Ervin of North Carolina to head the investigation. Sam Ervin was a partisan political Democrat and the next four years would be difficult.

The P.O.W. predicament deeply persuaded Nixon to work to bring all the prisoners of war home. The presence of the widow Lt. Colonel Nolde and her five children at the Nolde funeral in Washington emotionally moved Nixon. Colonel Nolde was the last American to die in Vietnam.

President Nixon had been working to obtain release of every war prisoner in an overseas jail. He had discussed these matters with Premier Chou En-Lai last year in Peking, China. The last American prisoner was John T. Downey who was held by the Chinese for twenty years. He was captured on Chinese territory during the Korean War.

In 1952, our government denied Downey was a CIA agent to set up subversive maneuvers operating behind enemy lines. It took great courage for Nixon to confess publicly the truth about the Downey involvement. The Chinese heard the confession and assured Nixon that Downey would be released along with two other American air force pilots who crashed in China after raids in North Vietnam. All the American P.O.W.'s held by Hanoi, Vietnam, would be released. At last all living American war prisoners would be coming home.

With all President Nixon had to think about, Atheist Madalyn Murray O'Hair filed suit on February 23rd against President Nixon, chaplains of the House and Senate, and other congressional officials to stop the use of religious church services in the East Wing of the White House and other use of government buildings for religious services.

Madalyn Murray O'Hair had previously won a lawsuit in 1963 banning compulsory prayer in public schools. She accused Richard Milhous Nixon of pushing Christianity as the official civil religion of the United States by holding church services in the East Wing of the White House. So in this second lawsuit she thought she would ban prayer in the White House. We had to wait to see how this would happen, but time would tell that Nixon would win out on this one against O'Hair.

President Nixon liked to get away from the White House. He retreated as often as possible to places where he would have fewer distractions where he could buckle down to intense concentrated reading and determined decision makings.

In Washington, D.C., February 26th, the 21st Women's Forum on National Security met to award women for their distinguished service in the cause of national security. The forum acted for five million women members of seventeen national patriotic societies.

Pat Nixon was nominated for an award for her trips to Africa, China, and Russia. The women applauded heartily when Maxine Chilton of Superior, Arizona, presented the Molly Pitcher award to Mrs. Nixon. Pat smiled and accepted the award in appreciation. She deserved it. As First Lady she did more for our country than any other woman and was admired for her selfless service for others. I was sure everyone she contacted, signing every autograph and shaking the hand of the last person in line, they knew she cared deeply for them.

Earlier in March, President Nixon had Sammy Davis for his "Evening at the White House," and everything went okay. Nixon thought music critic reporters should have been invited to the event, as the White House could have been credited for his administration. However, that night he gave orders that Sally Quinn of the "Washington Post" be barred from any activities at the White House—East or West wing. This reporter had violated all the rules and it irritated Nixon.

If anyone checked the White House calendar each year, Pat's birthday would be always celebrated on St. Patrick's Day, March 17th. Since Pat was an exceptional First Lady, no wonder they wanted to plan each time a special party for her. Because of this distinct date, the ambassador from Ireland always managed to come to visit the President and give Pat a beautiful green shamrock plant. Pat appreciated my gift of Avon Fresheners, and my remembrance added greatly to the joy of her special day.

That night of Pat's special day, President Nixon had another "Evening at the White House." Merle Haggard, a country western star, was the special entertainer. Everyone was wearing green, including Pat. President Nixon made everyone laugh when he came out attired in a gigantic green bow tie. Apparently, he borrowed it from one of the employees who worked there. I liked country western music. Some didn't care for that kind of music, but they perked up when Haggard sang "Okie From Muskogee" and other western favorites.

My heart was burdened for President Nixon and Pat. I wondered what else I could do to help. All I could do was pray for them. So, I was inspired to start "Operation: Paul Revere." My mother and my stepfather helped with the project.

I sent a letter to every church in America and other individuals. Postage was costly, but I thought President Nixon's request for prayer was important and what God wanted me to do.

So, this national prayer chain went out across the nation. President Nixon was aware of the project, and he became encouraged.

As time went by, sacks of mail came in with replies from all over the nation. My stepfather, mother, and I were truly blessed reading all the comments and answers. My Republican "Pueblo Grande Club" was helping, too. Then, it spread to the other Republican women's clubs. I was on the Arizona State Board of Republican Women, and I made my voice for Nixon heard there, too. By this time, everyone knew that a personal friend of Pat and Richard Nixon was standing up for them.

The Democrat Congress had ignored President's Nixon's warning about the energy problem in 1971. Twenty four months later the situation became worse. Nixon had looked down the road-so to-speak-and saw the critical predicament ahead. On April 18,1973, he asked Congress to deregulate natural gas and let prices rise with the market; tax credits for oil exploration and ended the compulsory import quotas. The office of Energy Conservation was created and ordered that this office would step-up to be a new cabinet office.

By the middle of May, Nixon asked all retailers and dealers to voluntarily participate together in supplying and reserving gasoline. Then, he asked all of us to reduce our speed to fifty miles an hour, instead of the seventy miles an hour, which we were used to when we were driving. By October, Saudi Arabia issued their full-scale oil embargo against us.

By November, President Nixon announced on television that we were headed for the most severe energy shortfall. He called for a conservation effort by everyone—federal, state, county, city and Congress and the rest of us out in the country. Heat would be lowered in all federal government buildings to 65-68 degrees. This applied to all of us in our private homes. We were urged to car-pool and drive at 50 miles an hour. Asked the states to return to daylight saving time.

The lower speed limit and daylight savings time, the construction of the Alaska pipeline made it out of Congress. But the Democrat Congress failed to pass one other important energy legislation.

I had to get up early to get in line for gasoline. If a service station did not get their usual allotment, I had to hunt one before they ran out of supplies on hand. Sometimes they did run out while I was in line. Then, President Nixon banned the sale of gasoline on Sundays and cutbacks on outdoor lighting. Then, we were asked to voluntarily ration our gasoline allocations.

By spring, I saw my gasoline costs jumped a big leap. It

took a big bite out of my budget. I had to travel to the college 25 miles away and then back home. I was wondering if I should move my bed to the college. Bread and a gallon of gasoline were now costing me about a dollar each. Since 1947 the food and fuel costs were increasing and this was the biggest jump from past years.

Everyone I talked to couldn't realize that this situation was real. But, it was! It wasn't the oil companies' fault. Their foreign oil imports had risen from $4.00 a barrel to $12.00 a barrel. As consumers, we were paying for the extra cost as it was passed on to us. Before long the energy crisis became an economic crisis. Nixon was working to end the Arab oil embargo with King Faisal and President Sadat. It would be a long year of hard work ahead for Nixon.

Every time I read newspapers or watched the TV news, the "Watergate" word dominated the news. I knew it would be difficult for Pat Nixon to carry-on her many duties as First Lady. Her calendar of state dinners and teas kept her busy in spite of the news reports about the all "going-ons" in her husband's Oval Office. The "Watergate" affair was still a mystery to her.

By Nixon 's second term of the presidency, Haldeman took over every detail in the office. Most of Nixon's first group of supporters and assistants had little meeting with him. Bob Haldeman blocked everyone's access to the President. He wanted to be the only channel for conveying what he thought was best for the President. Even Rosemary Woods, Nixon's personal secretary, ran into trouble with Haldeman's obnoxious power control.

Finally, it took close personal friends to leak confidentially to Nixon what was happening. At first, Nixon thought all what was going on was jealousy among staff members. However, when too many irresponsible decisions by Haldeman came to Nixon's attention, he became angry and annoyed a bit, and he called Haldeman "on the carpet." Many of us could not forget the manipulation going on behind President Nixon's back. It was his steadfast concern about ending the Vietnam War, which kept him many times from being aware of other things going around him.

I did not know how Pat performed her duties as First Lady during this skirmish about the Watergate event. On April 20th, before the full-blown frenzy of Watergate descended on her, Pat decided to open the White House grounds to a tour by the public. It pleased the people, and they were excited about visiting the many gardens there.

How many people had the chance to stop to smell the roses in the Rose Garden? They didn't, until Pat initiated their first tour. It was a thrilling, beautiful sight. The pink crab apple trees were in full bloom and red tulips delighted their eyes. Twenty-five Presidents had planted trees on the grounds. Information brochures were given to the public, so they could locate the presidential trees. Many of the trees were flowering and other trees were budding ready to burst in bloom. The crocuses were up and announced to everyone that spring had arrived.

Pat said her busy schedule gave her comfort and support during this critical, crazy time. It helped her to do as much walking as possible to encourage her to stand up underneath the daily stress of White House duties. The Watergate affair was something she couldn't do anything about, but she would continue on in what she could do best.

John W. Dean, Nixon 's counsel, was ordered by President Nixon to investigate the Watergate affair. Throughout March, Dean reported falsely that no one at the White House was involved. But they were! The noose was surely tightening around Bob Haldeman, John Ehrlicman, and John Dean's necks.

President Nixon was trying to sort out the many detailed staff stories about Watergate. He knew something was wrong. It worried him. Everyone around him observed him as more nervous and less talkative than usual. At times he was oblivious to his family and personal friends around him. We knew he was deeply troubled. It bothered Pat, too. She felt helpless because she could not help her husband in this situation, which was created without his personal authorization.

In Washington, D.C., I learned to listen and to not talk with others. This is a gossip town. The many whispers going around made it difficult to sort out what was a falsehood or the truth. I took notes on whatever I heard or saw.

Richard Nixon had been the target of the press since Alger Hiss days. He had proved the press and media that they were wrong long before the Watergate episode. It bothered me that they never forgave him and took matters in their own hands.

The burglars who went into the Watergate Hotel were professionals who left tracks all over the place. To me, they looked like they wanted to get caught on purpose.

Everyone on Nixon's staff was blaming each other for the Watergate break-in and what happened afterwards. John Dean, Nixon's legal counsel turned on the President and blamed Nixon for obstruction of justice and the cover-up. Tapes contradicted Dean's testimony. As Jesus Christ had Judas Iscariot as a traitor in his midst, Richard Nixon had John Dean whose actions betrayed the President and blamed him for everything that he did himself. As for me, I thought Watergate was a set-up and a plot to destroy Nixon. Surely the Nixon staff had sabotaged the affair from within the White House.

After making phone calls to his staff on Easter Sunday morning, President Nixon and Pat attended Easter church services. Even though the Vietnam Wars was not over, signs about Watergate appeared. The signs were nasty and repulsive. They targeted Nixon whether he was honest or a crook as the press were implanting in people's minds. Thank goodness President Nixon 's supporters were always there to counter act the disagreeable, unpleasant demonstrators.

On April 30th, President Nixon on nationwide television announced the resignation of Bob Haldeman, John Ehrlichman, and the firing of John Dean. By looking at Nixon 's face, one could tell that this circumstance wasted him emotionally. It was etched in his countenance. Nor did he tell us how he allowed this predicament to get out of hand.

When I called the White House to voice my words of support, Pat answered the phone. Pat was strong with encouragement for her husband. I felt as she did that this was a political harassment by others whose views were different than theirs. I never knew how she could stand steadfast and show strength in the days ahead. My heart ached for both to them.

All I could do is pray and write articles of support to newspapers. I promised the Nixons I would do just that. The family was very grateful for my standing in the gap for them. It was difficult for them to conceal their anguish completely.

I knew Richard Nixon had a very high sense of moral ethics and obedience to the law. He was a too efficient skilled a person to approve such illegal acts. In my heart I knew Haldeman and Dean and the rest of the crew had overstepped their bounds this time. Their blunders came back to haunt President Nixon. He took their blame even though he did not know all about it.

Nixon accepted the responsibility and a course of action concerning it. He asked for my prayers and I assured him he had mine. March 22nd, I followed it up with a letter.

Then I published an article, "Is This The Way To Run A Congress," and other articles in support of President Nixon in newspapers throughout the country. It did some good. Many people responded to it. It inspired a businessman out in Urbana, Illinois, to put up three billboards in the Champaign/Urbana area for Nixon.

Each billboard had a picture of President Nixon on it next to the assertion that read: "I have more faith in this man than

I have in any of his accusers especially the press." It was signed: "Dwight Dobbs, a proud American citizen."

Nixon read about the billboards in the newspaper and decided to call Dobbs and thank him for his support. Dobbs was thrilled with the telephone call from the President. However, Richard Nixon was more aroused with encouragement by this man's single act of support. He told Dobbs over and over what he did for him in this time of crisis. No one knows what can be done by one little act of kindness. It encouraged a President when he needed it.

Nixon had toyed with the idea of resigning several times. He was torn between two decisions what to do. With the scandal of the Watergate break-in clouding the Washington scene, the White House banquet gala for the American P.O.W.'s was a fragrant perfume in the air. It gave a vexed President a pick up.

More than 90 percent of American servicemen in Vietnam supported President Nixon's decision to attack the enemy forces there. When the prisoners of war came home, Nixon wanted to thank each one for serving this country so honorably. On May 24th, Richard Nixon as Commander in Chief gave the prisoners of war an elaborate White House party in their honor.

More than 600 P.O.W.'s came-many were weak and then, malnourished and showed signs of their mental and physical afflicted torments. Each one brought a guest. It was the largest sit down dinner ever held at the White House. P.O.W.'s and their guests amounted to 1,280 people. Everyone was served in a huge rain-drenched, red and yellow striped tent with chandeliers on the south lawn.

Pat and President Nixon moved around the tables greeting all the P.O.W.'s and guests. They were enjoying the festivities as much as their guests. Tie clasps were given to the men and brooches for the women. Both bore the presidential seal.

This banquet was a climax for the P.O.W.'s full day. They

had breakfast at the Washington Hilton Hotel—a sharp contrast to their horrible prison days at "Hanoi Hilton." In the afternoon Nixon spoke to the P.O.W.'s and shook hands with each one. Pat, meanwhile, entertained the wives and other guests in State Department Jefferson Room. Lt. Commander John S. McCain came on crutches on the mend from surgery on his injured leg. Two P.O.W.'s enjoyed a joyful reunion. While in prison they had never seen one another, but had conveyed messages by tap code in the next cell. Their face-to-face meeting at the banquet was a very emotional social gathering.

The main attraction was a handmade flag created from a white handkerchief. Thread from red underwear and a blue jacket was used to fashion this flag, which was flown secretly in the Vietnam prison. The flag was given to President Nixon.

The P.O.W.'s cheered President Nixon when he said "It is time to quit making national heroes out of those who steal secrets and publish them in the newspapers. Looking toward the balance of the second four years, I think I have some allies and I think I can rely on you."

The P.O.W.'s rose and gave Nixon a long applause and acclamation.

At that moment, Nixon did not think of resignation in this enjoyable festivity.

After the banquet, the most pretentious entertainment I had ever seen staged. Bob Hope was master of ceremonies. He kept everyone in "stitches." He had entertained troops in Vietnam many times. John Wayne, Jimmy Stewart, Sammy Davis and the New Christy Minstrels kept the joy of the evening at a high pitch. At the end of the program, Irving Berlin led us in "God Bless America," the song he wrote. In all it was a day of patriotic celebration event. Anyone who was able to dance did so until 2:00 a.m.

However, the Nixons departed at 12:30 a.m. to go to their personal quarters upstairs. In spite of the delightful entertainment and laughter, Nixon 's eyes portrayed the discouragement and dejection, which we never had seen before. Even when he laughed, the pain was there.

Pat did not think her husband should not resign as President. She recommended that he should "Fight, Fight, Fight!" I urged him to do so, too. After all it was his staff who thought up all this mischief and misdeeds.

It bothered Nixon, though. If there had been someone else beside John Dean and Bob Haldeman, there would not be any painful troubling thoughts of resignation. He wanted to find out what really happened at the Watergate break-in. His dependency on John Dean and Bob Haldeman to tell him the truth did not help President Nixon. They did not want to tell him their personal involvement in the matter of the Democrat National Committee break-in.

By end of May, John Dean failed to get immunity from the federal prosecutors. "The Washington Post" and the "New York Times" churned out stories everyday concerning John Dean and his allegations about President Nixon and Haldeman and the rest of his staff's involvement. However, Dean did not want to state his own part in the cover up.

I wrote a letter of encouragement to President Nixon noting his concern in the difficult situation ensuing around him. He responded knowing how I felt personally.

The Senate Watergate Committee wanted John Dean to give his testimony on June 18th. But, Sam Ervin chairman, agreed to postpone the Dean's testimony because of conflict of Leonid Brezhnev, the Russian Secretary General's arrival at he White House.

Stories of the Watergate affair clouded the Summit II meeting of Nixon and Brezhnev. The Soviet could not understand how Americans could tear themselves apart. It was puzzling to them. The Russians wanted the United States to abandon Israel to an Arab settlement on their own terms. However, Nixon felt the Israel and the Arabs should sit down and talk over each item in question. But, on other things such as agriculture, trade, and atomic energy and trade the U.S.A and Soviet Russia they were able to reach agreements and signed the Mutual Communication.

On June 25th, Leonid Brezhnev returned to Moscow and John Dean was called before the Democrat Senate Watergate Committee to give his testimony. For five days, the television media bombarded us with coverage from morning to night regarding the Dean testimony. We could not escape it.

John Dean turned on the President. He was applying everything he had been doing to Nixon himself. The mud of untruth by Dean about intelligence-gathering enterprise and the "Enemies List" stuck to Nixon. The press picked up each item mentioned without checking for the facts. His falsehoods were intermingled with a bit of truth. It was like the game of Gossip—what came in at the end did not resemble the truth at all at the beginning. The "Enemies List" was originally composed by Dean for dealing with people who he thought was a political enemy. Pat and President Nixon were not aware of the lists until Dean's revelation about it. Some people on the list wondered why they were even on the revealed list at all.

I was shocked by Chairman Sam Ervin's behavior. His treatment of many persons who came before him and his committee was despicable. They were humiliated and badgered. Reputations were being destroyed. What happened to innocent before being prejudged until all the facts are found? So I decided to research information about Sam Ervin and others involved in the hearings to learn if there would be anything about them to help President Nixon in his defense.

June 21st was Pat and Richard Nixon 's thirty third wedding anniversary. After all they were going through, I thought it was appropriate to remember their special wedding day. This close intimate couple was entwined in love. They appreciated my friendship, which remained constant over the years. I was a true friend who stood by them regardless what was going on in their lives.

I was delighted and proud of Pat Buchanan's testimony before the Ervin's Watergate committee. He really turned things around for the Nixon administration. Anyone who knew Buchanan would be aware that he would back up what he states by facts and documents. He told how the Democrats were the authors of dirty tricks. Buchanan named Dick Tuck, their Democrat trickster who was on the payroll of McGovern campaign during the 1972 Republican Convention. It made the Democrats uncomfortable. Of course, they didn't call Dick Tuck before the committee, or any other persons Buchanan mentioned. It was most embarrassing to Ervin's committee and they didn't want to hear anymore of Buchanan's revelations about what the Democrats had done. Unfortunately, not all networks were carrying Buchanan's testimony at the Senate hearings. If they had the public opinion would have been much different.

The Ervin Committee did not want to bring up the 1960 Kennedy-Nixon campaign vote fraud case. Surely, the Democrats covered up their involvement in that one. If I had been called up as a witness regarding it, I would have exposed the whole thing. No one wanted to listen to the truth and was silent. The Democrats thought it was all right if they did anything wicked, but anyone else did what they were doing they were guilty and should go to prison. It all depended on who was doing it.

Julie's 25th birthday was July 5th. My warm congratulatory message of friendship was appreciated. She was glad to learn I planned to write letters to newspapers across the country as soon as my classes ended.

In the wee hours of the morning, July 12th, Nixon was awoken with a sharp, piercing pain in his chest. It kept him awake and uncomfortable. His breathing was difficult and his fever escalated. The doctor's diagnosed his case as viral pneumonia and ordered him to bed for 5 to 8 days in Bethesda Naval Hospital.

He made a valiant demonstration of operating the government from his bed and shattering his 102-degree fever and the pain in his chest. Nixon declined to remove his self from active duty as President by reason of his viral pneumonia sickness.

On the second day, Pat Nixon, along with Julie and David Eisenhower, visited their husband and father and spent an hour with him. She was encouraged by hundreds of messages wishing the President to get well. However, Pat was distressed by the Watergate scandal and her husband's illness with pneumonia added to her worries. When she emerged from the hospital with sunglasses on and a strained look on her face after visiting her husband, Pat refused to talk with reporters.

Pat visited her husband daily, except for one day. Her half-brother, Matthew G. Bender died on Saturday. Bender was the son of Pat's mother, Kate, who was widowed before she married William Ryan, Pat's father. She attended the rosary service in California and could not visit her husband at Bethesda Naval Hospital.

July 18th, I received a thoughtful note from Pat regarding the get-well card and inspirational poem I had sent. Both of them were grateful for my constant friendship.

Television newsmen approached a Senate Watergate committee member and asked if Nixon was really sick. I thought that question was immoral, offensive, and a contemptible action and not very responsible by the press. It made me realize the vengeance and hate, regarding President Nixon, was running unrestrained and out of control in Washington. To my delight, several Republican congressmen agreed with my analysis of the press's behavior regarding Nixon's illness.

When Nixon finally appeared looking underfed and

healthy, White House staffers welcomed him on the South Lawn. There, Nixon read a get-well note he received from John W. James III, an 8-year-old boy from Livermore, California. He treasured this get-well letter, which he selected from the many letters he received.

The boy wrote:

"I heard you were sick with pneumonia. I just got out of the hospital with pneumonia, and I hope you did not catch it from me.

'Now you be a good boy and eat your vegetables like I had to do. If you take your medicine and your shots, you'll be out in 8 days like I was."

Afterwards, President Nixon grasped the importance of the time to give a stimulating talk disavowing any ideas of resigning for the cause of health scandal, or any other mortification. That, Nixon said, "is just plain poppy cock." He spoke about controlling crime, the drug problem, and prosperity without war. What he was elected to do he was going to do. "Let others wallow in Watergate, we are going to do our job."

After John Mitchell had resigned as the campaign director, Clark MacGregor became the 1972 campaign director for the re-election of President Nixon. However, on July 20th, MacGregor dropped a bombshell at the Senate Committee hearing about the involvement of the White House, and campaign staffers lying, misleading, and deceiving him about the Watergate affair. He sharply criticized John Ehrlichman and H.R. "Bob" Haldeman. Haldeman was the channel of communication between President Nixon and MacGregor concerning the re-election campaign. MacGregor blamed Ehrlichman for being unwilling to disclose relevant information on the Watergate matter. This put MacGregor in a situation to emit press announcements without having all the information accessible.

He denounced Ehrlichman for not telling him about the

break-in at he Ellsberg psychiatrist's office, the June meeting with John Dean and acting FBI director Patrick Gray, or his meeting with CIA (Central Intelligence Agency) with Richard Helms, CIA director.

John Ehrlichman counteracted by stating it was all done for national security reasons and did not want to publicly reveal lawful CIA actions because of ex-CIA workers entanglement in the Watergate affair.

However, when I heard all this it only confirmed my suspicions about the involvement of the White House staff and U.S. government agencies to remove the President from office. I decided to do some research of my own to help uncover the true facts about those who were working against President Nixon and our country. We were at war, and our President was being sabotaged from within.

I had promised the Nixons I would write to the newspapers all over the nation about support for them. As a daughter of a veteran, I even contacted the military "Stars and Stripes" paper to enlist veterans for Nixon 's side of the cause.

My article, "Remember Bobby, Sam" appeared in the Arizona Republic paper and other large newspapers. Friends I had across the nation were on the alert about the article. They clipped and mailed each one to me. In response to the article, people flooded Congress and the White House with their answers to the situation and Sam Ervin's hypocrisy.

On August 1st, the Attorney General's office announced that Vice President Spiro Agnew was being investigated for bribery, tax fraud, and kickbacks from contractors while he had been a county executive and governor of Maryland. The press tied Agnew's dilemma in with the Watergate affair and tried to make it stick to Nixon.

Apparently, the Nixon critics were running out of things to pin anything on Nixon. They started first on the Nixon's homes. The investigators on the Senate committee believed that the San Clemente property was purchased with leftover 1968 campaign funds. Of course they didn't check the facts about it. Therefore, the Nixons had ordered a much-detailed independent audit to diffuse the falsehoods that campaign funds had been used to buy the property in San Clemente.

Pat and President Nixon bought the $1.5 million estate in 1969 with their own money, bank loans, and $625,000 loan from Robert Abplanalp, and industrialist friend and C.G. "Bebe" Rebozo. As all of us who buy property to own, we know from our experience we have to borrow money and pay the current interest rate and similar to everyone else, we still owe money on our property.

But that didn't stop the critics and the media. They couldn't find anything about the Nixon's spending on their homes; so they started on the ITT anti-trust case, and on to the bombing of Cambodia, and to anything else they could jump on to complain about. If Nixon was not living up to their own personal agenda, they wanted to destroy the Nixons at any cost.

In 1973, the Democrats controlled the Senate and the House. Nixon became the first president since 1849 to start his presidency without the Republicans being in majority in either house. The Democrats were claiming they were robbed in 1972 when Nixon won by an enormous landslide against their candidate.

In late August, President Nixon flew to New Orleans to speak at the Veterans of Foreign Wars Convention. Pat and the President were planning on warm friendly greetings from the crowd there, as their motorcade would proceed through out the city. However, plans changed when proof was presented by the Secret Service that there was a plot to kill them in New Orleans. Therefore, they drove them a different way. Nixon needed an extra lift from all the pressures he was enduring. He was so frustrated with the actions of the press, Nixon lost his temper and pushed Ron Ziegler, his press secretary's back, with an order to take the journalist to a room reserved just for them. Of course the press picked up this outburst and action. They did not forget it.

As the convention, President Nixon was presented the Peace Award by Mrs. James Reid, the National Auxiliary President of the V.F.W. The award read; "Unity Foundation For Peace to Richard Milhous Nixon, 37th President, United States of America.

'Whose leadership and efforts toward World Peace are recognized and appreciated by the more than half-million members of the Ladies Auxiliary to the Veterans of Foreign Wars of the United States.

In newspapers and the television media, they manufactured stories about President Nixon. The gossip mill about Nixon drinking alcohol continued on and on. Apparently, they thought the President lived like one of them. Richard Nixon did not drink in excess because he could not hold his liquor and had no tolerance for alcoholic beverages.

The press latched on to the phone calls and the loud mouth expressions of Martha Mitchell. I first met Martha, the wife of Attorney General John Mitchell at a woman's meeting. She was pretty in her ruffles and bows pink dress. Her pink floral umbrella added the touch to remind others about this Southern belle. However, Martha had a problem. When she became intoxicated and drink loosen her tongue to excess. Even Pat could not help Martha. She would not listen to Pat's advice and turned a deaf ear toward her helpful counsel.

Martha was a sad case who added fuel to the Watergate affair. Whether it was true or not she would talk to anyone. John Mitchell had to spend more time with his wife Martha instead of managing the campaign store. He was so pre-occupied with her that he was not aware of other things done around him. By September, John and Martha separated, and Martha was left alone with her alcohol drinking.

Back in May, Archibald Cox was appointed Special

Prosecutor to supervise the Watergate investigations. He chose eleven men to be on the Special Prosecution Force. All were anti-Nixon except one. They threaten and frighten individual Nixon staff members and his personal friends. Cox asked for White House tapes and appointment logs. Never in the history of our country was any president treated like they did Nixon. As far as I was concerned Cox and his bunch were partisan zealots abusing the power they promised to uphold. I was shocked when they would not allow Nixon to state his point of view.

I remember when I substituted for a secretary who was on vacation. Even though I was a fast typist, I had to run each section of the dictatape several times in order to make out what he person was actually saying. The quality of the White House tapes was so faulty and the voices were so difficult to recognize and make out what they were saying at all. Apparently the acoustics in each room made it easy or hard for a person in it to hear distinctly. At spots on the tapes, no voices sounded. What were they really saying? Did the transcriber have to fill in to read what they were actually saying? That was anyone's guess.

On October 9th, Spiro Agnew resigned as Vice President and pled nolo contendere on failing to report income for tax purposes in a Baltimore, Maryland federal courthouse. He was sentenced to three years' probation and a $10,000 fine. I was saddened by Agnew's resignation. He was an inspiration to all who heard him speak. Agnew really was a strong patriot whose courage and candor reached our hearts to be better citizens.

Overshadowing the Agnew resignation news was the October 6th war in the Middle East. Egypt and Syria attacked Israel territories, which Israel had possessed since 1967. Israel was surprised by the attack, as well as our own CIA. The chairman of the Joint Chief of Staff at the Pentagon, Admiral Thomas Moorer was opposed to Nixon and Israel. They were using all kinds of excuses that the Arabs and the Soviets would be hostile and didn't want to do much about the situation.

This made Nixon very angry. He picked up the phone and stirred up the military who were putting obstacles before action. Nixon was not concerned with Arab and Soviet reactions. He told them that sending a large number of American planes was his decision. If Arabs cut off oil supplies in repayment of the airlift. After all, he was the commander-in-chief.

The Soviets were sending their own airlift to the Arabs-the other side. We were faltering. Finally, the military at the Pentagon woke up and decided to comply with Nixon's orders. Nixon's decisive action saved Israel. As for me, I thought this was his greatest foreign policy achievement. I was really proud.

When some of the Republicans heard President Nixon wanted John Connally as his choice to fill the Vice President vacancy my phone rang off the hook. They did not want Connally, but Ronald Reagan or Nelson Rockefeller. They knew of my friendship with the Nixon family and thought my opinion might hold some weight in the decision. I knew the Democrats in Congress did not like Connally from dropping from the Democrat fold and changing to the Republican side. He wouldn't have a chance for confirmation in Congress. Nixon would have to choose someone who could be confirmed by both sides.

That would be difficult, but I knew Nixon would find the right man for the office. He chose Congressman Jerry Ford for Vice President, and Ford accepted the nomination. By Friday, October 12th, Nixon announced in the East Room to the public regarding Jerry Ford as the new candidate for Vice President. Pat approved of the decision and so did I. Ford was not controversial and he had many friends in Congress on both sides of the aisle.

Senator John Stennis, Mississippi, chairman of the Senate

Select Committee on Standards and Conduct, a Democrat agreed with President Nixon he would verify accuracy of the summaries of the tapes. Archibald Cox had ordered Nixon to deliver nine tapes. He did not support the Stennis Compact plan, even though Senator Sam Ervin and Senator Howard Baker had approved it along with Elliot Richardson's Nixon's Attorney General.

However, Archibald Cox hated Nixon 's guts. But, I saw Cox and his staff of men as partisan liberal snakes in the grass. They were trying to destroy President Nixon unfairly at any cost. It made me angry that the media had overstepped their bounds by fueling the lies and misstatements. Without the facts they neglected to find, I was wondering what the public was thinking when they were fed this poison.

When Nixon ordered Archibald Cox to be fired as Special Prosecutor, Attorney General Elliot Richardson and William Ruckelhaus, Richardson's deputy, refused to fire Cox and resigned instead. However, Solicitor General Robert Bork became acting Attorney General and carried out Nixon's orders to dismiss Cox from his duties as Special Prosecutor and transfer all operations to the Justice Department.

From then on, the television media assailed us with all inflammatory discussions they could find. The Democrats were remarking to the public anything they could dig up whether it was true or not. In all the hot air expressed, my heart was saddened. November 3rd, I wrote a letter of encouragement with prayerful concern. November 13, Nixon quickly thanking me for my prayers.

In all this turmoil, Pat was honored at a Nevada Society black-tie dinner, as one of "Nevada's outstanding women of the century." President Nixon made a surprise ten-minute appearance at the 800 gathering. He praised his wife and two other women. Helen D. Bentley, Federal Maritime Commission Chairman, and Eva Adams, U.S. Mint. He repeated as he did on the nationwide radio television speech in which he stated he would not resign and would continue working as long as he was physically able to do so. He made mention about his present dilemma by recollecting his mother's deathbed counsel which Nixon had told often before.

His mother was near death, and he tried to cheer her up by telling her, "Mother, don't you give up." Nixon said, she answered and elevated herself up and saying "Richard, don't you ever give up."

Many Democrat politicians were there and Gerald R. Ford, the future Vice President. They gave him an outstanding applause.

Three hundred guests were at the Sunday White House church services. The inspiring speaker was Rep. William H. Hudnut III, an Indiana Republican and also an ordained United Presbyterian minister who had come to Congress in January. Before he was elected to Congress by the Indiana's 11th district voters, Hudnut was senior minister of Second Presbyterian Church in Indianapolis for 10 years.

His sermon was named "The Religion of Abraham Lincoln." He said, "There is a great difference between humbly praying, as Lincoln did that we might be on God's side, and self-righteous asserting that He is on ours. I think this humility can alone save us from the tyranny that inevitably results when the state or a ruling oligarchy within is deified."

His sermon was wonderful because of its appropriateness. It brought tears to our eyes.

December 10th, Pat accepted an 18-foot Fraser fir from North Carolina. She told us they would be in Washington for the Christmas holidays to enjoy the big fir tree. Pat was wearing a brilliant green wool coat, and she looked like a beautiful Christmas tree herself. In referring to the fuel shortage, she said, "People are staying home, buying trees and enjoying it more, and we will be doing much the same." Pat loved Christmas in the White House, the decorations, and for the family to be around them.

On December 15th, Tyna A. Lee, a Camp Fire Girl and Warren Tilgham, a Boy Scout, helped push the button to turn on the light for the national Christmas tree. It was a beautiful sight to behold!

December 16th, Billy Graham spoke at the pre-Christmas worship service. Snow was falling steadily outside while guests were listening intently as Graham spoke on the dark days of Watergate, the energy crisis, and the Mid-East War. He warned that there would be worse times ahead if we didn't repent as a nation and turn from sins. The hope of Christmas is that God has promised eternal life, healing, and forgiveness. Our greatest need is a change in the hearts.

The thirty voice Army Chorus delighted and encouraged us about the true concept of what Christmas was really about. After the benediction, President Nixon assured us that there would be enough gasoline to drive to church on Sunday.

Lights were dimmed for the holiday season to go easy on electricity. We were in an energy crisis. Gasoline could not be purchased on Sunday, and we had to wait in long lines to get it.

A lot of us had to car pool to work and lower heating temperatures. Many of us had to put on extra clothing just to keep warm. We were hoping this energy crisis would end soon.

Four hundred children of foreign diplomats were honored with the customary Christmas party on December 17th. Two days later, on December 19th, Pat had a tea for the wives of the White House Fellows and acted as hostess for the affair. She never forgot those around her.

This Christmas the White House looked more "natural." There were more pinecones, candles, and greenery than in past years. Any tourists could still marvel at the beautiful decorations. To evade all unnecessary use of electricity outside lighting was removed from bushes, trees, and windows. Indoors the trees would carry the smallest tiny lights.

Gold and silver ornaments and bright tinsel would give a more sparkling effect.

On this Christmas all of us were down and crushed by all the events of Watergate. Pat tried to cheer up everyone around her in spite of how she felt inside. Pat said Julie was ill with the flu and could not participate in the Christmas dinner. Nixon had made telephone calls to friends and other people across the country. He was glad he did not have to make calls to parents or wives regarding men who were killed in Vietnam.

Pat and President Nixon felt they had to get away from Washington after Christmas. San Clemente would be the destination. They decided to fly on a commercial airliner to set an example to the nation because of the energy crisis. All eyes were glued on them.

The next day, I picked up the "Washington Post" paper. On the front page there was a picture and article of Charles Colson, one of Nixon 's aides. Colson had a change of heart. He was let to Christ by Tom Phillips,a Graham convert and an old Boston friend.

When the press heard about Colson's conversion they 'poo-hooed' his personal decision. But there was a change. That ex-Marine, who would walk over his mother's dead body to get what he wanted, was now so different. I couldn't believe that God had made such a transformation in Colson. He had now joy and freedom from fear, in spite of all the turmoil around him.

It was President Nixon, who brought to the nation's attention in 1971, regarding the energy problem. Of all the energy programs Nixon had sent to Congress by September, only one had been passed.

Within a few months, I realized that the House Judiciary Committee—mostly Democrats—would vote for Nixon's impeachment. The Ervin committee kept the media provided with stories to fuel the harassement and attacks. When each one was attacked, we felt their pain.

In spite of all the stories the press had manufactured and blown out of proportion, Pat Nixon won the "Good Housekeeping" magazine "most admired woman' for the second year in a row. She won twice as many first-place votes as Mamie Eisenhower, the runner up. Even Julie Nixon Eisenhower achieved tenth in the polls for her vigorous defense of her father. I was determined more to stand in the gaps for my friends, and help the Nixon in anyway I could. This was a difficult but sad time at this holiday season.

Chapter 19

THE TOPPLING OF A PRESIDENT

In 1974 the headline stories about the Nixons persisted. The many rumors drove me to my knees in compassionate prayers and gratitude. I didn't see the Nixons as the media did. The Nixons were real people with hurts and fears much like my own. I was wondering if the press had skeletons in their own closets? If they had stories and the rest of the media found out, would it make them an idiot or fools of us all?

As vicious charges arose against the Nixons it was easy for me to get angry at both the injurious woe and those who have blamed and assailed with doing it. It was my goal to continue to be in constant prayer and stand up for them in their time of need.

There were various organizations out there, which wanted to drive Nixon from the presidency by impeachment or a technical conviction. They were deterred by the fact that they could not prove Richard Nixon personally guilty of any crime to remove him from the office of the President.

They were floating a legal theory around that Nixon would be liable for the wrong doing of his staff. If they were able to establish criminal liability attached to Nixon, whose staff through the president's oversight and omission, to commit criminal acts, then Nixon would be technically guilty under the loose interpretation of "high crimes and misdemeanors." If any Nixon's White House staff or Cabinet appointees were convicted then Nixon would be guilty too. They felt that President Nixon was criminally responsible for any illegal acts of his presidential office workers. Surely, they were not friends of Nixon.

I was glad Julie was speaking out and fighting back at criticism of her father. Sometimes I felt I was the only lonely voice in the country sounding off, too.

Pat said her husband would play the piano at night. The White House is such a pressure-box. One has to get away from it all to relax. Piano playing was moments of relaxation for Nixon. He still like to tease his daughters and son-in-laws. Nixon was still affectionate with his family. He would put his arm around their shoulders and pat them on the back, and said "We're-gonna-make it."

However, not all Democrats were trying to destroy Nixon. On January 10th, Rep. Otto E. Passman, (Democrat) from Louisiana put his article as he saw it in every newspaper. "Facts As A Democrat Sees Them." He was a Democrat but an American First and asked the American people to contact their congressman and protest the unwarranted action that few propose against President Nixon.

In all that was going on, Julie took time to write a short story, "Pasha Passes By" for the "Saturday Evening Post." It was her first literary endeavor about Pasha, one of the Nixon's three dogs.

January 9th, the Unification Church of America group came to Phoenix from Washington, D.C. There were speeches and a brass band. They were co-sponsor to National Prayer and Fast for the Watergate Crisis. The rally at Washington west of Central displayed a huge "Support Our President" banner. They also organized a pro-Nixon demonstration at the annual White House Christmas tree-lighting ceremony.

January 13th, the Nixon administration was investigating the story of a military spy ring inside the White House, especially the National Security Council. The spying enterprise implicated the unauthorized passing of exceedingly classified important matter to the Pentagon from the National Security Council.

The interrogation began after columnist Jack Anderson's publication determined there was a military spy ring going inside the National Security Council. Nixon was concerned about national security and was wondering what documents were stolen. He wanted all information leaks stopped.

At that time, Rear Admiral Robert O. Welander was the military liaison officer attached to the council. Apparently the spy operation was centered in his office. The secret intensive planning by Henry Kissinger was not provided to the Pentagon and the State Department. Therefore, certain military persons rifled National Security Council wastebaskets and briefcases for information.

Then Admiral Thomas Moorer, chairman of the Joint Chiefs of Staff, acknowledged he had received illegal unauthorized documents passed on by Yeoman Charles Radford, a clerk in his office. The Joint Chiefs were frustrated and angry because Kissinger did not share with them regarding the new diplomacy with China and Soviet Union, and the winding down of the Vietnam War. Therefore, they took things in their own hands and worked against President Nixon.

The more I listened to all what was proceeding in Washington, I began to realize that there was something more going on than irresponsibility by Nixon's White House staff. Here was our military doing things without authorization and under minding the role of the commander-in-chief.

January 28th, Monday Pat came down from Camp David, Maryland mountain place of seclusion where President Nixon had sequestered himself to welcome 150 wives of the National Religious Broadcaster at a reception in the state dining room. Her hands tightly closed together, she responded to reporters about that Nixon had not been sleeping well lately. Pat said, "He doesn't sleep long, but he sleeps well. Sometimes his sleep is interrupted by telephone calls."

They added, "Does he get up in the middle of the night to play the piano?" Pat replied, "He plays before he goes to bed. He is in great health. I love him dearly and I have great faith."

Most of the women who had come through the reception line told Pat they were praying for her husband and had faith in Nixon as President. She said, "I told them to pray for the press, too." A reporter asked, "Does the press need prayer?" Pat replied quickly, "We all do. Who doesn't?"

In her active schedule of receptions afterwards, Pat stood in the receiving line at a party at Meridian House greeting new diplomats and wives and children. Many of the events Pat was involved in were not reported by the press. It was frustrating to Pat what the media was doing to her family. She felt helpless, but she resolved to do something about it.

January 30th, President Nixon gave his State of the Union message at 9 p.m. I was wondering how Congress would receive him there. Would they receive him courteously or would there be a demonstration of unfriendly hatred.

As he arrived to deliver his address, President Nixon received a standing applause from most of Congress. Rep. Thomas O'Neill, Democrat, Massachusetts declined to applaud along with the other hard-liner Democrats. But Nixon congressional supporters—whether Republican or some patriotic Democrats—applauded so loudly that the hard liner Democrats finally had to stand even though they didn't clap their hands.

As Nixon progressed in his speech, he was interrupted 30 times by warm applause. It delighted all of us that there was still support for the President still in Congress. However, we realized he had enemies there, too, and we knew they were working against him.

Nixon added a personal word to his State of Union message. He believed one year of Watergate was enough and the investigations should come to an end. At that time he had no intention of walking away from his job as President.

All of us were overjoyed by result of the positive reaction to his speech. We were hoping against hope that more support would pick up in Congress.

The next morning January 31st, the Nixon family attended the National Prayer Breakfast at a Washington Hotel. Tricia Nixon Cox and her husband attended too. Senator John C. Stennis, Democrat from Mississippi presided over the prayer breakfast, but Rev. Billy Graham spoke to the audience. After Nixon left the prayer breakfast, he beamed and waved at those outside. Apparently, he was more encouraged about things around him.

The Watergate Committee decided to call former Central Intelligence Agency Director Richard Helms to appear before them and ask why the CIA ignored a Senate request not to destroy Watergate-related tapes? I was very concerned about the CIA involvement, indirectly or directly in Watergate and the destroying of CIA tapes.

February 17th, the "Washington Post reported that technical experts were casting doubt on the authenticity of two subpoenaed tapes. They were suspected of being re-recorded conversations rather than the original recording. It may be impossible to determine whether it was or not. Of the nine White House tapes originally subpoenaed, two never did exist. One tape had an 18 ½ minute gap.

Regarding the tapes, I knew what it takes to alter tapes whether for the good or evil. Someone would have to listen to a tape over and over again until that person would know the speech patterns, breathing spaces and voice modulations.

One would have to know the voices as his own voice. Then, cut out certain words, or a sentence with a razor blade and splice the tapes together. Background noise such as coffee cup clinking with desks or ashtrays, shutting of doors and other sounds can be duplicated or counterfeited by playing a second tape in back of the voice tape. When the tape is ended, it is recorded on a different unspliced tape.

This procedure of modifying a tape is excessive time exhausting. To change a word may take one hour, and one day for a full one-hour tape. There was a record floating around then on one of Nixon's talk vindicating his part in the Watergate affair, on the other side was a falsified rendition of the speech in which Nixon admitted that he was responsible for Watergate. Same words only arranged differently in the same speech.

Some audio experts were asked to identify the parts of the tapes, which had been altered. Ninety percent could not detect any changes. All of them agreed that none of them would be able to testify in court whether a tape had been altered or tampered in anyway or not.

With all the ex-so-called CIA men working for the Nixon White House, I had qualms and suspicious about what they were up to. Whether they were really retired—were they working for themselves or the CIA still?

At the Senate Watergate Committee hearing, Howard Hunt, one of the men involved in the break-in at the Democrat headquarters, told them he spied on Barry Goldwater, an Arizona Senator for President, Lyndon Johnson in the 1964 presidential campaign. At that time Hunt was working for the Central Intelligence Agency (CIA) and was permitted a leave of absence from the CIA agency to conduct surveillance on Goldwater. The CIA is barred by law from conducting domestic operations. But, here they were breaking the law.

Here again I was openly suspicious of their contention

that CIA had no involvement in the Watergate break-in. I guess several Congressmen had many questions as I did.

February 18th, Pat and President Nixon flew to Indianapolis, Indiana, from Huntsville, Alabama, after a public appearance there, to give Julie their daughter a lift back to Washington, D.C. Since September 1973 Julie had worked as an assistant editor at Curtis Publishing Company, which published Saturday Evening Post and other magazines in Indianapolis.

Julie had undergone surgery for a bleeding ovarian cyst. The Indiana University Hospital permitted her to go home three days earlier after this kind of operation. Even though she was in a very weak condition, she would need at least 3 weeks of convalescence at the White House before continuing her duties as an assistant editor. David and the whole family were there to escort her home at the White House. Julie hugged many of the nurses who took care of her there. She said farewell to doctors and the rest of the hospital staff.

On March 1st, Bob Haldeman, John Ehrlichman, Chuck Colson, John Mitchell and three others from the Committee to Re-Elect the President were charge and arraigned on obstruction of justice and conspiracy. It was Alexander Butterfield, a former White House appointments secretary who first revealed the existence of President Nixon's taping system, was instructing Watergate prosecutor Leon Jaworski on which tapes to ask for. He counted off certain dates and times of meetings and talks the president had with the staff, businessmen and other politicians. Apparently, many were not taking into count, that Butterfield had been in the CIA, and so I was suspicious because of his previous occupation (or whether he was still in the CIA?). Apparently, once in the CIA, there was not such thing as an ex-CIA agent.

The Nixons gave a black-tie dinner party for about 115 guests, March 7th, including 41 governors who were in Washington for their annual mid-winter conference. Singer

Pearl Bailey was invited to sing at the dinner. Prior to her performance, President Nixon presented Pearl Bailey the black singer, a pearl presidential pin and bestowed on her the title as "ambassador of love."

She enticed President Nixon to accompany her on the piano. Pearl really livened up the night's entertainment. During the impromptu performance, Nixon played three songs and managed to play and sing "God Bless America" with everyone at the party joining in.

President Nixon appeared a bit uneasy in his unforeseen part as a performer and jokes, but he enjoyed Pearl Bailey's impromptu touches in her performance. Everyone was in a warm-hearted mood and laughed all the way through the Bailey performance. It was a delightful evening no one could forget.

Then, when I picked up the Arizona newspaper, I noticed that Kathryn Graham, publisher of the "Washington Post" accepted an award in Tucson for exposing the Watergate affair. It made me so angry, I wrote another letter to newspapers in March telling the facts about the "Washington Post" publishers. Apparently, many people did not know the Graham family were friends of Alger Hiss, the spy, and supported his actions.

President Nixon joined several hundred air force men and their families gathered at Homestead Air Force Base, Florida, for a send off ceremony for Pat Nixon, on a six-day goodwill trip to Venezuela and Brazil.

Pat Nixon was the best ambassador the United States ever had. Once again she was leaving for Caracas, Venezuela, where she and her husband (then as Vice President) were spit upon and intimidated by angry crowds sixteen years ago.

Although Pat had tight security, a friendly reception was expected.

As Pat emerged at the close of the inauguration ceremonies for their new president, Charles Andres Perez of

Venezuela, the crowd stood to their feet and gave her a standing tribute worthy of any foreign dignitary. They admired Pat Nixon for her courage to return. Her mission was critical as well as diplomatic.

After Venezuela, Pat flew to Brazil for the inauguration of its new President, retired Army General Ernesto Geisel.

When I turned on the ABC evening news, March 14th, I heard Harry Reasoner, the television news commentator, lash out at "Newsweek" and "Time" magazines for their "unprofessional handling of the whole Watergate story" which he said has embarrassed all journalists.

Mr. Reasoner found in that week of "Newsweek" more than 30 instances of phrases that any editor should automatically strike out, and he assumed they had editors. He didn't like how the seven men were dragged in before Judge Sirica like common criminals for a formal reading of the charges. Nor did Reasoner question the right of magazine editors and columnists to have opinions and put them in their editorials and columns. Most citizens would deeply resent without the help of journalists, any similar undertaking to feed them their deductions. The revolting story of Watergate was little by little writing its own story.

Pat returned to the United States, March 16th, on her sixty-second birthday. It was arranged that she could stop over in Nashville to celebrate the "Grand Ole Opry's" opening of their new building. It was interesting to watch President Nixon play "Happy Birthday" on the upright piano. The excited audience joined in the celebration and sang lustily.

Pat was so ecstatic and thankful that her husband had staged this delightful surprise. However, neither knew what the other had planned. When Pat walked toward her husband with stretched forth arms in thankfulness. Nixon had already turned to talk to the person who was the host of the entertainment program. Nixon did not see Pat.

Of course, some of the news media misconstrued what

happened and thought the Nixon marriage was heading for the divorce court. This event added more fuel to the other false stories churned out daily. The Nixons were very private persons and rarely showed any moment of affection in public. The press and others did not want to acknowledge that the Nixons had one of the best husband-and-wife relationships ever in the White House.

I was wondering how each of them could stand up under the onslaught of the press and of the Congressional hearings concerning their staff. Even, some conservative supporters were urging President Nixon to resign. I was not one of them. I stood with them and prayed they would have the strength to endure whatever may come. I sent President Nixon a letter of encouragement and I received a letter of grateful appreciation for my support.

When Pat arrived back at the White House from her South American trip, my birthday card and cologne greeted her. At this time Pat was always glad for dear friends to remember her in a special way.

Untrue rumors plagued Tricia Nixon Cox and her husband Eddie. The latest story had Tricia in the hospital with a broken rib and two black eyes. Much was left to imagination that Eddie had inflicted the injuries. The gossip ran on and on. That they cheated on their income tax, their marriage was on the rocks, had three children and Tricia had come down with a bad fatal disease.

Many stories were manufactured by the press looking for any information they could.

It kept us glued for hours to the television as the so-called news spewed out their stories about Watergate and the White House going-ons. The Eastern newspapers printed so many false items it was impossible to get a retraction. It kept me busy writing to newspapers and the TV networks correcting their falsehoods.

John Mitchell and Maurice Stans, Nixon's former cabinet

members, stood trial in New York for over two months regarding the Robert Vescoe campaign contributions to influence the Securities and Exchange Commission inquiry. All of us were worried they were in difficult and serious problem. John Dean's witness at the trial and their testimony collided. What would the jury believe in this case? The jury acquitted Stans and Mitchell much to our relief. But, John Dean was not off the hook as yet.

President Nixon, on April 3rd, was open to attack on allegations of tax evasion because of his donation of his private vice presidential papers to the National Archives in return for a tax deduction in 1969. Unfortunately, the staffer who was doing the documentation paper work for Nixon neglected to process the papers until five months later. Nixon was not aware that he staffer had backdated the deed of the donation and waited so long to process the papers. He had delivered the vice presidential papers, March 27, 1969, long before the deadline of July 29, 1969.

Everyone was arguing which was the proper thing to do. Was it the date of the deed or the date of the delivery of the papers, which made it eligible? That was the question disputed. The Congressional Committee on Internal Revenue resolved it was not a proper deduction. Nixon tried to get the papers back, which the government possessed since 1969, but they declined. Nixon paid the $300.000 difference and lost his vice-presidential papers. No wonder he was frustrated and disturbed by this tax evasion. I wondered what all this had to do with the Watergate break-in. I came to the conclusion they were after President Nixon—he was the real target!

The same month, the House Judiciary Committee's Impeachment Inquiry requested that Nixon send them 42 tapes. Nixon decided to send them transcripts of the conversations the committee wanted on April 29th.

Later the "New York Times" published verbatim the

transcripts. But Nixon had purged words or conversations, not relevant or disgusting remarks about individuals, and profanity. He had instructed that any place where he or anyone else used a swear word, it was to be replaced by the words 'expletive deleted.'

There was an outrageous reaction by the public when they read the published transcripts. It was not what was mentioned that caused the uproar; it was the left out words, which caused the commotion. The "Blue Book" of transcripts was splattered all through the book. The public's conception ran wild. They thought their President was using pornographic terms in his talk.

I knew Richard Nixon since 1958, and I never, never heard him use a swear word around me, other friends, or any of his family. What I heard on the tapes was not the man I knew.

On the tapes, it was typical of Nixon to let off steam in his private office—as any other man does—with his staff. On the tapes, Nixon was not a good swearer. The expletive words deleted in the transcripts were read in and not common talk with Nixon. The deleted swear words on the tapes consisted of "Hell, Damn, For Christ Sake, Oh God, or crap and shit." He had avoided any rough, locker room, and pornographic words on the tapes. I'm sure if Hannah, his mother, was alive she would have been shocked and embarrassed that her son used even those words, even in private conversations.

I had many telephone calls about those swear words on the tapes. It took a lot of explaining and defending the situation. It was difficult to go to church and hear Nixon denounced. Nixon was being condemned for bad words that he not spoken. I was wondering why he removed them from the transcripts? Was it because he remembered his mother? Or-was it because of his many Christian supporters. Would the uproar be more gigantic if Nixon had left them in? Who knows?

Richard Nixon had not consulted with Pat, his wife, about the tapes, even before anyone knew they had existed. Surely, Pat would have suggested that the tapes be destroyed, since she knew they were very private conversations. As all the reaction and news flooded in, Pat became troubled concerning her husband and family.

In spite of all the hullabaloo concerning Congressional reaction and the press, the conversations on the tapes, and the Nixon 's tax problems, drowned out what was going on in the Nixon administration for the good of the country and the world.

When the "going" got rough, Pat and the President took to the road in April and May for a tour of the country. They took a tour of Michigan's "Thumb" area. President Nixon kidded with children. A Michigan candidate for Congress, James Sparling, rode with them as the Nixons met residents of about eleven communities along their motorcade route.

Then, they went to Jackson, Mississippi. The Nixons received a very warm welcome in their brief visit to the Mississippi state.

In Jackson, President Nixon met with the Mississippi Economic Council to have a lengthy discussion about economics in the state and country.

Around the world in Cairo, Egypt, May1st, Salem Shanab, 30 year old and Mayor of Malania, a village south of Cairo, Egypt, offered $2,500.00 to help pay Nixon 's tax bill. In a letter to President Nixon, May 1st, he wanted to help him this way when he heard about his tax plight. Shanab received a reply from the U.S. Ambassador thanking him for the offer of money but explaining that President Nixon intended to pay the tax bill hearing.

May 3rd, Pat and President Nixon came to Phoenix, Arizona. They stepped from the airplane into a warm welcome from Arizonans. I was so happy to see them once again. Julie had hitched a ride with them as far as Phoenix enroute to Los

Angeles. Pat looked beautiful in her royal blue silk suit, and smiled as she accepted her bouquet of yellow roses. Pat was happy to be in Phoenix and she thought the weather was beautiful.

During the flight, the Nixon family had joined the Arizona delegation. They talked about Indian art and jewelry. Their motorcade sped to Camelback Inn, where a youthful mariachi band greeted them as they walked to J. Willard (Bill) Marriott home where they would be staying.

Pat still had her smile when she and the President entered the Coliseum to the music of "Hail to the Chief." An enthusiastic crowd of 15,000 gave the Nixons a standing applause and tribute.

When her husband made a point in his message with the crowd's endorsement, Pat smiled and clapped. In the upper rows of the Coliseum, Pat refused to notice the hecklers and protestors there. But when Nixon supporters shouted words of welcome, she smiled.

At the end of his speech, President Nixon motioned for Pat to join him at the podium for smiles and pictures, and waves before heading for a party at Barry Goldwater's home. The next morning Pat was as bright as the Arizona sun. As I said goodbye, Pat still had that same warm, happy smile.

It was difficult to see her go and bid her farewell. President Nixon found his departure was just a few minutes away that Saturday but he still found time to shake hands with Air Force personnel. The Nixons flew from Sky Harbor International Airport to the opening of Expo '74 in Spokane Washington.

A Jesuit priest, John McLaughlin, on President Nixon's staff as a speechwriter adviser, and fact-finder, and a spokesman, stated that the White House transcripts proved that Nixon performed honestly in coping with a stinking affair—a murky commentary on his executive part of government.

When the transcripts were released McLaughlin defended Nixon against any increasing censure from Democrats and Republicans. He said, "The conclusion that the transcripts are amoral or immoral is erroneous unjust and contains elements of hypocrisy. When anyone considers the circumstances and the total context, the President exonerated himself throughout these conversations.

Nixon's morality should be determined not by scraps and fragments of recorded discussions, but by magnitude to which he has brought about an atmosphere of charity in the country at home and relations between nations."

By the time the Nixons had returned from their cross-country tour, The Blue Book of transcripts had caused a swell of criticism from several newspapers such as "The Chicago Tribune" and "Omaha World-Herald," suggesting Nixon should resign. Some Republican Congressmen echoed what the newspapers were saying. However, I did not endorse that sentiment. I suggested he stay in there and fight! Personally, I knew there was more to what was going on. It was a set up and Nixon was the target. How could I get people to listen?

The Capitol Hill Club, Republican social group, decided to give Pat Nixon a reception in her honor, May 9th, after her whirlwind tour. There was Pat Nixon smiling and hand shaking as if there were no problems at all descending upon her and her husband.

I was surprised John Rhodes, Congressman from Arizona, had showed up at the reception. Few hours earlier he suggested to President Nixon he should consider resigning. Apparently, he had changed his mind from earlier in May.

However, that didn't bother Pat Nixon. Pat gave Rhodes a warm welcome and said, "Let's look like we're friends." She even posed with him for pictures.

Several hundred guests were there as well as many well-known Republican Congressmen, Pat saw to it she had her picture taken with all of them. She was getting the necessary lift from the warm welcome she received.

When some women came by wearing sashes that said, "Support The President," Pat wanted the photographers to get pictures of the women. She was encouraged by the sight.

People still wanted to hear President Nixon in spite of all the media talk and criticism. Not all the people went along with the press. The Oklahoma State University in Stillwater asked him to address the commencement excercises Saturday night. As he departed from the Vance Air Force Base, Oklahoma for Washington, D.C. throngs of people came out to watch him and shake hands. This really pleased Nixon.

However, in California, a poll was taken among Californians if President Nixon should resign or be impeached. Forty one percent were in favor of him leaving office. Twenty four percent said he should not resign, but Congress should proceed with the impeachment process. But, thirty two percent said the impeachment should be stopped and Nixon should stay as President.

In Arizona, Governor Jack Williams warned guests at the Pima County Republican Club by saying that the impeachment and conviction of President Nixon would be a miraculous feather in the cap of forces of evil and benefit communism. He said he was not a Red hunter, but we should keep our powder dry and understand that what is going on around the world is not always good for us.

But, the students at Whittier College in California, President Nixon's alma mater, had assembled together in support. They said he was a good president and was proud of him. They wanted the Presidential Library to be on their campus.

More than 1,000 of the 1,600 students signed a petition expressing their pride and support in Nixon's time of hardships. It was endorsed by the Student Body President, Richard Jacobs.

After three weeks of silence, Billy Graham, personal friend and adviser, spoke out about the transcripts of Nixon's conversation about Watergate. Graham said, "What comes through on those tapes is not the man I have known many years. Other friends have said the same thing. He continued saying, "Nixon remains my friend and I have no intention of forsaking him now. Nor will I judge him as a man on the basis of a few hours of conversation under such severe pressures."

Billy Graham was conducting an Evangelistic Crusade in the Phoenix area when Nixon was briefly in Phoenix for a rally. Nixon called him early one morning just to say hello. Billy said he had spent several days reading the released White House transcripts and then prayed about it before making a statement.

Graham added for all to hear. "If this nation is destroyed, it will be the result of more decadence within. Therefore this should be a time to come to our senses, to return to God and his law. It would be nothing less than hypocrisy to call for a moral house cleaning at the White House unless we are willing to do the same at your house and my house.

'Our repudiation of wrongdoing and our condemnation of evil, however, must be tempered by compassion for the wrong doers. Many a stone is being cast by persons whose own lives could not bear scrutiny. Therefore, we dare not be self righteous."

There were many frustrating endeavors to free Syria and Israel from difficulties and perplexities to settle down to a settlement of peace. There was much hatred between Israel and Syria. Nixon was confident that the Israelis and the Syrians would sign the peace agreement. After much exhausting work, at the end of May, Syria and Israel accepted the terms of the agreement. He decided to have several summit personal visits in the Middle East to securely fix in place the achievements they had attained.

June 10th, President Nixon and Pat departed for Salzburg,

Austria, where they would stay overnight. It was a good thing they stayed there overnight to get use to jet lag because of the time change. But, Nixon was also afflicted again with phlebitis in his left leg. It was very red and swollen twice the size of his right leg. Apparently, one of the White House physicians had looked at it before the trip, and he said there would be no danger as of now for a blood clot to break loose. The doctor recommended that warm compresses be used on the leg and elevate it. It was best for Nixon not to stand on that leg as much as possible.

He made Pat swear to secrecy about his ailment. Nixon thought the problem would go away like it did before in Hawaii. After all, he didn't want the press to make it a mountain out of a molehill. He paused long enough in Austria to discuss problems with Austrian Chancellor Bruno Kreisky. Secretary of State Henry Kissinger accompanied Nixon at this meeting.

Later, Kissinger was upset about a "New York Times" editorial denouncing him for giving an erroneous testimony concerning the 1969 wiretaps. He was enraged about the charge; Kissinger called a press conference. After giving his side of the testimony, he added, "When the character and credibility of the Secretary of State is in question—if it is not cleared up, I will resign!" It rallied some supporters for Kissinger, but he had his critics in spite of what he said. The Nixons journeyed on to Cairo, Egypt, which featured the first portion of a weeklong five-nation tour of the Middle East. More than two million people welcomed Pat and President Nixon. One Egyptian young man climbed aboard a traffic light to get a good look.

An Egyptian belly dancer danced on stage at the Cairo Kublach Palace after the official state dinner party. Other Egyptian performers entertained them, Sadat and Nixon turned to the performers to have his picture with them. The troupe was so excited they surrounded him from all sides.

This caused the security guards to rush in remove Nixon and Sadat from the crowd.

They boarded an old special train for a three-hour train ride form Cairo to Alexandria. Egyptian villagers along the way stood with their animals to get a glimpse of Nixon. The President, on the train ride, was becoming irritable. He had stood on his leg too long and it was giving him trouble. It was good that a doctor was aboard to attend to Nixon.

From Egypt the Nixons arrived in Jidda, Saudi Arabia and came into humid temperatures over a hundred. King Faisal met them at the airport.

President Nixon discussed with him about the high oil prices, which was created by the Arab oil embargo and to see, if possible to help moderate oil prices. Nixon thought Faisal was a wise man and was encouraged by his remarks concerning the United States.

In the evening President Nixon went to an all-made dinner in his honor. Pat was hosted at a separate dinner by the Queen Iribat in her own palace overlooking the azure-colored Red Sea. The Moslems thought women were lower in rank than the males. Women are secondary inferior in their view. Men were not allowed in the Queen's Palace. That included Pat's Secret Service, much to their dismay.

At their last stop in Saudi Arabia, the reception in Damascus, Syria was more reduced than the excited welcome that millions gave the Nixons in Egypt. Syrian girls wearing uniforms of their school welcomed Pat and President Nixon at the Damascus airport. President Assad told Nixon "no peace can be established in this region unless a real and a just solution is found for that Palestine question. Nixon told them that I do not bring any instant solution. The Israel and Syrian troops along the Golden Heights along the Golan Heights— a good beginning. He stated we must move forward step-by-step as each case permits until we reach our goal of a just and equitable peace."

After dining on Arab-style lamb—an whole roasted sheep served on a platter, the two presidents exchanged remarks about a lasting peace.

As Pat and President Nixon were touring the Arab world, Pat Nixon was carefully protected in her public appearances. She had only trips or tours of one hour on her own. Many of her activities were social and ceremonial appearances with President Nixon at nightly dinner parties. She was often secluded in guest palaces.

Pat appeared bone-tired as their journey proceeded. The torrid humid heat caused much discomfort to travel.

In winding alleys, she found stall shops in a downtown market. Pat was fascinated with array of goods from all over the world and she would like to spend many days just shopping. Because she was surrounded by news reporters and heavy security Pat would like to spend more time without the security and reporters. She just wanted some fun.

Pat planned to visit the 12th century Omimayed Mosque and to tour Azzem Palace, a one time Showplace.

Before returning to the United States the Nixons visited Israel and Jordan from June 16-18th. On June 19, they departed for home.

I was wondering how either of them could make another exhausting trip. I knew Pat was very tired and President Nixon phlebitis was causing his leg to be painful and very swollen.

The secret about the President suffering from phlebitis slowly leaked out to the media. Now everyone knew that President Nixon was doing his job in spite of his affliction.

Pat and President Nixon departed June 25th for Moscow, Russia. They stopped enroute in Brussels to attend the NATO twenty-fifth anniversary ceremonies. The purpose of NATO was the Communism threat and its terror. Now it must find other reasons to keep it together.

Morning Russian shoppers were surprised to see the President of the United States standing outside his bubble limousine waving at the beaming Miscovites and shaking hands with them. They gathered and crowded closer to him. Before going to Summit III talks with Leonid Brezhnev, Nixon decided to meet the people in the streets of Moscow. Nixon spoke in his best Russian—Ochen Khorosho—"very good." Some in the crowd called out in English "Good Luck" and "We don't want war again."

President Nixon had just finished laying a wreath at the Tomb of the Unknown Soldier beside a Moscow Kremlin wall. He stood attention along with two U.S. military aides and a Soviet officer.

Pat Nixon received a bouquet of carnations and a Russian doll from one of the teachers at the Moscow circus school where she visited. In spite of her extreme weariness, Pat had that delightful smile, and the Russians smiled back and greeted her among the American and Byleorussian flags.

They journey on to Oreanda, a suburb of Yalta to visit Brezhnev in his villa overlooking the Black Sea. After their rest that night, President Nixon met with Brezhnev for serious talks. The conference was difficult and long. Both men could agree on ABM restrictions and environmental limits, but neither one could coincide on the MIRV. (Multiple-warhead nuclear missiles) Also, the Russians thought the Chinese were a threat to peace and would do anything to accomplish their aspirations.

After their long ride on the Black Sea in Brezhnev's yacht, Pat and President Nixon dined for dinner along on gallery platform outside their guesthouse. The next day, the Soviets finished Summit III with a flowery, formal observance and ostentatious display as they bid Nixons farewell at the airport. Nixon was glad to be going home, but they were not anxious what might lie ahead for both of them.

In the latest Gallup Poll, most of the people believed the news media were devoting too much time and print to the Watergate affair. They considered it excessive. Even those who claimed to be Democrats 43 percent thought the media coverage was profuse. Among Republicans the survey showed that 75 percent viewed the coverage was too much. Even independents with no party affiliation 54 percent considered the media coverage was unfair. After their arrival from overseas to Washington in a few weeks, the Nixons flew to San Clemente for relaxation and meditation—just to get-away from everything.

While there they heard via the television media that the House Judiciary Committee advised that President Nixon should be impeached. When I heard that news, I felt a pain in my heart. It was something I feared that the Democrats in Congress would hatch up anything to remove President Nixon from office.

What really puzzled me at that time, why weren't the men who burglarized the Watergate DNC—caught in the very act—were not investigated thoroughly? How come the Ervin's Senate committee did not call in men and women who worked at the Watergate Hotel and the Democrat National Committee office for testimony?

Also the FBI and CIA Watergate documents were omitted from review by the committee? Shouldn't all evidence be presented and not hidden? Many questions were left unanswered. It was all so unfair and tragic.

Because the House of Representative Judiciary Committee had already begun impeachment proceedings. Special Prosecutor Leon Jaworski decided that it would be inappropriate to charge a sitting President for such a crime as a cover-up participant. Nixon was named as an undicted co-conspirator. To indict President Nixon, Jaworski believed that if the case went to the Supreme Court it would be overturned there. So he decided to defer any decision about indictments and take more time to investigate all the related elements.

I was concerned about my friend, Pat Nixon. She wanted to escape the commotion and the flurry of actions at the White

House. What was really new for Pat, she was taking late-night walks a couple of times a week on deserted, quiet streets nearby. In this troubled time, the leisurely strolls offered her relaxation and privacy. Most of the time she walked alone, except for the Secret Service agents tagging along. When Julie was there she accompanied her mother.

The stress of the Watergate affair was causing Pat to show signs of strain. Deeply, she felt that certain persons were excessive in their pursuit of her husband. Pat had gone through many crises in their life and now there was one more tragic crisis to think about.

Pat loved to laugh instead of crying. At every function, all we saw was Pat being warm and friendly with everyone. Her smile was always there regardless of her being in pain or under strain of a situation. She was a perfectionist who cared about other people.

The news media was always trying to get Pat Nixon to discuss Watergate at every social event. She was troubled, Pat had complained that reporters had often neglected and overlooked her events at the White House. She only wanted volunteers and other entertaining groups to have more recognition. Thousands of letters were pouring into Pat Nixon's office from people urging President Nixon not to resign. She found encouragement in the response.

While criticsm from others mounted against Nixon, there was none spoken against Pat. The critics did not link her personally to any of the Watergate-related problems.

Pat had promised the public that they would open the White House to all who wanted to come. She kept that promise and entertained more people at worship services and social events than any other Presidential family.

The last few troubled months in the White House, Pat Nixon was working with Curator Clem Conger re-decorating the Queen's bedroom, the East Sitting Hall, and the Garden Room. In the family dining room on the second floor, she placed new draperies to match the rug. She renewed the matter of the 150-piece cobalt blue and white Nixon china and checked out the silver flatware service. Even though everyone was strained and nervous, Pat was working as if she was going to be at the White House for along time.

Clem Conger, the curator, admired Pat Nixon more than any First Lady he had worked for. To him, Pat was a warm, realistic person. He thought Pat Nixon did more for the genuine renovation of the White House than Jacqueline Kennedy. He only hope Pat would get credit for her beautification accomplishments some day.

On July 12th, President Nixon signed the Congressional and Impoundment Control Act of 1974 in the Oval Office and called it an important instrument in fighting inflation. It meant that Congress and the President would work together to keep down the cost of government and help every family to hold down their budgets.

The major problem facing all of us was inflation. Nixon thought the biggest problem was over spending by Congress, and hoped they would face their responsibility to hold down the cost of living.

The constant stream of headline gossip stories in the mass media drove me to my knees in compassionate intercession for the Nixons and all concerned with the Watergate affair. The press was distorting the facts that no one out there was supporting the Nixon family. But, that was not true!

On July 23rd, many hundreds prayed, sang and fasted on the steps of the U.S. Capitol for two days in support of President Nixon. It was sponsored by Rabbi Baruch Korff of the National Committee for Fairness to the Presidency, and also Rev. Sun Myuong Moon of South Korea. It was interesting that Rabbi Korff hadn't even voted for President Nixon, but God had led him to support and pray for Nixon. He was only asking everyone to seek the guidance of God in the matter.

Rabbi Korff led the fight for President Nixon in persuading

many persons to support and contribute money for Nixon's many legal bills. Thousands poured in from all the little people in the grass roots of the country who did not believe the noise of the mass media circus against Nixon.

Then, the House Judiciary Committee voted 27-11 and approved the first impeachment article, July 27th, against President Nixon. They decided that he interfered with the investigation of the Watergate occurrence.

As I heard this charge, I was wondering how Pat was holding up when she heard the news about her dear husband. She was the most gracious First Lady who conducted herself with distinction and calmness in this tragic affair. In her lifetime, she had been through a lot. I didn't know how she overcame each crisis, except for her quiet faith in God, which gave her strength to carry on. My prayers and support were with her.

On Article III the Judiciary House Committee indicted the President for abuse of power of his office. Legal and illegal actions were lumped together in the Judiciary House Committee's accusations. If there was no infringement of the law why did Congress consider it improper? That is why for political purposes, they pursued Nixon for impeachment.

When Senator Joseph Montoya, a Democrat from New Mexico, suggested that President Nixon should pay his own legal expenses in any Senate trial, he did know that the public would react to his announcement.

For example, Lewis and Sue Tortariello from Newark, New Jersey on August 3rd decided to help President Nixon pay his bills. They jumped in their car and drove up to the White House gates to give money for the President.

Bruce Herschensohn, one of President Nixon's assistants, who was in charge of stimulating anti-impeachment encouragement for Nixon, was astonished by their gift. They brought in a large crate of 22,000 pennies, plus their $10,000 savings bank book.

Nixon appreciated their gesture, but politely declined their offer. It had been the White House policy to refuse such gifts or give the donations to charity.

However, the Tortariello's took their crate of pennies and saving book back to New Jersey, along with two books and Presidential mementoes, such as cuff links, tie tacks and pins in appreciation of their generosity.

After my many visits to Washington, I became more puzzled by the many stories and remarks issued by persons I encountered. The Watergate mess was an intriguing mystery. I loved mysteries and this one made me to try to solve the puzzle.

When I arrived back to Phoenix for what I thought would be the last time to see Pat in the White House, my luggage was not aboard at the luggage pick-up. I reported the loss. They told me it should come in on the next flight. But, it was not.

After six days, the TWA airline called me and said the baggage had arrived. When I opened it, I discovered someone had searched my suitcase. It was not packed as I had precisely done in Washington. I was wondering what they were looking for. I knew Pat was concerned about anyone knowing about our personal friendship. Did this leak out, too?

Then, my stepfather told me that he was suspicious that our telephone lines were tapped. He could tell someone was on the line. John warned me to be careful. "Someone knows of your friendship with the Nixons. What they want, we do not know. Notify the police."

I told the police about my missing baggage and the tapped phone lines. I didn't want the police to leak the story to the press. Whoever was doing this illegal stuff might be chased away and we couldn't find out what they were planning. My stepfather took further precaution by keeping his loaded gun nearby where he could obtain if quickly.

But nothing came up in the police investigation. In a few

weeks the quiet mysterious breathing on the tapped phone lines ceased. I was really concerned about what really happened at the Watergate. Who was involved in this tragic affair?

John Dean, Charles Colson, and H.R. Haldeman hinted about CIA involvement at their Watergate trial. However, Sam J. Ervin, chairman was not convinced that the CIA had anything to do with the break-ins. The committee ignored the many CIA stories and didn't check out each story to find out which was the truth.

What was really interesting and part of the puzzle was the testimony of Frank Sturgis at the Senate Watergate Committee. He was one of the five men who broke into the Democrat National Headquarters. Also, he was an informant for the CIA and became a spy to gather intelligence information.

President Nixon knew what the CIA was in involved in, but he needed documented proof on file to expose them. They didn't like President Nixon because he threatened to reduce their budget for operation. Somehow the CIA fought back and wanted to control the Nixon presidency.

The plot was thickening! Because they could not repress Nixon, they decided he had to be removed from the office of President. Nixon had names of all the persons who were involved in government and foreign relations in the country. He had suspicions, but he wanted documents to back up his uncertain thoughts.

A breach between the Central Intelligence Agency and Nixon had been cooking along time. He knew the CIA was responsible for the flow of secrets national security information to become known. Nixon determined to find out the facts, but still he couldn't get those documents. The CIA leaked things to the Washington Post, which had no love for President Nixon. The Post added more fuel to the CIA leaked information. It caused President Nixon to fight back. Can you imagine when a President gives a direct order to obtain certain documents for the CIA or any other government agency, why would they refuse his request?

I was determined to know what was on the 18-½ minutes of the tape. Perhaps, with some new technology in the future that mysterious erased gap will reveal the information I needed to know. I always thought the information on the 18-½ minute of tape would help President Nixon. It would show who was plotting to remove the President from office.

I remembered Richard Nixon raising the issue concerning FBI forcible entries. He said the break-ins were extensively sanctioned by the Democrat administrations of John F. Kennedy and Lyndon B. Johnson. Apparently, the illegal actions of the FBI were well known. Even some ex-FBI agents told stories about unauthorized break-ins they had to participate in. If they had been caught, nothing found on them would link them to the FBI.

Pat was the strongest woman in her family. When reporters kept asking her about the Watergate affair, she politely ignored their questions. In spite of the ordeal, she never lost her sense of humor. It kept shining through.

Pat was tormented and distressed with persons downgrading her husband the President. She knew he had accomplished much for the country and she refrained from interfering with the gigantic dilemma he was coping with. Pat would not figure out why all this was happening.

On July 30th, the House Judiciary Committee in Article III charged President Nixon had perpetuated an impeachable transgression by opposing and challenging the committee's request for documents and tapes. They had added two more impeachment articles concerning Nixon's personal finances and the Cambodian bombing. Then, the committee recessed to debate the issues again, August 19th.

After hearing what the Judiciary Committee did, I called the White House to continue to fight—fight! I did not want

President Nixon to give up. Especially, I did not want him to resign his office.

While President Nixon had a sleepless night, I could not sleep either. I spent the night in prayer to decide what else I could do to help. Personally, I felt frustrated and helpless. The President had many choices on what to do. By morning each of us had come to the decision what was the right thing to do.

Pat was not told right away of her husband's decision to resign. When she heard the news, she was still determined to fight to the finish. Tricia and Julie didn't want their Daddy to resign either.

Julie was angry and fighting back. She considered her daddy her closest friend. It disturbed her when her father's integrity was questioned. She insisted that her father had done nothing to sanction impeachment with misbehavior in office. I agreed with her and decided to help her in her intensified public defense of her father.

Then, Senator Hugh Scott, Barry Goldwater, and Congressman John Rhodes told President Nixon in his Oval Office, they could find very little support left for him in the whole Congress. Even, some Republicans had deserted Nixon in his hour of trial and voted with the other side. When the going gets rough, I guess one finds out who your real friends are. I was more determined not to act like one of them. Throughout all this, my goal was to find out the facts and set the record straight.

I thought it was unthinkable when Haldeman pleaded with President Nixon to pardon all the men involved in the Watergate affair and all Vietnam draft dodgers. Nixon was not interested in a pardon for himself, or any bargaining deal for the others.

But President Nixon always prayed a silent prayer in the Lincoln bedroom before a press conference or any speech he was to give. When I picked up the "Washington Post," lo and behold that day there was a story regarding Nixon and Kissinger praying in silent prayer. Regardless, whatever Nixon tied to keep certain things private, the stories were leaked to the media by others. No wonder Nixon was perturbed how these things happened whether it involved national security or some other private event.

The evening of August 8th, Thursday, arrived sooner than was expected. President Nixon was to make his TV and radio broadcast telling us he would resign as President. It was very emotional; I could feel the tension in the room. Many friends and supporters were on hand. Some of us had been friends of the Nixons for years. When one started to cry we all had to join in and sob.

I never saw so many men cry. It caused Nixon to choke up and break into tears. He told us, "I hope I haven't let you down." I marveled how tearful Pat upheld her distinction and grace through this heart breaking ultimate outcome. As First Lady she exhibited unbelievable inner strength and dignified courage throughout this tragedy. Even when devastated President Nixon was reduced to tears, Pat showed remarkable courage. Her face full of agony, Pat watched her husband, President Richard Nixon make his farewell speech. When I saw the terrible pain in Pat's eyes and face, I broke down and cried.

It made it more difficult for Pat and the rest of the family and friends to have this sad farewell televised. It took a lot of us to fight for control and not completely break down. We did many deep breathing exercises to subdue our tears, which wanted to come.

Before President Nixon began to give his resignation speech, the East Room reverberated with our approval expressed by our much clapping. He was under such emotional tearful stress, I was wondering if President Nixon would pull himself together for the speech. But he did compose himself.

He told us who served him for many years that only a

man in the deepest valley can know "how magnificent it is to be on the highest mountain" when things do not go right, when a man suffers defeat, some think that all is ended. "Not true. It's only a beginning always."

"Greatness comes to a man not when things go good, but when he is disappointed, when he takes some knocks."

Nixon said, "He was proud of every man and woman who were in the East Room. "No man or woman came into this administration and left it with more of this world's goods than when he came in. No man or woman ever profited at the public expense or the public till."

"Mistakes yes, Nixon continued on, but for personal gain, never." I only wish that I were a wealthy man. I would like to recompense you for the sacrifices that all of you made to serve in government."

At first, I thought it strange and unusual Nixon talked about his mother and father, Frank and Hannah Nixon, instead of Pat, his wife. I remembered Hannah, his mother, was a godly Christian mother who put God first in her life and her son's life, too. He praised his parents because they were the guiding stars in his life.

When I looked at Pat, Julie, and Tricia's faces, I was glad that Nixon did not mention either one in his talk. Each one of them would have broke down. I was on the verge of doing it also. I knew it wouldn't take much to push us over the edge.

I remembered what Nixon said, 'Never be petty; always remember others may hate you, but those who hate you don't win, unless you hate them and then you destroy yourself." In ending his talk, Nixon was grateful for our support, and that all of us would be remembered in their prayers. May God's grace be with all of you in all the day's ahead."

We applauded and wept at the same time. Then, Pat and Richard Nixon walked to "Marine One," the presidential helicopter. They said goodbye to Gerald Ford and Betty Ford who would be the new President and First Lady.

As Richard Nixon climbed up the helicopter steps, he turned around with a painful smile and gave his last firm, determined wave of undulation. Then they were gone from view.

The television media kept running the event of Gerald Ford's oath of office as Chief Justice Warren Burger administered it for the new president. The only things I remembered Ford speaking to us was "Our long national nightmare is over. In the beginning, I asked you to pray for me. Before closing, I ask again your prayers for Richard Nixon and for his family. May our former President, who brought peace to millions, find it, for himself."

The Nixon's plane landed at El Toro Marine Base in California. Thousands of people were waiting with small flags to greet them. Many were singing "God Bless America." Some were weeping. Outside, crowds were trying to get in the Marine Base to see them.

The Nixon's were overwhelmed by the support of the people who came to see them. He thanked them, and he said he would continue to work for peace and freedom and everything he believed in for the good of the country.

Then, they boarded another helicopter for La Casa Pacifica home at San Clemente. The Nixons smiled but no one knew the pain that lingered in their hearts.

At their Spanish-style estate many close friends greeted them at their arrival.

Phone calls and telegrams of good wishes flowed into their family home. The staff was unable to handle the flood of phone calls. The volume of telegrams was unbelievable.

Julie and David remained in Washington to oversee packing and manage the family effects at the White House. Tricia and Edward Cox had accompanied Pat and Richard on their flight west.

Pat and Nixon were relaxed and in very good spirits in spite of their dramatic and abrupt departure from the White

House. Even as Nixon relaxed, he found himself in a new situation. No longer would he be immune from prosecution or called as a witness in any Watergate legal proceedings. The Secret Service would be with him the rest of his life.

Nixon did not know what had happened in all of the events leading to the Watergate break-in. However, he felt bad about the whole thing. He was so tortured and so down. Even though he had neither ordered the break-in at the DNC nor had any before hand knowledge, Nixon was ready to assume the guilt of the whole thing himself.

If the Nixons thought the worst was behind them, it was not to be. Some twenty lawsuits were filed against him, and legal fees rose to more than a million. The Congress seized all his Nixon papers and tapes. No other President ever had their presidential notes and reports taken without his personal authorization to do so.

The American Bar Association rebuked and upbraided Nixon. They had been considering formal hearings to determine what was Nixon's role in the Watergate affair. The California State bar had the power to hold hearings on a lawyer's behavior and actions and refer to the state Supreme court that it take disciplinary action which would involve expelling from the bar or suspension.

Instead of terminating their pursuit of Nixon, the Special Prosecutor's office continued to investigate close friends such as Bebe Rebozo. Nowhere would they leak to the media about their innocence. They were guilty in the eyes of the public because the people did not have all the facts or bothered to find out what the results of the evidence were. The television media had done their untruthful job and did not correct their falsifications on the Nixons and their friends.

Because of what happened to President Nixon, I decided I was going to devote full time to clear his name and to find out evidence to do so. So I offered my resignation in September from the Arizona Federation of Republican

Women State Board. I felt Nixon was innocent, and I couldn't understand why others couldn't figure it out or ask Congress to cool down their partisan talk to find the real truth.

Many overseas and at home had never understood what the Watergate scandal was about. It was the excesses of the Vietnam War that caused Watergate. I was sure if the Democrats hadn't been in the majority in the House or Senate, President Nixon would not felt inclined to resign. Personally I thought the jury was rigged or stacked against Nixon.

Then, Joan Wood, a Republican friend, called me on the telephone, and said President Gerald Ford on September 8th was issuing a proclamation granting a pardon to Richard Nixon. I didn't know whether to be sad or to rejoice at the news my friend gave me. I knew Nixon had done nothing wrong. I wondered why had President Ford decided to issue a pardon. I knew Pat felt as I did about the pardon. We knew that it was just a yielding and submitting to those who did not love her husband.

To accept a pardon from President Ford was revolting and despicable to Nixon. It would only give the impression he was guilty of the charges. Neither Pat or Richard Nixon knew in advance of President Ford's decision. When Pat heard the news she reacted violently in rage. The pent up pressure inside Pat came rolling out. She did not know of what the pardon would be for what? Pat did not know what this was all about.

Because of Pat's outburst, Nixon tried to give the pardon back to Ford. But President Ford did not endorse Nixon's idea of relinquish the pardon. Nixon told us that he was wrong in not acting more decisively and more forthrightly in dealing with Watergate, particularly when it reached the stage of judicial proceedings and grew from a political scandal into a national tragedy. No words could describe the depths of his regret and pain at the anguish his mistakes over Watergate had caused the nation and his presidency-a nation he so deeply loved and an institution he so greatly respected. The way Nixon tried to deal with Watergate was the wrong way. It was the burden he would bear for every day of his life, which was left for him.

September 11th, Richard Nixon wrote a letter to the California State Bar and resigned as a member of the State Bar. It was rejected because Nixon refused to admit he would encounter possible disciplinary action by the bar.

But Nixon wrote another letter to remove himself from the State Bar. However, upon receiving the second Nixon letter conceding a possible interrogation-the board accepted Nixon 's resignation. But, they warned him that disciplinary proceedings would be reinstated against Nixon should he decide to become a member again of the State Bar.

The mental excessive tensions that Nixon was enduring became a counterpart by a large blood clot forming in his left swollen leg. Phlebitis had set in his left side of his lower abdomen. Nixon 's doctors warned him that the pain indicated the blood clot in his leg might move to his lungs.

September 23rd, Nixon entered Long Beach Memorial Hospital at the advice of his personal physician Dr. John Lungren. He prescribed anti-coagulant drugs to shrivel the growing clot. For five days the Heparin treatment—a slow drip of the anticoagulant drug—was given. But, the drug did not work.

The clot grew bigger and was threatening his life. The pain from the swelling his left leg caused sleep to evade him. He was terribly weak. When I called the hospital, I was wondering if Nixon would make it. All I could do was pray for him to survive this crisis.

The doctors convinced Nixon that surgery was necessary for him to live. Early in the morning, October 30th, he underwent surgery at the hospital. Several hours later his recovery turned worse. His condition deteriorated and declined sharply. Nixon collapsed into unconsciousness. His

blood pressure pushed him into critical shock. Blood had crept into the cavity between the chest and pelvis. The doctor gave Nixon hours of blood transfusions and other necessary measures before his condition became more stable.

When he finally awoke, Nixon focused his eyes on Pat. She had been by his side everyday. Pat slept at he hospital and continued her meals even though Pat felt helpless, she had a great faith in God. She had prayed to God for her husband's recovery and to trust in the doctor's ability. Pat gave God and the doctors the credit for her husband's turn-round.

If Pat was in a state of shock, she showed no signs of strain in public because of her husband's condition. She was cheerful and was completely in control of herself. The only time she got upset was when reporters asked her "Is your husband really ill?" only she knew how sick he was. That question brought tears to Pat's eyes. Otherwise, Pat cried in private.

President Ford paid Nixon a visit in the hospital. He was appalled at Nixon 's dismal condition. Then Ford knew Nixon was really ill. However, Judge Sirica was skeptical. He sent three doctors from Washington to investigate Nixon condition. They decided that Nixon was unfit to testify or even travel to be a subpoenaed witness at the trial of Haldeman, Ehrlichman, and Mitchell. Even the "Washington Post" made fun of Nixon 's condition. It was disgraceful!

Richard Nixon on November 14th left the hospital in a wheelchair, literally exhausted and under travel restrictions. He was very tired often losing sleep having all those tests and enemas to clear his digestive tract. Nixon's condition was worse than when he came in the hospital.

For several months he would take coumadin, a blood thinner, for his phlebitis. However, Nixon would be still in danger of hemorrhaging if he encountered any physical trauma of any kind. He was to restrict his physical activity, such as protracted period of sitting at home, airplane, or a car.

Nixon told us it was his wife, Pat, who kept him alive. He doubted that he would have made it without her. Just having her there was the best medicine for him. He testified that the best decision he ever made was when he chose Pat to be his wife-a partner in life.

It was Pat who nurtured and fed her husband back to health. She would always eat with him to persuade and cause Nixon to eat more, even if she wasn't hungry herself. His doctors were anxious that Richard Nixon would gain some more weight he had lost. However, Pat saw to it he stayed on his low-cholesterol, salt-free diet.

From the public eye, Pat Nixon had vanished from the scene. Few people heard from her. Mail at San Clemente piled up and did not reach her for reply. This time she would enjoy her privacy. Although, Pat missed having people around her, she did have a few friends in for dinner. It made sense that they stay at home for dinner, instead of going out to eat and generate a commotion with the press or certain sections of the public.

One time Pat invited a few old friends to dinner. Even friends did not know what really happened at the Watergate affair. As I learned not to bring up the subject of the 1960 election to Pat, I knew how embarrassing it would be to bring up any word about Watergate. I didn't discuss it. When someone is ill, no one should bring up any subject that would disturb their mental or physical condition or well-being.

However, one old Nixon administration friend made the mistake to do so. It made Pat angry. She did not think her husband's physical condition shouldn't be subjected to that kind of questioning or influence.

Evangelist Billy Graham was starting a new religious crusade and could not be with the Nixon 's family. But, he called and talked to Pat and found out Richard Nixon almost died. Nixon, who had helped in many of Graham's evangelistic crusades, wanted Billy to stay at the crusade and continue his work.

I became depressed at the November election results for Republicans. Four members of the House Judiciary Committee who had voted against Richard Nixon's impeachment were defeated at the polls. Innocent men's lives were in disorder because they worked or were friends of Nixon. It was a very sad time.

The Watergate prosecutors continued the cover-up trial without Nixon in Washington.

Many questions remained unanswered about two tape recordings that didn't exist. Eight members of the Nixon administration were to testify about two conversations that went unrecorded.

On back of the box containing a tape ran out on an unattended recorder, a Roman numeral appeared. No one knew who wrote the notation—"Full, Tape Removed," for April 16,1973. In it Dean was indicating President Nixon in the Watergate cover-up. The notation "Full" could be read that the tape ran out or almost ran out.

The Secret Service technician Raymond Zumwalt who was in charge of the tapes, said on other times he wrote "Tapes Ran Out" on back of the box. However, the Secret Service technician changed his testimony in the course of the court trial why two days of presidential conversation were recorded on a six-hour supply of tape on a single machine. First, Zumwalt said he failed to turn on a second machine for that April date. Later, he changed his statement. He remembered the switcher hadn't been set to operate because it was on a weekend. Discrepancies between Zumwalt's initial notes and his later listing of who took out tapes and when they were returned to storage.

Secret Service Agent, Louis B. Sims who was in charge of White House technical services told that some memos concerning who checked out tapes appeared to be missing. His remembrance didn't agree or match exactly with Zumwalt's account.

Rose Mary Woods, President Nixon's personal secretary said the tapes were very poor in quality and that every word was impossible to hear on them. When she was transcribing tapes, Rose Mary found it very difficult. Despite working until 3 a.m., Sunday, and again the rest of the day. After rising at 6 a.m., she could not complete a transcript of even one September 29th conversation.

The Watergate Prosecutor recalled Alexander Butterfield, a former White House assistant, to their witness stand. He resumed the time-consuming procedure of verifying 26 tapes they want the jury to hear. Butterfield, who disclosed the existence of the White House tapes, approved 197 changes in voice identities of voices or words on transcripts.

U.S. Judge John Sirica wanted to be sure the voices on the tapes are the voices of the people they say they are. Because President Nixon was hospitalized in California and H.R. Haldeman, John Ehrlichman, John Dean, and others could not be forced to testify against themselves. Without testimony from those speaking in the tape conversation, there would be no way to prove the tapes had not been tampered with, or that the conversation ever took place.

By Christmas time, Richard Nixon was still bed ridden. They checked his blood pressure three times a day. When he could walk, it was just a few feet away. Because of his blood-thinning medicine and the humid sea air at San Clemente, Nixon felt the cold air more. He appreciated the warm heat from his fireplace in the living room and Pat's company.

The Nixons planned to spend a quiet Christmas at San Clemente, Casa Pacifica. The media was trying to tell us all, that no one cared about the Nixons anymore. But, they were wrong. Two days before Christmas, they received more than 14,000 Christmas cards. At a rate of about 10 packages a day had been coming in for several weeks. They had a large tree decorated with ornaments they had collected over the past 25 years. Most of the staff left for the holidays. On Christmas

Eve, Julie, David, Tricia and Ed were the only guests with their mother and father. It was not a very happy time.

By telephone, Billy Graham called the Nixons while vacationing in Jamaica at the country music singer, Johnny Cash's home. He inquired of Pat about Nixon's condition. She said Nixon was a little better, mentally and physically. The pressure of the last months almost crushed him. Billy Graham could tell that Nixon was not a well man—even on the telephone.

Later, Billy Graham said at a new conference that the felt he had been "used" by President Nixon's administrative staff. He explained that Nixon himself never tried to utilize unfairly their relationship, but some of his staff may have tried to do so.

In spite of Watergate, Pat Nixon was voted number one winner in the Good Housekeeping national magazine poll of the world's 10 most admired women. Even Julie Eisenhower, her daughter was ranked fourth. U.S. homemakers showed support for the Nixon's family. Jacqueline Kennedy Onassis slipped to number 26. Ever since Pat Nixon was Second Lady and moved up to First Lady, she was always in the top ten polls. People just loved and appreciated who Pat Nixon was and what she did. Jackie Kennedy never received that attention.

Chapter 20

1975
THE CIA, POW'S,
DEDICATION OF
PAT'S SCHOOL

The economic skid dominated our nation. All of us were asking, "How do we get out of this recession?" Inflation had climbed to an extremely large amount of 14.1 percent, and unemployment surpassed 9 percent.

The story of illegal Central Intelligence Agency (CIA) spying topped the daily news. Dozens of evidence included wire-tapping, break-ins, and secret inspection of mail and other activities. Many burglaries and other break-ins were not solved. All were linked to activities of the CIA or the FBI.

In 1947, when the CIA was first setup, it was forbidden to have law enforcement powers or internal security activities. The Federal Bureau of Investigation (FBI) was to have those responsibilities.

Participants in protest demonstration were followed. Their informants pierced ant-war groups. Members of

Congress were spied on by the CIA. Even President Nixon did not escape their onslaught.

Senator Howard Baker, Republican from Tennessee, also vice chairman of the Senate Watergate Committee, spoke out on his suspicions of the CIA link to the Watergate break-in. He had the same suspicious idea as I was thinking about this mysterious link to the CIA.

In reviewing the June 23, 1972 tape, Nixon was reported to have said to Haldeman, "Well, we protected Helms from one hell of a lot of things."

Richard Helms was director of the CIA until February 1973. He was a Johnson hold over. Nixon did not trust or like him. Neither did Helms have any love for the Nixon administration. Many of us wondered why Nixon agreed to let him stay on. I guess he had his reasons.

Did Helms inform Nixon about the clandestine enterprise? Or did Nixon's staff initiate the surveillance without telling Nixon? Perhaps, that is why Nixon was disturbed by the rumors and the bits and pieces of evidence he had collected about the CIA. Be assured there was widespread shedding of paper at the agency, even though no one gave an official order.

In 1969 President Nixon ordered that chemical and biological warfare would be limited and stockpiles of nerve gas, biological agents, and certain toxins to be destroyed.

Then, in 1970, Nixon ordered shellfish toxins and cobra venom to be destroyed. A very small amount of it would bring instant death. There was no known antidote. In violation of Nixon 's presidential orders to destroy the stockpiles of toxins and other chemical weapons, the CIA disobeyed again and retained the poisons. No source or memo could be found who was responsible for the retention of toxins.

Three days before the Watergate break-in a secret CIA memorandum was discovered. Those, who knew about the memo, kept it quiet. Because a public relations firm, which was a front for the CIA, didn't want their cover blown.

What was interesting, the CIA planted false stories and made up something about anyone or a group to discredit them. Then, if someone hears the untruthful story and reiterates it in a publication. If the CIA director reads the false story and believes what he read which his own CIA workers circulated in the first place, he is believing their own lies.

The information which, I had found out, showed the CIA was in continual contact with the "Washington Post." What were they trying to do there? Were they blocking certain stories from being published, or revise and amend what had been given; or to provide the Nixon administration their explanation of the occurrences and happenings?

By trying to substantiate stories with the Central Intelligence Agency, the "Post" warned the CIA beforehand of any stories they were about to crack. The buzz around Washington that there was much bargaining between the "Post" and the CIA. There was much discussion concerning matters of national security, and sometimes the "Post" would back down regarding it.

My suspicions were being aroused as I tried to put the mystery of the Watergate puzzle together. There was more to the Watergate break-in story than was told. I was hoping I could find out the rest of the story and match all the pieces of the puzzle.

January 3rd, Special Prosecutor Henry S. Ruth, Jr. told the House Judiciary Committee's criminal justice subcommittee that any legislation to publish Richard Nixon's extensive part in the Watergate affair would be unconstitutional.

He said, "Much of the evidence is one-sided and unsubstantiated and its public disclosure would be challenged in court as unconstitutional within an hour. If I am ordered to do it, I'll do it and throw it into court. That's all I am saying."

The panel wanted to have full exposure of Nixon's

involvement in the break-in. Even Leon Jaworski added his thoughts on the situation. He said any requirement to permit the former president to listen to some tapes would be most embarrassing to people in public office and convince that they were not relevant to the investigation of Watergate.

On January 9, 1975, Richard Nixon noted his 62nd birthday. Nixon did not want any birthday celebration. Pale and weakened by an acute depression, he was in no mood to commemorate the special day. But Bebe Rebozo and four other friends decided to surprise him by flying out with big steaks and a large special birthday cake.

It was the saddest party. Jokes and stories by his friends did not liven up the evening. Nixon did not regain his vigor or spirit. Pat watched her husband carefully. If he showed any signs of being weary she was ready to end the party. When the cake was brought out, Nixon blew out the candles on his cake. Everyone sang "Happy Birthday," and then, they left before midnight dawned.

As Nixon looked out at he Pacific Ocean, he was determined to recover his health. He knew he must do it if he would have to solve his other financial problems. Nixon faced civil lawsuits not protected or concealed by the pardon. He set up a schedule for walking and swimming and an occasional golf game. Because he was so fragile emotionally and physically, Nixon had to be careful in what he did. It terrified Nixon if anyone would heap verbal abuse on him. By bringing him in contact with people who supported and cheered him up, it did more for his morale.

As far as I could remember, Pat never had a serious illness, and Nixon was one of our healthiest Presidents. It was a difficult job for Pat to cheer up her husband. He was so very low. She knew any excessive mental tension or exertion would bring on another attack of phlebitis.

To see that her husband gets his daily walks, Pat would go along with him. She checked to be sure that Nixon would take his medicine every day and to keep in contact with his physicians, Dr. John Lungren, in case any problems showed up.

When I talked to Pat on the telephone, she seemed to enjoy life at her home. It was wonderful for her to feel the breeze on her face and enjoy the California sunshine. Pat enjoyed her gardening, weeding, and digging in the dirt. The hummingbirds and doves gave her much joy as they flew around her courtyard.

In February, Walter Annenberg, former U.S. Ambassador to Great Britain, invited the Nixons to his estate for five days to rest and enjoy the sunshine. This was Nixon's first social appearance away from his seaside home at San Clemente.

A quiet private dinner was given for the Nixons and other old intimate friends. Mr. And Mrs. Bob Hope, Frank Sinatra, Ronald and Nancy Reagan, and Mr. and Mrs. Leonard Firestone were included as Saturday night dinner guests.

For ten minutes Richard Nixon talked about how important his friends were to him now. He didn't talk about the past, but he said friends were very important when you are at the top but more so at a time like this.

Richard Nixon enjoyed the evening. He needed a lot of rest and many friends. As he was still recovering from his phlebitis surgery, the dinner guests arrived around 6 p.m. and left about 10:20 p.m. They didn't want any affair to tax Nixon.

Pat Nixon celebrated her 63rd birthday on March 16th. Since I couldn't be with Pat on her special day, I wired her a dozen of beautiful yellow roses as a birthday surprise. I knew she needed something to boost her spirits that someone really cared. It did brighten her day because of my kindness at that time.

March 29th, U.S. District Court Judge Noel Fox ruled that President Gerald Ford's pardon of former President Richard Nixon was constitutional. The ruling came as a result of a lawsuit filed by an attorney George Murphy of Marquette,

Michigan, urging the Court to announce last fall's pardoning of Nixon void and unconstitutional.

Judge Fox said Nixon and his aides were in rebellion and the U.S. Supreme Court decisions gave the president vast leeway in handing out pardons. President Ford's was constitutional but prudent public policy judgment.

Fox based his decision on the Federalist Papers #74 by Alexander Hamilton in 1788. In that Federalist paper, Hamilton argued that the president's pardoning power should be unrestricted because, "in seasons of insurrection or rebellion, there are often critical moments when a well-timed offer of a pardon to the insurgents or rebels may restore the tranquility of the commonwealth."

The period from the Watergate break-in, June 1972 until August date of Nixon's resignation was considered by the Judge was a season of insurrection or rebellion by many actually in government. He also wrote that many top Nixon administration officials had violated the civil liberties of individual citizens and violated campaign laws to preserve and expand their own and Nixon's personal power beyond constitutional limits.

Nixon usually arose at 7:30 a.m. in the morning. He enjoyed a light breakfast—a cantaloupe or grapefruit segments, a glass of fruit juice and a bowl of wheat germ and light cream. At his table, he turned the pages of the newspaper. The sport pages interested him more to check out the latest team scores.

After breakfast Nixon would usually go to his second floor workshop to work on his memoir book. He was working arduously to get part of his book finished by the fall for his publisher.

In an hour he would go to his office at the Coast Guard compound next to his home. A small, metal American flag was still visible on Nixon's blue business suit, as it was when he was President.

Among the stack of mail on his desk, many are from invitations from foreign countries. Nixon had rejected any lecture tours in the United States. It was his belief that no former President should take money for any speaking engagements. Neither, did he take any for himself.

Foreigners couldn't understand why Nixon had to resign as President. They were stating that it wouldn't happen overseas. Much of his mail went unanswered because he did not have the money to reply to everyone. Nixon tried to keep in touch with his personal friends mostly by telephone or brief notes.

Often Richard Nixon would take barefoot strolls with his wife, Pat, on the beach. They would chat and pose for pictures with beach goers.

Nixon didn't plan to write his memoirs right away, but his financial legal problems forced him to start putting it all together. Three former White House staffers became his principal researchers. The researchers worked long and strenuous preparing materials for his memoir book.

The Democrat Congress had cut half of all the economic and military aid in 1974 to South Vietnam, and they cut it some more in 1975. As the result, the Soviet Union poured in heavy support for Hanoi in North Vietnam.

President Ford was powerless to act because of tying the hands of Nixon and Ford to use air power against the Communist attacks. No wonder in April 1978, Pat and Richard Nixon were depressed at the news of the fall of South Vietnam. It was the U.S. Democrat Congress, which delivered and committed twenty million Vietnamese people to their death-knell or fleeing for their lives.

At the end of May, Pat Nixon attended the dedication of the Patricia Nixon Elementary School in Pat's hometown of Cerritos, California. She had turned down many invitations before, so no one knew if she would really come for the dedication. However, ten days before the actual dedication,

Pat surprised Margaret Skilling, the principal of the school that she would be there for the ceremony. Of course, everyone was thrilled, except William Watt, a local Democrat school board member, who had opposed naming the school after Pat Nixon.

Eight hundred people had shown up for the dedication ceremony. They thought Pat looked much better than she ever did.

As she beamed, she captivated her audience. Pat hugged several children and joked with the student choir, who sang music as a compliment to her as a real lady. Smiling, she enjoyed the lovely music. When the children gave her flowers, Pat quickly bent over and kissed each one of them. The children responded in kind to her real love for them.

Pat Nixon told her audience "I thought that only those who were gone—I mean really gone—ever had a school named for them. I am so happy to tell you that I am not gone!"

While Pat was enjoying the dedication of Pat Nixon Elementary School, Washington was buzzing with the latest news about whether the CIA was involved in the Watergate case. Alfred C. Baldwin III, a former agent of the CIA and also a worker in the Nixon administration, was questioned again about whether he played any part in his mention of the "CIA" from a court record in the Watergate case.

The deletion question had become the issue in confirmation of Earl J. Siebert as U.S. Attorney for the District of Columbia. Siebert was the head prosecutor in the Watergate break-in case. The deletion question involved the substituting of initials "CRP" (Committee to Re-elect the President) for "CIA" in the transcript of the "Los Angeles Times" interview with Baldwin.

Seymour Glanzer, and Earl Siebert, and Democrats had told U.S. District Court Judge John J. Sirica that referenced to "CIA" should be changed to "CRP." They said Baldwin told them to do so. The Democrats were concerned that the

Watergate defendants would use this as spurious bogus CIA argument in their trial.

However, Baldwin said he would not rule out that CIA was involved in the Watergate. Many had felt there was a good possibility that this was a CIA operation. Baldwin denied that he urged the changing of the initials of CIA to CRP on the transcript document. It was the CIA. The Democrats were divided on who said what. Baldwin set the record straight.

On June 30th, in San Antonio, Texas nearly 200 former American Prisoners of War (Vietnam) met for their first national reunion. They praised Richard Nixon for transacting their release with "dignity and pride" from the POW's camps in Vietnam. It was Nixon's decision to order gigantic bombing of North Vietnam compelled the North Vietnamese to negotiate.

The former POW's passed the following resolution:

"This assembly publicly extends its most sincere thanks and appreciation to Richard M. Nixon, for his singular display of courage and resolution in this moment of great adversity in our nation's history by taking the affirmative action necessary to affect our release."

They also said:

"We further convey to President Nixon our best wishes for his return to good health, great success in future endeavors and long life and happiness in our beloved country."

The litigation against Richard Nixon continued. Lawsuits were filed by individual seeking compensation from government exploits, which had never included President Nixon 's determination anyway. As far as I was concerned, I knew the Democrat lawyers in the Special Prosecutor's office hated Richard Nixon. They would try anything to pursue him at any cost.

Bebe Rebozo was a close friend of Nixon. These disgraceful bunch of attorneys enmeshed Rebozo and Nixon into a painful legal trial. Nixon was questioned for eleven hours. The scrutinized quizzing was an ordeal for both of them. It was an abuse of power by these U.S. lawyers. No evidence could be found against Rebozo.

All this legal mess cost much money. Legal bills of over $750,000 stared Nixon in his face. Then he owed his staff more than $150,000; on his San Clemente house he owed $37,000 in property tax; plus overdue payments on his mortgage loan and $23,000 medical bills from Long Beach Memorial Hospital.

I knew Nixon was not a wealthy man. It broke my heart to see Pat and Dick in this situation. I really had to pray to God many times to cool the anger, which was exploding inside. How could anyone do this to any human being I asked? But, they did.

Bob Abphanalp and Bebe Rebozo suggested that Nixon sell his beach house at Key Biscayne, Florida. Which he did to relieve his cash flow crisis. Most of his staff had to go. Household and garden expenses were cut to the bone.

Pat seemed to take things in stride in spite of the troubled financial dilemma, which enveloped them. She created a beautiful home at San Clemente. Everywhere flower arrangements in the house were very pleasing to everyone who saw them. Even certain kinds of weeds graced each bouquet and made it delightful to the eye.

Gardening was Pat's emancipation. It kept her free from any distractions from the past and to concentrate on making a beautiful home for her husband and family. The beautiful roses below the dining and living room were examples of Pat's handiwork in her gardening talents.

When Pat was not working long hours in the garden, she read and reread many books. Historical fiction and biographies were her favorites. She was intrigued by the secret scheme of a literary work she was reading.

However, I noticed that Pat was distressed because all her letters address books, mementoes, and remembrances were still impounded in the White House. All the things she cherished and appreciated had not been sent to her.

July 19th, Tricia and her husband, Edward Cox, came to visit. The Nixons were a close family and often visited one another. On the way back from Camp Pendleton golf course, Thursday, Nixon with his daughter and son-in-law happened upon an auto accident on the northwest edge of the base.

The Secret Service agents intended to pass the accident because of their concern to protect Nixon. The head-on accident occurred about two minutes before the Nixon car had arrived.

But president Nixon saw the accident and said immediately, "Stop, stop the car."

He asked the officer in charge of the rescue operation, "Can we give you any help? We do have first aid equipment."

The officer replied, "Yes, Sir. We can sure use that."

Nixon took charge and ordered his Secret Service agents to call for a Medivac helicopter. Everyone was working at getting two injured Marines out of one of the cars. The Marine in the other car was presumed to be dead. He was badly hurt and was not a very pretty sight.

One of the Marines had his foot forced into the brake pedal trapping him in the wreckage. Nixon commanded the Secret Service agents to get a crowbar from his backup car.

In this one car both Marines were still breathing. The helicopter took them to a nearby hospital where they died later.

The tragedy really affected Nixon. He knew the Marines were going off the base for a good time in their blue dress uniforms. The dead Marines were in their 20's and so very young.

Many people recognized Nixon but they kept working to save the trapped Marines. When Nixon left the accident scene, the officers saluted him and shook his hand to thank Nixon for his help.

Nixon was so concerned about the injured Marines, he called the Camp Pendleton commander the next morning to learn the outcome of the three men whom he tried to save. Pat was downhearted but peaceful. She was always wondering if the public would ever recognize the wonderful things her husband had done. Pat did not want the people to forget. We all hoped one day they would remember.

Chapter 21

PAT'S STROKE AND NIXON'S LEGAL BILLS

At the invitation of Ambassador Huang Chen, the People's Republic of China's representative in the United States, Julie and David Eisenhower journeyed to China. They celebrated the New Year in China just like any other traveler. Julie and David told the Chinese government that they appreciated the invitation, but they insisted on paying for their trip.

The purpose of their trip was to find out what the typical common Chinese people were thinking. While in China, young Chinese people were photographing them everywhere. They appeared to adore and revere them there.

On their visit to Peking, Chairman Mao tse-tung told them that their father was welcome to visit China at any time. Detailed accounts and photographs of the Eisenhower's meeting with Chairman Mao controlled every page one of the newspapers, stressing Peking's regard of Nixon's role in the opening of relations with Communist China and emphasizing interest over U.S-Soviet relaxation of strained relations.

Then, it was discovered that the Ervin committee had withheld documents showing President Lyndon Johnson had ordered the FBI to serve as a channel for wiretaps, bugging, and break-ins to spy on Martin Luther King and Robert Kennedy in 1964. Johnson wanted to know if those in the civil rights movement had foreign connections, which would endanger national security. Also, he wanted to obstruct and defeat any endeavor by Robert Kennedy to compel his nomination as vice president at the Democrat national convention that year.

This 1964 occurrence was an even serious outrage than the original Watergate break-in. It represents the turning of a police agent of government to criminal actions for political intentions.

What I wanted to know was:

Why was this bit of information and other important facts were kept secret by the Ervin committee? If it had been revealed, would it have made impossible to accuse Nixon with transgressions, which would dwindle to insignificance in contrast to other presidents before him? It appeared to me that the Democrat Congress did not want to reveal their own misdeeds.

In February 1976, the Republic of China sent an airplane for the Nixons at Los Angeles. The Chinese were friendly with the Nixons. They never forgot Nixon's friendship with them. They celebrated the anniversary of their first 1972 visit to China. By all the bands, banquets, and tour of the country given to the Nixons, the Chinese remembered him and recognized who he was. Nixon was given the privilege of meeting the new successor Premier Hua Guofeng that no one else had ever met.

At the end of May, I graduated from Grand Canyon College and had the desire to enter the teaching profession. The Nixons sent a large bouquet of flowers for a graduation present, which I adored. With a change of administration at the college where I worked as Assistant Registrar of Computer Services, I felt led to go to Tyrone, Pennsylvania in June to work with Claude Grannas at North Eastern Bible Conference grounds and to teach at the Prince Academy of Christian Education.

Also, David Eisenhower graduated from George Washington University Law School at the end of June. Julie and David decided to visit for a month at San Clemente. It was a good thing they decided to do so because Julie didn't know what lay ahead for her mother.

When the film "All The President's Men" based on Bob Woodward and Carl Bernstein's book, I was really disturbed about what it contained. How can anyone believe what was described? Fiction and fact were weaved together, so everyone thought it was the truth. But it was not. Then, their second book, "The Final Days" came out about the last days of the Nixon White House. It was a book blended with a garbage of lies and distortions of facts. The hatred of the Nixons stemmed back to the Alger Hiss case. Once again the prejudice was showing. The real true friends of the Nixons were never asked for interviews or for any other information. It was a fictitious, untruthful book paraded as a fact.

In July I was in Pennsylvania when I heard Pat had a stroke and had to be hospitalized. I felt so sad inside to be so far away from my special friend. In my mind, I was wondering what triggered the offset of the stroke. Pat had been through so much more than others.

Then, I found out Pat Nixon had been reading "The Final Days." Apparently, she had borrowed the book from someone else—over Dick's objections. Pat was portrayed as a drunken, erratic drinker on the verge of divorcing her husband. What they wrote about Pat Nixon was absolute nonsense—not true. What can anyone do about the irresponsibility of those two men who had no regard for the truth?

After Richard Nixon's resignation, Pat was in fine health. She believed in her husband and all he had accomplished. But on the day of the stroke, her blood pressure went sky high and bounced off the chart. Pat was not aware that she was having a stroke. She thought she was exhausted from doing all the extra house cleaning. Her servants were gone on a month's vacation, and she was filling in for them until they arrived back.

It was Richard Nixon who recognized her symptoms and contacted the doctors. They urged that Pat should be taken to the Long Beach Memorial Hospital. Pat protested, and said she was only very tired. For the first time she was depressed and frightened.

More than 100,000 letters and telegrams and 50 floral bouquets were received during Pat's hospitalization. More than thousand pieces of mail and telegrams were sent to San Clemente. At Pat's request the flowers were given to other patients in the hospital.

Was the book "The Final Days", Pat had been reading the cause of the emotional stress, which led to the stroke? Also, on that Fourth of July weekend, Pat had been watching on television the Bicentennial coverage. Both of them had looked forward to the two hundredth anniversary of our country. They had worked so long on it together. It was to be a splendid, elaborate, outstanding finale for their efforts. To observe some other President presiding at the ceremony, was that too much for Pat? Or was the news, Richard Nixon shared with Pat before he left for work early in the morning, that the New York State Bar would disbar him from practicing as an attorney?

None of Pat's doctors could pinpoint the accurate detailed cause for her stroke. But they emphasized that emotional stress could be a cause to elevate high blood pressure.

The stroke left Pat with some slurring of her speech, and her left side temporarily paralyzed so she could not walk. Some said Pat would never recover from this cerebral accident. But I knew different because they did not know the real Pat Nixon. Pat refused to be a burden. She determined to walk again and get well. Every morning she turned her exercise therapy wheel over and over again to strengthen her left arm and leg. Going up a few steps was difficult for Pat, but she never gave up in her strides toward recovery.

Messages of concern from friends meant a great deal to the Nixons. The outpouring of concern gave Pat the strength she needed to get well. Everyday Richard Nixon would sit by her bed and help her read the many letters, telegrams and the newspaper editorials. He was a great source of strength for Pat.

Pat Nixon had very few visitors at the hospital and her home. Just a small amount of time exhausted her completely. The fatigue showed on her face. Her energy was gone. She didn't want to take time to see anyone. No one knew the battle Pat faced ahead, but she determined to win it.

A gala event was planned by the United States Citizen Corporation Board for Pat Nixon. Because of her stroke, it was postponed until Sunday, November 14. Her doctors were confident that Pat would be sufficiently recovered to appear at the event. She was scheduled to receive "The First Lady of the Century" award.

I knew Pat would not be able to dig out in her garden and enjoy the flowers she loved so much. So, at Thanksgiving time, I asked the florist to send a large bouquet of flowers to Pat at San Clemente. To my surprise, Pat answered. The stroke had not affected her handwriting at all. She gave special thanks for my cherished friendship. I was glad my courageous friend was on the way to recovery.

At the beginning of the 1977 years, Nixon encountered the dilemma of his lack of money and his physical health. I remembered his critical sickness, which influenced Nixon's political profession two times. His infected knee in the 1960 campaign made him appear weak physically in the Nixon/Kennedy debates. Then, the viral pneumonia impaired his health and judgment in 1973 and kept him from destroying the tapes. If he had been in good, normal physical health, I was sure he would have listened to Pat and other friends to destroy the tapes. Would the results in 1960 and 1973 been different than what actually happened?

Nixon was harassed and pursued by individuals in many civil lawsuits, which had no connection to Nixon's presidential actions. Nevertheless, whether the alleged charges were true or not, he had to defend himself. Many were dismissed, but the lawyers had to be paid. Legal bills, property and back taxes, the mortgage loan on his house, and staff salaries kept mounting. Richard Nixon was not a wealthy man. He was facing a financial crisis of bankruptcy.

In his mind he was mulling over what to do about this financial problem. He came up with a solution to part of the crisis by signing a contract with David Frost for a twenty-four television interviews. In March 1977, I watched the Nixon interviews on television with David Frost. Anything I thought previously about the media came true at this television broadcast. It showed a cruel anti-Nixon prejudice and slanting of questions and selection of issues. I felt downhearted that Nixon had to go through this defamation on nation wide television. The money crisis did not give him any other option. Nixon did not keep one penny of the proceeds for himself. His lawyers inherited it all.

Pat celebrated her 65th. Birthday on her adopted namesake's day, March 17, St. Patrick's Day. Hundreds of cards, bouquets and gifts arrived from around the world in admiration for her as the former First Lady and best wishes for return to good health. As a birthday surprise I gave her a gift of perfume, which would remind Pat of all the flowers she adored. It brought back memories of our constant friendship. Pat was feeling fine for her birthday. She was looking more terrific each day as she determined to make a comeback to good health.

She was walking unaided and did not appear to limp as

she did for many months. However, her speech was still slightly slurred. No one knew that the pain was still in her left hand and shoulder, which would come to be better through therapy. Then, Pat would get relief of pain and lack of sleep.

My parents were getting up in years and longed to be nearer to me. Then, Ray, my good friend, thought I should be in Arizona instead of Pennsylvania. This way I would be closer to the Nixons in California, as well as my aged parents. At the end of the school year, I made my journey home. Everyone was glad to see me once again. Pat was elated about the prospects of me coming to visit.

As time went by, Ray proposed marriage on top of the Ferris wheel at the Arizona State Fair. We decided to have the wedding in November at the Chapel of St. Paul's, Globe, Arizona. Invitations were sent out to family and friends.

Pat and Dick were excited about my upcoming marriage. They wanted to be at the wedding, but their traveling days had to be limited because of their health problems.

Instead, they sent their love and good wishes. A package was sent to us for the wedding. It was a framed Lincoln Memorial needlework autographed on the back by Pat Nixon from the Nixon family. We were so grateful and proud of that treasured wedding gift, because we knew it came from dear friends we thought so much of, and we cherished their special friendship.

Chapter 22

NIXON'S BRITISH
AND USA TRIPS
PAT AND THE
GRANDCHILDREN

By Nixon's sixty-fifth birthday in January, the months
ahead did not appear favorable or promising. The media kept
relating to him in the news as the disgraced ex-President.
The press kept harping on it until people were tired of hearing
the expression.

All the polls regarding Nixon was mixed. There was a
growing minority, which believed Nixon was railroaded, but
the majority hoodwinked by the media thought Nixon was
guilty of obstruction of justice. At that time the fabricated
reporting took its toll on Nixon with the public.

Somewhere down the road, the public would be waking
up to the fact that the media was making mistakes with their
inaccurate reporting. The public was less likely to believe
what the media was saying. For the first time, they were
questioning what the media was spoon-feeding them.

Nixon's money predicament began to abate as some

international business transactions came through financially. Each day his health became better. His long walks on the beach and his swims in the ocean brought him more robust health. In fact, his golf game bought him more exercise which he needed, and a improved golf score as well.

Pat was perturbed when she learned in January her childhood home was flattened by a firebomb in Cerritos, California. This was the third time it had happened. When Pat moved away, several families overtime had resided there. A few years ago the Cerritos city government bought and made the encompass area into a park.

There was nothing elaborate about this humble, unpretentious five-room house, which had been turned into a museum. It had been home for Pat for seventeen years. Often she would visit it to recall memories of a happier time for her. Now she was sad because of what happened. It was an act of lewd manners against a special lady.

The town of San Clemente celebrated its 50th. Anniversary in February 1978. The Nixons consented that buses of people could enter the area around the Nixon place to gape and stare. No one could get out of the buses to say hello to the Nixons.

By March 1978, Richard Nixon's memoir book was on its way to the publisher. When the book came out, everyone reading it knew it was Nixon's own brand of work. The memoirs became a success. For the moment the book rescued Nixon from financial debt. It was the best presidential autobiography in our lifetime. The first six months, 330,000 copies were bought by the public. They like it. This was encouraging to Richard Nixon. He thought there were many persons out in the heartland—the silent majority—who never voiced their opinions in polls but remembered him in spite of the media rhetoric.

Pat celebrated her 66th birthday in March. I always remembered my special friend always, which meant so much to Pat.

Ray and I were planning a trip to California when our two boys would be out of school. I wanted my husband to meet the Nixons personally. When I contacted Pat, she was overjoyed that we wanted to visit them. From then on, my husband and I were counting the days until we could be with the Nixons.

The boys' Spring Break had arrived. We piled into our car for our journey to San Clemente enroute to our California vacation in San Diego, which we had planned for our two boys.

As we approached "La Casa Pacifica" the Spanish style Nixon home in San Clemente, I noticed a volleyball net was spread across the abandoned helicopter pad. Even, the miniature golf course had weeds developing around it. Now it was more home-like. The official presidential trappings were now gone. It was more peaceful and quiet.

When we came to call, at first I did not notice the results of Pat's stroke. However, I did observe both had aged. Then, I perceived Pat was dragging her leg a little bit due to some weakness in her arms and legs.

Pat and I put our arms around each other and told how good it was to see one another. She looked slender and healthful.

Ray, my husband, shook hands with President Nixon. He was in a state of shock and awe in meeting President Nixon for the first time. Richard Nixon was real gracious and invited my husband to watch a ball game with him.

Pat and I went out in the garden to look at the roses and other flowers she enjoyed so much. She was in very good spirits. I heard her laughter when we joked about certain things. There was a cheerful jingle in her voice.

Nixon told us that Pat, his wife was the best medicine he ever had. She was concerned constantly about him. He saw to it that Pat's blood pressure was checked regularly because of her hypertension.

The quieter life was good for her. Pat appeared to be content. For now, she was unable to be in large crowds. Too much agitation was not pleasant for her. It would make her blood pressure to zoom. At that time, she didn't realize the pain in her left shoulder and pain was due to insufficient physical therapy—not her arthritis.

It was time to say goodbye to the Nixons. Our visit was too short, but we had to make our motel commitment in San Diego and see all the other sights in Southern California. It was visit my husband never forgot.

If the media thought all Americans had forgotten Richard Nixon, they had to retract those statements. Nixon received an invitation from Hyden, Kentucky, which wanted to name their new gymnasium and swimming pool as the Richard Nixon Recreation Center on July 2.

Nixon accepted the invitation. Six thousand people turned out for the dedication. When Nixon delivered his forty-minute speech, the citizens screamed and shouted their approval. Those enthusiastic Kentuckians cheering warmed Richard Nixon's heart that he was not forgotten.

He felt so good about the Hyden incident, Nixon re-did it again at Biloxi, Mississippi. The large crowd bellowed and hollered that they were still for Nixon. This really perked Nixon up.

Then, the town of Shreveport, Louisiana, did not want to be left behind in all the enthusiasm for Nixon, a huge barbecue party was held in his esteem and admiration. This gathering bolstered and reinforced Nixon's spirit that he determined to make more friendly travel plans in the future.

By summer of 1978, Pat was able to attend a Republican fund-raiser party at their Las Pacifica home. She enjoyed the Congressmen and the movie stars who attended the fun party. It appeared that the party did her good. Everyone enjoyed her smile and friendliness. Nixon was elated by the support of everyone at the party.

Julie and David Eisenhower were living close by at Capistrano Beach. Julie was a devoted daughter and visited her mother often. Pat became overjoyed when Julie told her that she would be a grandmother sometime in August.

The thought of being a grandmother inspired Pat to fully recover from the effects of her stroke. She determined to keep up her physical therapy—daily turning a large wheel and swimming in their indoor heated pool. Pat had the volition to overcome the results of her stroke. And she did!

On August 15, 1978, Julie and David's little daughter, Jennie Elizabeth Eisenhower, was born at San Clemente General Hospital. Pat and Richard Nixon were happy grandparents and vied with one another who would take care of Jennie when their grand daughter stayed overnight. There would always be a bedroom for Jennie at the Nixon's home.

I heard from Pat. She said they were enjoying the beauty of the lovely flowers I sent for Thanksgiving and my kind thoughts of them. They also enjoyed the latest news of my activities. She thought my great spirit would keep me young forever.

On November 29,1978, Nixon journeyed to Great Britain as a private citizen. He had received an invitation to speak to the Oxford Union University and three other groups. Nixon was pondering in his mind whether it was the right thing or not to accept. All British Government Ministers, except the Minister of State for Energy, declined to see Nixon or to be present at any assembly where he was supposed to speak.

Nixon was unaware of the turmoil his arrival in Britain was causing when his airplane landed at the airport in the morning of November 29. Even, our U.S. Ambassador to Britain, who met Nixon at the airport, was rude to the ex-president.

As Nixon's car entered the grounds of the Oxford Union University, several hundred-student demonstrators encompassed his car. They jumped on the front hood of the car and repeatedly beat the doors of the Nixon car. It was a vicious student mob. It reminded Nixon of the Caracas, Venezuela, motorcade attack when he was Vice President in 1958.

However, the gathering inside the hall was different than outside. The crowd welcomed Nixon with much tribute and applause. None of the students tried to shout him down before he addressed them.

Afterwards, they participated in a tough question-and-answer session for Nixon. One of the student questioners asked him if he had any misgivings about his decision to attack Cambodia in 1970. Nixon replied quickly that his only regrets he had was he should have acted much earlier.

"Why should we accuse the United States of attacking the North Vietnamese occupied Cambodia would be like blaming and denouncing the Allies of invading German—occupied France in 1944?"

His quick reply brought down much cheering and applause. Nixon did admit to one question about the Watergate affair that he did not handle it properly and screwed the whole thing up.

Afterwards Nixon drove to the House of Commons to visit with Speaker George Thomas and Margaret Thatcher, Leader of the Opposition. He was pleased with the warm welcome Thomas bestowed on him, Nixon was impressed with Margaret Thatcher as a woman leader and her talents and predicted she would go far in the British government.

Next, Nixon gave a talk at the Conservative Philosophy Group. It was a meeting of literary scholars, news editors, and persons actively engaged in government and business. Once again, several men thought they had the chance to bury Nixon so he would not rise again. However, after Nixon had presented his oral discourse on foreign policy, the men were ready to extol and commend him instead.

There were several private dinners Nixon attended. At

all of them, Nixon had fun and was very relaxed socially. It did bolster him once again. Some thought Nixon sounded as if he was out campaigning for some new office.

On his trip to Britain everyone noticed that Nixon went out of his way to be especially kind and thoughtful to waiters, hotel maids, policemen, taxi drivers, and anyone else who were of service to him. They remembered Nixon. He was quite different than some other Americans who had traveled abroad.

When Nixon arrived back from his British trip, Pat united with him in New York City at the Waldorf Astoria hotel. Tricia took her mother shopping which she adored doing. It was a great treat for her.

It was the Carter administration, which had been unfriendly and indifferent to Richard Nixon since he resigned. However, in December 1978, there was a turn-a-round by President Carter. Apparently, Richard Nixon sent a letter in the interest of peace and freedom to President Carter advising him regarding foreign policy on China and Taiwan. Instead of being outraged about Nixon's criticism of his foreign policy, President Carter surprised Nixon by accepting his recommendations. Three days before Christmas, 1978, the Carter letter arrived in San Clemente. This letter was good news for Richard Nixon, and it really perked him up.

Then, the Washington Post reported that China's Vice Premier, Deng Xiaoping would be coming January 29, to the Carter White House. The Chinese told the Carter administration that they wanted President Nixon to be given the hospitality of being on the guest list. It was their request. For the first time since Richard Nixon left the White House, it was the Chinese who forced the Carter administration to acknowledge Nixon's recognition to be bestowed on him as a former President.

When Nixon returned to the White House, January 29,1979, he was greeted outside by some demonstrators carrying signs—"You belong in jail not the White House." After meeting with Deng Xiaoping, the China's Vice Premier, for a few hours, Nixon was invited for the third time to visit China again.

As usual, the media kept attacking Nixon. They wouldn't leave him alone. The publicity about the dinner with the Chinese was another step up the ladder to regain Nixon's status as a former president.

As the year of 1979 began, Pat looked great. She was relishing her garden, friends, and Jennie, her grand daughter. Although, she had put on some more weight, her size was still her customary size six. Her face, some times thin, was now softer and fuller. I wasn't sure if her arthritic medicine caused this or not. In her talk, there was no indication of slurring of speech.

In climbing stairs, Pat had to be careful because her weak leg might give away and disintegrate.

She moved her left leg a little bit slower than normal. Sometimes one could hear a tiny, clumping sound when her foot stepped down.

As long as I knew Pat, I never heard her complain about anything. She thought to sit around and think on one's own woes would only result in morbid thoughts. That would not accomplish anything for the good. Her internal self-control kept everything inside. No one would ever know if Pat was in pain or about to die.

Nixon always had physicals when he was President, but Pat decided to avert having any of them. After both of their illnesses, they decided to seek medical advice when either of them noticed symptoms, which didn't appear just right. I knew Nixon was concerned about Pat's health, in spite of his optimism. Both of them knew that strokes could occur again.

After rising early for a small breakfast. Pat went to the gardens at La Casa Pacifica and transplanted flowers and pruned and trimmed shrubs. She thought this was excellent therapy for her after the stroke. When Nixon was President, they had several gardeners, but now only one gardener helped Pat.

Often, Pat would go with her close friend, Helene Drown, to shop at Newport Beach or to Beverly Hills. When they would lunch they would sit at a far-out secluded corner table of a restaurant. This way Pat could avoid meeting people or some nosey reporters looking for a story. She didn't want all that attention, but to be left alone to enjoy her husband and family.

At first, Nixon shared the same thoughts of privacy as Pat. He enjoyed the California sunshine and working on writing his books. As always, he did his best thinking when he was alone in seclusion at his office or garden.

After his British trip, Nixon decided he would like to travel more to express his thoughts on issues of today. He had something to believe in and worth fighting for. He never gave up. It wouldn't be Nixon to sit on his rump constantly at San Clemente, nor to retire just to fish, play cards or to golf. All that would bore him to death. Nixon did not plan to retire to a pasture, but to take a stand on world peace issues. He considered that living.

Tricia Nixon Cox lived in New York City with her husband, Eddie Cox. In March she was expecting her first child. That would make Pat a grandmother for the second time.

The last week before Tricia was to give birth, Pat flew to New York City to be with her. Tricia had to have a cesarean delivery at the New York Hospital. Little Christopher Nixon Cox was born March 14, 1979 at 3 a.m.—just two days before Pat's sixty-seven birthday. Pat was overjoyed for the second time about her new grandson.

When Pat returned from New York, I heard from her again. My birthday remembrance awaited her return from her delightful journey back East. She enjoyed photographs of my two sons, Raymond Scott and James Darrell. Pat thought they looked happy and well as proof of my loving care.

While Pat was in New York, the city of Cerritos, California, decided to put a large plaque in her honor where her childhood home was fire bombed in 1978. Grass had grown over the fire scars. The bricks from the fireplace were used in the rose garden. Many people still come there and view the place where once Pat Nixon lived as a child.

In mid 1979, Pat was able to model for her official White House portrait. She was averse in having it done, but her daughters convinced her in having it done for them and her grand children. Since every President and First Lady had their portraits placed in the White House, Julie and Tricia thought it was important not to give in to the enemies who never wanted anything Nixonian in the White House.

Each day Pat posed for the four-hour sittings. She was annoyed a little why the sittings took so long. The artist, Henriette Hurd, realized that Pat would rather be working in her garden instead of posing for her.

When the portrait was finally completed, it showed Pat Nixon wearing an embroidered blue, chiffon long sleeved evening gown. She decided to wear a three strand large pearl choker. The rose shaped pin was midpoint inside with petals made of a small platinum decoration by inlaying with diamonds. Pat loved that piece of jewelry because it was a special designed gift from her husband.

Her lovely eyes showed great strength. As I looked at the portrait, Pat's mouth appeared sensitive and sad. I agreed with Pat the mouth in the portrait looked too sad. The person I knew all those years did not look that way. Maybe all the things, which happened to her, finally emerged and turned up.

Pat did not want her portrait hung in the White House until her husband's painting would be put up beside hers at the same time. She did not want anything done apart from him.

Sometime in the year Richard Nixon would have his portrait painted. Whether he would have it painted from photographs or take the time to sit for an artist to paint, Nixon did not let anyone know then of his desires.

When Richard Nixon journeyed to China once again in September 1979, he took along Tricia's husband, Ed Cox. While both of them were gone, Pat stayed with Tricia and her grandson, Christopher in New York. They had a delightful time shopping and enjoying blue-eyed blond Christopher. According to the family, little Chris looked a little like both of his parents and all his grandparents combined.

La Casa Pacifica always supplied the privacy that Pat wanted. In time the isolation became a penitentiary. Just to leave her home she had a struggle to avoid the press and the prying snoopy people. Pat did not want to be recognized or being asked personal questions about Watergate or her health.

Since Pat's stroke, she became very concerned about the upkeep of such a large place as the La Casa Pacifica. This Spanish style house cost extremely large amount of money to heat and cool. She could not give the garden the attention as she had in time gone by. Pat and her one lone gardener could not keep up the work needed in the large garden. Shortly, after Julie's baby girl was born, Fina and Manolo Sanchez, their valet, cook and maid for years, decided to retire.

Then, Julie who was living with her husband, David, in nearby Capistrano Beach, told her parents they would be moving to Pennsylvania in January. Their decision prompted Pat to make a move to New York to be near her children and grandchildren. Richard Nixon was also uneasy at San Clemente and finally thought La Casa Pacifica was too much out of the way for activity and influence which he needed now. It usually took a two-hour drive from Los Angeles. It was not a handy place for friends to find their way there.

Before their move to New York, I received a glass paperweight with pictures of the Nixons and their two grandchildren, Jennie and Christopher and the dates of their grandchildren's birthdays. The Nixons adored their grandchildren and were very proud of them.

Julie's little girl, Jennie, at this time was an adorable 18-month-old child. She had beautiful blue eyes and her face looked just like Julie. Little Christopher, now 11 months old, was a blue-eyed blond resembling both of his parents. Pat did not want her girls and grandchildren too far away. She couldn't live without them.

Chapter 23

THE ERROR OF
THE WATERGATE TAPES
AND THE OPENING OF
THE NIXON LIBRARY

Last year the Nixons sold La Casa Pacifica estate for 1.2 million. They put down payment on a co-op apartment at Madison Avenue and 72nd. Street. The tenants disapproved, and the Nixons had to cancel the purchase in New York. Then, they put another payment down on an apartment at 817 Fifth Avenue. Again, the apartment residents protested. They even filed a lawsuit to compel the Nixons to give up some of the security. No one liked the F.B.I. to check into the private lives of the apartment tenants. Once again, the Nixons had to withdraw their offer

Since they couldn't find any suitable co-op apartments, they bought an attractive four-story, brownstone town house at 142 East 65th.Street in one of New York City's fashionable, neighborhood communities. They would be just a few blocks from Tricia and Ed Cox, where the Nixons would be able to visit little Christopher, their grandson. In Pennsylvania, Julie and David would be less than an hour and half apart from them. In February 1980, the Nixons moved to New York. Now Pat would find it easier to go out of her New York house and stroll down Park Avenue than it would be to saunter down on any street in San Clemente.

Most of the furniture and accessories, which were from all their former apartments and houses, were conveyed to their New York town house. Pat always utilized everything she had on hand. When required or as needed, she would have the item re-upholstered or painted to harmonized in the new background. The surroundings were radiant and pleasant. Pat's favorite golden, yellow color could be seen through out the home. Several historical and personal keepsakes and remembrances were chosen as accessories. Many porcelain figurines were included.

Gardens were always a source of pleasure for Pat. Here in this 45 x 20 "postage stamp" garden patio of the townhouse, she could pursue the joy of gardening—regardless how small the space. A little wading pool for Jennie and Christopher was in a corner of this very small patio for their enjoyment.

They were enjoying the fascination of New York and specially the joy of being near their children and grandchildren. Nixon had his office in the Jacob K. Javits Federal Center, #26, in lower Manhattan, New York. Often, Pat would come down for a surprise visit or to spend lunchtime with her husband. Both of them would enjoy visiting now and then to a museum or a nearby play. They delighted in eating out in restaurants and walking in Central Park. Pat liked to shop. Sometimes Tricia or Julie accompanied their mother on some of her shopping trips.

When I picked up the latest newspaper, March 13,1980, it stated that the National Archives would preserve the record of the Senate Watergate Committee and some of it would remain secret for 75 years. I thought 75 years was a long time, but no one on the committee objected about that condition. The Watergate records had to be transferred from the Library of Congress to the Archives. Some of the material was sensitive and classified and would be closed to public access for security reasons, or because it might invade a person's right of privacy. Otherwise, most of the material would be open to examination under guidelines drawn by the committee. Anyone denied access to the record could appeal.

In June 1980, the Nixons spent their fortieth wedding anniversary in Europe visiting Switzerland and Germany. Pat desired to get a glimpse or a look at her mother's German birthplace. It was a little too far for Pat to go, but she was tired and happy.

That summer of 1980 Richard Nixon's new book, "The Real War" was published. It was a universal and domestic best seller. Nixon said the United States must return to a tough U.S. Diplomacy and our military strength must be increased. That the next American President should convince the Soviet Union that the United States would display military troops to stop aggression wherever needed.

It was Ronald Reagan, who was reading Nixon's latest book during the 1980 presidential election. All of the men who worked on the Reagan campaign had worked in the Nixon administration. They admired Nixon for his knowledge of foreign policy issues.

At a six-half week trial of W.Mark Felt and Edward S. Miller, top F.B.I men were charged with approving nine illegal entries in hope of finding fugitive radicals of the Weather Underground, a militant, anti-war terrorist group. Tuesday, former Attorney-General Richard Kleindienst testified he never gave Miller and Felt his consent for the break-ins.

The prosecutors had called Nixon as a rebuttal witness in this case. When Nixon, on October 29,1980, walked in the courtroom, the supporters of the Weathermen Underground shouted at him. Even members of the federal jury observed him in excited surprise. Nixon just smiled at the jurors when he acknowledged that he was retired.

Nixon, in this remarkable court presence, said he always delegated authority for national covert entries to the F.B.I. Director, J. Edgar Hoover. At that time in 1972 and 1973, the F.B.I. Director did not need such approval. In his testimony, Nixon said the F.B.I. Break-ins were justified because America was at war in Vietnam. The F.B.I. Agents had secretly entered individual homes in a pursuit for elusive members of the Weather Underground. All this was done without Nixon's knowledge.

A few minutes after Nixon's continued in his testimony, the Weather Underground followers sitting in the courtroom suddenly erupted into a loud outcry, "War criminal!" "He's a liar!" and "Genocide!" U.S. Marshals had to evict them from the courtroom.

Nixon turned up at the trial because White House authorization or the favor of the break-ins was an important decisive question in the F.B.I. Case. He described the climate of the country at the close of the Vietnam War.

Nixon said, "What I am saying is that at that time, as far as my actions were concerned and the actions of others, we must recognize that things were quite different than they are today."

The Weather Underground took credit for terrorist bombings at government buildings. Nixon was always concerned about terrorism wherever it occurred.

He said, "When you have it in wartime, it may create attitudes in this country that delays the end of the war, the end of the killing, then it makes it much worse."

Nixon kept in touch with Ronald Reagan, the new President-elect, and his circle of advisers and staff. On November 1980, he sent a letter to Reagan regarding recommendations for appointments to his cabinet. Reagan thought highly of Nixon's confidence and trust. Out of Nixon's list of appointment instructions, Reagan chose William Casey as head of the C.I.A., Alexander Haig, as Secretary of State, and William French Smith as Attorney General.

Reagan realized that Nixon had special experience in certain fields, and so he accepted Nixon's advice for those areas. Because Nixon loved his country, he was willing to help where needed. For the next remaining eight years of the Reagan's presidency, that channel of communications between Nixon and Reagan stayed open for advice.

Pat and Dick had lots of mail stolen. In 1981, some of the books Nixon mailed out did not arrive at their destinations. One of the packages I mailed to Pat for her birthday, she did not receive either.

Just when I thought the Nixons had decided to locate permanently in New York and enjoy life there, they sold their townhouse in June 1981, and bought a country home in Saddle River, New Jersey.

I asked Pat, "Which one of you decided to move to New Jersey?"

She replied, "Both of us did. Sometimes the traffic became heavy by our place and was disturbing. I couldn't walk outdoors without being recognized. There were tourists and buses and people with cameras. We liked living close to Tricia and Eddie in the city. In New Jersey, we will have complete privacy which we don't have here in New York."

Saddle River, New Jersey, is a charming little town just under an hour journey to New York City. The new Nixon's home in Saddle River at 15 Charlden Drive was a fifteen room, redwood and fieldstone, multilevel house which lay on a wooded four-acre lot, with a tennis court and a swimming pool. The house was barely visible from other neighboring houses and the road.

For the first time, the Nixons did not have any of their previous old furniture. They sold it all with their New York town house, except for the memorabilia and small household decorative ornaments. Now Pat had to start from scratch. She engaged two interior designers to work closely with her in decorating the house. Throughout the house, it reflected Pat's good colorful taste. It reminded me of a beautiful French garden.

While workers supplied alarms, cameras, and underground power lines for security reasons, and a massive metal gate across the driveway, the Nixons spent the past several weeks at a Manhattan hotel and then at Julie and David's home in Berwyn, Pennsylvania.

Just a few days before they move in October to their new home, the Nixons stayed at the Hilton Inn in Woodcliff Lake. The Secret Service agents checked in with the Nixons and set up a base in a room next to their suite. The protectors of the Nixons always had a button in their ears. Every time one walked by in the hotel, everyone knew who they were. They stuck out like a sore thumb!

Several Republican Nixon supporters in the area planned to have private welcome parties after the Nixons moved into their new home in Saddle River. This happened in spite of the Eastern press denunciation of President Nixon. The tide was turning!

January 9, 1982, Nixon held his 73rd. Birthday occasion at "Lutice" restaurant in New York. This restaurant was noted for its excellent good food. It was one of his favorite places to eat. His two daughters, Tricia and Julie, surprised him by bringing their children to the birthday party.

Nixon was astonished. Pat was radiant with her smile. For two hours they talked with others dining there. He blew out the one candle situated on his dessert. Everyone applauded loudly. The Nixons left the restaurant very happy.

Pat turned 70 years of age in 1982. She looked much younger than her stated age. Her vigor and endurance was not what it used to be. One could still perceive the slight problem she had with her left arm and leg. Otherwise, Pat was fine. However, Pat did not want to go on long distant trips.

She did enjoy going to Disney World in Orlando, Florida, with her children and grandchildren. Pat laughed when Mickey Mouse welcomed her family. Her grandchildren loved their grandmother. She would make up games and play with them. They loved that attention. As Pat had given so much love and discipline with Julie and Tricia, her two daughters, when they were growing up, she gave the same love and affection to her grandchildren. Little Jennie liked to play "shoe store" with Pat. She could try on all Pat's shoes and decide which shoes she would buy. Both of them had lots of fun.

When it was not feasible for the grandchildren to play outside, the Nixons allowed them to play in the basement family game room. It was filled with games, toys, and tricycles they could enjoy.

On Wednesday, April 21, 1982, the Orange County Republicans held a G.O.P. fundraiser at the Disneyland Hotel in Anaheim, California. Richard Nixon was the guest speaker. A private pre-dinner reception was held before the fundraiser dinner and was sold out at $1,000.00 a couple. The $150.00 plate dinner raised about $120,000. It was Nixon's first West Coast schedule appearance since he moved to New York City.

When Nixon arrived, appearing robust and light hearted, with a Republican woman party official on each arm. Everyone gave him a standing ovation. Just before he gave his speech, the band played "Hail To The Chief."

Nixon said backers of a nuclear arms freeze are sincere in their desire for peace but fail to realize the United States must first rebuild its military might to bargain from a position of strength. The United States should demonstrate it has the will to restore the nuclear balance with the Soviet Union. They lure Soviet leaders to the bargaining table by tying arms control to economize cooperation."

"The Soviet Union needs a deal. Lets give them one—but for a price. The United States can bargain from a position of strength. Although, the United States has an edge in some areas of nuclear weaponry, such as submarines and launched missiles, I agree with President Reagan that the Kremlin now has edge in the most powerful and accurate weapons of all, based missiles."

"The Cuban missile crisis under President Kennedy and the 1973 Middle East Crisis during my administration are occasions when Soviets back down because of U.S. nuclear superiority."

Nixon continued, "it's never been any secret the Soviet Union is bent on world domination. Make no mistake; they want to rule the world, but not a world of dead cities. They are aggressive and expansionist, but they are not madmen."

Yearly, Nixon was churning out his many books. Numerous foreigners and Americans found his autographed books arriving in the mail. The receiver found their opinions and beliefs were being influenced and swayed. They changed their opinions of Richard Nixon.

It was difficult to keep up with Nixon's travels abroad and his other speeches at home in America. Every time I picked up the newspaper or listened to the TV media, a Nixon article or item was there. When he sent one of his books to me or copies of his newspaper accounts of certain events he attended, I was thrilled that the public was finally appreciating Richard Nixon.

Nixon was invited to be part of the delegation with Carter, Ford, and Kissinger to Sadat's funeral in Cairo, Egypt. After the funeral, he visited Saudi Arabia, Jordan, Tunisia, and Morocco on a tour of his own. The rulers of these countries received him warmly. Whenever Nixon could help any of the countries on his tour, he passed the word along to the President or Congress.

He still kept his office at 26 Federal Plaza in New York

City. Every morning he would get up at five o'clock. Then, Nixon would walk for thirty minutes, have breakfast next, and then, take a fifty-minute drive into New York City to his office.

Many times Nixon would join Pat and Tricia for lunch when Pat would drive to New York City to have her hair done at Elizabeth Arden Beauty Salon or just to visit Tricia at her apartment.

The Nixons watched very little television. Both enjoyed reading and considered television a waste of time, except for some important political event or ball games. When Pat was not engaged in reading novels and biographies, she was working with many different flowers in her garden.

Nixon had a fireplace in his study as well as the rest of the house. On a cold and wintry night, it made the house warm and cozy with fires crackling in the fireplaces. He did his best studying by a fireplace or writing on a new book. Sometimes in the middle of the night he would get up and go to his study to write and read.

Pat had lived in houses in California, Florida, New York, and now Saddle River, New Jersey. She liked living in California in the summer, Florida in the winter, and New York in the spring and fall. Now Saddle River would hold something special for her.

The Nixons would rather entertain at their new home than dine out at a restaurant. When they did go out, it was only at homes of close friends.

Pat and Richard Nixon celebrated their 42nd wedding anniversary in June 1982. It lasted because of their same general beliefs and harmonious cooperation. It was truly an enduring love match.

A few days after their anniversary, Pat was not feeling so good. Then, on Sunday evening, she was admitted to the Valley Hospital for pulmonary infection and was expected to remain there for three days or more. Pat was to undergo a battery of medical tests to help find the solution to her health problem.

In June 1982, a hostile split Supreme Court ruled that Richard Nixon or any other President, could not be sued for activity executed as a principal leader—even for contemplated disregarding the rights of Americans.

This determination aroused angry disagreement from four justices, who attacked the ruling which imperiled the Constitution most fundamental statutes by putting the president "above the law" and reviving to the old concept that the king can do no wrong."

This contention by the Supreme Court was a triumph for Richard Nixon and a defeat for Ernest Fitzgerald, a Pentagon "whistle-blower", who made this lawsuit against Nixon. Justice Lewis Powell wrote the majority opinion. "There remains the constitutional remedy of impeachment. A rule of absolute immunity for the president will not leave the nation without sufficient protection against misconduct on the part of the chief executive."

Justice Byron White led the objection by arguing, "attaching absolute immunity to the office of the president . . . places the president above the law."

Fitzgerald believed he was fired in 1969 by President Nixon in retaliation for uncovering aircraft billions costs exceeding which was estimated in the contract. He had a thirteen year legal battle and than he was reinstated at the Pentagon. The Air Force had to pay $200,000 in legal costs, which Fitzgerald piled up to get his job back.

This decision came out at this time of the anniversary of the Watergate break-in. In a separate decision the Supreme Court ruled 8-1 that the aides of a president were allowed limited immunity-giving them less protection than a president.

In 1982, the other researchers, who studied the White House Nixon tapes within the National Archives in Washington, D.C., came to the same conclusion as I had when

I listened to the tapes. As far as I was concerned, the transcripts furnished by the Federal Bureau of Investigation on the tapes should not been presented as testimony and proof in the Watergate trials without studying human speech and the structure and development of the English language.

Because of the inferior bad condition of the uttered vocal recordings, no wonder anyone had to rely on the printed transcripts, which were presented. The tapes were too vague and unreliable. The use of the transcripts utilized during the Watergate trial was inadequate of picturing the distinct clear segments of the recorded dialogue correctly. Portions of the discussion were slanted in a way, which would make their usage in any judicial body extremely debatable.

The Watergate transcripts I discovered were not the truth as the Washington Post depicted them to be. There is a difference when listening to someone talk and reading a transcript. Everyone surmised that the transcript would help us understand the conversations on the tapes more plainly without altering or influencing our discernment and comprehension.

Some of Nixon's comments on the transcripts might be construed that he absolutely understood all the facts given to him. But in any uttered discussion, it may be just an example of a listener's input to the speaker expressing orally one's thoughts, opinions and feelings.

Then again, perhaps Nixon did not perceive any of the communication passed along to him. For every hour of conversation, it represented hundreds of hours of transcribing work. No one was sure in this tough job what to use. The tapes had to be rewound to make sure what was really said.

The F.B.I. transcribers misidentified persons who were talking. Lewd filthy words were not transcribed for the same grade of preciseness for various speakers. For words, which were absent, all together or obscure on the tapes, they invented words and filled in the gaps. Many of the conversations were constructed in a way to compel persons to do so. If someone did not know anything about the Watergate affair, one would find it difficult to understand what was said on the tapes.

I had to remind people that we don't talk the way we write. Words such as "that," "it", or "this" are often difficult to rebuild from the transcripts only. On some conversations, I heard indistinct sounds. I couldn't hear any words as listed on the transcripts. For the life of me, I couldn't figure out how they arrived at what was said.

Then, August 17,1983, Pat suffered another stroke which landed her in a New York hospital. She felt ill and was driven by a Secret Service agent to see her physician. The doctor diagnosed it as a mild stroke and put her in the hospital for five days. This time her speech was not slurred or no results of paralysis like her severe stroke in 1976. Now Pat was 71. She appeared to be recovering completely and in good health after many tests at the hospital.

In Yorba Linda, a group of civic leaders met with the Yorba Linda Elementary School District to arrange the purchase of the small white house where President Richard Nixon was born. The house was built by Nixon's father, and later, it was owned by the school district. Nixon was born in the front bedroom of the house. They hoped to turn it into a museum.

Richard Nixon had loved his devoted mother so very much. She meant a lot to him. In October 1983, my mother, who my husband and I took care of in our home, died because of her heart problem. We had difficulty getting her to the rural mountain hospital on Monday. The ambulance had a flat tire coming down the mountain road. A second ambulance had to be dispatched. Every day I visited her. Then, on Friday when I was going to the hospital twenty-five miles away, I had tire trouble also. It was time for mother to go, and she managed to stay until I could be with her.

Richard Nixon was so touched about my mother's death

that he wrote a personal handwritten letter about my mother. Nixon was glad that I cared so long for my mother in my home. I knew how he wished he could have done the same as I did then. I cherished that letter because I knew how compassionate he was.

Now, 71, in 1984, Richard Nixon was waging a difficult campaign to win back respect before history would write it differently. Once again he put himself in the spotlight by appearances on television and personal viewpoints around the country. Nixon had become witty and philosophical.

I remembered his interview on April, 1984, C.B.S. television, Nixon was joking. "They say it's the responsibility of the media to look at government—especially the President—with a microscope. I don't argue with that, but when they use a proctoscope, it's going too far."

He also propelled himself into planning a $25 million dollar presidential library to be built by private money in Yorba Linda, California. By selling three television interviews, he raised $500,000 to start the building fund for the library. Nixon unveiled a model of his future library for all the public to see and view.

Of all the presidents in the United States none have surpassed Richard Nixon in his ability to come back from defeat and personal reversals. Persistence was his middle name. He was leaving an indelible mark on our country and the world, which no one could erase.

I remember what he said while in the White House: "I believe in the battle, whether it is the battle of a campaign, or the battle of this office . . . . That is my way."

History will judge him as an ingenious diplomat who achieved détente with Moscow, Soviet Union and engineered ties with Peking, China. As I look at the tension and terrorism in the world today, Nixon's foreign policy looks much better. He had a superior record than any other president since World War II.

The Republican National Convention, which met on August 24, 1984, did not mention Richard Nixon's name at the meeting. However, one unidentified delegate wore his sentiment on his coat lapel. He wore a button, which said, "I'm For Nixon," and supported Nixon's views.

Nixon was an old master at the art of extracting and using information. He would use the political network and any back door contacts. After Reagan's 1984 re-election, Nixon sent a memo to Donald Regan, chief of staff, regarding his views how to organize the staff for the second term of the White House.

Nixon's mind was as sharp and immaculate as ever.

If anyone, who was a President in the White House, Nixon would be one of the people on the list, who he would call for advice in a world crisis. After President Carter had normalized relations with China in 1978, none of his people had thought the new arrangement would alter or change the bilateral coalition between the United States and its allies. Nixon brought this to Carter's attention and appraised each important ally. As far as I was concerned, Nixon was the only foreign policy leader at that time who had that kind of global outreach.

Now, seventy-two years old, Nixon did not show any signs of slowing down. He would be driven by one of the Secret Service agents from Saddle River, New Jersey, to his New York office. After arriving at his office at 7:30 a.m., he would spend the next two hours writing to relatives, old friends, to those who were suffering the death of a loved one, or persons who were sick in the hospital.

Nixon did not like to waste time. To do so, it made him feel culpable and blameworthy. Whatever he contemplated, he questioned whether it was the right thing to do. Would it make an impact on the world government or the people in it? That was how he saw the situation at hand.

The year of 1985, President Nixon voluntarily gave up his Secret Service protection. He decided that taxpayers did not need to pay the extra expense of protecting him.

In 1985, his sixth book, "No More Vietnams" was on the bestseller list for four and half months. He stated that the Vietnam War was a just war. Victory by the United States was unnecessarily thrown away by the Democrat Congress aided by the liberal media. Nixon declared we shouldn't back any anti-communist rebels unless we resolve to WIN! "The Chicago Tribune" and the "National Review" praised the book. However, the Washington Post" and "The New York Times" ripped it to tatters.

In September 1985, President Ronald Reagan spoke frequently with Richard Nixon in preparing for his summit meeting in November at Geneva, Switzerland with the Soviet leader, Mikhail Gorbachev. He agreed with Nixon that the United States desired peace, and that the Soviet Union needs peace.

Then, the press got wind of the Nixon-Reagan talks. They asked Reagan if he had taken or sought advice from Nixon. Reagan admitted that President Nixon had great experience and was most knowledgeable on international affairs. Nixon had a number of meetings with Soviet leader, Leonid Brezhnev. The problem with Reagan in his four years of his first term, all three Soviet leaders kept dying on him. Nixon was the one who had talked to them previously and had the information. Reagan agreed with Nixon that the Soviet Union and the United States had to live in the world together. It didn't mean that we had to love each other or that we had to change each other's system.

The year of 1986 began with Frank Sturgis, one of the Watergate burglar's, filing an lawsuit against his prosecutors to re-open his case to clear his name. He based his case on recently revealed F.B.I. records to prove that prosecutors withheld intelligence, and the F.B.I. Workers could not find no wiretaps planted on the telephones in the Democrat headquarters after the June 1972 Watergate break-in. His lawyer, Edward Rubin, charged that U.S. District Judge John

Silica compelled Sturgis and the other men involved into pleading guilty to the break-in. A writ of error Coram Nobis petition was filed to re-open a case based on inaccuracies and oversights on the earlier trial.

The annual convention of American Newspaper Publishers Association editors asked Nixon to address their group in March 1986. There he buried his hatchet with the new media. At this convention Nixon impressed many of the editors. One of the women attending was Katherine Graham, the publisher of "The Washington Post" newspaper and the "Newsweek" magazine, was so swayed by what Nixon said, she ordered her editors to write a story about Nixon. I wasn't sure about Katharine Graham's change of mind. In the past she had called Richard Nixon a Dr. Jekyll and Dr.Hyde and other mean things. I was glad Richard Nixon did not want to cooperate with that publishing company because of what they had done previously.

However, some political friends convinced Nixon it would be better to grant the "Newsweek" magazine their request for a story. Instead of an article, it resulted in a cover story, which surprised everyone. When all the journalistic enemies of Nixon saw the Washington Post change their position on Nixon, they decided to drop the fight, too. No way did Nixon admit anything to them or apologize. It was all done on his conditions and not on the terms of "Newsweek" magazine.

Reams of Watergate papers and tapes had been in legal limbo for twelve years. On April 29,1986, Assistant Attorney General Charles Cooper in the President Reagan administration wrote a legal thirty page memorandum that President Reagan was obligated to support any claims of executive privilege by Richard Nixon to prevent the release of the White House tapes and papers.

The Office of Management and Budget asked for the Justice Department for their opinion. It stated, "A former president's executive privilege would be of little value if it were dependent upon the ratification of his successors. He felt that an incumbent president should respect a former president's claim of executive privilege without judging the validity of the claim."

The opinion did not change regulations governing release of the papers and tapes. Even though, six sets of regulations had been proposed at different times to cover release of the papers by the National Archives, but many lawsuits were filed to block and halt disclosure. After the Watergate trial tapes were released, former Nixon staff members blocked access to release more documents stored in a warehouse.

By October 3, the House Government Operations Committee accused the Office of Management and Budget of subverting the regulatory process by giving the Reagan White House and Justice Department time to prepare a course of action, which could obstruct public release of Nixon's presidential documents. If the legal opinion had not been issued, Richard Nixon would have to go to court to uphold his executive privilege claim to combat anyone seeking release of his documents and tapes.

Nixon kept in touch with old friends by phone or letter. I was still glad to be on his list of contacts and supporters. It was a rare time if he visited others. If one would visit him at Saddle River, his dinners were less social than his White House affairs. His golf game did not get his attention as it did in the past. He even took time to visit a Saddle River second grade class talking about citizenship. If any child had a birthday, Nixon would celebrate that day by playing "Happy Birthday" on the piano. Each child was delighted that a president took the time to participate for his birthday.

In January 9, 1988, Richard Nixon celebrated his seventy-fifth birthday. His mind was sharper and more alert than ever. He was an inspiration to me-his excitement about life, not looking to the past but looking ahead to the future. I always regarded with high esteem his valiant spirit and his ability to contend with overwhelming hardship and trouble. In all the battles of life, he never gave up to fight back.

As I had discussed with Pat previously in our meetings, I wished he could have spent more time then with his family. When he did take time with the girls, it was quality time. Pat said he would go out of his way to always go to father-daughter events for them. Because as a father he always made everything so enjoyable, the girls always wanted to be with and for him. Now Tricia and Julie's children, Christopher, Jennie, Alex, and Melanie enjoyed the same fun.

The grandchildren didn't call Nixon, "Grandpa". They called him "Ba" because they couldn't enunciate the word. Therefore, the word, "Ba" stuck. Even, they called Pat Nixon as "Ma."

Christopher, Tricia's son, often went with grandfather Nixon to a "New York Mets" baseball game. If one of them watched a baseball game on TV, they would differentiate the results over the telephone to question whether it was a slide on first or second base or a home run.

Nixon had a strong sense of history and foreign policy, which made an important, striking collision on many views of world affairs. I always considered him a strong president and a great leader. He kept all his distress and torment inside. I admired Nixon for bearing all his pain and heartache in dignity and how he never complained to others.

When the story is fully understood, I hoped the people would agree that Nixon never profited or sought personal gain. Neither was he a womanizer like some other presidents we knew. All he wanted was to have a peaceful world. Surely, I hoped Nixon's achievements would not be dominated by the Watergate affair or by any mistakes he made. His major mistake was delegating too much authority to others. This caused abuse of that authority and proved unfortunate for the Nixon presidency.

As far as I was concerned, I never knew anyone who was

kind, thoughtful and unselfish as Nixon was. Instead of thinking about himself, he put his country first. His life's mission was to preserve a generation of lasting peace.

He relied on the book of Isaiah 2:4, "And he shall judge among the nations, and shall rebuke many people; and they shall beat their swords into plowshares, and their spears into pruning hooks; nation shall not lift up sword against nation, neither shall they learn war anymore."

It was his religious convictions, which carried him through life and his outlook personally and politically. He always remembered that the Bible was always open on his mother and father's breakfast table. At all times his parents impelled him to read the Bible everyday. It was Nixon's inner faith In God that gave him strength to carry on through the times of injustice and trial of crisis.

At 75 years of age, Nixon still guarded his privacy and loved to retreat to secluded places. It was there he could look up and meditate and think. By playing his piano or listening to classical music, he unwound and relaxed. Now, he would take Brownie, his dog, for a two-mile long walk each morning. Swimming also gave him exercise he needed.

He published his seventh book, "1999-Victory Without War" which he hoped it would influence the presidential election year and the debate on foreign policy. It also re-examined the twenty-first century and how we can make it a century of peace. The next twelve years will determine what we could do to work toward that end.

In 1989, I was stricken by a minor stroke the last of February. I had frightened my husband who was bedridden. Pat was very distressed by my medical problem. By May 2, my own husband passed away. The Nixons sent flowers for the funeral and their personal thoughts to help me through my grief. Since I was still on my walker, my life and body was quite muddled during the funeral and the rest of my time in recovery.

Richard Nixon turned seventy-seven in January 1990. He always appreciated my birthday remembrance and was grateful for my years of friendship. Then, his eighth book, "In The Arena", a memoir, was published. I believed that this book was one of the best Nixon had written. It had been written from the heart and personal experience. I was glad to receive this book from him. No wonder it stayed on the best seller lists for months.

Richard Nixon was in good health. In March, however, his medical doctor discovered that Nixon was experiencing a mild supreventricular heart-rhythm disorder, which at that time was only a nonlife-imminent heart condition. But, the doctor told him he had to cut down on his schedule and to eliminate his morning daily walks, and continue taking his medication. Except, for a slight case of hard of hearing, he was fine.

However, Pat Nixon suffered degenerative arthritis in her neck and was in continual physical pain. Her bronchitis and emphysema caused her to have a much-reduced breathing lung capacity and to tire easily.

In June, the Nixons celebrated their 50th. Golden Wedding anniversary Nixon was more devoted to Pat, his wife, than in the past. Their deep friendship was based on a very loving relationship. I admired his personal intimate concern with Pat. I knew they never demonstrated affection in public, but in looking at their eyes their love glowed for one another.

On July 19, the Richard Nixon Library and Birthplace opened for the first time. It had been paid for by $25 million private donations. To everyone's surprise, the Nixon Library did not take federal taxpayer money from the government. This is the only presidential library which does this.

The library, adjoining to the little white clapboard house, which his father built near the railroad tracks, tells the story of Nixon's life from Congressman, Senator, Vice-President and President. Now, 77 years of age, Nixon did not dream that the Library and Birthplace would become the third largest tourist attraction in California.

There is a place in the museum, which is dedicated to the life of Pat Nixon. The exhibit includes awards, personal letters, and many photographs depicting her journey through her private and public life. The red coat from her 1972 tour of China, and her bluish-green beaded 1973 Inaugural gown, and the 1952 black-and-white polka-dot dress she wore when Nixon was Vice-President with President Eisenhower.

As the Nixon Library and Museum was being planned, it was Pat Nixon who supervised the planning of the beautiful gardens there. Instead of having many rose bushes on the museum grounds, Pat wanted the natural beauty of the gardens be lovely all year. Therefore, all through the library and museum grounds, one can see Pat's love of beauty and handiwork.

The dedication of the Presidential Library and Birthplace was an important occurrence in the life of the Nixons. Forty thousand assembled outside in 90-degree heat and spilled over into the surrounding streets around the library grounds. Inside the building, invited guests could be seated on chairs and bleacher space.

Before the ceremony started in Yorba Linda, California, a welcome home banner had to be taken down. The sign was intended to honor Richard Nixon. It missed the mark with a misspelling of the Nixon name—NOXIN—just in reverse.

However, some protestors showed up for the event. Two of them were evicted. Outside on the boulevard, people marched and carrying signs saying, "Richard repent," "He's still Tricky Dick."

While we were getting settled in our seats, the Santa Ana Youth Band, the Disneyland All American College Band and the University of Southern California Marching Bands entertained us. The Indio Drill Tam and the Hispanic Dancers of Santa Ana supplied the fanfare and excitement to pep us up. Several hundred white doves were suddenly released when a flourish of trumpets sounded. In walked President Herbert Bush, Ronald Reagan, Gerald Ford, and Richard Nixon with all their wives. I couldn't remember when I had seen that many Presidents and First Ladies grouped together all in one spot. It was a historic moment. The audience roared their approval, and the applause was deafening.

The Yorba Linda Boy and Girl Scouts posted the colors. Then Vickie Carr sang "The Star Spangled Banner", our national anthem, which inspired us how fortunate we were to live in peace and freedom. In his opening prayer, Evangelist Billy Graham spoke of the upheavals and the uncertainties through which the world passed during the Nixon presidency.

William E. Simon, who was Nixon's Secretary of the Treasury and also president of the board of directors of the Library and Birthplace Foundation, gave the welcome to the audience. He mentioned the controversies, which surrounded Nixon's political career. Then, he said, "Despite all of that, as well as the unrelenting hostility from the national media, President Nixon managed to lead America out of the Vietnam War and bring back our P.O.W.'s."

Gerald Ford was the first of the three presidents present to give his remarks, "It does not diminish the roles many others in our country have played in the expansion of democratic freedoms to say that you, Dick Nixon, have the gratitude of men and women everywhere who cherish peace with liberty. Because you loved your country, and because you had the courage to serve this day is a celebration richly deserved by you and by Pat."

When Ronald Reagan was next to speak I remembered some of what he said.

"Richard Nixon is a man who understands the world. He understands politics, power, and the forces of history. Whether with Mao or Brezhnev, De Gaulle or Gandhi, President Nixon was the first among equals. A man whose foreign policy was universally acknowledged as brilliant. During my eight years in the White House, I relied on his insight and wisdom, and I will always be grateful for the benefit of his seasoned expertise. Pat Nixon, as the First Lady, is the true, unsung hero of the Nixon Administration, and our country owes her a great debt of gratitude."

President Bush gave the longest remembrance speech. When Nixon was President, George Herbert Bush had worked in different offices for him. They had a special relationship over the years. He praised Nixon and Pat as the First Lady.

"Richard Nixon helped change the course, not only of America, but of the entire world. He believed in returning power to the people; so he created revenue sharing. And that young people should be free to choose their future; therefore, Richard Nixon ended the draft. And he helped the United States reach new horizons in space and technology. He began a pioneering cancer initiative that gave hope and life to millions. And he knew that the great outdoors is precious but fragile, so he created the Environmental Protection Agency, an historic step to help preserve and widely use our natural resources."

"Future generations will remember him most, in my view, for dedicating his life to the greatest cause offered any President—the cause of peace among nations."

"As First Lady, we remembered Pat Nixon who championed the Right to Read program, helped bring the Parks to People program to the disadvantaged. And she was the most widely traveled First Lady, visiting five continents and twenty two nations, overcoming the poverty and tragedy of her childhood to become a mirror of America's heart and love. A gracious First Lady who ranks among the most admired woman of post-war America."

All of us were overwhelmed by all the praise heaped upon Richard Nixon and Pat that day. Nixon remained a hero to all of the women who worked in his campaigns or or

as a personal secretary. They were there that day. Along the Nixon journey, just common typical men and women, who had worked for him one time another along the way, wanted to be part of Nixon's celebrated dedication. They knew he spoke up for them. It was their turn to stand together for Richard Nixon.

Now it was Nixon's turn to speak. As usual he spoke from the heart, and did not use any notes. Nixon had a photographic memory and wrote all his own speeches. The rest of the presidents needed help from speechwriters to present their ideas and stories. I always admired him for his ability to speak without a script.

Nixon recalled the days when he was a young man when he used to lie awake in the white small clapboard house his father built and dreamed of far away places. "It was a long way from Yorba Linda to the White House," he stated. In his dedication speech, Nixon referred about Pat's childhood home in Cerritos was burned down because of arson, and many worried there wouldn't be a memorial to Pat Nixon. "But there is a memorial to Pat Nixon. Her memorial is her children and grandchildren."

Some of his other thoughts that day, I recorded for history.

"What you will see here, among other things is a personal life. The influence of a strong family of inspirational ministers, of great teachers. You will see a political life, running for Congress, running for the Senate, running for governor, running for president three times. And you will see the life of a great nation, 77 years of it. A period in which we had unprecedented progress for the United States. And you will see great leaders, leaders who changed the world, who helped to make the world what we have today."

If you take no risks, you will suffer no defeats. But without risks, you will win no victories. You must never be satisfied with success, and you should never be discouraged by failure. Failure can be sad. But the greatest sadness is not to try and fail, but to fail to try at all. Only when you become engaged in a cause greater than yourself, can you be true to yourself."

"Let history record that we just did not save the world from communism, but that we helped make the world safe for freedom. That is the great challenge for Americans today."

Many of us cheered and some of us shed tears as Nixon spoke. Then, it was Pat who put the "frosting on the cake" and surprised everyone by walking carefully to the microphone and speaking slow with careful thought. Her remarks were simple-"I just want to thank you for your years of loyalty and support."

Pat was astonished by the standing ovation the crowd gave her. Everyone stood up and gave her resounding applause. She even raised her arms trying to quiet the continuing cheers.

Richard Nixon and his daughters beamed with enjoyment. When Pat finally finished her speech, Nixon put his arm lovingly around his wife and accompanied her off the platform. The crowd gave her another standing ovation. Pat was happy but tired.

Finally, Nixon waved his hand and thousands of red, white, and blue balloons came down. After Dr. Norman Vincent Peale's benediction and Vickie Carr's rendition of "God Bless America," we felt we were on "cloud nine" of joy and inspiration. It was a grand finale for a wonderful day for the Nixons, as well as for his loyal friends and supporters.

That evening, as old friends and loyal Republican supporters we gathered at the Century Plaza Hotel in Los Angeles, California to continue to celebrate the roots, life and legacy of Richard Nixon, the architect of peace, marking the Library dedication festivities.

In the California Lounge at the hotel, we attended a private reception at 7 p.m. preceding the celebration gala dinner. I thought Pat looked more physically weaker than when she was First Lady. Her hair was much darker and shorter than in previous years. But, there was Pat ignoring her pain and standing for an hour greeting old friends.

I was amazed how incredibly sharp her mind was. She could recall where she saw each one of us. Pat was delighted I could come. I hugged her. At that moment, I didn't realize and not knowing some day in the future, she would be gone from my life as a very dear friend. Pat introduced me as a special friend to others in the room. She had not lost her sense of humor. We all laughed as Pat recalled old memories and many funny stories from the past. Her spirit had grown stronger. I could see how content and serene she was. The Library dedication events brought back all the delightful good things she enjoyed at the White House, which surpassed all the bad things, which happened to her husband. It pleased her that her husband finally received acceptance from others, and that his reputation was finally restored.

Nixon was the outgoing, social one. He was playing his public role as he greeted each one of us. Shaking hands and so friendly, I was wondering If he was planning to run again for some major office. Also, he remembered each one of us as Pat had recalled, too. It touched each one of us that Nixon never forgot those who worked for him one time another and became his loyal friends.

By the look on his face and the words Nixon was expressing, I knew the grand opening of his presidential library was a very happy moment in his life. However, I knew his restless energy would keep him busy in advising presidents, giving interviews, and speaking out for world peace wherever he could.

By the fall of 1990, Nixon became hard working and diligent in writing another book, "Seize The Moment: America's challenge in a one Superpower World" on foreign policy for America in the twenty first century. In the continuing changing world of the Soviet Union, Nixon had to do more research on what was happening there. This caused many re-writes as the book manuscript progressed.

I was wondering how many more books Nixon would continue to write. I knew when this book was published; I would receive another as I had in the past.

Nixon had to be the most important preeminent advocate to help Russia to recover from the Cold War. He had a vision for the Russian world, which the United States must not fail to lead. Nixon advised that we should get the public's attention focused on foreign policy. It would not be popular but necessary. Because Nixon loved his country and freedom first, he refused to vanish from the scene. He determined to speak out and warned what might happen if certain actions weren't carried out.

Pat told me I should come around in October, especially at Halloween time. She said this holiday was one of Dick's favorite events. They invite all of the children in the town and their parents to come. It would be a festive time.

Dick loved passing out candy to the children. She said it was good for Dick. Pat thought he needed this activity to bolster his spirits. Nixon would greet each child and their parents, as if he was still on the campaign trail. Both enjoyed it.

I mentioned to Pat that this warm display by her husband all through his life caused more people to vote for him more than any other person. She recognized what I was trying to say.

Some people were listening to Nixon. The Republican Congressional Committee asked him to address their group, December 7, 1990, on the Middle East situations of the Persian Gulf and in Lithuania. That speech was called "A War About Peace."

Richard Nixon continued to send copies of his speeches to me because he knew I would get his message out. When each speech arrived, I was impressed with his knowledge of the situation on hand.

He spoke about Mikhail Gorbachev of the Soviet Union—

"Gorbachev had no choice. He had to retrench abroad and reform at home. His first priority then and now, was to restore the health of the Soviet economy. This was the most revolutionary decision of a Soviet leader since the Russian Revolution, which brought the Communists to power in 1917. For seventy years, Soviet economic policy had served Soviet foreign policy. Now Soviet foreign policy had to serve Soviet economic policy."

This explains Gorbachev actions according to Nixon:

"He withdrew the Red Army from Afghanistan not only because it was costing men as well as money, but primarily because it helped create a peaceful image for Gorbachev which opened the door for good relations with the West and economic assistance he needed for his desperately sick economy."

Nixon continued, "We are in the Gulf for two major reasons. Sadam Hussein has unlimited ambitions to dominate one of the most important strategic areas in the world. Because he has oil, he has the means to acquire the weapons he needs for aggression against his neighbors, including at some future time, a nuclear arsenal. If he succeeds in Kuwait, he will attack others and will use whatever weapons he has, including chemical and nuclear to achieve his goals. If we don't stop him now, we will have to stop him later when the cost in the lives of young Americans will be infinitely greater."

"Always remember that where an insatiable aggressor is involved, while war is bad, a bad peace is worse because it can lead to a bigger war."

Chapter 24

1991-1994
THE FINAL YEARS

On Nixon's seventy-eighth birthday, (January 9, 1991) he was more concerned about what was going on in the Soviet Union. He thought the United States was too busy with the Persian Gulf War and not watching and observing what Gorbachev had used his Soviet armed forces to kill and terrorize the Lithuania people. Why weren't we standing up for the captive nations?

Nixon called the White House and let the Bush administration know that their policies on Gorbachev and the Soviet Union were very wrong. He told them to watch out for Gorbachev. The other republics would be next in line.

As Nixon predicted, the Soviet Union tanks moved into Latvia, January 20, causing terror everywhere. Then Nixon was flabbergasted and astounded when he heard the Secretary of State, James A. Baker, had arranged and transacted a joint Soviet/U.S. agreement with Aleksandre Bessmertnykko, the Soviet foreign minister calling for suspension of active hostilities in Iraq. Nixon was sure that Bush was angry as he was concerning the events, which had happened in the last few days.

Nixon knew that Gorbachev did not plan to take apart or wreck communism, but to arrange an impractical pursuit for a stamp of reform, which would be consistent and harmonious to communism. Many of those who were urging reform inside the Soviet Union did not trust Gorbachev. They backed away from him. Boris Yelstin was the one who started the organized activities working toward reform. However, they lacked a plan or process to affect a change in their country in spite of popular support throughout the Soviet Union.

There were those in the Soviet Union who advocated the people a choice between bread and freedom. They played on the Soviet people's fears by asking them if they wanted gross unemployment and massive inflation. So the Russian people there had to decide who would deliver them from the same outcome.

The disciplinary act of the Gorbachev regime on the republics did not terminate the people's support for independence and rebellion against the Kremlin's control. This was the climate and environment of the Soviet Union before Nixon decided to go there to visit with Gorbachev, Yelstin, and other Russian leaders. Nixon had done his homework by researching everything that Gorbachev had said or done. He was scheduled to give a speech in Moscow at the Institute of World Economics and International Relations on March 22.

The day before Nixon's departure, Pat celebrated another birthday, March 16. Tricia, her oldest daughter, had come down from New York City to be with her mother. On the kitchen table were many birthday cards. Bouquets of flowers from friends and admirers were displayed around the family room. My attractive "forever" flower bouquet which I gave her, made Pat's heart sing in gratitude for my birthday remembrance.

Pat also told me they planned to move from Saddle River to nearby Park Ridge, New Jersey, in ten days. The packing had already started.

What a job she said! I could sympathize with her because I would be moving to my new home about the same time. We wished each other's moves would go smoothly.

Their beautiful fifteen-room home on four acres in Saddle River, New Jersey was now sold to a Japanese businessman for several million dollars. They had bought a three bedroom, four-story townhouse condominium in nearby Park Ridge, New Jersey. Pat said that they would prefer to spend their time and energy on other activities than trying to keep up the Saddle River house.

The cost of security was tremendous. The new home would be less expensive to keep in existing state of repair and maintenance.

The new residence would be more comfortable and bright. Pat liked the extra garden space and the brilliant, yellow sun parlor, which was attached to the townhouse. She would still have plenty of room for her grandchildren to come to visit, and also for her to tinker around in the garden when she felt like it.

Also, Nixon transferred his office from New York City to 577 Chestnut Ridge Road, Woodcliff Lake, New Jersey. He would be closer to the Park Ridge residence and wouldn't have to endure the long drive to New York City.

Nixon had arrived In the Soviet Union prepared for his visit. The Soviet Union and the United States Press did not wish to cover Nixon's seventh trip to the Soviet Union. When he was talking with the common ordinary, Russian people, Nixon attracted the news media's attention.

The people told Nixon about their fears, plight, and expectations. The populace was still as poor as when he visited the Soviet Union in 1959.

Then, Nixon gave a speech to the Institute of World Economics and International Relations in Moscow, March 22, 1991. His speech, "Moment of Truth" was well received by the Russians. Nixon warned them, "Not to turn back to the 'so-called good old days', which would be tragic and futile. Those attempts would always fail. Great people show what they are made of not when the going is easy, but during the times of crisis, when the going is tough as you showed in World War Two. This is your greatest crisis, your moment of truth."

The New York Times newspaper gave better coverage than the Washington Post. I wasn't surprised at the Post's coverage. They hated to admit Nixon was still around.

Bernard Shaw of CNN's television media interviewed Richard Nixon (Live) in New York on Saturday, April 13, regarding America's mission. Then, Sunday Eve, I watched him on "60 Minutes" program to press the need for the U.S.A. to change their attention from Gorbachev to Yelstin.

On Monday Nixon met with President George Herbert Bush to discuss with him regarding the information he found out in the Soviet Union. Bush wanted strange ties to the republics, but he desired to rely less on Gorbachev. He was not sure that Yelstin was the best reformer in the Soviet Union. On this one point on Yelstin, Bush did not take Nixon's advice.

Three days later, Nixon took off for the Bahamas for a vacation. His frustration and disgust regarding the Russian situation drove him to a place where he could meditate and think for a while. But, that vacation was cut very short. He became very restless. Four days later, Nixon was back to work in continuing writing on his new book.

However, the Russians went to the polls in June and elected Yelstin as President in their first free Russian election. They also repudiated communism by changing the name of the city of Leningrad to St. Petersburg. Long before Reagan had called the Soviet Union "the evil empire", Nixon had stated these same words over and over. The opposition had been so occupied with the unpopular Vietnam War, they weren't listening or stopped up their ears at anything Nixon was uttering.

My neurologist surgeon recommended in July that I should have major surgery on my back. I told Pat and Dick regarding my hospitalization. They wished me well as I was to undergo surgery that week. I had a difficult time in coming out of the anesthetic. The nurses and doctors were talking to me trying to get me awake. After many hours I finally woke up.

What really surprised the nurse's station were the many telephone messages I received. The one phone call which I received got their most attention was the one from Richard Nixon. They were wondering if I was a V.I.P. person to receive such a call.

Later, I told them I was only a personal friend of the family. Again, Nixon was only being a thoughtful person inquiring of the health or the outcome of my surgery. I never forgot Nixon's kindness and thoughtfulness. From then on, some of the nursing staff wanted to hear the rest of my story. They were fascinated by it.

Pat would still keep in touch by telephone or by letter with friends. Since she didn't have any secretary to help answer her mail, her German housekeeper, Heidi Retter, aided her with other correspondence when necessary. Two days a week, Pat did the cooking. Nixon always enjoyed Pat's weekly meat loaf along with a salad she made. She always liked to have lots of fresh vegetables with the meal, and fresh fruit for dessert. Nixon relished Mexican food, but Pat enjoyed pasta. Both of them liked to eat in the kitchen while taking pleasure in watching the beautiful view outside.

I was surprised that Pat woke up at seven in the morning—just like I did. She said she only watched the morning TV programs if there was some important issue or a special guest she was particularly interested in. Pat always watched the evening news, and then she went to bed early. Neither did she go to the theater. In the family room, they had a large television screen and VCR. From their library of film classics, they could view whatever they chose.

Pat enjoyed reading books more than television. She would send Heidi, her housekeeper, to the library every week to get more reading material. At one time Pat was interested in football games. She now leaves the viewing of sports to her husband or the rest of the family.

In November, she attended the dedication of the Ronald Reagan Presidential Library in Simi Valley, California. Five other First Ladies—Betty Ford, Barbara Bush, Nancy Reagan, Rosalynn Carter, and Lady Bird Johnson came, too. But it was too much of an affair for Pat Nixon. She frightened everyone by collapsing there. Pat was much sicker than we all thought. Surely this would be her last public appearance.

When the "Good Housekeeping" magazine most admired women poll (1991) came out, Pat Nixon was listed as number five on the list. She had moved up to number five from number six. What was amazing, she had been in the top ten lists for twenty-one years. No other First Lady ever had that distinction. After the media put Jacqueline Kennedy on a pedestal, the people across the country still related to Pat Nixon. Doesn't that say something how the people really felt? Women knew Pat Nixon had her share of disappointments and defeats, and she did not have an easy life. They said this courageous lady is like one of us. Both related to one another and could understand each other's circumstances and situations.

By the look on her face, I was sure Pat was enjoying her warm, private life and a cherished relationship with her husband. She was relishing the time spent with her daughters nearby and the different times with her grandchildren.

Personally, I thought Richard Nixon would live to be in his nineties. I saw a beautiful eagle penholder in a bookstore. I thought it would be nice for his seventy-ninth birthday. He enjoyed the gift. He told me, "At this time when I have only one year to go before I celebrate my eightieth birthday. I have concluded that the most rewarding compensation for getting older is to hear from good friends-young and old."

After "Seize The Moment" book was published in January 1982, Nixon was out there promoting his latest book. Whenever he could, he was granting interviews, Nixon knew the press would be throwing questions about the upcoming presidential race for the White House, and also what he discovered on his trip to the former Soviet Union. But, he wanted the American people to center their watchfulness on what was happening in Asia. It would be crucial in how the United States should handle its relationship with China.

Enthusiastic reviews and criticisms were flowing in from the media and foreign policy makers around the nation regarding "Seize The Moment," Nixon's latest book. It was a complete prescription for peace, prosperity, and freedom in the post-Cold War period.

Nixon enjoyed taking his grandsons, Alex Eisenhower and Christopher Cox to sports events. One Saturday, they attended a basketball game at Madison Square Garden. The exciting game was going along really well. Then, at half time, the cheerleaders put on their dance show.

Suddenly, they discovered Nixon and made the whole crowd in the stadium aware of Nixon's presence. With all the jostling by the crowd and the cheerleaders, Nixon ended up with a couple of the cheerleaders in his lap. Because of this incident, he didn't get to see most of the game. The crowd swamped him seeking his autograph.

After that event, Nixon would rather watch sport games on his television. It pleased him that some people still remembered him.

By March, it was still snowy and icy outside. Nixon couldn't go outdoors for his long walks. He realized that he couldn't do things liked he used to do. Therefore, he had to be inside to take his daily exercise on his stationary health and fitness machine. Instead of moping about the cold weather, Nixon disciplined himself to keep up his daily exercise as his doctor suggested. Reading and writing kept his brain cells alive and running. He determined at his advanced age that his body and brain would be correlated and kept in good shape.

Nixon had another dog called "Brownie", which followed him everywhere. He had discovered this stray dog on their former Saddle River property. It was a mixed breed of some kind. I don't know who adopted who first, but this dog latched onto Nixon's affection. The dog was not well trained and his behavior was something to be desired. Pat didn't like the messes the dog created in the house.

This year Pat was sometimes healthy and other times very ill. Her bronchial emphysema made her breathing strained and arduous. She could not do anything vigorous or energetic. Otherwise, it made her cough much worse. But, every time she was ill, Pat bounced back until she recovered. It made everyone happy she was still with us.

Half a mile from the Nixon's home was an Italian restaurant, "Valentino's", Pat and Richard Nixon would take out the entire family once a month. All the lively and effervescent grandchildren came along with their parents, Julie and David and Tricia and Ed. When Pat didn't feel up to "par", she would order a veal dish she loved from the restaurant. She would send her cook, Heidi, to pick up the take-out.

Pat turned 80 on her March 16 birthday. I gave her yellow roses in a white wicker basket. She put the flowers in the sunroom for everyone else could admire and enjoy. Pat said the roses would chase the clouds of winter away and give a promise of spring, which would be a cheery note.

She always enjoyed for her birthday her favorite white cake with a lemon filling and whipped cream frosting. In Park Ridge she discovered "Walter's Quality Pastry Shop" which made lovely tasty cakes. It was so delicious, Pat ordered that kind of cake be delivered for her next birthday.

Nixon was always looking ahead. He never looked back. He knew he was getting older and he tried not to over exert himself. When he was recovering his strength to get back to health, the lack of exercise and any other action was a wretched time for him. It caused him to feel defenseless and ensnared.

In April, Nixon decided to visit Bebe Rebozo, his long time close friend in Florida. Down there he mis-stepped on the stairs and took an unexpected turn on his ankle. Bebe rushed him to the Miami Hospital. It was only a sprained ankle but so painful! Nixon never thought he would wind up in a wheel chair. He didn't like to take painkillers, because those kinds of medicine made him always feel upside down and screwy. Even with the soft cast on his foot, he couldn't walk without pain. Eventually, the pain subsided and he felt much better.

Nixon was frustrated that American foreign policy was being ignored during the campaign. The Bush/Clinton presidential campaign was marked by significant issues, but those were limited in scope. Bill Clinton was stressing the condition of the economy and other internal issues. Bush was compelled to give a rebuttal to Clinton's attacks and perform on Clinton's battle turf. Communication for the Bush campaign was mired and not getting the true message out to the people in the country.

The voters were exasperated and dissatisfied. They were unsure where to pin the blame. Nixon recognized that the people were looking for some undetermined person to really believe in. Bush's concern was with Ross Perot entering the electoral race.

Nixon felt as I did that too much consideration was paid on how the operation of the campaign was run and not enough attention what was being said. Communication was the problem. Was Bush talking directly to the people? Everyone was talking, but the people were not listening. It was Nixon who recognized that the public dissatisfaction was so powerful and zealous, and that Clinton and Perot used it to feed their political campaigns.

Surely, there was a weak economy, but America also was in a crisis of moral decay. Nixon pondered why wasn't the Republican Party enlivening up the Bush campaign? He thought all Republicans should unite behind President Bush. He questioned why they hadn't gone after the Democrat Congress and Clinton? He continued questioning the actions of the campaign committee and who was letting President Bush down. Personally, he thought Clinton was a moral disaster,

Nixon met with Patrick Buchanan and his wife, Shelley. Buchanan use to be on Nixon's White House staff, and he also had tossed his hat into the presidential race. Nixon told him to withdraw from the presidential campaign. Also, the United States cannot be isolated from the world. Besides that kind of talk, it doesn't work any more in our world today.

The campaign, Nixon thought, would become the most dirty, contemptible one of all. Voter apathy and dissatisfaction laid the foundation for the agitation tempest for the third party candidates, such as Ross Perot. Perot was a different unusual, populist candidate who knew how to touch on issues important to certain people. Most of the people out there didn't know anything about the electoral process or the U.S. Constitution.

Third party candidates in a presidential race usually get only 20 per cent of the popular vote, just enough to deny the right candidate the presidential prize. Perot had the money to finance a campaign organization. But, most candidates cannot overcome the vast financial and organizational leverage and power of the Republican and Democrat parties.

Nixon was following the presidential race very closely. He did not want Clinton to win. When Dan Quayle told the nation our culture was in a moral decline, and that we should restore the distinctive, moral values to reverse the drift, Nixon agreed with Quayle.

By June, Nixon received a phone call from Ross Perot. He wanted to have a discussion with Nixon the following day. As usual Perot was not on time for his Nixon appointment. As in the past, Nixon found out Perot didn't always say what he actually meant and keep his word. This time Nixon leaked the story to the press.

Then in July, Perot called Nixon and said he was dropping out of the presidential race. His main campaign workers had quit the campaign.

Also, people were writing and calling Nixon to enter the race to run for President. They were looking for leadership to replenish the barren space. They knew he was very smart and had a political comprehension of issues and other things around him. But that was not to be!

By August, Nixon felt that Bush would lose the election. He saw that most of the people believed our nation were going in the wrong direction, and they were blaming President Bush for the whole thing.

At the Republican Party convention President George Herbert Bush said the Cold War was won by the endeavors of Richard Nixon, Gerald Ford, and Ronald Reagan. This was the first time Nixon's name was mentioned at the convention since the Watergate affair.

Then, Ross Perot decided on October first to re-enter the presidential race. Nixon was not surprised at Perot's actions. He knew the man didn't always keep his original word.

Pat and Dick and the rest of the family gathered together to watch the election returns as they came in. They wanted Bush to win. The Nixons thought Clinton's election appealed to counterfeit goals resting on amorality instead of a morality base. Losing to Clinton would be very bad. Nixon couldn't believe that Clinton had really won the election. He tried to block the results out of his mind.

Then, Nixon wrote a complimentary letter to Clinton in hoping he might be helpful in advising Clinton about foreign policy issues for the good of the country.

Nixon won a unique lawful triumph on November 17,

when a three-judge U.S. Court of Appeals unanimously ordered a U.S. District Court that Nixon must be compensated for the government's seizure of his presidential papers and tapes.

The court said, "In the light of history, we hold that Mr. Nixon, like every president before him, had a compensable property interest in his presidential papers and violated Nixon's rights under the Fifth Amendment, which prohibits the seizure of private property for public use without paying the former owners just compensation."

The compensation would be a gigantic amount. No one wanted to speculate how many million dollars Nixon would be awarded.

By December, Pat became very ill. Her weight was under one hundred pounds. This was not very good for a five foot seven lady. Her breathing was difficult, and her cough made it even worse. All of the family urged her to go to see a doctor, but she didn't want to go. Her unconquerable courage and power of determination caused her to fight back until she recovered. I was wondering how long she would be able to fight back. It concerned me as well as Nixon did.

Nixon celebrated his eightieth birthday, January 9, 1993. I received an autographed picture of Nixon with his grandchildren.

Nixon said, "The secret to a long life is never to look back, but to look forward. You've got to have something to live for otherwise you cease to live. Who wants to live when you have nothing to live for? Always look to the future you may live to enjoy it. Look back and you die!"

He said he didn't like to wear glasses because it made him feel old. I thought this would be the last time any of us would mention his birthday. At his age, Nixon was having difficulty looking ahead. He didn't know how many years he had left.

The last of February, Nixon developed the flu. He had to sleep a lot and drink large amount of liquids. The doctor ordered medicine with codeine for his illness. It made him feel like he was walking upside down on the ceiling. His fever came back because Nixon decided not to take any more of the medicine, which was making him woozy.

Then Pat picked up the flu from her husband when she was making scrambled eggs and toast for him. Heidi, their housekeeper, was indisposed because of a broken ankle and couldn't be there to help the Nixons.

By March 2, Nixon took Pat to the New York hospital, because she had much difficulty in breathing. The flu cut off her breathing on top of her bronchial emphysema. Pat became better and returned home from the hospital.

When I picked up the "New York Times", I noticed Nixon's article, "Clinton's Greatest Challenge" urging aid to Russia. Then, I learned that President Clinton called Richard Nixon regarding the article Nixon wrote.

Because of the article, Clinton invited Nixon to come to the White House. I couldn't imagine a Democrat President asking a former Republican president for advice. On March 8, Nixon met with Clinton to talk about the issues he stated in the article.

After their discussion, Nixon thought Clinton was undisciplined and could not focus his attention on any problem. He discovered that Clinton did not have "steel in his backbone." It was Hillary, Clinton's wife, who was the most influential and resolute person. Nixon knew Clinton was relying on wrong persons around him. Clinton was making mistakes without checking out the consequences of his actions.

Following his talk with Clinton, Nixon appeared on the House floor at Capitol Hill and gave an arousing speech there. All the Washington papers covered it. This time the newspapers had only acclaim for Nixon and declared him a viable foreign policy advisor for our country.

When I found out that Pat had returned home from the hospital, I sent a basket of flowers hoping it would give her enjoyment for her birthday while she was convalescing. When I received a note from Kathy O'Connor, President Nixon's office assistant, I knew something was dreadfully wrong.

Pat always corresponded or talked by phone with me. Since she was unable to do either, I felt sad inside. Kathy relayed Pat's message, "Your warm expression of friendship and affection brightens my day."

However, Pat developed acute respiratory difficulties, April 25, and Nixon had to return her to the hospital. She was having a very severe problem with the high blood pressure and other respiratory complications. Then they discovered a spot of cancer in her lung. Every day Richard Nixon was at Pat's bedside. He could not spend too much time at his office to continue working on his latest book, "Beyond Peace."

Nixon was ready to cry. His life partner's health was dramatically growing worse. This was another crisis in their life and he couldn't do much about. Helplessness and sorrow continued to eat within him. Sleep fled from him. How could he go on alone without her, he asked himself! She was his encourager and supporter in the mountaintops and the valleys. Pat stood by him through many a crisis. She was always there for him.

After an eighth day stay at the New York-Cornell Medical Center, Pat was released May 3rd, to come home to be near her husband and family. She was hopeless ill. I did not know if she was aware that soon she would depart from this life. We all knew that one-day would soon arrive. Pat said she was feeling better but everyone around her knew it was only momentary. It was most difficult for Nixon and his two girls, Julie and Tricia.

Several weeks later Pat became more seriously ill. It was almost impossible for her to breathe. She had lost so much weight and the pain was severe and overwhelming. As her husband and children determined to cheer her up, Pat was the one who resolved to gladden each one of them and keep their spirits elevated.

Some days Pat felt pretty good and then on other times she did not. Nixon noticed that this was happening. On the days she felt better and didn't have to stay in bed, Nixon cared for her tenderly. He would sit with her outside to enjoy the flowers she adored. When they didn't watch television together, Nixon would read some special book to her, which Pat liked.

By June 14, Pat went to the hospital again for her check-up. In her weaken condition; she had difficulty in walking to the car. At the hospital, they put her in a wheel chair. The next day at home, she had difficulty in eating any food. Her strength was evading her each day.

Then, on June 22,1993 morning at the age of 81, Pat Nixon's life came to a quiet close. She died happy at home with her husband of 53 years and her daughters, Julie Eisenhower and Tricia Cox at her bedside.

Nixon was grief stricken. He was confronted now with Pat's death and how he lost his partner in crisis. No longer the "comeback kid" or a former president of the free world, Nixon felt defenseless, adrift, and full of anxious concern that he would be alone.

I was in amidst of preparing for a yard sale when I received a telephone call from the Nixon's office concerning Pat's death and her funeral. Of course, I was stunned. It made me sad that my special personal friend was gone. I never liked funerals, but here I was invited as a special guest to Pat's funeral in Yorba Linda.

I contacted, Carmi Becker, one of my political friends, and told her about Pat's funeral. But, I needed someone to drive me over there, and someone else to manage my yard sale for that Saturday. Pat's funeral was for family and personal friends only. On such short notice, I really had to scramble around to make arrangements to be there.

Carmi's husband, Robert Becker, said he would manage the yard sale while I was gone. Hannah Lafoon, a friend from church, said she would come over and help, too. Carmi made reservations at Country Side Suites in Yorba Linda near the Nixon Library.

Richard Nixon accompanied his wife's body to California Friday to be buried on the Nixon Library and Birthplace grounds. President Clinton provided the old Air Force One, a Boeing 707 for the transportation. It was the same plane Nixon had used for his trips to the Soviet Union and China.

Friday evening, we were among the thousands who attended the public viewing for Pat Nixon. It was amazing to see how many people turned out. We were pleased that people still remembered Pat Nixon.

On Saturday, we took our place at the funeral service an hour before it was scheduled to start at 10:00 a.m. It was set in the grassy amphitheater for family and friends. Carmi and I sat in silence on white lawn chairs facing the reflection pool, watching the rest of the invited guests coming in.

Outside the garden wall, the press was isolated with their telescopic cameras to view the private funeral. Hundreds gathered in the parking lot outside the Library grounds to hear the funeral service over the loudspeakers. Some protestors were outside parading around with obnoxious and hateful signs. Then, we heard reports about some group threatening to bomb the place because all the former presidents would be there. President George Herbert Bush was to be there along with Gerald Ford and Ronald Reagan. Someone had an" axe to grind" with President Bush policies. They thought this would be the occasion to get all four presidents at one time. However, Barbara Bush's brother had died. Because of all this going on, Bush sent his son, Neil, to represent him.

As I sat in the library garden waiting for the service to begin, I recognized many men and women from years gone by. Former President Gerald Ford and Ronald Reagan, former cabinet members, Senator Bob Dole, Mark Hatfield. Bob Haldeman, Charles Colson, Pat Buchanan, Rosemary Woods, Henry Kissinger, and Bob Hope and Buddy Ebsen from the entertainment world were there.

At the morning service, a deadly pale Richard Nixon walked into the garden with Billy Graham. He was afflicted with sorrow as he saw all of us there to pay our respects for Pat, his wife. Nixon put his hands over his face and cried. When I saw Nixon's grief, I was touched and felt his emotional situation deeply. Tears came up in my eyes, too. We all stood quietly when six Marine honor guards carried Pat's mahogany casket and placed it under a white canopy on a raised platform decked with flowers. As Billy Graham opened the service, the sun poked through the ashen, cloudy skies. He told us, "This a time for tears but also a time of smiles and happiness in our hearts."

Billy Graham and four other eulogists-Lt. General James Hughes, Cynthia Hardin Milligan, Governor Pete Wilson, and Senator Robert Dole took turns at the podium praising Pat Nixon as a wife who knew both adversity and jubilation in her life.

Graham said, "Few women in public life have suffered as she has suffered and done it with such grace. In all the years I knew her, I never heard her say anything unkind about anyone."

Their remarks were preceded by a musical performance by the Chapman University Choir and the chorale. The selections were "For All The Saints Who From Their Labors Rest," "This Is My Song", and "You'll Never Walk Alone."

Then, it was Billy Graham's turn to conduct the memorial service. He said, "When we are confronted with the death of someone we love, we all pause for one moment in time to consider eternity. Death comes to us all, and we need the hope of which Jesus speaks 'In my Father's house are many mansions.'

"The passing of Pat Nixon is not only sorrow at the loss and sympathy for her family and friends, but it also draw attention to all the great values of life which she demonstrated."

"For the believer the brutal fact of death has been conquered by the resurrection of Jesus Christ. For the person who has turned from sin and has received Christ as Savior and Lord, death is not the end. For the believer there is hope beyond the grave. There is a future life! I do not believe that God would have placed eternity in our hearts unless there was a future life."

After the memorial service, Nixon withdrew to the main lobby reception. At first, he was going to speak to us. But, his emotions got in the way, and he retreated from the lobby to compose himself. When Nixon came back, one could tell he had been in tears. He began telling us about Pat whom he had lived with for 53 years. The warm memories Nixon shared about Pat brought sunshine in our lives that day.

At the reception line, Carmi and I progressed along with others. Even at this sad time, I still stood in awe meeting President Nixon once again. Carmi, my friend and driver, had never met any president. Nixon knew me by name. He appreciated my years of friendship, campaign work, and always enjoyed my telephone calls and letters. Richard Nixon was now just a grieving husband for his wife who he loved and lost. Instead of shaking hands, I just wanted to give him a hug. I knew if I did, we both would break down because of our love for Pat. I was trying to keep back my own tears.

Then, I introduced Carmi Becker to President Nixon and telling him who she was. After shaking hands, Nixon told my friend, "Carmi, take good care of Helen. We don't want anything to happen to her."

Carmi assured him she would. Then, I told Carmi, "That was a presidential order, you know.

I found Julie Eisenhower, Nixon's youngest daughter, and

we hugged each other. She said, "Helen, friends like you make everything bearable." But my grief got in the way again, and I couldn't even talk to Tricia, the oldest daughter, and her husband, Ed Cox. I was really missing Pat. With her gone, it was leaving another vacancy in my life. Later, I talked to Billy Graham, Bob Dole, and Charles Colson at the reception, which helped me to finally overcome my own emotions of sadness.

Four days before Julie's birthday, I received a thoughtful note of appreciation from Richard Nixon regarding the beautiful flowers I had sent for Pat's funeral.

He said, "She would have been very proud that you remembered her so thoughtfully and that makes me doubly proud."

"For the past fifty-three years I have usually finished personal letters with the phrase, 'Pat joins me in expressing our appreciation and sending our best wishes.' I can't say that now in a physical sense, but there is no question that in a spiritual sense she joins me in saying that to you today."

After Pat's death, Nixon needed assurance from someone. His partner for life was not there to help him through the remainder of his journey alone. The years ahead would surely not be the same as before without her.

None of the press knew the real Pat Nixon. Some of them didn't realize Pat was the woman who was content with caring for her family and happy with the husband she adored and pleased. Even though, Pat was a teacher before marriage, she did not pursue a career apart from her family because that was the way Pat wanted it. It was her personal choice.

I was disgusted with "U.S. News and World Report" and "Newsweek" magazines

Regarding the obituary story of Pat Nixon. They were asserting she did not have any admiring public, and she was foolish to put her husband first instead of her own wishes and desires.

Nixon was angered as I was about those articles. We both had to watch anything stressful which would make our blood pressure rise. How could those news magazines get everything so wrong about Pat Nixon? Were they judging her by their own misguided lives? I was convinced that they hated Nixon and doing this piece about Pat was their way in getting back at him. It was really disturbing!

Americans across the land proved the news magazine wrong by sending in thousands of sympathetic letters to Nixon. They didn't believe what the news media had been saying about Pat Nixon. The people knew better.

Thank goodness Nixon had two girls he could turn to at anytime. They were a very close family and were always there for each other. It wasn't unusual for Nixon to use Julie's birthday, July 5, as a time without change for continuity of the family dialogue. If Pat were alive, she would still resume the custom. The family discussion with his two girls gave him the "pickup" Nixon needed.

When Nixon heard from the news media about all the malicious gossip of the Clinton White House, he resolved to contend once again to be in the political skirmish. He decided to concentrate on writing his latest book "Beyond Peace", on issues, which mattered most to him. It gave him the chance to turn from the pain of his loneliness to political controversies and arguments. Absorbing himself in the writings made him feel better each day. He determined not to give up.

By September 1993 Nixon was revising and proof reading his manuscript for his book, "Beyond Peace." However, the Clinton White House was constantly asking Nixon for advice, but President Clinton did not always listen to the advice given. One of the things Nixon told Clinton that American servicemen should not serve under the United Nations command. That the United States should use the United Nations, but we should not be used by it. Instead, Clinton compromised than to stand for the right thing. He did not listen to Nixon's advice. Maybe, if Clinton had listened, he wouldn't have encountered all the trouble he had laid down for his self.

Then again, Clinton had one of his staff call Nixon to come to the White House to attend a ceremony with all the former presidents to honor the signing of the peace agreement between Israel and Palestine Liberation Organization. Nixon refused to attend. He did not want to be a "showing" front made to create a good but sometime a false impression for Clinton.

A debate was raging in the country over the North American Free Trade agreement. Clinton favored N.A.F.T.A. and was trying to get all the former presidents to endorse it by signing a letter with him. Even though, Nixon supported the Free Trade agreement, he declined to sign the letter and attend the ratification ceremony. Ronald Reagan agreed with Nixon and both did not attend. Both of their positions on the subject were well known.

For Nixon, he realized he was getting old and was more determined not to let his mind deteriorate. After having lunch in September with his old friend, Ronald Reagan in New York City, he had keen enjoyment being with Reagan. Reagan's jocularity and the sharing of bygone times delighted Nixon.

But, he could see that Reagan's condition was getting worse mentally. Reagan would have trouble following his train of thoughts. He would start talking and then Nancy, his wife, would have to help him out. It made Nixon very sad. Somehow Nixon felt Reagan was not the same person he once knew. After seeing what had destroyed Reagan's mind, Nixon once again determined it shouldn't happen to him. All his life he used self-control and exercised his mind by reading, studying and remembering. Nixon's thinking was very sharp, and he wanted to keep it that way.

By November 1993, Nixon had completed his final book,

"Beyond Peace." He was pleased he had accomplished what he set out to do.

Nixon's strength of mind improved and had enabled him to bear adversity with courage. He was finally looking forward to the Thanksgiving holidays with his two daughters and grandchildren. It would be a happy time with the rest of the family. Of course, Nixon would miss Pat, but in all of his daughters he would see a bit of her. He was fortunate to have his two daughters and their husbands to bolster his spirits.

At Christmas time, Julie and Tricia spent the holidays with their families at home. This year Nixon would be alone without Pat. Every year he always enjoyed the Christmas production at New York's Radio City Music Hall. This year he was determined to see it once more. In fact, Nixon invited some friends to come along for this Christmas matinee show.

As his large, luxurious, chauffeur-driven sedan was trapped in Manhattan traffic, a tiny throng of people recognized who was in the car. They came closer to wish Nixon their very best for the Christmas season. By the time Nixon reached the Radio City Music Hall, he was met by a swarm of people to shake his hands, to get an autograph or just to let him know he was not forgotten.

Although, Nixon enjoyed the beautiful music and the Rockettes magnificent, dance routines, it was the ending of the show about the birth and life of Christ, which touched and enthralled him that day. The message of the true story of Christmas shook Nixon up and everything else was not as important as before. One thing his faith in God did not waver, and it sustained him through many a crisis.

When his eightieth-first birthday arrived, January 9, 1994, Nixon was not very enthusiastic about adding another year. It was difficult to be without Pat. He was lonely because of her absence. All through the house, he roamed alone. Thinking about his advancing age did not help Nixon's loneliness.

For comfort he turned to his King James Version of the Bible. Nixon never did like the newer translations. Somehow the new versions did not do anything for him spiritually or give him peace of mind and soul as the King James Version did.

Several weeks before he departed on his Russian trip. Nixon had sent his last book, "Beyond Peace" to his publisher, Random House. In it offered strong and firm solutions, coping with crime, health care, the entertainment industry, race relations and the environment.

Nixon observed that "The depiction of violence and explicit sex sells and Hollywood is in the business of making money." By foregoing its responsibility to observe basic standards of decency, Hollywood has accelerated the decline of these standards in the community at large. "He warned that unless Hollywood cleans up its act, it will inevitably face censoring by the government."

He said, "The news media bears a large share of the responsibility for the current loss of faith in American political institutions. An institutional bias in the press" makes for excessively harsh criticisms of all politicians and public officials," he wrote, "Competitive pressures to often push the media past the limits of responsibility, destructively and unnecessarily undermining the authority and credibility of government.

"While the news media would not have physicians certify themselves, we are taught to expect that editors, reporters and broadcasters have a unique capacity to ensure that they themselves act responsibility," he said.

Even though, Nixon started the Environmental Protection Agency to find a balance between economic growth and protecting the environment, he stated, "But as so often happens with government programs, the pendulum has swung too far. Measures designed to protect endangered species, such as bears, wolves, and the bald eagle, are now being used to force Idaho farmers off their land for the sake of the thumbnail-size Bruseau Hot Springs snail."

Nixon called, "All 1,342 impenetrable pages" of the Clinton healthcare plan a blueprint for the takeover by the federal government of one-seventh of the nation's economy." He maintained that the criminal justice has abysmally failed to deliver what should be the first freedom: freedom from fear."

He said most political leaders, in order not to appear racist, avoid the question of race as it effects crime. "What is truly racist is to avoid addressing the problems of black Americans for the sake of avoiding offending people's sensibilities," he wrote.

Nixon warned, "The nation must face up to the fact that the breakdown of the family is worst in the urban underclass. Blacks are not the only members of this underclass, but they are the largest proportion of it. In 1992, half of the murder victims in the United States were black. Ninety per cent were killed by other blacks."

Nixon said blaming crime as a cause of poverty is a copout that is 'morally corrupt and intellectually vacuous" and the solution lies in resolve that another lost generation will not take to the streets in the beginning of the next century."

It was early evening, March 7,1994, only nine months after I talked to Richard Nixon at Pat's funeral in Yorba Linda. I had just returned from a birthday luncheon, and then I flicked on the television to C.B.S. News. There, I saw Richard Nixon, 81 years old, still trying to solve the problems in Russia with President Boris Yelstin and his political foes. He was unsteady in his walk, and one of the men there was helping him down some stair steps. To me, Nixon looked very tired and not very well.

I breathed a prayer—"Dear God bring Richard Nixon home safely. Please don't let him die over there."

He did come home. But, Nixon warned that our country

must not abandon Russia. The Russian people deserve our support for their freedom, he said. This wise advice and pertinent information he provided for President Clinton as he offered in the past to President Reagan and Bush. Once again, Nixon had put his country first and not for his self!

Suddenly, on Monday, April 18, 1994, a friend called and asked me to turn on the radio news. The newscaster announced that Richard Nixon had suffered a stroke. They stated that he was stricken at home. Nixon had been relaxing on the deck before going to a dinner meeting. He collapsed on the ground. Heidi Retter, his housekeeper, discovered him there. In turn, he was rushed in an ambulance to the New York Cornell Medical Center. Nixon was unable to talk but was conscious and alert.

I was sadden—could only hope and pray. When I called the hospital, they stated that the next twenty-four hours would tell the fate of his stroke. When I called Nixon's office, Kim Taylor answered and said, "People were responding. Get-well messages and cards were pouring in from all over the United States and the world."

My mind flashed back in time to September 1974, at San Clemente when Richard Nixon was very ill with phlebitis. He had a stabbing pain on the left side of his abdomen. His left leg was severely swollen, and a blood clot broke off and was traveling toward his lungs. Since anti-coagulant drugs did not work, the doctors told the Nixons surgery was necessary to save his life. After the October surgery at the Long Beach Memorial Hospital, Nixon developed internal hemorrhage, which left him critically near death. Across the nation, a group of loyal friends, who believed in him, had all night prayer vigils on his behalf. Pat was by his side encouraging him not to give up. It was her strong faith which helped him to get well. He survived that health crisis.

At that time, I was so disgusted at the shameless behavior of some the press who did not believe Nixon was ill. They didn't take the opportunity to investigate the truth. They only wanted to print their bias thinking. Thank goodness the Chicago Tribune and the Pulliam papers let their readers know the true facts. Even, some of the Congressional Democrat committee was skeptical, and so they sent out two doctors of their own to check out his condition. Now, twenty years later, I was praying that Richard Nixon would beat the odds once again and survive this crisis. The doctors said after twenty-four hours, they would give their predictions on his prospects.

His condition was very critical. This time Pat would not be there. She had stood by Dick through crisis after crisis, heartbreaking setbacks, and the joy of many victories. Anytime, Richard Nixon said, "I don't think I can make it. Pat was always there by his side and said, "Yes, you can!"

Often, Dick had said if it hadn't been for Pat, he would not survive physically or politically. She was his life. Pat was the "spring" which made her husband tick. The trauma of her death was heart wrenching for him. I recalled that at Pat's funeral, his face was twisted in grief. I predicted after Pat's death in June 1993, Nixon would not last long. It would be just a matter of time.

Then, that time arrived. Nixon took a turn for the worse—his brain suffered a swelling—a most serious critical threat. For years, I knew his doctors had been treating him for irregular heart beats which makes a person prone to blood clots. As he faced a critical condition in 1974, death beckoned again. Richard Nixon slipped into a deep coma. As his condition rapidly deteriorated, Julie and Tricia, his two daughters, were by his side.

By Friday, he was gone. Tears flowed down my cheeks when the television networks interrupted the regular programming announcing his death. Now for the first time, I realized that we would not have his leadership and wisdom. Death did not actually write the final chapter of the Nixon unbelievable life, but it achieved what the media couldn't do.

Inside ten months, Carmi Becker and Cathy, her daughter, and I had to make another sad journey to Yorba Linda. We had arrived days early in preparation for Nixon's funeral. Thunder, lightning, and a heavy, unseasonable downpour of rain welcomed us to Yorba Linda. It was very chilly, as well. It rained and hailed and rained some more. The ground was covered with bead-size hail pellets. We waded through some deep puddles. In spots, the hail resembled snow. I never remembered it hailing like that before in Southern California.

The TV networks had fifty satellite trucks plastered all over the presidential library grounds. The reporters were interviewing anyone they could get a hold of there—and I was one of them.

Tuesday, some of the media were amazed at the thousands crowded under umbrellas and sheets of plastic waiting in a three-mile long line to file past the closed, flag draped casket of Richard Nixon lying in state. There were Indians, blacks, whites, Latinos, and Asians, old and young, and babies in strollers in that line. People were cold from the chilly moisture, but it didn't stop many persons from joining the ever-growing line. The press was still shaking their heads. They couldn't believe their eyes that thousands of people would come out for Richard Nixon.

Some of the people were singing and telling jokes and sharing with others their coffee and hot chocolate. I was surprised when I learned that some of the people had waited in the rain six and eight hours, just to show their devotion and love for a leader who had fallen. It was the populace from the heartland-the grassroots of America-who finally spoke what was on their hearts. I was glad the "Silent Majority" expressed their feelings once again and proved the disbelievers wrong. They were there for Richard Nixon.

About 50,000 people had gone through the line; and 25,000 persons were turned away at 10:30 a.m., Wednesday morning before the funeral of President Nixon. Hundreds of men and women would have liked to be one of the invited guests at the Nixon funeral on the presidential library grounds. Since they couldn't be there, they huddled around the television monitors set up in the street and listened quietly when the funeral service started.

When I heard the "Ruffles and Flourishes" played, and then the "Hail To The Chief," and finally the 21 gun salute which boomed across the grounds, it made me realize again that the captain of our army, Richard Nixon, our leader, had fallen. The services prompted displays of emotion and personal remembrances. Many of us had been with him a long time, in many a battle. He was "one of us" and our hero.

Senator Bob Dole's eulogy brought tears to our eyes. I was hunting for a tissue in my sweater jacket to help wipe away my tears. No more would anyone of us have a talk with him in person—or get a phone call—or written orders. For us, we always thought he would be with us—forever bounding back and never giving in.

At the funeral Billy Graham said, "And so we say farewell to Richard Nixon today with hope in our hearts, for our hope is in the eternal promises of Almighty God. There is hope beyond the grave, because Jesus Christ has opened the door to heaven for us by his death and resurrection. Richard Nixon had that hope, and today that can be our hope as well. And we look forward to seeing Dick and Pat some day in the future."

Following the solemn hour-long service, the honor guards bore Nixon's coffin to the burial plot where his beloved Pat was buried. Finally, they would be together forever!

As I was leaving the Nixon service, one display of photos and flowers caught my eye and I remembered it here.

"Farewell, Friend—Farewell
We say not Goodbye—No, Tis Not Final!
Soon, Very Soon
Under Golden Skies
And In Fair Clime.
We'll All Be There Again
To Meet And Greet You
Again—Til Then"

(Signed by Sanjay)

Richard Nixon left an indelible mark on our country and the world, which cannot be erased. When the television media keeps re-airing the life of Nixon, it makes us wonder if he really is gone. Many books are churned out to keep his name alive in our memories.

Most of all, Pat Nixon's legacy will be her family. The Nixon family was the definition of family values. She had an enduring relationship with other children-not just with Tricia and Julie. She was a wonderful, devoted mother and First Lady, who never wanted any credit for herself. Pat was the driving force behind her husband, Richard Nixon. When he was down, she kept him going in good and bad times and supported him in his many endeavors. Today, we don't find that in a wife. That speaks a lot of what a family ought to be and reminds us what we have lost through time.

As a war president, Nixon determined to win the Vietnam War at any cost and save military men's lives and to bring the prisoners of war (POW'S) home. The world today is far different and safer because of him. Nixon dared to take risks for his journey for peace and freedom, as no other man had done.

As Pat was the constant anchor in her husband's life, she was the only First Lady who gave stability to our country when it was in the turmoil of war.

As partners in crisis, they didn't pack their bags and fade away. As a nation we lost a world leader and First Lady. When they passed away from our view, it was truly an end of a remarkable chapter in our country's history, which should never be forgotten.

THE END

About the Author

Helen Montgomery is a former schoolteacher. She became a coordinator and speaker for all the Nixon presidential campaigns. This resulted in a 35-year personal friendship with the Nixons.

Mrs. Montgomery's writing credits include People In Time, A Journey of a War President, and Something To Think About, a monthly column for political newsletters.

She received her B.A. in Art Education from Grand Canyon University, and Bible from Moody Bible Institute. Montgomery is a frequent speaker at schools and clubs. Montgomery has appeared on Editorial USA, Party Line Talk Show, and interviewed on national TV at Nixon's funeral and the Commercial News paper.

She lives in Danville, Illinois.

Acknowledgements

My son, James Darrell (J.D.) Montgomery, was the one who encouraged me to take my Nixon journal out of the lockbox and write this book.

Thanks to Jeannie Crippen, Janet Moore, and Janell Noble for spurring me on to finish writing the Nixon story. Also, for Julie Nixon Eisenhower's assistance regarding her mother's article and White House photos.

Thanks to Sherrill Montgomery-Hammer for trying to get this on the computer.

Special thanks to Kathy Starkey for putting this manuscript on the computer and editing the final draft. Thanks to Kathy's husband, Morris, for putting up with us for the extra time spent in finishing this story.

Short Summary

Partners In Crisis is the most fascinating, revealing inside story written by a Nixon campaign worker and personal friend.

It is filled with dramatic revelations of the human and spiritual. Political and personal which Montgomery had known first hand—new light is shed on the 1960 Kennedy/Nixon presidential race which was the closes race in history—not the Bush/Gore race; how Pat Nixon was a better campaigner than her husband, and loved by people until the day she died; terrorism attacked the rule of law; and how the CIA fed false information to the Washington Post to topple the President.

BVG